PIMLIC

5 5

Hugh Brogan was for 10 years a Fellow of St
John's College, Cambridge. He is now a lecturer
in American History at the University of Essex
and is currently writing a book about President
Kennedy. His publications include *A History of
the United States*.

THE LIFE OF
ARTHUR RANSOME

———

HUGH BROGAN

PIMLICO

PIMLICO

20 Vauxhall Bridge Road, London SW1V 2SA

London Melbourne Sydney Auckland Johannesburg
and agencies throughout the world

First published by Jonathan Cape Ltd 1984
Pimlico edition 1992

Printed and bound in Great Britain by
Mackays of Chatham PLC, Chatham, Kent

ISBN 0-7126-5249-3

Dedicated
to my Mother
MRS CHARLES HACKETT
for she too has always been
an admirer of Arthur Ransome

Contents

Figures

Acknowledgments

The greatest pleasure in writing this biography has been the universal kindness and courtesy I have met in my quest for understanding and information. Even those people who, as it turned out, were unable to assist me, responded to my inquiries most politely, and the book would have been much the poorer, and have taken much longer to produce, but for the immense helpfulness of those who did have memories or papers to share with me. Even those who were gruff to start with afterwards proved, like Dr Johnson, to have nothing of the bear but his hide. So I am happy to acknowledge my debts. I earnestly hope that I have not forgotten any.

First and foremost I must express my gratitude to Arthur Ransome's literary executors, Sir Rupert Hart-Davis and Mr John Bell. Without Sir Rupert's immediate and continuous help and encouragement the book could not have been written. He and Lady Hart-Davis let me stay repeatedly in their house and lavished perfect hospitality upon me. I was shown all Sir Rupert's Ransome papers and books. He reminisced freely about his old friend and answered all my postal inquiries fully and promptly. Best of all, he went right through the completed manuscript, which as a result was vastly improved in innumerable ways. Then he volunteered to read the proofs. It is impossible to thank him adequately.

I was also lucky enough to be the guest of John Bell and his wife, the late Pamela Whitlock. They too helped me with memories, papers, books and encouragement. It is lamentable that Pamela cannot now be thanked for her kindness with a present of the book to which she and her husband gave so much. But I can and do thank John, most earnestly.

Arthur Ransome's papers are mostly deposited in the Brotherton

Collection in the Brotherton Library at the University of Leeds. I have lost count of the visits I paid there. I was always received with the utmost courtesy and helpfulness by Mr Christopher Sheppard and his staff; by the senior members of the university, who, all fraternally, let me use their common room and restaurant; and by Mrs Boag and the staff at Devonshire Hall, where I was happy to stay. Mrs Ann C. Farr must be given special mention. The Ransome papers are in her care, and without her work they would be almost unusable. I owe much to her knowledge, enthusiasm and efficiency; not least to her help with the illustrations.

There are other Ransome holdings at the Lakeland Museum in Kendal, and I must thank Miss Mary Burkett and her staff for their helpfulness and courtesy to me on my visits to Abbot Hall.

Arthur Ransome's daughter, Mrs Tabitha Lewis, was not only kind enough to let me interview her, and to read over those parts of the biography which directly concerned her – I am grateful for her helpful comments – she also let me read and make extensive use of her unpublished memoir of her childhood. It should be apparent to every reader of chapter III (not to mention some other passages) how much I have relied on her. She also allowed me to make use of some excellent photographs in her possession, and to reproduce one of her father's illustrated letters to her. Mrs Tania Rose passed on to me all the references to Arthur Ransome which she came across while working in the Public Record Office on the life of her father, Morgan Philips Price; she also talked to me about her memories of Arthur Ransome, and allowed me to quote from her parents' visitors' book. Taqui Altounyan (Mrs Robert Stephens) not only gave me lunch while I interviewed her, and allowed me to quote from her memoir of her childhood, *In Aleppo Once*; she also read and commented on all the passages of the biography which dealt with Arthur Ransome's relations with her family. Miss Josephine Russell talked to me freely of her memories of Ransome, let me make extensive use of her brother George's log-book of two voyages on the Broads with Arthur and Genia, and lent me her photograph albums to plunder for illustrations. My friend and neighbour Mr John Cole gave himself considerable trouble to put me in touch with the Young family of Wandsworth. The consequence was that we were both invited to a hugely enjoyable reception at the Ram Brewery, where Messrs John, James and Thomas Young not only extended munificent hospitality (I was particularly taken with their Special bitter) but shared with me their memories of Arthur Ransome, and showed me their relics: photographs, letters in code, and the Jolly Roger they once flew on the Broads. My friend and colleague Dr Simon Collier, while visiting Madison, Wisconsin, was kind enough to make a search of the Raymond Robins papers in the Wisconsin State Historical Society's archives, in quest of Ransome material. Mr Dennis L. Bird sent me copious cullings from his unique Ransome collection, and Mr Richard Davies, of the University of Leeds, furnished me with valuable translations of Russian material in the Ransome papers.

Miss Valerie Kettley, of Jonathan Cape Ltd, was most kind and helpful in enabling me to use the plentiful Ransome material in the firm's possession; so was Mr Anthony Colwell, who also began the ruthless business of knocking my manuscript into shape. The job was completed by Miss Jane Hill, whose skill and patience and good humour I cannot praise enough.

The University of Essex generously paid many of the expenses of my research. The Master and Fellows of St John's College, Cambridge, were characteristically hospitable whenever I needed to visit the Cambridge University Library, where it is always a happiness to work. Mrs Maggie Berkowitz kindly let me stay with her in Kendal.

For the rest, I can only draw up an alphabetical list of their names, and again say thank you to: Mr W. D. Amos, Dr Christopher Andrew, Mrs Georgina Battiscombe, the BBC Hulton Picture Library (for permission to reproduce plate no. 5), Mr and Mrs G. D. Caldwell, Dr Glen Cavaliero, Professor T. W. Craik, Mr Michael Cullen, Miss Caroline Downay, Miss Janet Gnosspelius, Mr I. E. Graham, Mrs Mavis Guzelian, Mrs Jean Harding, Dr Geoffrey Hosking, Mr George Jones, Mr Richard Kelsall, the Kenrick family of Blakeshall, Mrs Cecily Ledgard, Dr Richard Luckett, Dr Francis Lupton, the Rt Hon. Harold Macmillan, O.M., Mr and Mrs Hugo Meynell, Mr and Mrs Malcolm Muggeridge, Dr John Murphy, Mr Mark Paterson, Mr Peter Philips Price, Mrs B. H. C. Russell, Mr Richard Scott, Mr Adrian A. Smith, Dr S. A. Smith, Dr and Mrs Stephen Spackman, Dr Zara Steiner, Mr John Rowe Townsend, Dr Hugh Tulloch and Mr and Mrs John Tusa.

Wivenhoe, Colchester   H.B.
July 1983

I

Beginnings

There was a Boy; ye knew him well, ye cliffs
And islands of Winander!

WORDSWORTH

Arthur Michell Ransome was born on 18 January 1884 at 6 Ash
Grove, Headingley, Leeds, just across the big park, Woodhouse
Moor, from the Yorkshire College (later the University of Leeds)
where his father was then Professor of History.

The outline of his boyhood is easy to draw, and is largely unremarkable. He was the eldest child of Cyril and Edith Ransome.
Mrs Ransome's maiden name was Boulton. He was followed into
the world by Cecily, Geoffrey and Joyce. The Ash Grove house
was small, but rising prosperity enabled Professor Ransome to
move, and move again, to better property at the top of Headingley, near St Chad's, beyond the Shire Oak and the Skyrack Inn.
The family spent most of the year in Leeds, but passed all the
summer holidays at High Nibthwaite on Coniston Water. After
a period of private tuition Arthur was sent to prep. school at the
Old College, Windermere, and to Rugby in 1897, the year his
father died. He left school at the age of seventeen and entered the
Yorkshire College, but left that also, after two terms, to start work
as a publisher's errand-boy.

The history of his inner life during childhood, important in anyone's story, doubly important in the case of an imaginative writer,
and trebly so for a children's writer, is not nearly so simple. To
judge from the account given in Ransome's *Autobiography*, the
only source available, it was dominated by two presences.

The first was that of the lake.

Even today Coniston Water, or Thurstonmere, is magical in its serene beauty. Thanks to the efforts of the National Trust and the Lake District National Park its shores are much less changed from what they were in the last years of the nineteenth century than a prospective visitor might reasonably fear. The lake is large or small as each beholder decides. For an enterprising, imaginative child it is just the right size: an ocean to play with, not without danger; sudden squalls can capsize a small boat instantly. An adult visitor, prudent enough to travel to Coniston outside the holiday season, may discover a tranquil harmony of water, wood and hill that shapes the soul, according to Wordsworth, as nothing else can. It certainly affected young Arthur. The books he subsequently wrote for children show that for him the lake became a symbol of life and its fulfilment; but he was not an obvious subject for such natural promptings. The boy Wordsworth, even at his busiest, must always have been deeply introverted; such is not at all the impression given by Arthur Ransome's later account of his childhood, or by the words and actions of his manhood. Perhaps it is significant that he seldom refers to Wordsworth. For Arthur, life at Nibthwaite was one of constant, extrovert eagerness; a refuge from the painful tangles of home life at Leeds. Perhaps the main events of the Nibthwaite holidays were not unlike those of Wordsworth's boyhood, but the colouring given to them by Ransome's personality was vastly different.

It is not clear when he first visited the lake. His father carried him to the top of the Old Man of Coniston when he was a baby: 'I think no younger human being can ever have been there.' It is only an inference that he spent summers at Nibthwaite throughout his early life. When he and his family and the farm where they stayed come clearly into focus, Arthur seems to be seven or eight – the age of Roger at the beginning of *Swallows and Amazons*.

Swainson's farm would have seemed paradise to any child. Being in the fells it was not surrounded by the level wheatfields, green meadows and orderly hedges of the south, but by woods and rock, heather and bracken, badgers, grouse and sheep and drystone walls. Near the farmhouse were cowsheds, a hayloft, a damson orchard, beehives; safe perils for a child to explore (except the beehives, but there is no record of Arthur getting stung). Below the farm was the little white village; a beck with trout in it, and a stone bridge to wriggle under; and the lake. Arthur's parents seem to have had a sensibly relaxed attitude to the possibility of drowning, like that of most families who live by real water (it is suburban goldfish ponds that kill infants); at any rate, Arthur had no impediment to overcome in his love affair with Coniston. On every arrival at Nibthwaite, he records,

I had a private rite to perform. Without letting the others know what I was doing, I had to dip my hand in the water, as a greeting to the beloved lake or as a proof to myself that I had indeed come home. In later years, even as an old man, I have laughed at myself, resolved not to do it, and every time have done it again. If I were able to go back there today, I should feel some discomfort until after coming to the shore of the lake I had felt its coolness on my fingers.[1]

As he grew older he would explore further. The rocks above the farm provided a splendid watchtower over the lake; there was also the Knickerbockerbreaker,

a smooth precipitous rock easy to climb from one side for the pleasure of sliding down its face to the damage of my knickerbockers which, when they were threadbare, kind Annie Swainson used to darn *in situ*.

There were mushrooms and blackberries to pick, trout to tickle under Nibthwaite bridge, new friends to make – charcoalburners, gamekeepers, poachers. There was haymaking and butter-churning. There were birds and beasts to watch and identify, caterpillars and newts to collect. Arthur threw himself into all these activities with the zest that was to characterise him throughout his life and with a simple joy that still shines from the pages in which he describes them. The one thing that Nibthwaite may have lacked was literature. On the inevitable wet days the children amused themselves with transfers. Arthur's life by Coniston was not that of a bookworm. No one there would have suspected him of being a future author.

As he grew older the lake beguiled him more and more. The

---

1 Throughout this book I have drawn heavily on both the *Autobiography* (as here) and the various unpublished autobiographical papers in the Brotherton Collection and at the Lakeland Museum, Abbot Hall. Quotations, unless otherwise specified, may be assumed to come from these sources.

children fished for minnows off the Swainsons' stone jetty, and for perch from a rowing-boat. Sometimes the whole family went up the lake to Peel Island for a picnic. 'We spent the day as savages. My mother would settle down to make a sketch in water-colours. My father, forgetting to eat his sandwiches, would drift far along the lake-shores, casting his flies and coming back in the evening with trout in the bottom of the boat for Mrs Swainson to cook for next day's breakfast.' Peel Island, 'steep-sided and crowned with trees', and with a miniature island, a large rock, south of it, like a dinghy in tow, reminded the antiquary W. G. Collingwood of a ship of old times; with its little secret harbour and camping-ground it became one of Arthur's most sacred places. There were few to challenge possession in those days, though on one occasion the Ransomes and the Collingwoods, strangers to each other, arrived together. They decided to picnic in company. Mrs Collingwood's private thought, only revealed years later, was to wonder that such a pretty woman as Edith Ransome should have such very plain children.

Cyril Ransome is the second dominating presence in the early pages of the *Autobiography*. Arthur's portrait of him comes to life in such details as the account of a boating lesson on the lake:

My father had rowed at Oxford and from the beginning taught his children to row with their backs and to regard their arms merely as strings connecting the oars to the part that did the pulling. 'In ... Out! What are you doing with those elbows? ... Keep your eyes on stroke's shoulders ... Now then ... Ten strokes both together ... In! ... Out! ... In! ... Out! ... (Crash) You again, Arthur!' My feet had slipped off the stretcher or my oar had missed the water and I was on my back with my feet in the air. 'Nothing to howl about. That's catching a crab. Better men than you have caught them before now ... But not two in one day.'

'You again, Arthur!' In no way can Professor Ransome be compared to the great monster fathers of the late-Victorian age – to Sir George Sitwell, or Dean Worsley, or G. G. Coulton. He was too clear-headed, too upright, too sane. He was only too anxious to share the joys of life with his children. But he also wanted to mould his son. He found, as so many other parents have found, that the clay was resistant from the start.

He did his best to observe Arthur dispassionately, but unfortunately allowed his observations to fall into a pre-ordained pattern. The outstanding character trait to be inferred from the anecdotes that Arthur tells of his childhood is self-will. In no violent or assertive fashion, but in his own sunny way, the little boy was not to be influenced or diverted from his chosen path. Or rather, he insisted on doing his own choosing. His father was a Conservative, so he was a Gladstonian. His father tried to teach him trout-fishing by demonstration: instead of watching, he wandered off to catch loaches. He resisted all indoctrination – a healthy enough response. Unfortunately Cyril Ransome saw it as mere unteachability, and linked it with various other unsatisfactory characteristics.

> I was for ever after some new thing and, much worse, for ever planning that it should be the occupation of a lifetime. I spent every penny I had on coloured paper, made spills in dozens and grosses and formed a one-man company that should make spills for all Leeds, for all Yorkshire, for all the world, and put the match-factories out of business. In this my father saw at once a foreshadowing of something like my grandfather's disastrous venture as a manufacturing chemist. It seemed to him (and indeed was) a miserable, mercenary ambition.

This grandfather (succinctly described in the *Autobiography* as a man 'acute in considering all business except his own') had burdened Cyril Ransome with his debts, which took years to pay off. The professor felt the burden acutely. It does not seem to have occurred to him that perhaps it was his own resulting preoccupation with money and the dangers of poverty – Arthur formed the impression that his parents were 'very hard up', which can hardly have been the case – that induced mercenary ambitions in his son. Perhaps there had been too much talk of grandfather's debts. A small boy might well conclude that a large fortune was the best and most important thing in life. Being an ingenious Ransome – the delinquent grandfather was a talented inventor, and the collateral line of the family manufactured farm machinery – he set busily about making one.

> When I had glutted the spill-market ... spills were forgotten and I was practising day in day out the simpler conjuring tricks

that were to lead me to the prideful moments of a professional magician who, before vast audiences, should produce rabbits out of a hat (for the moment I was content to produce white mice). My father was still more disheartened. His hopes rose a little when I showed a deep interest in caterpillars and found and identified some of the rarer hawk-moths, but fell again on learning that I proposed to breed them on a gigantic scale and sell them sordidly to collectors. Then I had plans for making a fortune out of the monstrous multiplication of Belgian hares, which came to nothing because of my unwillingness to kill them. He was pleased when, after a visit to the Leeds museum in the Philosophical Hall, I set about making one of my own, but was once more disheartened when he heard that I saw my museum, temporarily housed in the drawer of a washing-stand, as already the nucleus of a collection that should fill a building something like the Leeds Town Hall, and attract pilgrims, at sixpence a head, from all parts of the world ... Alas, in almost everything I did with such enthusiasm my father saw not so much the enthusiasm as the traits which in his own father he had most deplored.

Thomas Ransome was a flibbertigibbet, who had thrown away a promising scientific career to make his fortune out of one hare-brained scheme after another, and it seemed that his grandson was going the same way. Cyril Ransome's father-in-law, Edward Baker Boulton, was not much better: he had been a sheep-farmer in Australia, but cared only for water-colour painting. He retired to Clifton to indulge the passion, and died while Arthur was still very young.

It was a disturbing heredity, and although we now know that Arthur would mint it into gold, both real and metaphorical, his father, who was intensely ambitious in a conventional way, cannot really be blamed for fearing the worst. His boy even showed signs of being a muff. When Cyril went out shooting, he took Arthur with him to act as a beater; but the screaming of a wounded hare reduced the child to an endless paroxysm of tears. He was not taken on a shoot again for many years. One day on Coniston the father dropped the son over the side of the rowing-boat to see if, like tadpoles, young humans could swim spontaneously; un-happily Arthur, in panic, went under at once and subsequently refused to learn to swim in the usual way. He was sternly told that next summer at Nibthwaite he would not be allowed out in the boat.

As it happened, this dreadful threat produced a happy ending. Arthur displayed his usual tenacity and, for the first time, a kind of inspired practicality that was to serve him well throughout his life. He went down to the public baths on his own, and taught himself to swim, by his own method, in three visits. When at the family breakfast-table he announced that he could swim, his father told him not to tell lies. Arthur insisted, 'and was grimly taken off to the baths to prove the truth. I do not think I ever saw my father more pleased with me than he was that day.'

Such an outcome was unusual. Almost all the stories in the *Autobiography* leave one feeling that Cyril Ransome was oppressively imperceptive. He sat perpetually in judgment on his son, and made his views felt. '*Treasure Island* we knew and loved, but I remember my father's shocked astonishment when I did not realise that *The Black Arrow* was in comparison a poor machine-made thing.' What makes the stories so sad is that Arthur was in many respects his father's son, inheriting some of his best traits, including his courage and devotion to duty. He liked and admired his father, indeed, it is clear, hero-worshipped him, modelling himself upon him (with considerable success) and longing for his approval. Love carried him so far as to claim, in the *Autobiography*, that Cyril Ransome was a born educator, although the same pages show him failing to teach his son Latin, French, swimming, trout-fishing, shooting, and also failing to notice that Arthur was miserable, and was learning nothing at his prep. school; worse, was losing 'the power of eager learning for its own sake' (to be sure, there were and are few schools in England where this power is not systematically eradicated, in Arthur's day because the masters cared for nothing but games, in ours because they care for nothing but exam results).

Cyril noticed, but did not see the meaning of, the fact that the boy picked up things, when *not* taught them, quickly enough. Arthur said, 'I cannot remember learning to read' – not a common boast; but he did remember that at the age of only four he was able to read *Robinson Crusoe* from cover to cover. His proud father gave him a copy of the book as a reward. Cyril Ransome's affection, hope and ambition for his son are not in question; only his insight. Insight had never been his strong suit. On the day after Edith Boulton accepted his proposal of marriage, he took round to her a volume of Bagehot's essays and a book of Wordsworth's poems, with some of them marked, 'and told her that he looked forward to examining her on both a week later'. Yet Edith does not seem to have minded this manner of wooing. She entirely accepted her lover's attitude to life and people, and made his doubts and anxieties about Arthur her own. Between them these devoted parents implanted a profound anxiety in their naturally buoyant son, a self-doubt which was to dog him all his life and probably had much to do with his chronic duodenal ulcer.

Yet it can hardly be said that the professor failed as a father. His influence was too pervasive for that. He introduced Arthur to the lake country, the great imaginative consolation of his son's life, and indeed his chief defence against his father's values. He introduced him to fishing, which eventually became a dominating passion. Many of Cyril's traits, including a difficulty in understanding other people's point of view, reappeared in the adult Arthur, who made a cult of his father's memory, his death having occurred before the conflict between them could induce, as it otherwise must have done, a strong and conscious rejection of everything Cyril believed in. As it fell out, the son mourned the father deeply, cherished his memory, and showed that he felt the slights he had endured only by describing them in his autobiography, and by missing no opportunity, in the rest of the book, of praising the kindness and encouragement he had received from various older men, substitute and more generous fathers, at various stages of his career: W. H. D. Rouse, W. G. Collingwood, Robert Ross, Harold Williams.

Cyril Ransome's death was like his life. One night at Nibthwaite he went fishing for sea-trout. On the dark bank he fell over an old grindstone and damaged a bone in his leg. He thought the injury was a sprained ankle, and ignored it, on the grounds that exercise would keep it from stiffening and spoiling his holiday. But it was not a sprained ankle. 'The doctors were slow in finding what had happened, probably because my father was so sure himself.' It was some form of tuberculosis. Eventually the foot had to be amputated. After that it was a contest between death and a very determined man, who contrived to go on shooting partridges, grouse and wild duck, and fishing, and writing (history books for schools, and political journalism) and looked forward to a political career. In 1897 he gave up his chair at Leeds and moved to Rugby, where he planned to be a sixth-form tutor before going into

Parliament. He entered Arthur for the Rugby scholarships – a last gesture of hope and ambition. Even the amputation of his leg at the knee, and then at the thigh, did not arrest his disease. Arthur failed abysmally in the scholarship examination.

A few weeks later, at the Old College, Windermere,

> the headmaster's wife came to me in the dormitory over the gateway in the old square tower that used to rock in high winds. She sat down on my bed and told me that I should not see my father again. He was dead and I lay and wept with my head under the bedclothes. I have been learning ever since how much I lost in him. He had been disappointed in me, but I have often thought what friends we could have been had he not died so young.

But at the funeral he was horrified at himself, because, mingled with his sorrow, was a feeling of relief.

The feeling did not last long. It is much less easy to forgive ourselves for failing the dead than for failing the living; besides, Arthur's mother survived. She determined to carry out her husband's wishes now, as when he was alive. She 'told me (though I knew only too well already) of my father's fears for my character and her hopes that from now on I should remember to set a good example to my brother and sisters.' As little as ever, if she had her way, would Arthur be allowed to be himself; and the family stopped going to Nibthwaite for its holidays.

Young Arthur's essential characteristics were evident from his earliest days. Before he was sent away to the Old College he seems to have been a spirited, warm-hearted, intelligent little boy, however naughty. Naughty he certainly was, as the stories of his friendship with young Ric Eddison demonstrate. Eddison was the son of a Leeds solicitor; he lived at Adel, a village two miles or so further out of Leeds than Headingley. Arthur went to Adel for lessons with Ric under tutors whom the boys mercilessly persecuted.

> Ric's favourite motto, often quoted in crises of our long war with our tutors, was 'Discretion is the better part of Valour', but he knew how to temper discretion with daring and sometimes showed an ingenuity and a power of assessing the behaviour of grown-up persons that, as a small boy, I looked upon

with awe. Consider, for example, the sad case of Mr A., one of the long series of tutors who endured for a while and disappeared ... Mr A. we disliked extremely and Ric decided to get rid of him. His plan depended on accurate timing and a knowledge of his mother's views on education. We knew at what time Mrs Eddison would be going upstairs to dress for a tea-party. That was enough, if she would be punctual, and she usually was. Ric and I sat down to arithmetic, one on each side of the table in the nursery with the victim-tutor sitting between us at the head of the table. Ric became more and more annoying, with a long series of stupidities, echoed by me, until we could feel that the tutor was at the point of explosion. A glance at the clock. The time had come. We simultaneously bombarded the poor tutor with idiocies until at last, outraged beyond bearing, he rose in wrath, smote right and left and brought both his pupils toppling, chairs and all, to the nursery floor. There was no need for us to raise the piteous wail we had in readiness. Steps were running up the stairs. The door opened and there was Mrs Eddison looking at the field of battle. Mr A. left that afternoon.

Ric dealt with Mr B. with equal efficiency. One detects in him perhaps the germ of Nancy Blackett's character. Arthur's solo naughtiness has more the flavour of Roger Walker.

I had a vindictive dislike of grown-up persons, however kindly, who tried to be witty at my expense (by asking, for example, 'who was the father of Zebedee's children?'). There was in Leeds a lecturer on agriculture called Archibald, the kindliest of men, whom we knew both in the lakes and at home. He was remarkable for the gleaming baldness of his head. He rashly, coming on me feeding my guinea-pigs, asked 'Do you know that if you pick a guinea-pig up by its tail, its eyes will drop out?' I had been asked that question before. I looked up at him innocently. 'Mr Archibald,' I said, 'if anyone were to lift you up by your hair, would *your* eyes drop out?' and the next moment was fleeing for my life.

Well might he flee; but the standard of repartee is high, the humour appealing, and the personality which could be so ruth-lessly cheeky was surely formidable. Not, however, more formidable than his partner in crime: indeed, Ric Eddison was ever the leader. He too was a future author, although the intricate, mannered fantasies that he produced in manhood (*The Worm Ouroboros* is, or deserves to be, the best-known: it is a forerunner, if not a prototype, of the works of J. R. R. Tolkien)[2] could not be more unlike the works of Arthur Ransome; but he seems undoubtedly to have been an imaginative stimulus to his companion:

> *The Worm Ouroboros* was a book of strange power, a story of fantastic heroes in a fantastic world, written in a consistent, fastidious prose that seemed devised for that purpose. The language, the place-names and the names of the heroes were for me an echo of those ancient days when Ric and I produced plays in a toy theatre with cardboard actors carrying just such names and eloquent with just such rhetoric.

This is the only example of creative play which Ransome mentions in the *Autobiography*; but in a publicity handout issued by his publishers in 1948 he told of a similarly revealing incident:

> I was a cheerful, small boy of action rather than of letters. Then one day we were playing at ships under and on a big dining-room table which had underneath it, in the middle, a heavy iron screw pointing downwards. It was my 'watch' below. My brother or sister was on the bridge, on top of the table, and suddenly raised a shout for 'All hands on deck!' I started up, and that big screw under the middle of the table made a most horrible dent in the top of my skull, altered its shape and so, in one moment, changed my character for life. I crawled out, much shaken; and that very afternoon wrote my first book, about a desert island, in a little notebook with a blue cover. I have been writing ever since.

According to the handout, this incident occurred when he was eight years old, therefore in 1892, which was the year before he went to Windermere Old College. No one, I suppose, will take

2 Tolkien met Eddison once; read and praised all his works; but denied convincingly that they were any sort of influence on *The Lord of the Rings*. After *The Hobbit* appeared AR wrote to the author, describing himself as 'a humble hobbit fancier' and questioning the use of the word 'man' to describe a hobbit at various points in the book—which was to hit where it hurt, and Tolkien accepted his criticisms.

the theory of the stimulating power of a bang on the skull very seriously. There were more important factors at work in the Ransome household pushing Arthur towards writing: the example of an admired father, perpetually at his desk (when not fishing); the family practice of reading aloud (warmly commended in the *Autobiography*); the absence of rubbishy books in the house.

> Children begin by being omnivorous. To them the miracle of being able to read makes any book miraculous. A course of second-rate books can blunt that new-found faculty of reading ... People say that a child must have 'free choice'. But how is a child to know the difference between good and bad, if all look alike and he has not by experience of the good so trained his palate as to reject the bad? We were never conscious that the bad was being withheld from us, but in fact it was ... We did not know that we were forbidden to read rubbish but we were given every opportunity of reading the best.

In such circumstances it was probably inevitable that Arthur would eventually try to turn childish games into written stories: the games themselves, after all, were acted stories. The incident of the table is important for other reasons. It enables us to date the moment of transition; and it is significant that the first tale he tried to write concerned a desert island. The last sentence in the anecdote is also noteworthy: 'I have been writing ever since.' Thousands of children every year try their hand at writing; almost none has the talent to make anything of it. Of those who have the talent, few have the persistence to keep going. It was to be years before Arthur met with any acknowledgment that he had talent; still longer before anyone recognised that his persistence was not simply misplaced obstinacy. His doggedness should have pleased his father, though there is no evidence that it did so. It was a sign of what was, at bottom, a character of granite.

That he had other mental virtues may or may not have been clear to his parents by the time the period of tutoring with Ric came to an end. He was sent for a time to a day-school half-way between home and the Yorkshire College. There he first learned Latin, and was so well taught that in after years he could say that it had never occurred to him that learning was an unpleasant form of toil. Everything changed when he was sent to the Old College. As usual, his father's intentions were of the best: in this case, he thought he was doing Arthur a favour by sending him to school in the lake country, to which they were both so devoted. It was perhaps the only comradely thing that Cyril ever did for his son. It turned out very badly. True, the lakes and fells were there; but now they were to be no more than a consolation in distress. 'I will lift up mine eyes unto the hills ... '

> From the date that the doors of his prep-school close
>   On the lonely little son
> He is taught by precept, insult, and blows ... [3]

Blows came heavy and fast upon Arthur because he was no good at games, being extremely short-sighted: another thing that his father did not notice (nobody did, until he went to Rugby). The headmaster was a Christian and a sportsman, so naturally he believed in the character-building virtues of football, boxing and cricket. Arthur was ceaselessly forced into these pastimes, and as ceaselessly disgraced himself:

> No great damage can be done by a small boy wearing boxing gloves but there is something dreadful in not being able even to try to parry blows of which you know nothing until they land one after another on your eyes and nose. I saw no worse when my eyes were bunged up and used to welcome the bleeding of my nose because as the blood poured down, my turn at fighting came to an end, so that I could use a handkerchief and save my clothes. The headmaster called me a coward. The other boys jeered at me and knowing my utter inability to retaliate used to attack me at any odd moment just for fun.

A mind chronically humiliated and afraid is unlikely to be very receptive in the classroom. 'Work here was not learning but the anxious avoidance of punishment.' Fortunately for Arthur he had some means of escape from the external horrors, and necessity drove him to make the most of them.

His Great-Aunt Susan Ransome lived in Windermere village, and he was allowed to visit her on Sunday afternoons and on special occasions. At church he could see Aunt Susan in her pew

---

3 Rudyard Kipling, 'The Waster'.

and tell himself that presently he would be, for a few miraculous hours, *not at school*.

> She was a spirited old lady. I remember coming in one day when she was playing hymn-tunes on the piano. Suddenly she struck a wrong note and the next moment with resounding crashes she brought down all ten fingers on the keys, again and again, with repeated volleys of sound, all the way down the keyboard from the treble to the base, when with a final thunder of the lowest notes she looked up, saw my startled face in the doorway and sat there laughing at herself.
>
> As long as she could scramble on the fells she could never resist the call of a fox-hunt. She was a great toxophilite and in dark green uniform with tabs and tassels, quiver and longbow, used to take part in the archery meetings on Belle Isle, the long island that stretches across the mouth of Bowness Bay.

They were good friends, but she could provide no more than an intermission in his unhappiness, unless of course he told her what he was enduring. This he did not do, neither did he tell his parents. Decades later his mother told him that in his letters home (which she had kept) 'there is a constant refrain of "white mouse" "white rat" "newt" etc!' Pets were a safe subject in letters that were open to inspection by the schoolmasters. 'When parents receive letters from their sons beginning "I am very happy" they must not be too sure that their sons are living in Elysium.' On the other hand, it would have taken a very perceptive parent indeed to read accurately between the lines of the first of Arthur's letters to survive. Undated, it appears to belong to the year 1895, when he was eleven, and more than bears out his mother's observation.

> My dear Mother: I could not write to tell you how the boots felt, As I only put them on yesterday. I have got them on now. They hurt horribly as I expect you will know. I have got a wofull piece of news for you. Mrs. Raikes says that nobody is to have any more money in the middle of the term. So could you send me some mice and my cage instead of the money. A lot of the boys are getting pets, And I will be awfully out of it if I do not have some. It does not matter what colour, but I like black and white or chocolate best. I would like some tremendously. If you send them you could get them at the

animal market on Tuesday. Then they would arrive here on Wednesday. I *would* like some. I have to go for walks just the same. I am just going for one now. Do not tell Mrs. Raikes that I said this. Or she would be very angry with me.[4] I am going up for a scripture competition in the Christian. My conjuring is getting on splendidly. I have got the Mesmerised Penny, the Multiplying Halfpenny, and the Penny pierced by your finger. I have got on quite alright in my work. I am going to keep on with my conjuring. I hope you will be able to give me the mice. The more I have the better I will get on with the other pet keepers. There are only six more weeks till the end of the term. I am already planning an entertainment with conjuring, juggling, and a set of performing animals, Mice, Rats, Guinea-pigs and Rabbits. I am preparing a set of apparatus for Performing Mice. It is a Race course with hoops to go through and Hurdles to jump over. I wonder whether the children will like it. If you cannot get mice Rats will be just as good. I have got a beautiful little cage made on purpose for the rats here. Please will you tell the children Habout the Rats and Mice and tell them that I am going to dress a Rat up like an old Woman and Ventriloquise it. Please tell Miss Sidgemore that I will write to her when I write to thank for the mice if they come. I am hoping for the mice. Your loving son, Arthur.

The handwriting is very large, which perhaps results from his poor sight; he seems a little over-anxious as to whether he will please or impress the other boys; but Mrs Ransome must have kept the letter because it struck her as the amusing outpouring of a happy child. She cannot be blamed.

He was unhappy, and he kept the information to himself. The same pattern of behaviour can be found in Rudyard Kipling's account of his own very similar childhood. Kipling too was nearly blind, though nobody knew it; he too suffered great unhappiness; he too was silent, when he might easily have told loving relations; and he too became a writer.

The coincidence is marked enough to be worth exploring a little. Kipling would probably have put it down to general causes: 'Children tell little more than animals, for what comes to them

---

4 This suggests that the censorship was not so rigorous as the *Autobiography* says, and that the young AR knew it.

they accept as eternally established. Also, badly-treated children have a clear notion of what they are likely to get if they betray the secrets of a prison-house before they are clear of it.'[5] Ransome agrees: 'Small boys are reticent and resilient and, not knowing the world, are ready to make the best of it.' It may be observed that Kipling was alleged to be a liar, Ransome a coward: they were not allegations that either boy would want to ventilate more than necessary. With Kipling it might have led to a dismissal of all complaints, and punishment for bearing false witness; in the other also it might have made things worse rather than better, by confirming Cyril Ransome's fears about his son. Besides, sensitive and intelligent children, knowing that there is something very wrong in their relation with the world, and not thinking to blame it on sensory deprivation, are almost bound, in their many dark moments, to fear that their oppressors are right to despise them: Kipling implies as much in 'Baa Baa Black Sheep', the short story he made of his experience.

The clearest inference is sanctioned by the express statements of both men. Each was saved by his imagination; one might say, by the birth of his talent. Kipling records that the mental bullying he endured forced him to give attention to the lies that, in self-preservation, he was forced to tell: 'and this, I presume, is the foundation of literary effort.'[6] During his periods of solitary confinement in the basement of the House of Desolation he began to play a private game, based on *Robinson Crusoe*, in which he pretended to be a trader with savages. Another punishment which proved valuable was that of being compelled to learn Prayer Book collects by heart, and chunks of the Bible. Above all, he read, with desperate avidity, even when his eyes began to trouble him, even when 'the Woman' tried to deprive him of books. It was the same when he spent his Christmas holidays with his Burne-Jones cousins: among all its delights the chief was being read aloud to by his aunt out of *The Pirate* and *The Arabian Nights*. On one occasion William Morris appeared suddenly in the nursery and told its denizens part of the story of Burnt Njal. It seems likely that Kipling's destiny was fixed before his tenth birthday.

Arthur Ransome did not suffer as much as Kipling, and he grew up into a writer of much narrower range, but the pattern was

5 Kipling, *Something of Myself*, Macmillan, London, 1937, p. 15.
6 Ibid., p. 6.

otherwise the same. With him it was his mother who read aloud: 'Fortunately for us [she] enjoyed this and read extremely well.' He does not specify which books or authors she read, except for Scott ('at the same time I was racing through him for myself at a speed that my father tried to check by cross-examining me on the book I had been reading before letting me take the next from the shelf'). But he gives a longish list of the books that came the way of the Ransome family: *Treasure Island* and *Robinson Crusoe*, the *Jungle Books*, 'hot from the press', *The Rose and the Ring*, *Alice*, *Jackanapes*, 'the whole spectrum of Andrew Lang's fairy books, which I collected one by one at Christmas and on birthdays', *Lorna Doone*, and *Thorstein of the Mere*, by W. G. Collingwood. Kipling gives a similar list, and tries to indicate which of the works he mentions were eventually to stimulate ideas of his own.

Readers of this biography, or of the *Autobiography*, *Old Peter's Russian Tales* and the *Swallow* books, will easily spot which of the titles on Ransome's list were eventually to inspire him. But one title, *Thorstein of the Mere*, requires more than mention, if only because it must be unfamiliar to most readers today. It was a book that might have been written for Arthur, or for any boy familiar with Coniston Water. One such, the author's son Robin, took it over so completely in the telling and writing that it had to be dedicated to him. The book exists on several levels. On one, it is a masterpiece of Pre-Raphaelite or Ruskinian design (W. G. Collingwood was Ruskin's partner, secretary and factotum). On another, it is a very acceptable pastiche, reading like a translation of a lost saga of the coming of the Northmen to the Lake District. The author's deep inwardness with Viking culture is impressive, though to an adult taste the antiquary in him comes out a little too often: he is incapable of passing by a place-name without explaining it or making an intelligent guess at its origin. Perhaps it is ungracious to carp, since the whole story originates in a guess as to how the lake came to be called Thurstonmere. And a splendid story it is, in which Collingwood's knowledge of the water and hills of the district is deployed to wonderful effect. Thorstein is the youngest son of a family of Norsemen who settle at Greenodd. Up-country is wild and unknown. Thorstein's destiny takes him north, where he discovers the lake that comes to bear his name. He is cheated out of his inheritance, and nearly out of his true love, but all comes well in the end. At the climax of the book he successfully withstands a siege on Peel Island. Eventually he dies valiantly, as a Viking should, in a glorious defeat; but his children survive, and their descendants after them, in their home at Nibthwaite.

Like Kipling, Ransome met the Bible — the Authorised Version, of course, the inspiration of England for three and a half centuries: 'there was a Bible Reading Society, joined by the whole school, and its members were given printed cards showing a passage to be read for each day of the year. These I enjoyed, and came to know the fine prose of the Authorised Version very well.' The school did little for his Latin, but he came to know the Second Book of the *Aeneid* well, with its thrilling account of the wooden horse, Laocoön's warning, and his killing by the serpents. Otherwise the only books of any value to which the school introduced him were Carlyle's *French Revolution*, set as a holiday task ('when set to write an essay on it after coming back to school, [I] stopped only when the headmaster said I had written ten times more than I should and cut off the supply of paper'), and Rolf Boldrewood's *Robbery under Arms*,

of particular interest to me because my maternal grandfather, though, unfortunately, not a bushranger, had spent much of his life on the very ranges where Starlight and the Morgans did their desperate deeds and I, alone in the school, had seen a blackfellow's boomerang and even thrown one.

Though entirely lonely at school, Arthur had his sisters and brother for playmates in the holidays: unlike Kipling, he had no need to invent solitary games. But he needed a refuge just as much during term, and found it in the countryside itself. When, after one particularly horrible experience, he ran away, he went north, by a road from which, as he had already discovered, he could see the hills he knew from Nibthwaite: over the Kirkstone Pass, down towards Ullswater, into the heart of the lake country. He did not get far: he was met on the road by a friendly coachman, a frequent visitor to Great-Aunt Susan's kitchen, and taken back to school. But nothing was said to him about the incident, or to his parents. He reasoned later that the authorities could not afford to let Professor Ransome know that they had driven his son to such a pitch of despair, and lesser punishment might simply drive him to try to escape again, or, worse still, tell tales. Best to overlook the whole matter. Arthur might well feel that his blind appeal to the hills had saved him.

On school walks in the woods between the Old College and the shore of Windermere he used to listen for the sound made by a little beck as it came down from the heights over many little waterfalls. 'Lingering dangerously I used to listen for it again to see if I could still hear it and then run hastily after the others.' He collected caterpillars as he had at Nibthwaite.

Best of all I had the great good fortune to be at school at Windermere in February 1895 at the time of the Great Frost, when for week after week the lake was frozen from end to end. Then indeed we were lucky in our headmaster, who liked skating and wisely decided that as we were not likely to have such an experience again (the lake freezes over only about once in every thirty-five years), we had better make the most of it. Lessons became perfunctory. After breakfast, day after day, provisions were piled on a big toboggan and we ran it from the Old College to the steep hill down into Bowness when we tallied on to ropes astern of it to hold it back and prevent it from crashing into the hotel at the bottom. During those happy weeks we spent the whole day on the ice, leaving the steely lake only at dusk when fires were already burning and torches lit and our elders carried lanterns as they skated and shot about like fireflies. I saw a coach and four drive across the ice, and the roasting of an ox (I think) on Bowness Bay. I saw perch frozen in the ice, preserved as if in glass beneath my feet. Further, here was one activity in which I was not markedly worse than any of the other boys. On a frozen lake in the grounds of the three Miss Fords at Adel, a kindly foreigner, Prince Kropotkin, had guided my infant footsteps. I had learnt to move on skates and was thus better off than most of the boys who had never skated at all. Those weeks of clear ice with that background of snow-covered, sunlit, blue-shadowed hills were, forty years after, to give me a book called *Winter Holiday* for which I have a sort of tenderness.

He was now, in fact, spending most of his time among the lakes, for this was still the period of the Nibthwaite holidays: Leeds was at best an interlude at Christmas and Easter. The country was printing deep; it was a secret joy, something for the most private contemplation. More than sixty years later he was to sum up in a sentence what it had meant to him throughout his life: 'No matter where I was, wandering about the world, I used at night to look for the North Star and, in my mind's eye, could see the beloved skyline of great hills beneath it.'[7] The hills of Coniston, or Windermere, or both? It scarcely matters. What is clear is that early experiences of this kind, duration and intensity – coupled, perhaps it should be added, with a passion for books, those other consolations – are almost bound to create a writer. Ransome's destiny was fixed as early as Kipling's: certainly by the time he was thirteen.

The drama of his life had been launched: the conflict of the forces symbolised or activated by the lakes and by his father, which one day he would resolve in his art. Meanwhile childhood ended. His father died, lake holidays ceased, he entered Rugby without a scholarship, and the struggle with his mother began.

Edith Ransome is mentioned frequently in the *Autobiography*, but always with such reticence that it would be easy to conclude that she was of little importance to her son. However, more than three hundred surviving letters to her from Arthur prove that such a conclusion would be entirely wrong. He loved his mother dearly, and in the years of his manhood, at any rate, found her a valuable friend and confidante. Their relationship was so important to him that he could say little about it for publication. So he described his youthful clashes with her, and one or two of his cruel blunders; he mentioned some of her characteristics, but made no attempt to draw her portrait. In describing his father he could not resist the unconscious urge to take his revenge. Almost all his anecdotes of Cyril Ransome show the professor in a bad light, but at least they bring their subject to life. By contrast, Mrs Ransome is not much more than a silhouette. She does not move or speak. And the few letters from her which have survived do not fill the gap.

At least it is clear that she was a much less formidable person than her husband. She was good-looking. She was a gifted and persistent painter in water-colour, like her father. Kindly, intelligent and firm, she was an excellent mother. Her self-effacing disposition explains her success as the wife of so overbearing a man as Professor Ransome. She was perhaps over-earnest: her

7 'Author's Note', *Swallows and Amazons* (1958 edition).

mother, a Gwynn, stoutly denied that there was any Welsh blood in the family, and Cyril found that he could tease his wife by pretending to prove her descent from Caractacus.

She was devoutly resolved to be as loyal a widow as she had been a wife, but she was no match for her elder son's determination to go his own way. She could use the name, memory and known views of the dead to help her in her battle; she could call on Arthur's love for her; she found in the end, as mothers so often do, that while these weapons might win a campaign or two, they were useless for winning the war. So she lost, and Arthur gave her cause for distress and anxiety for thirty-five years. But she lived to see him an established success, and perhaps came to feel that all was well since it had ended well.

In 1897 her programme for Arthur was that he should do well academically and enter a respectable, well-paid profession. He did neither, and never looked like doing so. For one thing, at Rugby he gained a valuable ally.

The school suited him. He might have been as unhappy there as he had been at the Old College, but luckily went into the form of Dr W. H. D. Rouse, later headmaster of the Perse School, Cambridge. Rouse was a great scholar of language and literature, valuing not only Latin and Greek and Sanskrit but also, amazingly enough, English, of which he thought well enough to teach it in the classroom. (F. R. Leavis was to be one of his pupils at the Perse.) However, Rouse's first service to Arthur lay in another sphere. A maths master noticed that young Ransome was unable to read the writing on the blackboard without going up to peer at it; Rouse had the boy's eyes tested, and his short sight was at last discovered. Arthur put on the spectacles which were thenceforward part of his appearance, and at last began to enjoy the life of a normal schoolboy. He took up Rugby football and managed to scrape into his house fifteen. He tried all other ball-games, and discovered billiards: 'even now, though I have only once made a break over thirty and call that a Red Letter Day on which, with the help of lucky accidents, I make a break of twenty, I will go a long way for the pleasure of a game.' He had to suffer the fagging system, then at its prime, but was lucky in his fagmaster, R. H. Tawney, the future socialist philosopher and historian:

I dusted his study with a feather brush, blacked his boots, made the toast for his tea and lit his fire for him, this last an accomplishment that has been of the greatest use to me in many parts of the world. I must say that I found him an admirable employer of labour.

The ragging, which at first he had to endure at Rugby as at Windermere, seems to have died out as Ransome grew used to his spectacles, though they were occasionally broken for him and frequently by him:

> I had to take them off for swimming, and then was so blind that unless I had been able to put them in a very safe place I had to beg somebody to find them for me, and more than once trod on them while looking for them.

He bounced out of the unnatural introversion which prep. school had forced on him so completely that we hear of some of the usual 'unforgotten, innocent enormities' of Victorian schooldays, such as an illicit excursion to some local races, and the manufacture in a test-tube of nitro-glycerine, which then had to be disposed of: it was poured down a drain in the roadway, Arthur and his accomplice fully expecting to destroy half Rugby in the process. He made several good friends, among them E. T. Scott, who would one day be his editor on the *Manchester Guardian*. He went on cycling expeditions about the countryside and collected ammonites for the school natural history museum.

Had this been all, there would have been no need for Mrs Ransome to be alarmed: it was the sort of banal existence which, coupled with a very slow progress through the lower and middle forms of the school, had shaped many a future solicitor, bank manager or schoolmaster. Unfortunately Rouse had not confined his attentions to Arthur's eyes. During the English lessons he had discovered that his pupil read books eagerly, and had formed the ambition to write them; even gave some promise of ability to do so. 'He saw nothing wrong in my determination ... and to the dismay of my mother did everything he could to help me.'

Nobody else believed in Arthur's literary promise. He enjoyed reading the Greek New Testament, but his Greek grammar was hopeless. He showed what he thought of Latin by having a copy of the *Essays of Elia* bound into a cover of Caesar's *De Bello Gallico*, so that he could have something pleasant to read during the interminable lessons. 'I remember being called upon to construe, and, with unthinking enjoyment, reciting aloud to an astonished class and master the praises of Roast Pork.'[8] He was not much good at English composition, once he moved up out of Rouse's form. Such promise as he showed was for science and engineering. The schoolmasters sneered at him, the boys teased him. When he was indiscreet enough to publish a piece of 'earnest doggerel' in the local paper, on the subject of the recent death of Queen Victoria, his schoolfellows set the words to a merry tune and sang it under his window. He listened 'with hot cheeks and eyes'. Even that did not cause him to waver in his course. For one thing, he knew perfectly well that his poor performance in the classroom was largely caused by his simple failure to do the work. Perhaps he meant to be a conscientious student, but somehow there was always something to distract him: making small engines of various kinds in the school workshop, editing a monthly magazine written by himself (like Kipling), going for an illicit cross-country run with Ted Scott, or simply, again like Kipling, taking 'intense delight in visible things' – elm-shadows in the Close at Rugby, a blue butterfly seen during a summer holiday in Wiltshire.

> This bad habit of absorption in anything other than the work that was my immediate duty has persisted all my life, and I have been most unjustly rewarded for it. I have been allowed, for example, to put into my books my pleasure in the sailing and fishing that have taken so many of the hours that should have been spent in other ways, and so have been able both to enjoy my cake and to keep it.

Mrs Ransome had reasons for deploring Arthur's choice of a career which, together, do not amount to much, and show her to have been conventional, if not timid, in her approach to life. But they also show her to have been an affectionate mother, only too anxious to do right by her boy.

It is nowhere stated, but it seems to be implicit in the *Auto-biography*'s account of the business, that the dying Professor Ransome took Arthur's failure in the Rugby scholarship very hard. It confirmed his worst apprehensions, and he passed them on. 'My mother had inherited my father's fears lest I should turn out as

8 *Bohemia in London*, p. 23.

irresponsible as my grandfather, and thought writing a profession likely to bring out the worst in me.' Her picture of the trade of authorship, as retailed by her son, seems unduly alarmist. To be sure, there was always the threat of New Grub Street; but in that golden age, before the rise of the free public library, when printing costs were low, middlemen were fewer, and the public had nowhere to turn for entertainment of an evening save to magazines and novels, or to the theatre, which could provide an excellent living for authors, even mere anthologists and critics could earn an adequate income solely from the sale of their writings. If Mrs Ransome seriously objected to the career of letters as such, she was not very well informed. Her objection was probably based entirely on her estimate of Arthur's character and talents. As to his character, we know what he was and what she thought of him. She seems to have believed that a steady routine job was what he needed. Why it was supposed sensible to thrust Arthur into the sort of profession for which he was unfitted by the deepest bent of his character is the sort of question which only parents can answer. Mrs Ransome was on much stronger ground in fearing that Arthur lacked the talent to succeed. His aunt Helen Boulton, herself a writer, was brought in to reason with him. She did not make the mistake of scoffing at his ambition; she merely suggested that it was something that he could pursue in his spare time. His immediate business was to put himself in the way of earning a regular income and so relieving the financial burden on his mother; perhaps it was even suggested that he ought, as soon as possible, to start contributing – there were the three younger children to bring up, after all. Rouse offered to coach Arthur for Oxford, but the offer was declined. 'There was no smallest likelihood of my winning a scholarship. Life at Oxford was costly. My mother could not be asked to keep me there while I prepared for what? for a profession that guaranteed no regular income.' Once again, the logic is obscure. For a professor's wife, Mrs Ransome seems to have had a surprisingly narrow, utilitarian idea of a university education. Clearly it did not cross her mind that at Oxford Arthur might enrich his spirit and his intellect, and perhaps, whether through contact with his fellow-undergraduates or in new fields of study, discover a vocation, as many men and women have done there, which would both satisfy his ambitions and guarantee his prosperity. The suggestion that she had the money (otherwise the debate was pointless) but would not spend it on a mere writer is unpleasant. The appeal to Arthur's guilt-ridden affection for her, disguised as one to his sense of responsibility, was illegitimate: after all, it was his education that was at stake, not hers (perhaps we should bear in mind that she had never had one, in the full sense, even during her engagement). But it was all quite innocently done, and Arthur caved in. He agreed to study a second-best subject, science, at a second-best institution, the Yorkshire College.

So at the age of seventeen and a half Arthur Ransome returned to his native city to study at his father's university. The inevitable happened. The Yorkshire College might be infinitely smaller, poorer and rawer than the University of Oxford; but it was quite as effective as the more ancient place in respect of what is, after all, the essential function of a university: liberation. Arthur sensed the change immediately. 'For the first time in my life I was not conscious of a surrounding atmosphere of doubt or disapproval.' He blossomed, but not as a scientist. He enjoyed playing with test-tubes, Bunsen burners and other apparatus in the chemical laboratory (in *Pigeon Post* he would one day make use of the knowledge he gained there) but that was all. He began to collect books, haunting second-hand booksellers', stinting his meals so as to have money to spare, and being encouraged in this latest enthusiasm by old family friends who did not take Mrs Ransome's view of the literary life. He shed Rugbeian pieties by going on pilgrimage every Sunday to a different place of worship – Unitarian, Anglican, Wesleyan, Congregationalist, Quaker – before giving up religion altogether, and by dropping team games in favour of long walks in the country. And he confirmed his vocation, quite as thoroughly as if he had been at Oxford:

The decisive moment found me in the College library. I had gone there from the laboratory to consult a book on mensuration or magnetism, and happening on some shelves where the books were classified not by their subjects but by the names of their authors I saw two tall brown volumes with richly gilt lettering and decoration on their backs: J. W. Mackail's *Life of William Morris*. I began dipping into one of them, sat down with it and never went back to the laboratory that day. I read entranced of the lives of the young Morris and his friends, of lives in which nothing seemed to matter except the making of lovely things and the making of a world to match them. I took the books home with me, walking on air, across Woodhouse Moor, in a thick Leeds fog, and had read them through before I went to bed. No second-best choice would satisfy me now. Nothing would change my mind. Nothing should stop me. From that moment, I suppose, my fate was decided, and any chance I had ever had of a smooth career in academic or applied science was gone for ever. For days after that I moved in a dream, reading that book again and again.

Such moments of conversion occur only when the soul has been thoroughly prepared for them. The decision to go to Leeds had not in the least altered Arthur's determination to write; on many nights he sat up late doing just that. The world of books had been growing more and more alluring. More and more he desired the education that he had not found at Rugby and that was not available at Leeds – or, indeed, at any other English university of the epoch. Not surprisingly, after the battering he had received, he was for a time waylaid by doubts as to the chances of realising his dreams; and his belief in the dignity of letters – the prop of his self-respect – was also tottering. Mackail's *Morris* reassured him on both points. It sanctioned a departure that, perhaps unconsciously, he was already contemplating. 'Nothing seemed to matter except the making of lovely things.'

Mackail's biography sent him to Morris's own writings, including *News from Nowhere*. It would be reasonable to suppose that they would begin his political education, but the *Autobiography* plainly states that they did not. Kropotkin had taught him skating, not anarchism; Morris taught him aestheticism, not socialism. His imagination was not caught by the idea of making a beautiful world. 'In 1901 and for many years after that I should have been astounded to learn that I should ever have to take part in politics. In those days in England it was still possible for a young writer to regard contemporary politics as a matter for the politicians.' He was particularly likely to do so if he was reluctant to grow up, which was very much the case with Arthur.

But perhaps events were moving too fast for political ideas to have any chance of taking root in his mind. The demands of the laboratory are inexorable, yet Arthur was beginning to shirk them. He was devoting as much of his time as possible to 'writing and reading, reading and writing', causing his landlady to exclaim at the frequency with which she had to empty his waste-paper basket. If this went on he would meet disaster in the examinations, thus disgracing the Ransome name in Leeds. Yet the writing and reading were equally necessary. He had everything to learn about literary skills. Besides, he wanted to write essays in the manner of Hazlitt, and fairy-tales in the manner of Andrew Lang and Hans Christian Andersen, ambitions which were not likely to bring in much money for years, if ever. So he did not feel entitled to ask his mother to support him as a student at the Faculty of Arts at Leeds, since she would not, thereby, be helping him towards financial independence. Anyway, he understandably flinched from the frightful row which such a request would provoke. All in all, it seemed best to start looking immediately for a job that would pay him his keep and leave him time to learn, somehow or other, to write. Having reached this conclusion he at once began to act upon it.

He got 'some small rubbish' printed in a Leeds magazine, and eventually asked for an interview with the editor of the *Yorkshire Post*, who had once been the Ransomes' next-door neighbour. The editor received him kindly but advised him not to think of entering journalism until he was older and had a university degree. He made an approach to R. and R. Clark, the Edinburgh printers: probably there was a family connection there too, for Geoffrey Ransome eventually went to work for them; they were the printers of Messrs Macmillan, and Mr and Mrs Maurice Macmillan were Cyril and Edith Ransome's closest friends. But they had no job for Arthur.

The approach to Clarks' seems to have been made with his mother's knowledge, so Arthur must have plucked up his courage to inform her of his apostasy rather sooner than is stated in the *Autobiography*. His first surviving adult letter to her tells the rest of the story, and since it also illustrates the young Arthur's character, and the scantiness of his literary attainments, it is worth giving in full.

(*16 February 1902, Yorkshire College, Leeds*) My dear Mother: the windfall has arrived. On hearing that you were coming to finally decide, I made a last and crowning effort and wrote to Grant Richards the publisher of the Worlds Classics etc setting forth my virtues and faults.

Result. He has written and says that if I could come up to see him some day next week, Thursday would be best, he could very possibly give me a start in his firm.

It is much better this than the Clark business and if I left here early on Thursday morning I could come back the same night in a sleeping train so it would only cost the journey and it is a pity to throw away such a chance. It would mean, no more expense, you wd be able to settle where you liked, I should be safe anyhow whether I turned out good at writing or not in a business connected with my beloved books!

He says I am to give him two days notice so if you could telegraph it would be a blessing. I know it would turn out all right in the end and although it is a risk of the journey money it is less than Edinburgh and far safer. It might mean a whole career.

Such is the power of Cheek. (I have also got a letter from Hall Caine very decent on the subject.). Do telegraph and say you'll risk it. Nothing venture nothing have. I told him I could begin work in June so as to get my whole year at Coll. It is an awfully good chance. Please telegraph to 29 Broderick Grove, as soon as you can so that I can let him know if I'm coming. Think of what we may be throwing away if I don't go. It would mean missing 1 lecture only, and I havent missed 1 yet besides the sore throat day. Please telegraph.

Believe me
your affec. son
ARTHUR M. RANSOME

Hope the excitement wont upset you.

What could poor Mrs Ransome do? She had gambled on Leeds and science, and lost. She took her defeat like a sportswoman (after all, publishing was a very respectable trade) and gave Arthur money for his fare. He went down to London and Grant Richards offered him a job as office-boy at eight shillings a week. Mrs Ransome also went to London, and was charmed by Mr Richards: Arthur was allowed to accept his offer. She decided to move to London herself, so that her daughter Cecily, who wanted to be an artist, could have a studio there, and Arthur could live at home. He could stay in lodgings until she had found a house. Suddenly it was all arranged.

II

An Education in Bohemia

On consulting a classic work to find synonyms for a Bohemian,
I find the following: 'Peregrinator, wanderer, rover, straggler,
rambler, bird of passage, gadabout, vagrant, scatterling, land-
loper, waif and stray, wastrel, loafer, tramp, vagabond, nomad,
gypsy, emigrant and peripatetic somnambulist.'

ARTHUR RANSOME, *Bohemia in London*

If Leeds was liberation, London was liberty itself.

The job at Grant Richards lasted only six months. Arthur threw
himself into it with enthusiasm: being a London errand-boy in
summer weather was pleasant work. He learned a lot about publishing, including a neat swift enviable way of tying up parcels,
and was given more and more responsibility, since the firm was
understaffed. At length he decided that he was worth much more
than he was getting in wages, and demanded a rise. The manager
seems to have regarded this as impertinence and, if he raised his
pay at all, it was only by two shillings a week. The episode left the
errand-boy somewhat disgruntled, and when he came across a
similar job, paying a pound a week, he took it. The people at
Grant Richards, that rising firm, thought he was making a great
mistake: the Unicorn Press, his new employer, was on its last legs.
But Arthur did not want to be a publisher: he wanted more independence than he could get on eight shillings a week, and leisure
to practise the art of writing. The Unicorn Press, where there was
less and less to do, answered his needs perfectly. He stayed for
about a year, and then resigned. He had begun to sell articles and
stories to the magazines, and rashly supposed that he could now

make his living as an author exclusively. The Unicorn Press disappeared a few weeks later.

The fair career in publishing, the prospect of which had pleased his mother so much, came thus to an early end. So did Edith Ransome's other device for keeping her wayward son in order. He lived with her in Balham for nearly two years (that is, until the spring of 1904) and then moved off to lodgings in Chelsea. He was still in law a minor, only just past his twentieth birthday; but from that moment we may date his adult career as a man of letters, entirely his own master at last. In the autumn of that same year his first book was published.

Arthur was to write two lengthy accounts of his early manhood, one for the *Autobiography*, the other diffused through his *Bohemia in London*. Both breathe an air, or rather a gale, of exuberant enjoyment. For six years he was like a schoolboy on holiday. The story of his escape from Balham and his mother catches the general spirit perfectly.

He spent a morning prowling round Chelsea until he found a room that suited him: it had four windows in good condition, cost only a few shillings a week, and had a water supply two floors down. He ordered a boy and a grocer's cart to arrive outside the Balham house after lunch, and when they did explained to Mrs Ransome what he had in mind. He loaded the van with his only possessions: a large wooden chair, a railway rug and dozens of books, and sat on the tailboard to make sure that nothing fell off. 'Of this I am now ashamed,' he commented in the *Autobiography*. 'I should have thought of my mother's feelings and not mounted the tailboard of that van in full view of all our neighbours who were watching from behind their lace curtains and their aspidistras.' At the time no such thoughts crossed his mind. He lit up a pipe and undid a couple more of his shirt buttons. 'The pride of it, to be sitting behind a van that I had hired myself; to carry my own belongings to a place of my own choosing; to be absolutely a free man, whose most distant desires seemed instantly attainable. I have never known another afternoon like that.'[1] The van carried him slowly in his glory through south London: he did not even mind the mockery of errand-boys and loafers, 'for was I not now a free Bohemian, on my way to the haunts of Savage, and Goldsmith, and Rossetti, and Lamb, and Whistler, and Steele, and

1 *Bohemia in London*, p. 22.

Carlyle!' The van went across Albert Bridge, up Cheyne Row, past Carlyle's very house, and so along the King's Road to the World's End, where boy and Bohemian each had a pint of beer (that was in the happy days before the law closed pubs in the afternoon). Arthur sat on his tailboard reading *Love for Love* ('Poor Innocent! You don't know that there is a place called the World's End? I'll swear you can keep your countenance purely; you'd make an admirable player') and drinking to Congreve's memory. Then off they went again, soon arriving at Arthur's lodging, which seems to have been somewhere between the King's and the Fulham Roads – Lamont Road, perhaps, or Limerston Street. The landlord (a greengrocer) was displeased by his tenant's exiguous furnishings, and not much soothed when they were supplemented by half a dozen grubby packing-cases from the nearest grocer's shop. But Arthur was in far too high a feather to stand any nonsense, and was presently left alone, arranging his packing-cases to make a cupboard, and a bed (with the help of the railway rug), and a chair, which he put by the window. There he sat and smoked over a book of poetry, savouring the hopes and fears of his freedom, and was so happy that he fell asleep leaning on the window-sill, waking in the morning with a cold in his head.

It did not take him long to become a full citizen of Bohemia. All his life he had a gift for making and keeping friends, and now (it was one of his special joys) he could exercise it to the full for the first time. Sending articles to magazines was a good way of getting to know other writers, even if the articles were often rejected (he knew what it was to go dolefully down the stairs from an editor's office, feeling like a schoolboy who had been whipped) and before long he was able to lavish his enthusiasm and his instinct for hero-worship on a dozen notable seniors. In a studio near The Boltons he drank in awe a concoction christened 'opal hush' by W. B. Yeats (claret diluted with lemonade out of a siphon); going home to Balham or Chelsea at night he used sometimes to take a detour through a quiet street behind Westminster Abbey to see if his cousin Laurence Binyon's light was burning, and to exult in the thought of the poems that might result from such midnight labour; sometimes he would glimpse G. K. Chesterton rolling up Fleet Street laughing to himself and bumping into other pedestrians without noticing. But it was G.K.C.'s brother Cecil whom he got to know really well at this period.

They worked together on a literary magazine, the *Week's Survey*, under an amiable editor, Paul Neumann, who printed whatever they sent him until the magazine lost too much money and changed hands. His closest friend of all the literary men was for a time the as yet almost unknown Edward Thomas.

Arthur could hardly have found a hero more worthy of worship. The two men had much in common. Both were countrymen at heart, with a passion for literature, and the moment was propitious for them, since this was the time when the Decadence was swiftly and amazingly modulating into what would come to be called Georgianism, the time when, as Yeats was to remark, 'everybody got down off his stilts; henceforth nobody drank absinthe with his black coffee; nobody went mad; nobody committed suicide; nobody joined the Catholic Church; or if they did I have forgotten.'[2] Beer and dog-roses and the open road would soon become clichés just as deadly as green carnations, but for the moment it was exciting to meet other able young men who shared your tastes and were ready to laugh, even if affectionately, at Gordon Bottomley (another new friend) for his continuing attachment to the views and attitudes of the Nineties.

Yet is is to be doubted if it was just their common tastes which drew Ransome and Thomas so close, though obviously they would not have been friends without them. Arthur seems to have found in Edward an elder brother, six years his senior, whose acute intelligence, fastidious judgment and solid literary accomplishment made him a star to follow and proclaim. Perhaps he was also touched by Thomas's underlying restless melancholy, so unlike his own puppyish enjoyment of life. For his part, Thomas found Ransome 'exuberant, rash, and Protean' as well as intelligent, and was attracted by a temperament so unlike his own. The high point of their early intimacy came in the autumn of 1904. Arthur had by now moved to a ground-floor room at 1 Gunter Grove, and Edward Thomas, on one of his frequent flights from his wife and children, took the room next to it, for ten shillings a week ('extra for washing, light and coal'). Both men were extremely hard-up, and lived for a week on cheese, for nourishment, and apples, to counteract the constipating effect of the cheese. Then Edward unexpectedly got a cheque for twenty-five pounds by the three o'clock post. He and Arthur, in Bohemian fashion,

2 Introduction to *The Oxford Book of Modern Verse*, 1936.

were unshaven and scarcely dressed (they being penniless, what had there been to spruce up for?) but the cheque had to be cashed immediately, if they were to have the money that day, for the bank closed at four. They took a hansom, cashed the cheque, paid off the cabbie, 'and walked the Strand like giants'. They had tea, then at half-past six went to Soho for dinner. After an excellent meal and a smoke they paid the bill, left the restaurant, hesitated in the street a moment, and went into a restaurant on the other side, not a word said, to have dinner all over again. Then it was port in a friend's room until three in the morning. Edward was in such high spirits by the time they got back to Gunter Grove that he sat on Arthur's bed singing Welsh songs at the top of his voice, to the accompaniment of Arthur's penny-whistle and his own heels drumming on the floor. 'Presently there was a deep thud that startled us for a moment into quiet.' It was their land-lord, a postman, who slept in the basement, and had been suffi-ciently roused by their music to fall out of bed, though not, it appeared, to wake up, for they heard his snoring boom out again almost at once; so they felt free to resume their hullabaloo.

Arthur too must presently have received a cheque, for soon after he bought a desk, which Edward helped him to carry through the streets to his lodging. They often walked to lunch at a cheap restaurant in Fulham. It was on one of these excursions that Thomas gave Ransome a needed warning: 'Have nothing to do with women!' He himself had married far too young, he said, and had a miserable life as an undergraduate as a result, bearing the burden of family responsibilities while he was still only a boy. 'I run away from home every day,' he said, on this or another occasion, 'but I always come back for tea.' What this meant was that he had got too much used to the comforts of domesticity to enjoy privations in Gunter Grove as the romantic young Arthur did. So after a month he retreated to his wife and children in Kent. Arthur used occasionally to visit him there, and go for long tramps with him and his dog.

Arthur was a tall, thin young man. He had inherited his mother's brown eyes and high cheekbones, and these, combined with his red moustache, occasionally gave him a Chinese air, some thought. The moustache would eventually become a walrus affair on the grandest scale, making up for all the hair he lost from his head. His externals and internals were closely studied, during his Bohemian period, by Stephana Stevens, a literary agent who later became an authority on Middle Asian folklore and religion. She was at this time making a name for herself as a popular novelist, and eventually put Arthur into one of her books. It has an infelicitous title ('– and what happened: being an account of some romantic meals') but it does give a priceless picture of the young Ransome as he appeared to a very intelligent, caustically observant, but essentially sympathetic young woman. He figures under the alias of 'Matravers'.

'Who is Mr. Matravers?'

'Matravers? He is a person who writes small books in large and beautiful print in which the t's trail down towards the next letter; books in which the first word on a page is printed below the last line of the page preceding. He contributes essays to quarterlies, and reviews novels in a literary paper without ever having written one. He is, in print, the most fastidious and meticulous creature. In person he is bombastic, Gargantuan, thunderous, explosive, brutal, and bouncing.'

'Bombastic, brutal and bouncing! It sounds like "I love my love with a B",' said Letty.

After this most accurate evocation (yet Arthur was a shy creature under the bounce) Letty is taken to meet Matravers.

A sonorous and volcanic 'Ha-ha-ha-ha,' proceeding from the hidden turn in the stairs, made her start, and the next moment … she beheld a large young man of shaggy appearance. He was quite young, and the shagginess was not so much due to hairiness, for his face was smooth, except for an untidy and somewhat undeveloped moustache, as to a general impression conveyed by his personality. Possibly his aura was shaggy. He wore an old and worn shooting-jacket, a yellow tie, leggings, and an enormous pair of boots; altogether Letty had never seen a man more unsuitably attired for the London streets. It was preposterous.

I am afraid that Letty was a dress-snob, for she had already objected to a friend's red tie. It is nevertheless true that normal middle-class street attire was then of a required formality which nowadays would be regarded as intolerable except in the stuffier regions of the City and the Inns of Court, and there was significance, as Bohemians well knew, in the eccentric manner of their dress. They were asserting their youth, their artistic status, their mental and moral independence; and Arthur was among them.

Matravers, like his original, is permanently hard-up: Letty discovers, on this first meeting, that his watch is in pawn. He is also inclined to fall in love for a week with every pretty girl who comes his way. His feeling for Letty herself is unusually durable. She is a prentice journalist. He sends her a bunch of white heather the day after she gets an article into print for the first time. Letty is ungratefully unimpressed: she thinks him a most self-satisfied young man, unworthy of womanly pity.

Matravers gives an evening party, and in the course of it utters a speech which is pure Ransome:

> I was down at Windsor. My publisher's kids live down there, and I'd promised to have tea with them. A jolly little girl, and a boy, and another youngster. We got playing a rowdy game with a mechanical steamboat in the fish-pond – I was a torpedo, you see, and I got pretty soaked. Then a man came in to tea, and we got to words, almost to blows when I told him he was an ass, and then I missed my train.

Matravers has a puppy, which eats the dinner and leads to a row with the landlady. The puppy is sent into the country. Matravers explains why, and again, in his White Knight way, sounds exactly like his model:

> I didn't want to leave Mrs Burgin, though she is such a harridan, because I've just fixed up some new bookshelves – I daresay you noticed them. Before, all my books were in sugar-boxes, and I could never find a book when I wanted it. I'm just editing a set of Russian authors for a series, and writing prefaces to them, and one likes to turn up a reference quickly.

This series is surely a transmogrification of the little volumes that were to form part of *A History of Story-Telling* which Ransome edited in 1909.

Matravers bullies Letty about her article ('It was beastly and journalistic') and boasts about one of his own works, which he gives her: 'the workmanship is careful. I rewrote it about fifteen times.' He offers to teach Letty Russian: Arthur was a great one for giving lessons. He tells a ghost story: with Arthur it would have been a folk-tale.

> He was very young, she discovered when she looked at him at her leisure, and he had a half-nervous, half-confident manner in playing the host which rather took her. He was so bursting with interests and enthusiasms and youthfulnesses that she almost forgave him his naive egoism. It was the egoism of a big puppy that bounces up to you wagging his tail and jumping up at you as much as to say 'I *am* a jolly creature, am I not? Of course you'll make a fuss over me!' She felt that the danger of intercourse with him would be that she might yield to the temptation of taking him at his own valuation just because he was such a happy, blundering piece of self-satisfaction.

He woos Letty earnestly, playing 'Summer is icumen in' to her on a flute (it was one of Arthur's favourite tunes, but he played it on a penny-whistle) and insisting on helping with the washing-up after she gives him supper. Over the kitchen sink he asks her to marry him so that they can live in a cottage on the Yorkshire moors. 'His short-sighted eyes, vague as brown moons in his young face, were full of enthusiasm, his face was damp and reddened with the effort of explanation.' Letty, after forcing him to admit that he has earlier proposed marriage to each and all of her women-friends, refuses him; so he goes off for a tramp with a gipsy, sending Letty a parcel from the countryside containing moss; two hedge-sparrow's eggs, blown; four plover's eggs, unblown; primroses, anemones and wood-violets; watercress; and a black stone wrapped in cotton-wool. 'The parcel breathed Matravers, and she recognised his small, clear writing on the label.' It does not induce her to marry him: perhaps she finds his 'room-shaking laugh' or what strikes her as his gigantic size too much to live with. But neither does she quite accept the verdict of one of her friends, that Matravers has all the trappings of genius without the genius. He is at least individual and vital – much the most vital person in the book.

The portrait of Matravers shows what a force was unleashed once Arthur had got free of his school and his family. Most of the traits it depicts were to be in evidence for the rest of his life (though not the excessive susceptibility: he was to learn in a hard school to keep his heart under control). It is avowedly the portrait

of a very young man: the worldly shrewdness, the keen intellectual edge, which were characteristic of the mature Ransome,
are hardly visible. But what Stephana Stevens saw she recorded
faithfully. It was not her fault if she never got more than a glimpse
of Arthur's real business in these early London years.

He was educating himself as a writer. His idea of self-training
was characteristically energetic, straightforward and so practical
as to seem Utopian. He wrote all the time, as he had at Leeds:
planning his evening's scribbling, in his Grant Richards days, on
his way back from the office on an omnibus, and throwing away
the results, or burning them (on one occasion he set fire to his
mother's chimney). Sometimes he would write a string of essays,
and then change over to write a string of stories. He found that he
could not mix the two pursuits: he could not, as it were, write an
essay before supper and a story afterwards. The genres seemed to
demand different skills, and his mind was too stiff to switch gears
promptly and easily. He was not always short of robust criticism,
of the Rugby kind. When he was lodging in Clapham, before his
mother arrived at Balham, one of the young men in his boarding-
house asked to see what he was writing. 'He read it and looked at
me with pity. "I say," he said, "if you think anybody is ever
going to *pay* you for stuff like this, you're mistaken. You'd much
better chuck it. Why not do fretwork instead? Then you'd have
something to show for all the time you're wasting." ' Arthur
slogged on: he rightly believed that if he was to acquire a style –
that characteristic aspiration of writers of the period – if he was
to master the art of words, so that he could say what he meant
and say it in such a way that people would read it, he would have
to practise incessantly.

In his maturity he did indeed have a style, one which never
draws attention to itself or the author, and is otherwise chiefly
characterised by a miraculous ease and lucidity. It was acquired by
years and years of the strict discipline which the young Ransome
imposed on himself, years during which he had to purge himself
of many bad habits, in particular a weakness for purple patches
which uneasily combined the lushness of the Nineties with that of
the Georgians. His taste improved with time. He was always
facile. This statement may seem inconsistent with the fact that he
took endless pains over his writing and rewriting. It is not. Many
writers, of whom Ransome was one, are driven by habit or
neurosis to tinker endlessly with sentences that do not actually

need their attentions. Others learn only with agonising slowness how to string words together at all – George Orwell was one such. Ransome never seems to have gone through this phase, and it was probably his facility (it can hardly have been anything else) which caught Rouse's attention when he was thirteen. The result was that all the labour of his nonage risked saddling him with a permanently bad style: pastiche might have become his natural language. Fortunately his verbal ease left him free to devote much of his attention to problems of form and content, and this saved him. There is nothing like hard honest thought for compelling a writer to say what he means without frills.

Arthur did not believe that constant scribbling was alone enough to make him a writer. He also thought that he would have to complete his interrupted schooling by reading omnivorously. Here he may seem to be rationalising his bookworm tendencies; but it is surely just as sensible to regard his hunger for books as evidence of a need. The sort of writer he was to become eventually may not have required all the baggage he now took on board; but the sort of man he was would have been incomplete without wide and deep study. He wanted to feel himself part of the literary tradition of England, and he could do that only by familiarising himself with the work of his predecessors and contemporaries. Books were the friends of his imagination, and he wanted as many of them as possible. His family believed that he had destroyed his worldly prospects for the sake of books; to vindicate himself he behaved at times as if reading books was the only thing worth doing in life. He wanted to prove his vocation, and did so as thoroughly as he did everything.

The result was impressive. For example, the *Autobiography* mentions the following authors as among those he read between 1901 and 1909: William Morris, Robert Blatchford, William Hazlitt, Arnold Bennett, M. P. Shiel, Sheridan, Laurence Binyon, Ernest Bramah, *Erewhon* Butler, Sir Thomas Browne, David Hume, J. B. Mayor (*English Prosody*), Keats, W. G. Collingwood, Balzac, Henry James, Alice Meynell, Kenneth Grahame, Carveth Read (*Logic*), Bishop Berkeley, Gordon Bottomley, Yone Noguchi, G. K. Chesterton, Congreve, Yeats, Cecil Chesterton, W. W. Jacobs, Edward Thomas, E. Nesbit, Richard Le Gallienne, Leigh Hunt, Kant (*Critique of Pure Reason*), Schopenhauer, Santayana, Bernard Shaw, George Borrow, Charles Leland, R. L. Stevenson, Sainte-Beuve, Gautier, Jean de Meung, Lascelles Abercrombie,

Hugh Walpole. Undoubtedly a complete list of his reading at that epoch would be much longer. The actual list should not be regarded as fully representative of Arthur's taste, but it does at least prove that in his twenties he was not afraid of tough reading, and had a liking – presumably therefore a measure of aptitude – for abstract thought: no one without it is likely to struggle with Kant for very long. He found Hume's *Enquiry concerning Human Understanding* delightful, not only at first reading but for many years afterwards. Perhaps it was Hume who completed the overthrow of his religious beliefs.

If he escaped the mental dryness that can afflict the university-trained mind, Arthur did not altogether escape the characteristic weaknesses of the autodidact. He was not always able to distinguish between commonplaces and real intellectual discoveries. He could be excessively solemn about ideas. But he was too genial a soul for the latter trait to do much damage. A passage from his *Bohemia in London* shows the human side of his book-mania quite beautifully:

> I remember the buying of my *Anatomy of Melancholy* (that I have never read, nor ever mean to – I dare not risk the sweetness of the title); two big, beautiful volumes, with a paper label on the back of each, they stood imperious on the shelves. I had seven-and-sixpence in the world, and was on my way up to Soho for dinner. I took one volume down, and turned the thick old leaves, and ran my eye over the black print, broken and patterned by quotations in italics, Latin quotations everywhere making the book a mosaic in two languages. To sit and smoke in front of such a book would be elysium. I could, of course, have got a copy at a library – but then I did not want to read it. I wanted to own it, to sit in front of it with a devotional mind, to let my tobacco smoke be its incense, to worship its magnificent name; and here it was in such a dress as kings and hierarchs among books should wear. If I were ever to have a Burton, this Burton would I have. I remember I laid the book down, and stoically lit a pipe, before daring to look at the fly-leaf for the pencilled price. Just then another man, one with the air of riches, walked casually up to the stall, and, fearful for my prize and yet timorous of its cost, I seized it and turned with trembling fingers back to the beginning.

The price, it turned out, was eight shillings. Arthur gave up all thought of supper, haggled successfully with the bookseller, and handed over his seven-and-six. He walked happily home.

> One of the volumes was uncut – UNCUT. My landlord met me at the door with my bill. 'The Devil!' my heart said; 'I will attend to it,' uttered my lips; and upstairs, penniless, by the light of a candle that is, after all, as Elia has it, 'a kindlier luminary than sun or moon,' I spent three hours cutting that volume, leaf by leaf, happier than can well be told.

Pity the heart that cannot feel for Arthur in this triumph. And we need not take seriously the assertion that the book was not for reading: he read everything. But even the most innocent pleasures are traps. Arthur's delight in owning books, and in the sacrifices he made to buy them, would one day bring him great unhappiness.

At what may be called the technical level, his education was rapidly successful. In those days it was almost impossible to stay out of print if you had ability, so many were the magazines; to be sure, they often failed, but others immediately sprang up in their place. Editors were not long in finding out that young Ransome could spin sentences agreeably into the sort of stuff they needed. He scraped a living, though it was a marginal business: on one occasion he was saved from having to pawn his bicycle only by getting employment as a ghost for a publisher of sportsmen's autobiographies and books of advice. He wrote whatever was wanted: it was all good practice. The first book to which he put his name was entitled *The A.B.C. of Physical Culture*. It was not a work which he ever mentioned in later years.

Usually he did not need to sink quite so low. In 1904 he was going to the offices of the *Week's Survey* every Thursday, where with Cecil Chesterton and others he lay on the piles of back numbers and made up the week's issue, 'improving the work of other contributors, curtailing their articles, filling them up with jokes or parentheses, till they swelled or shrank to the required space, and in their own special columns, over their own names, instructed the universe on everything under heaven, and sometimes made metaphysical excursions even there.'[3] They also rolled each other's logs assiduously. It was even better fun than editing *The Granta* or

3 *Bohemia in London*, p. 179.

The Cherwell would have been. Next year, or the year after, thanks to the kindness of Maurice Macmillan, head of the great publishing firm, who remembered his own friendship with Cyril Ransome and approved of his son Daniel's friendship with Arthur, Ransome was paid £50 for looking after the monthly magazine *Temple Bar* during the last twelve months of its life. It had outlived its era, but Arthur was able to get the work of several of his young, talented, but as yet unknown friends into its pages, and he enjoyed the business of putting issues of the magazine together and seeing them through the press.

All this was very good training for a journalist, but at that time Arthur was quite determined not to become a newspaperman. 'By this time I knew two or three reporters and had the liveliest fear of being irrevocably drawn into the spinning maelstrom that newspaper life seemed to be. At all costs I wanted to be free to go on with my own education, which had almost nothing to do with the writing for which I was paid.' All his life long he cherished his independence, and could find good reasons for not accepting regular work when it was offered him.

The drive to educate himself and the need to earn his living were not the only forces working on Arthur. The years since 1897 had dimmed neither the memory of his childhood nor his longing for the lake country, and in 1903, given a week's holiday by the Unicorn Press, he hurried north by night-train to Coniston. He had an idea that he might find he could write poetry, and took a notebook with him to receive his inspiration.

It was a mistaken idea. No one can do everything, and as is shown by a specimen preserved in a letter to his mother written in 1906, Arthur in verse could not avoid even the most glaring forms of pastiche and plagiarism:

> Pipe, pipe, my shepherd boy,
>   Wild bees are humming;
> Laugh loud and leap for joy,
>   Summer is coming.
> Blue bells in elfin chime,
>   Ring in the summer time ...

Yet on the first day of his holiday in 1903 he lay on a large flat rock between two torrents of the Copper Mines Beck on the side of Coniston Old Man, and scribbled away earnestly at his poetastery. An artist, who had been sketching higher up the mountain, saw the immobile body as he walked home in the evening and wondered if it was a corpse. 'Young man,' he called across, 'are you alive?' The body (which had perhaps been taking a nap) jumped up, and over the beck, and he had his answer; another question revealed that the live young man had been trying to write poetry. 'Instead of laughing, he seemed to think it a reasonable occupation, and we walked down to the village together.' It was the beginning of the most important friendship of Arthur's life.

The artist was W. G. Collingwood, and he lived during the spring and summer at Lanehead, a house on the north-eastern shore of Coniston Water. He might have been expressly created to fill the gap left in Arthur's life by the death of Cyril Ransome and by the tensions which, before then, had divided father and son. Like the Ransomes, he was not native to the lakes, but had come to know them intimately during his school holidays and later; he could truthfully boast that he had climbed every fell and swum in every tarn. He and Arthur could thus meet easily on the ground of their common passion for the magic country. In 1903, furthermore, Collingwood was fifty years old: just the right age for an avuncular or paternal relationship. Even more important were his other attributes. He lived exactly the life whose possibility Arthur had glimpsed in Mackail's *Morris*. As a young man he had abandoned all idea of an independent career to minister to the needs of John Ruskin, which he did until the sage's death in 1900. He had originally settled at Lanehead because it was only a mile or so north of Ruskin's house, Brantwood. He was second-in-command of all the enterprises that Ruskin launched. He painted a charming sketch of Ruskin in his study, still to be seen at Brantwood today; and devised the monument in Coniston churchyard, a noble Saxon cross in green slate (Collingwood's authority in the matter of such crosses is still acknowledged). Money, he held, was only important in so far as it freed you to do your real work. He and his wife Edith made their living by selling their landscape paintings; but Collingwood's central activity was as a writer and antiquarian. He was a walking embodiment of Arthur's most cherished beliefs, loves and aspirations; and he was infinitely kind, infinitely encouraging, to young ambition. He and Edith were able to give Arthur exactly that help and support which his own parents, from the best of motives, had always denied him.

Arthur was pleased to find himself talking to the author of

Thorstein of the Mere, but he was too shy to follow up the encounter until the last day of his holiday. On the evening of that day, however, he presented himself at Lanehead and got the sort of welcome which made it inevitable that, the following year, he should be back on the Collingwoods' doorstep as soon as he got to the North again.

1904, the year of this second return to the lakes, was also, it will be remembered, the year of Arthur's escape to Chelsea and of his first book (not counting *Physical Culture*). All this had a bearing on his relationship with the Collingwoods and on the pattern of life he established for the next few years. His friend Gordon Bottomley lived in the Cartmel valley, and, in partnership with a local printer, proposed to publish a series of books of *belles lettres* and poetry by new authors. Arthur was to act as talent scout for the project, and, unsurprisingly, as he remarks in the *Autobiography*, 'the first young authors who came into my mind were Edward Thomas, Cecil Chesterton and myself.' Thomas was to publish *The Rose Acre Papers* with the Lanthorn Press, as the concern was named.

When in Maytime, not long after the removal from Balham, Arthur came back to Coniston, it was as a man of letters, with serious business in hand: he had to oversee the publication of a book of essays of his own. But he was welcomed as an eager, charming boy, whose tastes and interests were largely the same as those of the Collingwoods, and whose loneliness was perhaps plain. At any rate it was W. G. Collingwood who began to speak of his wife as Arthur's aunt, and the aunt herself who made Arthur feel at home in Lanehead, first by inviting him to stay, then by allowing him to help with the washing-up, and finally by sending him on errands into the village. It was all ecstasy to him. Returning from his first errand,

> I passed a hawthorn tree that had shed its petals all about it, a patch of glittering snow on the dust. During all that time the leaves of the trees seemed more luminous than they are today and the hills had sharper edges. I would stand gaping at this or that as if I feared I should not remember it for ever. I need have had no such fear. On the lake or on the further side of it I used to look for the pale corner of the Lanehead house where it showed through the trees below the fell and tell myself that I could not really be one of that loved family.

On an earlier page of the *Autobiography* he summed up what this friendship meant to him: 'Those two gave me something I had not missed because I had not then known that it could be. The whole of the rest of my life has been happier because of them.'

It would be absurd to try to equal, let alone surpass, the glowing pages in the *Autobiography* in which Arthur Ransome tenderly records his debt to the Collingwoods and their children, Dora, Barbara, Ursula and Robin. Arthur, like many others, but luckier than many others because the experience was complete and long-lasting, had found a second family; one in which he was safe from the sore points and rough edges that inevitably afflict members of families linked by blood, who have no choice but have somehow to cope with each other, whatever their differing tastes and characters, as children grow up and parents struggle with their training. Arthur, as it happened, was by now on good terms with his own relations, especially his mother and his brother Geoffrey ('I am a buffoon,' he remarked, 'but Geoffrey is a wit'); but the tension of the past was unforgotten, and Edith Ransome still looked on his projects discouragingly. Whereas, though the Collingwoods had their own problems, they were nothing to do with Arthur, and he could enjoy himself idyllically. He fell in love with the whole family, but in particular (and, given his character, inevitably) with one of the girls – with Barbara, who took two years or so to make up her mind not to marry him – two years in which he was, therefore, immunised against making a fool of himself over other women. The Collingwood parents would have welcomed him as a son-in-law, but had the sense to let events take their course. It says much for all concerned that when Barbara made her final decision she and Arthur remained close friends. He was almost equally devoted to Dora; and as Robin grew up he too gradually became an intimate.

All the Collingwoods painted or wrote or both (Robin was to turn into a more brilliant version of his father, ending as one of England's most distinguished historians and philosophers) and took it for granted, as Mrs Ransome never could, that Arthur was right to devote himself to authorship. By their spirit and example they encouraged him to work at his art harder than ever.

Arthur's instinct pushed him in the right direction from the moment he reached London. For example, he met a charming artist, Pixie Colman Smith, whose party-piece was the narration of folk-tales which she had heard in her childhood in Jamaica. They were chiefly concerned with Anansi the spider-man, and, as told by Pixie, were always realised in exactly the same words and phrases: 'In a long before time before Queen Victoria came to reign over we there live in the bush one black fat shiny spider call Anansi ... ' It was this formal aspect of the tales which fascinated Arthur. Somebody else might rather have been struck by the anthropological aspect of these myths, transferred from Africa to the Caribbean; a historian or a sociologist might look for what they could tell about the development of slave and free black society. To an artist it was the economy of their presentation which mattered, the language, so unexpected and yet so apt, which made the tales memorable. Before long Arthur knew them all by heart and himself made party-pieces of them. He used to tell them to the Collingwoods at night before the fire in the Lane-head sitting-room. He never wrote them down: he would have regarded that as untrue to the genius of the tales. He held that, once heard, they were unforgettable. Unfortunately this does not seem to have been true. Only a fragment of one of the Anansi stories, as told by Arthur, survives, in the memoirs of Dora Collingwood's eldest daughter:

> One of the stories was about a witch who put a spell on Anansi, so that if he said the word five he would drop down dead. His enemy made five piles of yams by the side of the road, and then lay in wait for him. Along came Anansi. 'Please Anansi will you count these piles of yams for me, I am so blind I cannot see.' Anansi was so small that he had to climb on to one of the piles. He began counting, 'One, two, three, four ... *and* the one I'm sitting on.' 'No! no! that is not the way,' but he went on, over and over again, till the witch was trembling with rage, but he never said 'five'. My mother, counting washing for the laundry, or dealing out fruit to us at lunch, would say 'One two three four ...' 'AND the one I'm sitting on,' we would chant in chorus.[4]

For years afterwards Arthur tried to write tales of his own in the same style. He failed: folk-stories cannot be synthesised. More important is the reason why he tried. From the start of his career

4 Altounyan, *In Aleppo Once*, p. 162.

he wanted to be a story-teller, as distinct from a novelist. He never seems to have aspired to make novels, although in the end he found himself writing them about children. When he produced a series of studies of fiction-writers he called it *A History of Story-Telling*, although among the authors discussed was, for example, Flaubert, who seems absurdly diminished by such a rubric. There might be various reasons for this limited ambition. The prestige of the story was high in that age of Stevenson, Kipling, Wells, Doyle, Conrad. In his youth Ransome lacked the knowledge of men and women that is necessary for serious novel-writing. It is unlikely that this influenced him. What he wanted to do was to equal the enchanters of his childhood as a teller of tales. He was willing to branch out: much of the imaginative work that survives from his youth is quite outside a child's range. But he had no doubt as to where his imagination worked most intensely, although he had as yet no idea of how best to exploit the fact. He was still fatally attracted by whimsy. He much admired the children's tales of E. Nesbit, which were coming out in rapid succession (1904 was the year when both *The Phoenix and the Carpet* and *The New Treasure Seekers* appeared in book form), but he had no suspicion that he was to be her successor. Indeed he still had much to learn before such a succession was possible. The Collingwoods began to teach him.

Much of their charm for him came from their association with the lake of his childhood, and everything they did reinforced and embellished the link. In the mornings everybody worked, but in the afternoons the young people went off on excursions. Sometimes it was to a picnic on the lake-shore, where they made a fire for their kettle and ate bun-loaf spread with marmalade. Sometimes it was to go sailing.

Ransome nowhere states unequivocally that it was the Collingwoods who introduced him to the pastime which, next to fishing, was to be his favourite hobby, and was to provide so much material for his best writing; but as he never mentions the subject in the *Autobiography* until he comes to describe *Swallow*, the Collingwoods' boat, and to evoke the happy days which he and they passed aboard her that summer, his readers can hardly be blamed if they make the inference. There can be no doubt that for years most of the sailing he got was with the Collingwoods, and in Robin, six years his junior but soon his firm friend (Robin, too, was a Rugbeian with tepid feelings, at best, about his school), he had an ally who was as absorbed in the pursuit as he became himself. By the summer of 1908 (to look ahead a little) they were racing against each other, in *Swallow* and *Jamrach*, a boat which belonged to Tent Lodge, the house nearest Lanehead.

All this was not so much a second childhood as a reawakening of his first, a recommitment to pleasures and intensities that might otherwise have become irrecoverably overlaid by the complexities and excitements of life in Bohemia. To be sure, it had been Arthur who had sought out the Collingwoods: he had been well aware of what he needed. But if they had repulsed him he might never have found it. So they deserve full credit for keeping open the road which eventually led to the books that made him famous.

The second literary gain from association with the Collingwoods arose from the nature of W. G. Collingwood's concerns. His daughters might, if they chose, enjoy the mere sensual music of the lake country and look no further; he himself was also intensely interested in all aspects of Lakeland history and society. He thus opened another door to Arthur's imagination. It was already on the latch. *Thorstein of the Mere* had peopled the Lake District with Vikings for him. He had also shown himself responsive to the people of the lakes, for instance in his close, affectionate observation of his Great-Aunt Susan and her household. Collingwood's influence was most casually exerted. But living in the same house as such an admirable figure, Arthur could not fail to respond to his example. He read his books, and was sufficiently impressed by their author's insistence on the Norse origins of the Lake people to nickname him 'the Skald' – which became the regular family name for him. The Skald drew back the veil from the past. As a child at Nibthwaite Arthur had made friends with the local charcoal-burners, a friendship he now renewed; but it was Collingwood who could show him, under the encroaching trees, grass and bushes, the traces of bloomeries along Coniston shore, relics of the iron industry, rapidly dying out, which had brought charcoal-burning into existence. Peel Island was now revealed as more than a favourite picnic-ground: the Skald had excavated it and found traces of a small medieval settlement, perhaps the former home of outlaws. He knew everything of the region's history, and under his tutelage Arthur began to convert his spontaneous liking for the people of Cumberland, Cartmel and Furness into a deep love of a society of strongly self-respecting, independent folk, with a multiplicity of avocations, deep roots in the past and great warmth of heart. Class distinctions seem to have been comparatively unimportant. The men of the hills were still, as in Wordsworth's day, statesmen: democrats, one might say, by tradition (a tradition that no doubt Mr Collingwood would have loved to trace back to the Vikings).

So for the next few years Arthur's life fell easily into a pleasant pattern. Autumn and winter were for London and work: for securing the necessary commissions, and meanwhile earning enough by miscellaneous writing to stay alive. With the spring he would leave for the North. After 1905 he did not again stay at Lanehead, being too prudent to risk outlasting his welcome. But he lived close at hand: just outside Cartmel for three years, in a farmhouse called Wall Nook found him by Gordon Bottomley; in 1908 at a cottage in Low Yewdale. He was thus never more than a dozen miles from the Collingwoods – nothing for a vigorous young man as fond of walking as Arthur was at this period. Every day he wrote, and every day he revelled in the lake country: expressing himself sometimes by tinkling at the piano in Wall Nook farmhouse, or by wrestling with young men getting into training for the Grasmere sports, or by cultivating gipsies and the charcoal-burners (who used to sweeten his clay pipes for him in their fires and leave them at a pub to be collected) or simply by watching otters playing in water-meadows in the moonlight. Here, he concluded, was his home. Gradually he harmonised the two sides of his life, through his friendships. When the Collingwoods came to London in the winter of 1904 he made sure that they got to know Edward Thomas; Thomas and Bottomley were already friends, so it was natural for the former to visit Cartmel, 'to walk with me and talk with Gordon Bottomley', as Arthur was to put it. Before long the little circle of writers at Cartmel was sufficiently conspicuous to attract attention among the natives. Arthur was remembered for his appetite for marmalade and for his habit of walking about hatless, coatless and even waistcoatless in hot weather. The circle was not dispersed when Arthur moved to Low Yewdale: indeed, it grew, and the critic Dixon Scott not only emulated Arthur's then unusual habit of sleeping in a tent in good weather, but devised a slogan which emancipated this group of budding Georgians from Gordon Bottomley's notions: 'Roast Beef and Rose-buds!'

opposite 1 Arthur Ransome shortly after his first marriage, *c.* 1909

Long before then, at Wall Nook, luck had brought Arthur another enduring friendship. Lascelles Abercrombie, who was courting his future wife at Grange-over-Sands, came to stay at the farm. He and Ransome were very soon breakfasting, walking and arguing inseparably.

Abercrombie was a poet, now unfashionable, who in his commitment to his art was forever speculating about how it would and should develop. Arthur, searching for a way to realise himself, was quite as interested in the subject. The debates he began with Abercrombie sharpened and enriched his mind, making it possible for him to emerge, in a few years' time, as a critic.

Before then he still had to serve out his apprenticeship. His first appearance in book form (for he did not count *The ABC of Physical Culture*) gave proof that he still had a lot to learn. *The Souls of the Streets* (1904) was greeted by its author with rapture, by his mother with silent despair (she 'could not disguise her feelings that this was yet one more nail in the coffin of the respectable future she had hoped for me') and by Edward Thomas with a sigh:

> I suppose that if a man can write such things he should be encouraged to publish them. That he should want to publish them, amazes me. In book form, I can only endure them when I think he has made a tolerably good mould of sentences &c into which he may some day find something to pour. I know something about sugar in prose, but this is prose in sugar.[5]

Thomas was nearly as good a critic as he would one day be a poet: here he put his finger on the essential point. *The Souls of the Streets*, a collection of 'little papers' – some of them had already been printed in the *Week's Survey* – shows that Ransome had acquired great skill with words. Otherwise it is almost without merit; the essays are not only trite, but sickeningly sentimental, as is shown by an extract from 'A Tuscan Melody':

> Lastly to prove that all this is true, was not the old song sung to me to-night, when dusk caressed the apples in my orchard? Two girls, who looked like spirits in their pale dresses against the darkness of the trees, sang to me leaning on a bough whose

5 All quotations from correspondence between Edward Thomas and Gordon Bottomley come from R. George Thomas (ed.), *Letters from Edward Thomas to Gordon Bottomley*, Oxford University Press, 1968.

faint pink blossoms still showed dim in the twilight. Only an hour ago, when I passed into my cottage, the stars sang high in the heavens above me and the echoes of those two sweet girlish voices were clinging round my heart.

There is a great deal about girls in *The Souls of the Streets*, as if the twenty-year-old author simply could not keep away from the subject.

The book nevertheless still has a certain charm; none of Arthur's friends was unkind enough to tell him how bad it was (as he matured, he found out for himself); above all, the Skald was encouraging; so the next year Ransome brought out another collection of essays, *The Stone Lady*. If anything it was worse than the first. Edward Thomas, reviewing the book, was courteous but damning:

> Though there was much gallantry and tenderness in his attitude towards men and women and nature, and no insincerity, there was yet a lack of sincerity ... Mr Ransome has gathered lovely flowers and has no water to put them in. For a moment the reader thinks them fresh, and in another he knows that they are dead.

Yet both these early books were clearly the works of a writer: of someone who could handle language, tell a story, expound an idea. There was promise in them. That promise became much clearer in Arthur's next significant undertaking, a series of little nature books for children (later collected into one volume) that appeared in 1906.

Ransome was still at the stage of scribbling to order; a dangerous practice, but one which can sometimes have stimulating and surprising results, as with the new books. A small publisher commissioned five short volumes on, respectively, the garden; ponds and streams; the seasons; woods; fields and country lanes. Each was to have a few illustrations by some struggling artist, and a text by the equally struggling Arthur Ransome. The market they were aimed at was that of the unimaginative (always the largest) those parents, teachers and librarians who have no idea what children really like, and accept unquestioningly the current assumptions. In Edwardian England those assumptions were predominantly coy.

Had Ransome found himself, he could hardly have undertaken this commission as conscientiously as he did. The first book, on the garden, hit exactly the desired treacly note:

This is a little book all about two children who live in a grey house with ivy on the walls, set in the middle of a garden with an orchard at its back. It is going to tell you about some of the things that there are in the garden, things that the two children love ... But first of all it is going to tell you about the two children and the other people who belong to the garden, and about the garden itself. When you have heard all this you shall know about the feathered people, and the insect people, that the two children love, and also about the two gardens that are theirs for their very own.

There are four people who belong to the garden and to whom the garden belongs – the Imp, and the Elf, and the old gardener, and me.

Ransome follows this prospectus remorselessly. By the time we have been taken to visit the snails and slugs (lovable, even though they damage the lettuces) we are likely to have been put off nature study and children for life. Words like 'wee', 'fairy' and 'jolly' pepper the text. Maiden aunts must have loved this volume.

Ransome next tackled the book of the seasons. Someone who could take the sex out of pollination –

'Look at his legs,' said the gardener, and they looked. The bee's legs and part of his body were golden with fine yellow dust. ' ... that is pollen dust, that is, and the flowers want the bee to come to them to carry it about to other flowers, for unless the pollen is carried about from flower to flower the seeds do not ripen.' 'Oh,' said the Imp.

– should have had no difficulty in making spring and summer boring, but the writer's instinct began to assert itself, and any reader with knowledge of the mature Ransome can see odd signals in the text, like bubbles as a pot starts to boil. There begin to be symptoms of characterisation. Ransome abandons the description of the life of birds and animals, at which he was not very skilled, and tells instead about the things in which his touch never failed: the activities of humans, especially country humans (haymaking, sheep-shearing, ploughing); and, his especial genius, how to do things – in this case, how to make a cowslip ball. The Imp shows traits of the kind that would later distinguish Roger in the *Swallow* books, wriggling through corn-shocks, and losing a blackberry race to his sister: 'The Imp is like me, and eats nearly as many as he picks. Blackberries are easier to carry that way.' The Ogre remembers that when he was little he liked wriggling through corn-shocks himself.

He recalls himself strictly to business at the opening of the third book of the series, *Pond and Stream*. Tadpoles, newts and caddis-flies fill the foreground; but in the background the new music becomes stronger and stronger. We may guess that Ransome could not spend so much time in the company of the Imp and the Elf, however loathsome their sobriquets, without getting interested in them, or at least without trying to make them interesting; and the only way he knew of doing that was to try and place them in the real world – in other words, in the only childhood he knew about at first hand, his own. Where else were 'the becks that trickle down the valley. You know what a beck is? The Imp and the Elf are north country children, and they would not understand you if you called the beck a stream.' His uncertain grasp of the children's reality is illustrated by the fact that a few pages later the Imp actually uses the word stream; but immediately afterwards he and his creator escape to the banks of a beck, and the magic begins. As Ransome was later to demonstrate so frequently, he had an acute sense of the individuality of streams and rivers, and the beck in this book, though schematically conceived (it was meant simply to illustrate the varieties of waterlife), suddenly acquires reality when it runs under a little bridge made of a slab of solid slate, which the Imp, still Rogerish, insists on wriggling below himself, under the scornful supervision of his sister. Then the party climbs the beck and meets a dipper, painstakingly described; but Ransome still had a lot to learn, and the passage has none of the charm of Titty's encounter with the same bird in *Swallows and Amazons*. Then, by one of those turns that seem accidental, or merely mechanical (after all, the children having inspected a duckpond and a beck, where else is there to go?) but are really determined by the deepest forces of an artist's nature, they get into a boat and row out upon the lake.

The lake comes from nowhere, suddenly, like Keats's perilous seas forlorn, but like them it is instantly recognised as enchanted.

'Half way down the lake there is a little rocky island.' Natural history is thrown to the winds, and Ransome describes a journey thither.

> We run the boat carefully aground in a pebbly inlet at one end of the island. We take the baskets ashore, and camp in the shadow of a little group of pines. There is no need to tell you what a picnic tea is like. You know quite well how jolly it is, and how the bun-loaf tastes better than the finest cake, and the sandwiches disappear as if by magic, and the tea seems to have vanished almost as soon as the cork is pulled from the bottle.
>
> As soon as tea is over we prowl over the rockinesses of the little island, and creep among the hazels and pines and tiny oaks and undergrowth. Do you know trees never look so beautiful as when you get glimpses of blue water between their fluttering leaves? When we have picked our way through to the other end, we climb upon a high rock with a flat top to it, and heather growing in its crevices; and here we lie, torpid after our tea, and pretend that we are viking-folk from the north who have forced our way here by land and sea, and are looking for the first time upon a lake that no one knew before us. The Imp tells us a story of how he fought with a red-haired warrior, and how they both fell backwards into the sea, and how he killed the other man dead, and then came home to change his wet clothes, long, long ago in the white north. And the Elf, not to be beaten, has her story, too, how she rode on a dragon one night and saw the lake – this very lake – far away beneath her, like a shining shield with a blue island boss in the middle of it. And how the fiery dragon flapped down so that she could pick a scrap of heather from the island, and how here was the very heather that she picked.

This passage demonstrates the profound impact of the lake country and the Collingwoods on Arthur's imagination: in the last passage the Imp and the Elf might almost be infant Collingwoods, and the Ogre, who has clearly at least read *Thorstein*, might almost be pretending to be the Skald himself. It also contains, in suspension as it were, the essentials of the *Swallow* books. The narrative tone is still unsure, but for the rest we have the deep feeling for Peel Island and Coniston Water; the fantasising, which was to make the lake, for the Swallows, a vast unexplored ocean; the feeling for actuality which prevents the fantasies from boring or getting out of hand; and finally, in the relationship of the Ogre with his charges, the relationship of Captain Flint with his nieces. It does not matter (we are dealing with the imagination) that the Imp is a boy; what is described here, though at the time of writing Ransome did not know it, is an early expedition of the Amazons to Wild Cat Island.

Before the book ends the children are taught a little more natural history, but Ransome's real achievement has been to convey the magic of a day spent in the open air.

> As the two of them go off to bed, very happy and very, very tired, we can hear the long kr-r-r-r-r of the nightjar in the pinewoods up on the hills, and below us in the woods at the head of the lake two owls answering each other.

In these words Ransome almost achieved his true literary identity. But the owls would not answer again for many years.

The nature books, if not exactly failures ('Not bad for a little town boy,' said Mrs Collingwood), were not successes either. They were useful practice, but they led to nothing immediately. For one thing the publisher went bankrupt and Arthur was paid nothing but his small advance. So he did not finish the series. Perhaps it was just as well: had the Imp and the Elf continued to preoccupy him he might have invented the 'Arthur Ransome book' before he was fully capable of exploiting the form, and so have gone off at half-cock. Instead he travelled in a completely different direction.

His next work, published in 1907, was *Highways and Byways in Fairyland*, about which the less said the better. It earned Arthur £10, was the apotheosis of the coy, and was arguably his worst book. Then one day in the winter of 1906, when Arthur was sitting at a table in a tea-shop with Cecil Chesterton, Stephana Stevens came up and said to him, 'There's a book that ought to be written, and you are the one who ought to write it, a book on Bohemia in London, an essayistical sort of book, putting Bohemia of today against a background of the past. Think it over. I've got a publisher waiting for it.' She showed true insight in making this suggestion, and Arthur went to work eagerly. A year later (autumn 1907) *Bohemia in London* appeared: his first real book; for though it is by no means without blemishes of tone, the conception is sound (it was Stephana Stevens's, after all), the execution competent, the matter interesting and the overall effect undeniably individual.

Only a year previously Arthur had been complaining to Edward Thomas that he could not get anything of himself into his stories. He got himself abundantly into *Bohemia in London*, as earlier passages of this chapter amply prove. The book is essentially one long discourse in which the writer feels free to introduce any topic related, however loosely, to his theme, and personal reminiscence necessarily takes up a large part of his utterance. Yet the work is not simply autobiographical. It is what it professes to be, a guidebook to Bohemia as it existed in London in the early years of the twentieth century, midway between the eras of Enoch Soames and Ezra Pound. The guide's free flow of anecdote serves to convince the reader that he knows what he is talking about; so does his flow of allusion to earlier denizens of Bohemia (Hazlitt, above all, but also Johnson, Lamb, Dryden, De Quincey) and his comprehensive survey of Bohemian geography: Chelsea, Soho, Hampstead. For the first time Ransome confronted a task which made the fullest demands on his powers, and although he was only twenty-two when he began the work, and had only mediocre writings behind him, he showed himself adequate to the challenge. His style is still somewhat overblown, but it is muscular compared to what it had been in *The Stone Lady*. There are some unfortunate passages (for instance, an evocation of Ben Jonson and other dead Bohemians, who obligingly sing drinking songs) but the picture of artistic London is on the whole convincing. It is suffused with the author's intelligence, warm feeling and perceptive humour.

The book clearly foreshadows Ransome's journalism, which is chiefly distinguished by its ability to convey, vividly, clearly and economically, what it felt like to be among certain people at a certain place and moment. Its effect is enhanced by excellent illustrations. Ransome had taken some pains to find the right artist: Fred Taylor, who produced a splendid series of black-and-white drawings, including two showing respectively Arthur in his cart on the way to Chelsea, and Arthur among his books after he arrived there. These designs make *Bohemia in London* easily the best-looking Ransome volume ever produced. All in all it is no wonder that it was his first success. It won him good reviews and respectable royalties, from North American as well as English publishers (Stephana Stevens had seen to that); but he had to eliminate a slightly bawdy ballad from his text before it could appear in Canada and the United States.

Bohemia in London was more good practice for a journalist, but Arthur still did not want to be one. Arthur Waugh, of Chapman & Hall, thought he might make a discursive essayist (others were to get the same idea in later years) and suggested a book modelled roughly on *Bohemia*, to be called *The Book of a Thousand and One Pipes*. He had probably noticed Ransome's addiction to tobacco. This was an idea that Arthur was willing to test, but it was no good, he could never get started, let alone finished. So it remained unclear, to himself as well as to others, what sort of a writer he had it in him to be.

His own bias was still towards story-telling. In the winter of 1905–6 he moved from Gunter Grove to lodgings in Chelsea Studios, on the King's Road, and from there he wrote to his mother (now living in Edinburgh) that he was not going on with his murder tale, whatever that may have been. 'Fairy stories suit me better ... I am busy reading Folk Lore. I am going to read all the English Folk Lore books that there are. With that knowledge behind me, I shall be better equipped than any other fairy merchant going. It is the one subject that it is possible to excel in without a degree.' *Highways and Byways in Fairyland* hardly bore out this confidence, however. Arthur's conclusion was that something was wrong with his technique: he does not seem to have suspected that the trade of 'fairy merchant', or even that of purveyor of murder tales, was not his. His long debates with Lascelles Abercrombie, though valuable, provided no better clues. Edward Thomas might perhaps have put him right, but Thomas was himself more and more hopelessly at sea: not until the arrival of Robert Frost in 1913 was he to discover that he was a poet. Besides, Edward was becoming disenchanted with Arthur. He had taken to referring to him, behind his back, as 'the Electrician', in disdainful allusion to Ransome's vitality, which he had once found so refreshing. He had enjoyed playing the patron to his young follower, but now that Arthur, all bumptiously, and still so young, was setting up successfully on his own, he could not repress twinges of resentment. 'My liking was never without artificiality. I cherished him because he was the nearest approach to a blithe youth I happened to know and it is natural that I should be angry with him for a rather speedy disillusionment.' Then, Arthur's scrambling in and out of love was so undignified, and his literary taste so uncertain – he had actually not admired one of Edward's favourite passages in his own writing until forced. He was writing a profile of Edward for the *Bookman*. It was all too much.

So there was no one to save Arthur from his next false start. He turned critic; and he got married.

III

Entanglements

You may carve it on his tombstone, you may cut it
   on his card,
That a young man married is a young man marred!

RUDYARD KIPLING, *The Story of the Gadsbys*

Arthur belonged to a decently reticent generation, and said no more than he had to, in his *Autobiography* or anywhere else, about his sexual and emotional history. Yet the essentials of that history are plain.

He was a sexual innocent until at least the age of twenty-four. After leaving Rugby he found himself powerfully drawn to women, but did not know either how to manage his feelings or how to satisfy them. In the late-twentieth century it may well seem inconceivable that such a normal young man could still be a virgin in his mid-twenties, but at the century's beginning there was nothing particularly unusual about it, at any rate in the ranks of the professional, public-school middle classes to which Arthur belonged. In Bohemia, it is true, there was every opportunity to break free from middle-class conventionality in sexual as in other matters, but Arthur did not do so. In this single, immensely important respect he failed to emancipate himself from the official simplicities of Rugby. And then he fell in love with Barbara Collingwood, but after two years of inconclusive courtship at Lanehead he was very little wiser about women and himself than he had been before.

He was young for his age, he says, and needed reassurance; needed it, apparently, so much that he decided that almost any woman would do, so long as he could have her company at home:

he had now moved into a large, comfortable flat in Baron's Court, just the thing to share with a wife. He took to writing love-letters, in the Matravers fashion, to almost every girl he met; and sometimes, if the letters seemed good enough, he posted them. This led him into endless scrapes. One girl, the future Sylvia Lynd, had the wit and kindness to suggest that he repeat his proposal the following day in person, 'and then we'll have tea'. On another occasion he came to his senses just in time and pursued the offending letter – successfully, it appears – to the banks of the Clyde. Far worse were the occasions when girls took the letters seriously: two or three times his unfortunate mother had to rescue him from unsuitable engagements. Soon any mention of a pretty girl was likely to disturb Mrs Ransome's peace of mind. For instance, when Arthur went over to Paris to prepare his *History of Story-Telling*, he wrote home enthusiastically about a young artist he had met, Jessie Gavin, who eventually made some excellent illustrations for the *History*. Edith Ransome wrote back warning him to be careful, and he had to confess, 'I am afraid it is too late to tell me not to fall in love with her.' The story had a happier ending than many. In the spring of 1908 Arthur left Paris for England and the lakes, and although Miss Gavin later visited him in Low Yewdale the affair (if that is what it was) seems to have died out painlessly soon after.

Then he met Miss Ivy Constance Walker.

She was brought to his flat by some friends that autumn, and promptly made the rather vulgar assertion that she was not a barmaid – 'alluding, I suppose, to the impropriety of coming with young men to a young man's rooms'. She was delicately beautiful, with a slight build, light brown hair and light brown eyes; men found her exceedingly attractive. So it was natural for Arthur to respond to her lead with *badinage* about saving her character by marriage. They carried on the joke for some time – the *Autobiography* is exceedingly imprecise about how long – and the end of it was that soon afterwards, if not that very evening, Arthur fell seriously in love.

He seems never to have been happy in this love. He and Ivy[1] were entirely unsuited to each other. It is not surprising that for a time he came under her spell, for she was probably the first

---

1 So Arthur always called her: no doubt his unconscious early detected what was, for him, her true nature. After he deserted her she called herself Constance.

middle-class woman who had ever projected her sexuality at him. To be deliberately enticed by a beautiful woman was a heady, an irresistible experience, the more so as the woman knew well how to heighten her attractions with touches of mystery and melodrama. What is harder to understand is what this Queen of Air and Darkness saw in an innocent, bookish boy.

He was not bad-looking; he was exuberant company; he was upright, good-natured, intelligent and promising. But it is impossible not to suspect that it was his unworldliness which was his real charm. Ivy had a dreadful home, from which she was eager to escape, but she was herself palpably unstable. Although she always plumed herself on the number and devotion of her admirers, she was not the sort of woman whom prudent men marry, and by the time she met Arthur she must have realised it, for she was twenty-six. So she entrapped him. Whether or not she prolonged the marriage-joke, she soon let him see that she took their relationship as seriously as he did himself. He discovered that she was unhappy, and depended on him to rescue her. After that he could never get free: He felt bound in honour to stand by her as long as she wished it, and she exacted her bond. In later years he blamed himself bitterly for this quixotic weakness, which did nobody any real good, and at the time, realising their mutual unsuitability, he more than once asked to be freed. 'She refused that and there were horrible scenes that made me feel at the same time a villain and a rabbit.' He gave in to her violence: it seemed there was nothing else to do.

He discovered that she was a wild and elaborate fantasist.

Presently we became engaged, whereupon she told me that she was already engaged to her cousin who was abroad. Then she told me that she was looking after her cousin's mistress and illegitimate child. She told me of her home life. Of her mother, who was partly Portuguese, she told me that, to keep her happy, she had persuaded her mother that the Sun God was in love with her, and that her mother had allowed herself to be decked with flowers to receive him, when a sudden thunderstorm had frightened mother and daughter alike. Of her father she said that he had a passion for power, and used to tie up her dog and beat it under her bedroom window.

She took Arthur down to Bournemouth to meet her parents.

They lost no chance of blackening each other's character to their daughter's fiancé. Arthur saw that throughout her childhood Ivy had been used as a weapon by Mr and Mrs Walker in their war against each other. 'She had had no chance of growing up like a normal human being.' Yet he was going to marry her.

Arthur and his future mother-in-law soon learned to loathe each other, but he was not afraid of her, nor of her husband. George Graves Walker was a rich, idle man who had been trained as a solicitor but seldom or never practised. 'I got on well enough with him when he realized that he amused me, and I showed that I did not mind amusing him. I think he was glad to engage in single combat with his wife, without feeling that his daughter's support might be given to either at any moment.' He seems to have had something of Ivy's taste for complicating life; or perhaps he was simply mean. At any rate, his only stated objection to the proposed marriage was that it might entail an expensive wedding from his house. So he refused to allow a public announcement, and according to Ivy wanted her to 'elope' with Arthur to Scotland. The marriage settlement was drawn up by a solicitor friend of Ivy's, behind her father's back. However, the finished document was shown to Mr Walker, no doubt by the bridegroom, anxious to do the right thing at all costs; and he said that in his opinion Arthur ought in no circumstances to agree to it. In later life Arthur thought himself an idiot for having done so nevertheless; but it is a fair guess that at the time he supposed that Walker was merely making mischief, and he may have been right, for after all the marriage settlement never seems to have given him any trouble. He rushed on his fate. Elopement to Scotland proved impossible, so on 13 March 1909 he married Ivy in a registry office. They travelled that day to Paris for their honeymoon, and returned to England to be married again in church on All Fools' Day.

There is no record of what Arthur's family thought of all this, but Edith Ransome must surely at some stage have wished she had spared herself the trouble of rescuing Arthur from unsuitable engagements. None can have been so unsuitable as his marriage.

The newly-weds settled in Hampshire, in a cottage which Edward Thomas had found for them: Stoner Hill Top near Petersfield, half a mile from the beautiful little house that Geoffrey Lupton had built for Edward himself to live in. It was a friendly action, and suggests that Thomas had overcome his disenchantment of the year before and was looking forward to Arthur's company as much as Arthur, we may be sure, was looking forward to his. They resumed the habit of taking long walks together. Unhappily Edward did not like Ivy. He described her to Gordon Bottomley:

> She belongs to the higher orders and no connection of hers has ever been in trade. She paints herself. She has many rings. But she is pretty and spiritual and clever but not clever enough to do her own hair. Unfortunately I never venture to limn the higher orders in my sketches.

Which suggests that Ivy had offered herself as a subject for an essay, and that Thomas had rejected the idea. Perhaps Ivy did not take the rejection kindly; at any rate, a month and a half later he was reporting, 'we see little of them. Arthur is a little uncomfortable in his new glory, I think.'

Arthur's idea was that by getting Ivy into a normal life, well away from her parents, she might become normal herself. It was a vain hope. For one thing it was no easy matter to make the separation. George Walker had approved of the Petersfield house, 'thinking it about the right distance, as he said, so that he could easily come over if he wished and we, without a car, would find it hard to meet him uninvited.' But invited they were, less than two weeks after their church wedding. 'Thank God,' wrote Arthur in the diary he had begun to keep, on getting back to Petersfield after a three-day visit. A few nights later they had supper with Helen Thomas, and on 20 April Edith Ransome came for two nights. She was soon followed by Mrs Walker:

> (*Diary, 29 April*) Arrival of mother-in-law.
> (*5 May*) Awful row.
> (*7 May*) Exit the mother-in-law. Thank God.

Mrs Walker was clever in a way, he reflected in later years. 'Once when I was playing "Summer is icumen in" on the piano, she said "You put hatred into that – hatred of me!" and, of course, she was right. As I played that lovely old tune I was thinking of Cartmel and Coniston and the life I had known before the disaster had happened.' But she was not his real problem.

(*Diary, 10 May*) I have had today information which suggests that Oliver Carr, W. S. Du [illegible] and Blake, have met and discussed a plan for the abduction of my wife, and her detention in a lighthouse to be bought by Carr.

The source of this delightfully ridiculous tale was of course Ivy. She also got Arthur to agree to buy a revolver to defend her. It shows what a powerful hold she had on him that he could take the story seriously for a moment; though he never actually got round to buying the gun.

In later years he usually chose to forget, or not to mention, how much he had wanted her. Even very young, innocent men do not marry girls out of pure quixotry, except in the novels of E. M. Forster. Mulling over his drafts of the *Autobiography*, Arthur noticed the point himself:

I do not think I have made it clear that she was extraordinarily attractive to all men, including myself. My very efforts to escape must have seemed to her (as indeed she said) wilful, and wrong-headed. It was as if she felt she had to cure me from being myself. How could I not perceive that all the others envied me for being married to her?

Years later he told his daughter that he and Ivy used to 'entwine like serpents on the lawn, and made love up an apple-tree', the implications of which are confirmed by some sour comments from Edward Thomas:

(*4 June*) Nor is there much to tell of the Electrician. Perhaps you caught the smell of burning in the startled air – for I hear he was at Coniston. We see little of one another, as the Two rise for breakfast (when they do rise) between 1 and 5 p.m. while we are bourgeois in such matters. Although he is a lightning author and transformationist there are not yet any small Electricians that I know of.

(*16 July*) They frequent Petersfield and other pubs enlivening the countryside with song. We like the 'painted lady' less and less and call her the Unicorn because she has a small ivory horn in the midst of her forehead. We feel very bourgeois beside them but deferentially expect *Bohemia in Froxfield*.

This is catty. Even if Arthur and Ivy were trying to solve their problems in bed, they were not the first young couple to do so; and after all they had not yet been married six months. What is interesting is the implication that they were enjoying each other's company (a point confirmed for a later period by their daughter's memories). Arthur's natural exuberance took a lot of quenching, and Ivy, it seems, could respond in kind. Singing in pubs, or on the way home from them, is not quite what one expects to hear after reading Arthur's gloomier retrospects ('it was as if a guillotine had fallen to cut off for ever the life that I had known'). At the time he was perhaps less fainthearted. Indeed, in the *Autobiography* he remarks that he took Ivy to Coniston (it must have been in May) to make her a present of the life he loved so much. Unfortunately the visit was not a success. As Edward Thomas had so promptly noticed, Ivy was a snob, proud of her descent from the Pochins of Barkby Hall, Leicestershire. 'Three days of the North were enough. She could not see the kindliness of the north country folk because, though they would call a cheerful greeting, it never occurred to them to touch their hats.' So back they went to Stoner Hill Top, where Arthur hurried on with his *History of Story-Telling*, now several months overdue.

The *History* was a by-product of Arthur's interest in the theory of narrative art, itself a by-product of his failure to write publishable stories. It came out in two forms, as a series of little volumes of extracts from eminent story-tellers (for instance, Rabelais, Balzac, Gautier, Flaubert — Ransome was suffering from an acute attack of French flu) each with an introduction by Arthur; and as a single-volume collection of the introductions, with additional essays. In its periodical form the work impressed Edward Thomas, as fair and clear a critic as ever: he noted that it was very carefully done, and found in the writing 'a kind of merit though I am not clever enough to define what'. The book is written in the same unbuttoned, personal manner as *Bohemia in London*; the style has shed many pointless rotundities. The author is always pleasantly intelligent about the writers he discusses; sometimes he is better than that. All in all, the *History* was evidence that Ransome was still advancing as an author; but its chief importance was that it led to further commissions, which had the effect of turning him for a few years into a full-time critic. Martin Secker, just starting his own publishing firm, commissioned a book on Edgar Allan Poe; Messrs Jack, the publishers of *Story-Telling*, commissioned two anthologies: *The Book of Friendship* and *The Book of Love*. Arthur did not struggle against this turn of fate: 'If that was what was wanted, who was I to refuse to supply it?'

The summer of 1909 was one of sustained literary effort. Ivy took a hand in the work. According to Edward Thomas, she and Arthur worked at the *Friendship* anthology together, and borrowed a dozen books from which to make prose or verse extracts. This is confirmed by the work's preface, for though the *Book of Friendship* is dedicated to Lascelles Abercrombie in sentences that reek of nostalgia for bachelor freedom and the North,[2] Arthur also thanks his wife, 'without whose help this book would never have been done, for incredible labours in transcribing and correcting'. Arthur would one day remark that he had done his best to make a success of his marriage; the evidence suggests that at this stage Ivy was doing her best too. In the intervals of writing they shared little adventures: sleeping in the open, after supper with Edward and Helen; motoring over to Roland's Castle (in whose car is not explained).

Nevertheless, she was not making Arthur happy. Her husband's ideal of marriage was a thoroughly domestic one: he liked Hazlitt's phrase about gathering mushrooms together 'to drop into our hashed mutton at supper'. Ivy wanted something altogether more startling, or at least a responsive audience. Once Arthur was called to her room, where she was having breakfast in bed, to see her take a plate of poached eggs and tip them on to her head. He did not applaud. Yet she did not give up her efforts to enhance life by performance. 'Any audience would do. Once in the train a young man was reading a religious newspaper. Presently she leaned forward and asked him "I think you are a preacher." The young man blushed and said he was. "I knew it," said she, "You have such holy eyes." ' It all makes entertaining reading and was presumably intended for a contribution to the general gaiety, but it painfully embarrassed Arthur. He was not exactly a conventional man, but the value he set on sincerity, his dislike of affectation in all things, his need for a supportive friend-

2 'I am glad that the man for whom I have made this book will know, while we both live, that I value his friendship ... I would give many meals to meet that man again on Lowick Bridge, and walk with him to the Hark to Melody; and I send him this book in memory of those old walks and talks and pleasant inn parlours, and also in the happy knowledge that it may not be long before we enjoy those things again.'

ship within marriage (to make up for childhood deprivations) were all so great that he could not have been more distressed by Ivy's antics if he had been a banker. In this he was a sad disappointment to his wife, who wanted him to play up to her. He came to think that she should have married an actor, or should have been an actress herself.

They were unsuited to each other in almost every way, and the thought must arise that Ivy was in some way a stupid woman, since she attached herself so obstinately to a man so unlikely to make her happy. Yet there is a pathos about her too. Her actions can be seen as partly inspired by a terrible insecurity, a desperate wish to test affection, in the hope of receiving that total reassurance which in the nature of things is unattainable. She had trapped Arthur, but in her way she loved him (her daughter says she adored him) for he was the only man who ever tried seriously to be kind to her.

She was as bad at managing him as he was at handling her. She noticed enough of his real nature to try to change it, rather as his parents had, but even less wisely, for she was not dealing with a schoolboy but with a man. Perhaps she was misled by the fact that she had had so much more experience of love affairs than he. But in the end she did him a great service. There was indeed something unformed about Arthur until his marriage: he was zealous, amiable, mediocre, juvenile. The sufferings that Ivy brought him forced him to focus himself. He was compelled, first, to recognise his limitations, then to accept them, then to defend them against her assault. He emerged from the experience deeply scarred, but with a clear identity that thereafter never blurred. This enabled him to become a true writer.

In August 1909 Ivy conceived. This was probably Arthur's reason for being in a 'violent stew' in mid-September, when she went off to Bournemouth and did not instantly send a letter to say she had arrived safely. But her health was perhaps less problematic than his own. On 15 July, for instance, his diary reads: 'Very very bad in my guts. They scorn a liquorice powder.' The intestinal ulcer which was going to cause him so much pain and distress for the rest of his life had announced its coming. Arthur always attributed it to his neglect to eat proper meals in the days of Bohemia; but it seems just as likely that it was caused by the impact on an anxious, sensitive man of a disastrous engagement and marriage.

The Book of Friendship and *A History of Story-Telling* appeared in the autumn, and were to be followed by *The Book of Love* and *Edgar Allan Poe*. Arthur settled down to work on these new projects not in Petersfield, but at Peak's Farm, near Semley, Wiltshire. Perhaps the lease on Stoner Hill Top had run out; or perhaps the Thomases and the Ransomes were getting too much on each other's nerves. Arthur, like his grandfather, was always shrewd about other people's affairs, if not about his own; living at such close quarters to Edward and Helen he seems to have detected the strains between them, of which, anyway, Edward's gloomily cryptic remarks in London had given him clear warning. He did not think Helen worthy of her husband. On his side Edward was constantly irritated by the Electrician and the Unicorn. It was a sad ending to what had seemed such a promising experiment.

The retreat to Wiltshire may also have been suggested by a desire to get further out of range of the Walkers; whether or no, by March, as the birth drew close, Ivy felt the wish to be near her mother; besides, she and Arthur had both been ill in February. The seaside might do them good. So off they went to Bournemouth, where their daughter was born on 9 May 1910 at about 2.40 p.m., as Arthur carefully recorded in his diary. It was a difficult birth, made worse for Arthur by Ivy's schemes to heighten its drama.

> My wife had insisted that I should be in the room while my daughter was being born but, just before the delivery was complete, her doctor had the humanity to send me to his own house for a bottle he pretended to have forgotten. He too, poor man, had been given a place in the general fantasia. It had been explained to me that my mother-in-law had been allowed to suppose that he was in love with her while he was in fact in love with her daughter – and so on, and so on.

This is one of those incidents which show in a sudden glare the distance that we have travelled in two generations. Few husbands nowadays would find it particularly *outré* to be required to assist at their wives' childbed, but in Arthur's eyes Ivy had done something self-evidently appalling. Her 'fantasia', on the other hand, he found merely wearisome.

In the last stages of pregnancy Ivy had been so large that she was told to expect twins, and, asked what she would do, had replied with spirit, 'Oh, drown the black one and keep the tabby.' As is the way with such jokes, the name stuck: the little girl was duly called Tabitha. Her safe delivery had removed at least one source of anxiety, and soon Arthur was pressing ahead with the book on Poe. He sent off sections to be printed as they were written, and by August half of it was in type. The family moved for the rest of the summer to lodgings near Godalming, where Tabitha was unwell for a few days and was bitten by a flea. Much more important was what happened on 27 August (the date must be recorded): in his own phrase, Arthur's ancestors at last had their way with him. In his usual democratic fashion he had struck up a friendship with the local postman, who persuaded him to try angling in the Wey. Arthur had not handled a rod since fishing for perch in his father's time; but the postman advised him, and enough of his skill came back to enable him to catch two roach. Never a man to do anything by halves where technique or pastime were concerned, he threw himself into this new hobby with passion. Perhaps he felt it was time, now that he had a child himself, to stop rebelling against his father and to start imitating him. At any rate, fishing soon became his chief occupation, next to authorship, and by the last years of his active life had even taken first place. In the interim a substantial amount of his writing had been devoted to rod and line.

By early September *Edgar Allan Poe* was finished, and there was nothing to do but wait for the last batch of proofs. Arthur felt he deserved a holiday; besides, he was planning a book on roads and walking. He decided to go off for a solitary camping trip in the lake country. Once he was away from Ivy, his marriage seemed like 'a bad, incredible dream'. Waking, by contrast, was heaven, and that meant Lanehead. He camped in the garden, sailed with Robin Collingwood, and corrected the last batch of *Poe* proofs on Peel Island. They were brought to him by Ursula, the youngest Collingwood girl (Dora and Barbara were not at home), who swam across to the island with the proofs tied to her head.

That feeling of intense relief at escape from his wife was a very bad sign; but Arthur's next action shows that he had still not given up hope. The Collingwoods, who would be away from Coniston until Christmas, offered him the use of Lanehead, and Arthur (thinking to make Tabitha a proper Lakeland baby) readily agreed. So did Ivy, now stuck in Bournemouth lodgings ten minutes' walk away from her parents. She and Tabitha and Tabitha's black Jamaican nurse arrived on 7 October, the day the Colling-woods left, and Arthur settled down to a winter of hard work in the place where he had always before been happy.

The work project went well enough. *Poe* was published on 4 October, and got much better reviews than its author thought it deserved. He was perhaps too severe on it. It is true that his exclusive emphasis on Poe's thought, on Poe as 'a philosopher of aesthetic' rather than as an imaginative writer, seems somewhat perverse, but it was deliberate: he felt that unintelligent praise of Poe as a writer of Gothic tales and verse had produced serious misunderstanding. His own modest claim for the book was just: 'It had at least considered Poe's theories and his self-conscious technique in writing stories ... It had also, for the first time, given a detailed account of the strange position, almost that of a French writer, that Poe had won in France.' The book reads swiftly and easily, and if it provokes the reader to argue with the writer, that is all to the good. In sum, it shows that Ransome had thoroughly mastered the craft of criticism, and he was soon to show that he had something original to say.

Even before the publication of *Poe* Secker and Ransome had begun to discuss a successor. The difficulty was in choosing a subject. Ransome wanted to write about Hazlitt, had indeed planned and made notes for a book about this favourite author, and approached Methuen about it; but Secker did not think it would be marketable. So Arthur proposed to follow his study of Poe with one of another self-conscious word-artist, Robert Louis Stevenson: 'at that moment "native wood-notes wild" did not interest me.' Secker agreed. The whole thing seems to have been arranged during a flying visit to London at the end of September. Then, on 10 October, a telegram came to Lanehead from Secker urgently asking Arthur to write a book on Oscar Wilde rather than Stevenson, and demanding an immediate reply. Arthur, stipulating only that the book on Stevenson follow that on Wilde, agreed to the proposal the next day. Oscar Wilde was a splendidly artificial, opinionated author: just the right subject for dissection by an opinionated critic. Secker sent the Methuen edition of the complete works to Lanehead, and Arthur settled down to read them through. This was not his only occupation. There was *The Book of Love* to compile; a book of essays to write (eventually he destroyed it); and the small collection of bad, fanciful stories to be assembled which was published next year as *The Hoofmarks of the Faun.* He kept up his more serious experiments with narrative art by turning proverbs into stories. The idea was in the air, for Edward Thomas, unknown to Arthur, was doing the same thing at much the same time, only with greater success. Arthur's stories had titles like 'A Rolling Stone Gathers No Moss', and, to judge by the eight which survive, were more the result of toil than inspiration. Their chief interest today is that they represent a clear though unsuccessful attempt to apply the Anansi technique to original work, and are thus a step on the road to *Old Peter's Russian Tales.* They have never been published.

Family life went less smoothly than work. On 7 November Tabitha was rowed across the lake to be christened in Coniston church, but the magic did not take: the baby was never to be a lake-dweller. And her father, as his diary shows, was thoroughly blue-devilled that autumn:

(*12 November*) Evening spoilt by Ivy's Mother. Night ditto; by the sheer ugliness of remembering her.
(*13 November*) Blues.
(*14 November*) Blues.
(*18 November*) Belly bad.
(*19 November*) Belly.
(*20 November*) Ill belly.
(*1 December*) All ill.

Neither were matters any better when they went to Paris for Christmas.

(*25 December*) Blues.
(*26 December*) Blues.
(*27 December*) Blues. Improvement.
(*28 December*) Jolly day. Row about my rudeness when at dinner with the Gordons.

This stark record of emotional and physical discomfort leaves an impression which the more cheerful reminiscences of the *Auto-biography* do something, but not all, to counter. The charcoal-burners were still sweetening Arthur's clay-pipes; he went on walks to the Duddon, Windermere and Cartmel; he nearly ship-wrecked himself on Coniston, when the *Jamrach* would have

broken on the rocks off Peel Island but for the magnificent calm
resourcefulness that Arthur always displayed in such crises:

> ... the jaws of the gaff had smashed, the mast and sail had
> slapped into the water, and poor old *Jammy* was lying on her
> beam ends ... I had not come out prepared to do repairs, and
> there was very little time to spare. Luckily I was wearing boots
> with stout leather laces. I took them off under water and with
> the laces roughly fettled up the gaff-jaws until I could hoist a
> bit of sail, enough to get her moving. She cleared those jagged
> rocks that would certainly have holed her had we touched by
> about two yards, and drifted while I baled and got things more
> or less to rights.

For a moment he came into his kingdom.

To outward appearance, 1911 was his most successful year so
far. *The Book of Love* and *Hoofmarks of the Faun* were published.
He had literary articles – mostly reviews – in half a dozen magazines, which brought in £54 17s., a solid, useful sum in that
remote age; though his first article on fishing, for a journal called
The Tramp, was never paid for. He read four manuscripts for the
house of Macmillan, at two guineas a time. The royalties for
Edgar Allan Poe came in. The Ransomes appeared quite comfortably off, a fact noted by the ever-faithful Edward Thomas. They
stayed in Paris in quest of Wilde throughout January, where
Arthur enjoyed himself talking over his project with Rémy de
Gourmont and Anatole France; but Ivy fell ill. Her health was to
be bad off and on until the summer. On their return to London
they established themselves at 120 Cheyne Walk, and Arthur
began to bring his Bohemian friends home for supper. In later
years Ivy told Tabitha that this forced her to learn to cook, if only
to avoid the humiliation she felt when one evening Arthur asked
her to make an apple tart for his guests, and she had not the
vaguest idea how to do so. Meanwhile Arthur, on the advice of
Laurence Binyon, sought out Oscar Wilde's literary executor,
Robert Ross. Ross proved immensely kind and helpful, introducing Ransome to Wilde's two sons and to Ada Leverson, and not
only letting him read *De Profundis* in its original, unabridged, unpublished form of an endless epistle *ex vinculis* to Lord Alfred
Douglas, but allowing him to take the manuscript down to
Wiltshire, to the Ransomes' new home.

In a sense it was the first real home they had had together. Ivy and Arthur moved house at least six times in the first two years of their marriage, but neither was really of the gipsyish disposition that this might suggest. Tabitha was a puny, sickly baby, who might benefit from country air; perhaps her parents would too; and no doubt they found living in London expensive. So in May they transferred by stages (Arthur on the 2nd, Ivy on the 15th, Tabitha and her nurse a fortnight later) to the Manor Farm at Hatch, a hamlet a few miles from Salisbury, just down the valley of the Sem and the Nadder from Semley, where they had spent the first winter of their marriage.

It was a delightful house and suited them all. Hatch was such a tiny place, and the Farm, next to the churchyard, with its garden and paddock, was such a good house that Ivy could indulge her genteel fantasies. In the *Autobiography* Arthur says only that it was two-storeyed, grey, with mullioned windows. He was better pleased by the fact that it was in excellent fishing and walking country, and well clear of the influence of London. It gave him scope for all his enthusiasms. His study, says his daughter, was sacred, he was not to be disturbed when working there. Ivy told her that he once threw a small wooden chair at his mother-in-law when she persisted in disturbing him. Tabitha describes the study as a small room with a low window looking out on the garden with its lilac tree. The walls were lined from floor to ceiling with Arthur's collection of books; his collection of pipes was displayed round the whitewashed fireplace. He made himself a square table, and a desk so designed that he could work at it either sitting or standing – the latter perhaps the more desirable posture, as he was now suffering from piles as well as his ulcer. Aesthetics, such an important deity for a writer on Oscar Wilde, was given its due by a good kitchen table covered in red baize and crowned with a pair of heavy silver-plated candlesticks and a tall lamp. Arthur made himself snug for reading by sitting at this table with his back to the fire, his book propped on a small book-rest, and no doubt one of the pipes stuck between his teeth.

Tabitha's unpublished memoir also records that he left his mark on other parts of the house. Fishing-rods stretched along the stone-floored passages, suspended from hooks. He suddenly developed a craze for breeding mice, so a whole room, once the monastery's privy, was devoted to their numerous cages. Ivy kept them clean and fed, Arthur showed them, and the prize certificates which they won were tacked up on the walls of the 'Mouse House'. The penny whistle was now used to charm snakes in the woods, Arthur lying along a low, moss-covered wall to do so; he brought one such snake home and kept it in a teapot which was put on the table at teatime. He was far from being a perfectly considerate husband. Ivy could be a surprisingly docile wife. If the day was to be devoted to fishing she would find herself baling out either a leaky rowing boat on the lake at Wardour Castle, or a leaky punt on the lake in the Shaw-Stewart woods, while Arthur fished from the opposite end of the vessel, as often as not in pouring rain. Once home, he would step into the slipper bath prepared for him, 'surrounded by kettles and cauldrons and saucepans of boiling water', and then light up his pipe, while Ivy sponged him down and soaped him 'with what was called a face-glove (made of bathtowelling), and whilst the fire roared away my father would read poems, often holding out the same leg twice to be soaped.'

Tabitha's memories are vivid and convincing, although she was only one year old when the family moved to Hatch, and no more than three when her father went off to Russia, never to return for more than a few months at a time. It is difficult even to guess what year any particular reminiscence should be assigned to. It is perhaps likely that Ivy's behaviour was more amiable when it was a question of winning back an errant husband rather than of keeping one on the spot. But the over-all picture is notably consistent, and makes it impossible to accept, without qualification, the stark picture of undeserved domestic misery painted in the *Autobiography*.

Father and daughter delighted in each other. The Jamaican nurse might have been a rival for Tabitha's attention. The child nicknamed her 'Gig-gee' and happily pulled out tufts of her black curls, which Gig-gee displayed to Ivy as evidence that 'Missy Ba-Ba' was stronger today. After a fortnight at Hatch Gig-gee gave notice (and finally left at the end of September): perhaps she missed the stir of London. So when Tabitha needed to be coaxed to eat, or to drink her milk, it was Dor-Dor (her father) who was called in with his penny whistle, to charm his daughter as he charmed the snakes (her favourite tune was 'The Lincolnshire Poacher'). At breakfast a year or two later she watched him filling up with a large bowl of porridge and thick cream, followed by scrambled eggs and tomatoes, and coffee. For his part, Arthur enlivened the meal by reviving some of the conjuring tricks he had learned as a child. He would throw up the loaf of bread so that it stuck to the oak beam, or do the same with lumps of sugar. When Tabitha took to making what she called elderberry wine he nobly pretended to drink it. It was only by chance that she discovered that he was really spitting it out of the dining-room window as soon as her back was turned.

She was fascinated by all his eccentricities. There was the occasion when he had to catch an early train, and overslept. The fly arrived while he was still in bed. He leapt out, clutching his clothes to him; Ivy snatched up those he missed; owner and garments were flung into the cab together, and there he dressed while the old horse jolted along as fast as possible to make up for lost time. On another occasion Arthur decided to stuff and mount some fine carp and perch which he had caught in the Shaw-Stewarts' lake; but to keep them fresh he stored them, alive, in the bath until he could take them up to London. On the day of the journey (perhaps he had overslept again) the village woman who cleaned the house was told to collect the fish and put them in portable cans while Arthur dressed. The job was quite beyond her. Soon the bathroom floor was awash, the fish had leapt out of her clutches, and she herself was prostrate, having fallen over the cans.

Of all the stories that Tabitha tells, perhaps the most significant is that of the maid Bulpit, who broke one of a pair of heavy cut-glass goblets. In tears she confessed to Arthur. He told her to bring him the goblet's fellow, and when she did, dropped it to the ground himself so that it too smashed. 'Now, Bulpit,' he said, 'don't worry. I've broken the other, so now we are quits.' What Ivy thought, whose goblets they were, we do not know.

Clearly life was never dull while Dor-Dor was about. And he seems to have taken pains to protect Tabitha from being hurt by his bad relations with Ivy. When he moved into a separate bedroom, it was made into an adventure. Tabitha left her cot and started to sleep in her mother's bed, Dor-Dor explaining to her that her job was now to be a hot water-bottle and keep Mum-Mum's back warm. He himself would come in every morning immediately after taking his ice-cold bath, kiss Tabitha, and take pains to let her know that he had dutifully lain right down in the water. So she accepted the change without difficulty, and did not wonder that her father should be happier in his new bedroom, with its charming view and furniture, and (inevitably) a huge book-case. The only sad note in their relationship at this time is that when Tabitha caught mumps Arthur did so too.

Tabitha was interested not only in her father. There was the drunk cook, who always spent her pay at the nearest pub, five miles away, and on her return would walk round the house putting out all the lights. There was Moab the donkey, who drew the cart in which they all travelled about the country, whether to go fishing, or on picnics, or for longer excursions. There were the rats who stole the eggs which the chickens laid in the hay-barn: 'one would lie on its back, and hold an egg in all four paws, and another rat would tow it away by its tail.' She seems to have been as happy as her father had been at Nibthwaite. But she did not know all that was going on.

In the *Autobiography* Arthur describes that first summer at Hatch as one of desperate worry. Since the book on Wilde was progressing smoothly the reason can only be that his relations with Ivy were nearing crisis-point. The year before he had taken to calling her Bébé (he had a weakness for infantile nicknames): perhaps we may read it as an attempt to put their marriage on a footing of fantasy, with Ivy playing the lovable irresponsible child to Arthur's wise old father. If so the device did not work. A struggle for dominance was in progress, and Ivy was not to be bought off by baby-talk. If Arthur's weapon was his exuberance, which tended to sweep all before it, hers was her genius for making scenes. It was much the more effective, especially when blended with her continuing, obsessive, theatrical fantastication.

The farmhouse had originally been part of a monastic grange, and according to Tabitha the monks still walked: she heard their habits rustling in the scullery, and once saw a tall white figure standing beside one of her father's book-cases. Arthur could have been forgiven for thinking that if the house was haunted it was by unquiet spirits of a more recent date:

> It was a little like living in a lunatic asylum. Every now and then ... for example, a telegram would come, unsigned, naming day and hour and the Trocadero. The first of these telegrams included a warning against trying to discover the sender. She insisted that the telegram had come from a mysterious well-wisher, possibly someone who intended to leave her money, for which reason we had no right to disregard it. We used to keep the appointment, and found a table booked and a dinner

ordered on a scale much more lavish than I could have afforded. I am inclined to think, now, that she had arranged the whole affair herself.

So she had. Tabitha's reminiscences confirm the story in all essentials: she heard it from her mother, and adds the detail that Ivy paid for each outing by pawning something. Arthur found the whole thing in very poor taste:

> Dramatisation, and penny novelette dramatisation, went on unceasingly. She could not live without it and I was perhaps the cause of much of it because I was quite unable worthily to sustain the role of the hero of a melodrama. I believe that if she had herself been an actress able to release her dramatic talent on the stage she would have had less need for drama in what was, for her, a lamentably private life ... I was extremely unsatisfactory and she tried hard to build for me a character very different from my own, even telling and attributing to me stories very unlike any I should tell. Friends who had known me from boyhood were astonished to hear that I was a hard drinker. Until I was quite old I used to meet people for the first time who, after they had become friendly, told me the fantastic tales that they had heard long before.

Yet this incompatibility was no new thing. What made the summer of 1911 so anxious was that as Tabitha began to put babyhood behind her Arthur began to fear for her future, brought up between two such antipathetic parents. The fonder he grew of his daughter, the worse became his anxiety:

> By the end of 1911 it was clear that unless we separated (that is, unless I ran away) things might easily become much worse. I could not forget the background of the mutual hostility of her father and mother which seemed to me to explain and excuse much of her own character. Anything, I thought, would be better than for my daughter to grow up as her mother had grown up, for ever playing her father against her mother, her mother against her father.

But it was no easy matter to nerve himself to run away from the daughter he was coming to love so much, or even from Ivy, with whom he still occasionally enjoyed tender moments:

(*Diary, 2 January 1912*) Long and intimate talk with Bébé. Both very happy. Corrected proofs of Wilde. Bébé helped.

The question of his health was now also too serious to be neglected. Nevertheless he neglected it. Perhaps there was little that medicine, at that date, could do about his ulcer, but piles were a different matter. This painful and humiliating disease responds best, short of surgery, to a carefully gentle regime and a quiet life. It got neither from Arthur. He was his father's son in this as in so much else. He was not quite so suicidal as Cyril Ransome, though in the end he nearly did die of piles; but sitting for hours in cold wet boats, or walking fifty miles across country in one day, or participating in the local tug-of-war competition on Coronation Day (the Hatch team, trained by Arthur, would have won but for foul play in the final) might have been calculated to make his condition worse. It was to torment him for the next five years, culminating in the first of the many major operations that he had to undergo.

His literary career also began to run into bad difficulties, largely of his own making. In Martin Secker he had been lucky enough to acquire a first-rate publisher. Ransome was on excellent personal terms with Secker, and soon after his settlement at Hatch went to great trouble (that fifty miles' walk) to introduce him to Lascelles Abercrombie, who thereafter always published with the firm. The barometer seemed set fair. Then Arthur fell in with a mysterious literary operator who called himself Charles Granville. (For some reason he called his publishing firm Stephen Swift.) Granville was the expansive, munificent sort of publisher, very different from the prudent novice, Secker. He was the publisher of two magazines, the *Oxford and Cambridge Review* and the *Eyewitness*, which was edited by Cecil Chesterton and Hilaire Belloc. He was full of large ideas for Arthur Ransome's future. Arthur contributed regularly to the *Eyewitness* (later the *New Witness*) and his most important critical article, 'Kinetic and Potential Speech', appeared in the *Oxford and Cambridge*. He listened appreciatively to Granville's schemes while enjoying Granville's hospitality. The upshot was that he agreed to leave Secker, even before *Oscar Wilde* had appeared, and to transfer to Granville the right to publish all his works, past, present and to come, in return for a guaranteed steady income. In December 1911, *Wilde* being finished, Arthur began to make a translation of Rémy de Gourmont's *Une Nuit au Luxembourg* for Granville.

Oscar Wilde was published on 16 February. It marked the climax of Ransome's critical career. It has some of the faults of *Edgar Allan Poe*: in both books artists are discussed as if the most important things about them were their critical doctrines; perhaps Ransome succumbed to the temptation of treating his subjects as if they shared his own order of priorities. He had little to say about Poe's symbols or Wilde's wit, rather in the spirit of the writer who devoted most of his treatise on Schubert to the composer's operas. But as in the case of *Poe*, perversity was strength. Wilde's very intelligent speculations, above all those in *Intentions*, were taken as seriously as they deserved. Indeed, they seem to have put Ransome on his mettle. The year before, in his essay on kinetic and potential speech, he had put forward a theory which, taken up a few years later by I. A. Richards (who talked of the 'tenor' and the 'vehicle' of poetry), entered the mainstream of critical discourse. He was now able to apply this distinction to Wilde's writing; but he also made use of other ideas which he had evolved in his conversations with Lascelles Abercrombie. *Oscar Wilde* is built on a solid foundation of critical investigation, it is both a portrait and a speculation, is intellectually tougher and more rewarding than the laboriously purple prose of its style would suggest. As that style showed, Arthur was not altogether at ease with Oscar, but his discussion triumphantly transcends his awkwardness.

The book was well received. Helped by extraneous circumstances (soon to be set forth) it went into at least eight impressions, and was still being reprinted in the 1920s. One reviewer hailed it as 'just that sane, dispassionate, clear-eyed, and clean-minded book about Wilde ... which needed doing competently and finally.' To be sure, some of Edward Thomas's friends greeted the book with derision. Thomas was in a gloomy mood, and to cheer him up Clifford Bax and Herbert Farjeon composed a parody of John Masefield's *The Everlasting Mercy*, the poem of the moment, called *Walking Tom*, about Edward himself, in which Tom, a lost soul, sinks from crime to crime. The climax of his degradation comes when he murders Arthur Ransome by hitting him on the head with

> His latest work, called 'Oscar Wilde, a Study',
> A bloody book his blood made still more bloody.[3]

The poem seems to have done its work in lightening Edward's mood, and there is no reason to believe that he took its view of Arthur's achievement.

Unfortunately for Arthur the drama of Oscar Wilde was still not over. The book had concerned itself as much as possible with the works rather than the life; still, there had to be a biographical summary, and it was not long before objections were raised to it. Ransome had given a rather cruel sketch of Wilde's marriage, in which he referred to Constance Wilde as 'sentimental, pretty, well-meaning and inefficient'. Reasonably enough, her brother, Otho Holland, wrote to Arthur to protest; but in the process he also blackened Oscar's name, saying that he brought no love to his marriage, which he entered on only for money, that in the days of his prosperity he neglected his wife and kept her short of funds, that he adopted an attitude of 'pitying contempt' to her and had, in fact, 'practically divorced' her from 1885 onwards. These were monstrous falsifications, but Arthur (who can have made very little use of the introduction to Wilde's sons) swallowed them whole, wrote a grovelling reply to Holland, and asked permission to use the 'information' in the second edition of his book.[4]

Worse was to come. Less than a month after the publication of *Oscar Wilde*, on 12 March, Martin Secker agreed to sell his rights in that book and in *Poe* for £60 to Arthur Ransome and Charles Granville. Next day Arthur wrote in his diary, 'Lord Alfred Douglas served Secker with a writ for libel (including me).' And so a *cause célèbre* began.

Arthur was entirely taken by surprise, which would itself be surprising if it were not already clear (the Holland incident shows it) that he was out of his depth in the Wilde *milieu*. True, he had

3 Eleanor Farjeon, *Edward Thomas: the last four years*, p. 37.
4 In a letter to me Sir Rupert Hart-Davis (who is the editor of Oscar Wilde's letters as well as AR's literary executor) comments: 'I am quite certain that Oscar was in love with his wife, and didn't realise his homosexual propensities until he met Robbie Ross, some two years after his marriage. I think Arthur was horrified by Oscar Wilde, was terrified of what the book let him in for and wished he'd never written it. This explains his acquiescence in Otho Holland's suggestions, many of which are quite beside the point.'

observed certain precautions when discussing the more sensational aspects of Oscar's career. He said as little as possible about the celebrated trials in his book, and carefully labelled homosexuality a vice, a disease, 'a malady of the brain'. He was not prepared to endorse the prosecution of Wilde, and indicated his dislike of the Philistine rejoicing that attended poor Oscar's fall; he never mentioned Alfred Douglas by name. But as events quickly demonstrated, this care was wholly insufficient. What little Arthur had said about the unnamed Douglas was unforgivable, for it amounted to twin assertions that Douglas had lured Wilde to his ruin and abandoned him afterwards. Ransome ought to have been prepared to be attacked in return. Not only were the allegations serious enough to have angered and alarmed a man of much less vulnerable character than Bosie; not only was the whole *affaire Wilde* shot through with vindictiveness, notoriety and melodrama, so that there was no likelihood of libels going unobserved; but Douglas, having abandoned the follies of his youth in favour of a fine new set for his middle age, had already started a career as a semi-professional litigant.

Secker and Ross had not anticipated trouble either. Presumably they felt that Ransome's statements dealt so gently with facts so notorious that Douglas would not dare to sue. Unfortunately they did not allow for the possibility that some of the statements – based, as they largely were, on *De Profundis*, the bitter outpourings of a disgraced prisoner in Reading gaol – were inaccurate, and that Douglas might believe he could disprove them. Then there was the matter of Douglas's hatred of Ross, to whom *Oscar Wilde* was dedicated. According to Arthur, Ross said afterwards that 'he ought to have foreseen that this would enrage Douglas who had been engaged in a feud with him. But I think Douglas would have attacked the book, dedication or no dedication.' Ross, however, insisted on bearing the costs of the defence: he believed that he had led Arthur into a scrape, and felt he should do what he could to get him out.

Douglas took the view that Ross was the mastermind of an elaborate conspiracy to ruin him, and his resort to the courts was almost automatic. He and his shady associate, T. W. H. Crosland, thought the case would be a walkover, and looked forward eagerly to the damages they would be awarded. Lord Alfred was always short of cash.

On Ross's advice Arthur instantly sought out Sir George Lewis, son of the famous and fashionable solicitor who had been deeply involved in the affairs of the Wilde family for more than thirty years. Lewis thought that perhaps the matter might be settled quietly if it was left to him. It took him some time to learn his mistake, and meanwhile Arthur saw him daily.

This gave Ivy her opportunity. Arthur was filled with deep dread of the publicity he would have to endure, however the case went; and he might lose it. Ivy saw it as an opportunity to be embraced. At last her life with Arthur was taking the right turn. She acted at once. Taking the hint from Arthur's conferences with Lewis she cabled to Edith Ransome that a warrant was out for his arrest, and that he was hiding in London. Fortunately Mrs Ransome, who had endured much from Ivy, knew better than to believe the story. Arthur's return to Hatch on 20 March put an end to such fantasies for the time being.

It was *sauve qui peut* for the defendants. Douglas was suing Ransome, Secker, the printers and The Times Book Club, which had ordered thirty-four copies of *Oscar Wilde* for distribution to its members. Secker, no doubt feeling sore because of the way Arthur had treated him, wrote to Alfred Douglas explaining that he would prefer not to defend the case and had by mutual agreement cancelled his contract with the author. He later said that he had come to doubt Ross's motives and to believe that Douglas was being unfairly treated; a statement which we are free to disbelieve, or at any rate find self-serving. Douglas graciously dropped him from the case, whether or not in return for payment is unknown. The printers made a settlement out of court. So poor Arthur was left naked to his enemies, except for such aid and comfort as The Times Book Club might bring. He could not even count on a speedy settlement of the business: the case would not be tried for another year.

1912 was a nightmare for him. The anxious side of his temperament had all too much trouble to feed on, and more was to come. 'There was nothing to be done but work and, with the quicksands of my marriage under my feet and a most unsavoury law-case ahead of me, I was finding work more and more difficult.' But his enthusiastic side could not be repressed entirely. It surged to the fore in the late spring when a friend's casual challenge led him to lay out five pounds on a donkey-cart and a donkey in the Caledonian Market. The cart was painted green with yellow roses, and the donkey was Moab, already mentioned. Arthur and his friend, Ivar Campbell, set off from the courtyard of the British Museum – Arthur had been working in the Print Room on a book on the grotesque, never completed – and reached Hatch after ten leisurely days on the road.

This experience touched off a donkey-cart craze (in some ways Arthur was exactly like Mr Toad) which Tabitha, precocious child, though only just over two, was to remember vividly for the rest of her life. She called Campbell 'Camel' and rode on his shoulders. The cart was laden with tents, rugs and other camping equipment, and the grown-ups walked along beside it. When Camel tired, Tabitha was put in the cart, and when it went downhill the rest of the party climbed aboard. To Arthur's mind a donkey and cart moved at exactly the right speed for land travel, and Moab was an intelligent and obliging animal: she tended to get ahead of the pedestrians, but always stopped to wait for them at the next pub. She did not like to be ridden, however. In mid-June Ivy mounted her three times and was thrown each time; Arthur too made three attempts, and on the last occasion stayed up, which he recorded gleefully in his diary. At the end of the month Arthur, Ivy and Campbell (presumably Tabitha too) went on a journey of a week or more, ending at Yeovil, from which they made a train journey up to town to spend the night in the Argyll house in Bryanston Square. Then Campbell went to Scotland while the Ransomes returned to Yeovil to reclaim the donkey and cart. Two days later Ivy told Arthur that she had become Ivar Campbell's mistress.

Her sorely tried husband leapt at his chance: 'I suppose that means that you will be wanting a divorce. We had better go back to London to see a lawyer.' This too-prompt response surprised and displeased Ivy. Arthur had called her bluff. She quickly withdrew her 'confession', substituting for it a less risky fiction, which Arthur had to pretend to accept. The marriage continued.

But he had shown his hand, which can have done nothing for Ivy's sense of security. She began, half-intentionally perhaps, to frustrate all his attempts to work, as if she were jealous of his vocation. Perhaps that is why she made no objection to the mouse craze, which began in September. Mice were her allies against books.

As if things were not bad enough already, in early October Granville absconded. He was wanted for embezzlement and bigamy, and fled the country. Arthur now risked the loss of title to all his work of the past five years – to everything worth republishing – that is, to everything since, and including, *Bohemia in London*.

Fortunately this was the sort of crisis which always brought out the best in him. He went up to London immediately, found Granville's offices in chaos, and simply sat there, day after day, until he had established his interest as a leading creditor of the bankrupt firm. He appealed to the Society of Authors for help, but was snubbed by the secretary (which, since he thought it worth mentioning in his *Autobiography*, forty years later, perhaps has something to do with the fact that in the end it was the Royal Literary Fund which inherited most of his estate). Arthur was not to be beaten by such an incident. Authors having let him down, he turned to publishers. He temporarily sacrificed control of his earlier copyrights, but kept the most valuable – *Poe*, *Wilde* and a collection of essays, *Portraits and Speculations*, that was just then being printed by Geoffrey Ransome's firm at Edinburgh. Methuen agreed to take over *Poe* and *Wilde*, which they proposed to re-issue as soon as the Douglas case had been heard. Macmillan's, his father's publishers, agreed to issue *Portraits and Speculations*. It was not a bad piece of salvage, which perhaps explains why, in a despairing memorandum that he wrote in his notebook at the end of this dismal year, he did not mention the Granville business at all:

Dec. 12 1912. This last year has been the worst year in my life. On this date last year my *Wilde* was finished. Since then I have done nothing but the three essays on Nietzsche, Pater, and Art for Life's Sake.[5] I have not been able to work. I have allowed myself to keep my wife's times rather than my own. I have found it increasingly difficult to filch or force time for study of any kind. I have risen late, too late for a morning's work, I have played cards after lunch till it was too late for an afternoon's work. In the evening, for fear of hearing my wife's complaint that I have been away from her all day and might at least spare her the evening, I have played cards again. Nor has there been any satisfaction in this, for an ill conscience has made me ill-tempered and my wife unhappy. I have been unhappy almost always myself.

5 Not quite accurate: in late August he began work on a long narrative poem for children, *Aladdin*. The essays were published in *Portraits and Speculations*.

I am not accustomed to praying. But if I were to pray it would be for understanding. Ought I to sacrifice my job in life in order to be a better husband? Or ought I to sacrifice my conscience as a husband for my conscience as a workman?

This fact – of steady loss of ground since last year – is unalterable. Perhaps I have already taken the step, made the choice, and determined without knowing it to be a good husband.

But of course he had not. For one thing it was impossible to be a good husband to Ivy, or at any rate impossible for Arthur. For another, his commitment to writing was too deep to shake off; and indeed it is hard to imagine how else he could have earned a living. Publishing would hardly have cured him of his calling.

Even though he eventually came through, the terrible year left its mark. On many occasions during the next few years (which were going to be quite trying enough from other causes) thoughts of his marriage and associated ideas were to plunge him into deep melancholy. A still blacker mark was the effect of his various distresses – the lawsuit, his bowels, his belly and his wife – on his temper. There is little evidence about his disposition in early life, to be sure; but from about 1912 onwards stories about his irritability multiply, though he could still be overwhelmingly jovial. In his prose he was almost always to be fair-minded and even-tempered; in his life, not so.

The day of the Douglas trial drew near. Ransome might perhaps have wriggled out of the action, as Secker had done, but if he had, Douglas, now bearing proof that he had been libelled, would have been in a strong position to prosecute Ross for, among other things, having circulated the libel by showing Arthur the unpublished parts of *De Profundis*. Arthur was incapable of leaving a man like Ross, who had been so helpful to him, in the lurch; so the trial had to come on, and come on it did, even though in January 1913 Douglas was declared a bankrupt on a moneylender's petition and although in February he was charged with criminally libelling his father-in-law. These occurrences only made it more important to the plaintiff to get his hands on some damages if he could.

Arthur had many sympathisers. Robin Collingwood had nobly offered him all his savings; thanks to Robert Ross, Arthur was able gratefully to decline. Gordon Bottomley and Edward

Thomas agreed in deploring Ransome's victimisation. Thanks again to Ross, Arthur was invited to tea by Bernard Shaw, who told him the story of the celebrated meeting in the Café Royal in 1895 between himself, Oscar, Frank Harris and Alfred Douglas at which Harris warned Wilde quite specifically of what would happen to him if he proceeded with his libel suit against Douglas's father, the Marquess of Queensberry. Shaw was entirely of the opinion that Wilde had been kept on his desperate course by Alfred Douglas, which was exactly what Wilde himself said in *De Profundis* and one of the things which Arthur's counsel would try to prove in court: perhaps there was some idea of calling G.B.S. as a witness. So Arthur was cheered up, but not much. He wrote to his mother that he was working at a dialogue between a philosopher and a homunculus, and reading St Augustine, but 'it is getting so near the time now that I am not fit for much'. He went to the courtroom as if going to hospital for an operation.

The trial opened on 14 April 1913. It was the first time that Arthur was involved, with a leading role, in a drama larger than that of his own life. The case of *Lord Alfred Douglas* v. *Ransome and Others* was a crucial event in the post-mortem legend of Oscar Wilde. It brought into the open Douglas's hatred of Robert Ross, which had originated in their rivalry for the living Oscar's companionship and affection; it made public some of the unpublished passages from *De Profundis*, so that the dead Wilde was able to make his own fresh contribution to the legend;[6] and it depicted the character of Douglas in such sharp detail that the tragedy of Wilde's fall began to acquire the deeper interest that arises when a drama contains more than one fully-realised figure. But what had all this to do with Arthur Ransome? His reputation and literary career were at stake; he had been made wretched for thirteen months by the prospect of the trial, which was yet another source of friction in his marriage. His misery is understandable. Outside his family and small circle of close friends, nobody cared what happened to him. The public, great and small, was too much agog

6 This was important, because the complete *De Profundis* could not be published until 1959. In the mean time the manuscript rested, under a fifty-year embargo, in the British Museum, where Ross had deposited it to keep it safely out of Douglas's hands. It took a court order to make it available for the Ransome trial. Not until 1962 did the definitive edition of *De Profundis* appear as part of the Hart-Davis edition of Wilde's letters.

over what in a way was a re-run of the trial of Oscar Wilde. Arthur felt his irrelevance, and resented it.

His resentment seems to have clouded his judgment of the whole affair. To his mind he was being dragged through the courts on an irrelevant charge. He had written a work of pure criticism; the biographical details in it had been completely secondary to his main purpose; he believed that the court should recognise his intentions, indeed his achievement (for no one disputed that *Oscar Wilde* was a most creditable effort), and pardon him for any merely incidental transgressions. This view, which he still held when he came to write the *Autobiography*, was totally naive about the English law of libel, and might have proved fatal to him had he not been in good hands. But he never seems to have recognised what he owed to them, and consequently is unjust, in his account of the affair, to his counsel, J. H. Campbell, KC. Campbell was a highly respected barrister, who subsequently became a judge. His plan of campaign was excellent. He knew a vexatious litigant when he came across one. He knew that such cases as Douglas's usually come to court only because of spite or greed or both. Ransome's remarks about Lord Alfred had been 'colourless', as F. E. Smith was to remark to the jury (he was representing The Times Book Club), and clearly meant to be as little offensive as possible; wounding nevertheless. For instance, Ransome had observed that Douglas was a man 'whose friendship had already cost him [Wilde] more than it was worth'. Given their author's character, let alone the craven attitude of his publisher, there can be little doubt that a private approach would have led to the elimination of the offending passages without the expense and parade of a trial; indeed Ransome might easily have been induced to put Douglas's conduct to Wilde in a comparatively favourable light. But Douglas wanted money, and vengeance on Ross. He would have a trial and blast Ross's character. He realised neither that this approach compelled the other side to attack his own character; nor that Ross, not being a party to the suit, could be kept out of the witness-box; nor, above all, that in the full text of *De Profundis* 'Ransome and Others' had an invincible weapon.

Douglas, in a way, was as naive as his intended victim. He had been enraged by Ransome's statements, because he had convinced himself that they were untrue: Oscar was the predominant architect of his own ruin, and Lord Alfred had stuck to him loyally after his release from prison. But rage is a bad councillor. It drove

Douglas to blacken the motives of everyone in sight, and his counsel was too inexperienced to abjure these tactics. So it was insinuated that Arthur had personal malice against Douglas, because he had once applied for a job on Lord Alfred's paper, *The Academy*, and not been given it. Douglas also said that Sir George Lewis was guilty of unprofessional conduct because he had been Lord Queensberry's solicitor, and was now using letters in his possession against his former client's son. Lewis, by leave of the judge, instantly rose to say there was not a word of truth in this allegation, which certainly cannot have helped Douglas with Mr Justice Darling, whose summing-up, when it came, leant decisively to the side of the defence. The incapacity of the prosecution, and possibly the bias of the judge, were most clearly shown by the fact that the dubious foundations of Ransome's specific assertions were never brought inescapably to the jury's attention. This was because Campbell, for the defence, was able to make the issues much more dramatic than anything that could be settled by the production of Lord Alfred's bank-book, which showed that between Wilde's release from prison and his death Oscar had received at least £580 from the plaintiff. Instead, Campbell raised the fascinating question: had the adored Bosie been the real contriver of Oscar's downfall? The answer that prevailed may not have been the true one, but it was the one expressed, in prose of unrivalled strength and point, by the late martyr himself.

Campbell had the unabridged *De Profundis* read out. The opening pages of that immense letter,[7] a shattering *exposé* of Lord Alfred's faults, were all Campbell needed or intended to put in evidence. He was unexpectedly assisted by the plaintiff and his counsel, who reasonably but mistakenly believed that the full text of the letter would show anyone that it was so inconsistent as to be quite unreliable as evidence of anything except Wilde's fluctuating state of mind in prison. As a point of literary criticism this is undeniable; but the endless text, read out by Campbell's junior, bored the jury and further irritated the judge. They rebelled, and the reading was broken off; but the unalterable impression that it left in everybody's mind was that Bosie was, in Labouchère's words, a young scoundrel and that he had ruined his great friend.

Furthermore, Lord Alfred Douglas, writhing with rage, injured

7 *De Profundis* takes up eighty-eight pages of the Hart-Davis edition of Wilde's *Selected Letters.*

vanity, shame and impotence, had made a deplorable impression in the witness-box. At one time during the reading he could bear it no more and simply disappeared. For this he was roundly rebuked by the judge. He was impertinent to Campbell, and had to endure another rebuke from His Lordship. He denounced Oscar as a devil incarnate, and then had to listen while Campbell reminded the jury that he had written to the dying Wilde to pledge 'undying love and affection'. He was, he discovered, in a trap of his own devising. Campbell not only produced *De Profundis*. 'Like all leading Counsel who from time to time had to cross-examine Lord Alfred',[8] he went painstakingly through Douglas's writings of the early Nineties to show that he was homosexual, and had left England at the time of Wilde's arrest to avoid being arrested himself. Lord Alfred was desperately anxious to prove that he was a reformed character, converted to heterosexuality as well as to the Church of Rome, and indeed that he had never been guilty of more than boyish mistakes. It was a thin story, and would have been shot to pieces had he produced the affectionate and indiscreet letters that Oscar had written to him after his release from prison. Yet without those letters he could not convince the jury that he had not betrayed Oscar and that therefore Ransome's libels were unjustified.

After this performance counsel for the defence felt they could rest their case. They summoned no more witnesses (Arthur was never called). Instead, F. E. Smith rose to make his final address to the jury. He had listened as impatiently as Arthur to Campbell's performance, at one time saying in a whisper (and not a very quiet one), 'never mind that old sheep. I'll put your case for you.' This he did, in a bold, slashing style. From the point of view of history, he said, the world was entitled to know what were the main facts in the history, literary or otherwise, of well-known men, and how those facts could be stated less offensively than in Mr Ransome's book he was at a loss to understand. The hysterical protests from the plaintiff in the witness-box made it necessary to bear in mind, on the question of damages, who it was that had chosen, on account of his reputation, to produce a rehash of the whole odious story. Alfred Douglas was a man of infamous life who did not deserve a verdict or damages, since these would supply him with a misleading testimonial to his character. Camp-

8 Derek Walker-Smith, *The Life of Lord Darling*, p. 163.

bell followed this up by calling the prosecution 'a piece of tremendous bluff' and did all he could tu ram home the impression left by *De Profundis*. Wilde had been sacrificed to the plaintiff's inordinate hatred of his own father, and Ransome was justified.

Mr Hayes, for the plaintiff, did his best, but his worst could scarcely have been more damaging for his client. Trying to discount Douglas's homosexual sonnets, he unwisely ventured into literary criticism. He mentioned Shakespeare's twentieth ('A woman's face, with Nature's own hand painted, Hast thou, the master-mistress of my passion').

DARLING: Do you mean the jury to infer that Shakespeare was guilty of the same practices as Wilde?
HAYES: Certainly not. I meant that Shakespeare's sonnets were perfectly innocent, and anyone is at liberty to write sonnets of the same kind without any meaning being attributed to them.

The whole affair was a plot got up by Robert Ross, which must be why the defence had not called him as a witness.

DARLING: I have listened in vain for any reason why he should have been called. He was only Wilde's literary executor.

Hayes tried to defend his client's moral character; the judge forced him to admit that Lord Alfred's wife had just left him. Altogether Darling did Arthur proud, not only by this sort of intervention, but in his summing-up, when he went so far as to say that no one but Ross had read the full text of *De Profundis* until the trial (the implication being that Douglas had only himself to blame if he was now without a character under his stains) although in fact Ransome had based part of his book and his libel upon it. In the circumstances it is perhaps surprising that the jury took nearly two hours to find for the defendants. The words complained of, they said, were indeed a libel, but were true. Judgment for the defendants was entered, with costs.

Arthur sat through the four days of the trial in such misery that afterwards he could remember only certain highlights: F. E. Smith's stage-whisper; T. W. H. Crosland trying unsuccessfully to intimidate him with a ferocious glare, 'not knowing that I could not see him without recalling the rather endearing story of his first arrival in London from Yorkshire, by road, pushing a perambulator that was shared by manuscripts and a baby'; the hapless Mr Hayes suggesting that Rémy de Gourmont did not exist, and that therefore *A Night in the Luxembourg* must be an unhealthy concoction by Ransome himself (fortunately Arthur had been warned that some such tactic might be attempted, so he was ready with a copy of the French original, which he placed conspicuously on the table in front of him, under the eye of the judge); Ivy sitting in the public gallery throughout, to the scandal of the delicate-minded, angry because Arthur refused to let her sit beside him in the body of the court; Daniel Macmillan taking lunch with the Ransomes every day during the trial so that Ivy was obliged, by mere good manners, not to go on quarrelling. Then suddenly it was all over; it was spring, and congratulations were raining upon him. He was characteristically grumpy about them. Win or lose, the struggle had meant nothing to him but thirteen months of wretchedness. His indignation was not assuaged by victory, and he did not see what there was to shout about. An American journalist was asking him what he was going to do now: 'you have the ball at your feet.' Arthur replied that he was going to get rid of it 'as quickly as I can'.

That meant more than the American can have guessed. The victory in the Douglas case revived Arthur's energies, if not his spirits. He felt ready to take control of his destiny again; and that meant not only making fresh literary plans, but solving the problem of his marriage.

Evidence is extremely scanty; one must read between the lines of the *Autobiography*, the autobiographical memoranda, and Arthur's few surviving letters to his mother; but it seems clear that relations between husband and wife had deteriorated sharply even since December. Ivy was eventually brought to admit as much, and was induced to call on Sir George Lewis to see if a separation could be arranged. She bid for the solicitor's sympathy by declaring, as she swept into his office: 'Tell me what he wants me to do. If he wants me to go and be a prostitute in Piccadilly Circus I will do it for his sake.'[9] Lewis was too worldly-wise to be

---

9 Ivy's speech oddly resembles her remark about not being a barmaid (see above, p. 59). The two together suggest that she was both fascinated and frightened by her sexuality, associating it with the danger of loss of social status, always one of her preoccupations.

impressed by this sort of thing. 'I thank you, madam,' he replied.
'You have shown me exactly why it is advisable that he and you
should separate.' The rest of the meeting was stormy and led to
nothing, except that from then on Arthur was able to count on
his solicitor's support and help. But there are more ways than one
of engineering a separation, and Arthur was no longer dependent
on lawyers.

He was feeling mutinous about all aspects of his fate. He still
meant to write the book on Stevenson (it was the only solid commission he had in hand); but after that he would abandon criticism. It had brought him nothing but trouble, of a kind he meant
never to risk again. Ivy did not understand this at all: criticism
had brought notoriety, how could he abandon it? He was hankering after story-writing once more. In the London Library he had
recently come across a translated collection of Russian fairy-tales,
and the idea that became Old Peter was stirring in his mind. Then,
he had promised himself that after the trial was over he would go
away for a long walking holiday; to Touraine, perhaps, or to
Sweden. It occurred to him: why not Russia? He could combine
business with pleasure there by learning the language and studying
Russian folklore; and he could escape, perhaps for good, from Ivy.

Life contains few clean breaks. Arthur's marriage dragged on
in substance until 1917, and in form until 1924. Nevertheless
the decision to travel to Russia marks the moment when he
answered his question of the previous winter, by putting his job
in life before his conscience as a husband. The actual sojourn in
Russia brought home to Ivy that he meant what he said, especially
as she had no idea where he was going to when he vanished.
Never again would he consent to sacrifice himself and his work
to her tantrums, or even, if the choice had to be made, to his love
for Tabitha. The decision was to cost him dear in later years, but
there can be no doubt that it was the right one.

It was right even as a means of averting further deterioration in
the marriage. Arthur went up to Leeds to see his mother, who
had returned there, and to Edinburgh to see his brother and, most
probably, to get a commission for a book of Russian tales from
Messrs Jack, who would eventually publish Old Peter. Then back
to Hatch. What happened next is best told in quotation from the
letter in which he poured out his heart to his mother after reaching
Russia:

(*30 June 1913*) Three days before I left, in one of her terrific scenes (in this case because of a mistake I made in the name of a servant, a mistake I instantly admitted) she took up the two lighted lamps from the dinner table and beat them to pieces, narrowly escaping setting the house on fire.

I told this to Lewis before I left, and he agreed that it was more than unwise to remain in the house, as in another such scene she might, without meaning it, go a little further. He is going to try to arrange a peaceable separation, at least for some months so that I can have a chance of getting some work done.

Well: I did not want to worry you with all this: but, remembering what you told me about her absolutely untrue letters and telegrams on a former occasion, and her hatred of you, it occurred to me that she may try and get at you in some way now: so that it is better for you to know all about it beforehand ...

If only Ivy would give me a little peace I should be able to work here like anything. As it is, I live in constant terror of the post. Tabitha has been poorly, and Ivy has refused to have any nurse, even her own choice. Fortunately, however, Tabitha is better again. How I wish that infant were not going to be brought up in an atmosphere of lies, and dark stuffy rooms.

My dear Mother, when I think of Ivy's deliberate efforts to separate me from my own family, the censorship of my letters, and all the rest, I am surprised that I am still fairly sane ... If only Lewis can arrange a peaceable separation, I do hope that in a calmer life you and I will be able to be the friends we used to be before that unfortunate marriage. I am so glad we had that talk in Leeds before I left England.

One piece of very good news I have for you. Douglas has withdrawn his appeal. So the whole of that trouble is at an end. Lewis has done most extraordinarily well.

Perhaps it would be a good thing if you sent this letter on to Geoffrey. I should like him to know exactly how things stand. And in case you are at all worried it will be a satisfaction to you to know that he also knows. I told him when I was in Edinburgh how things were: but the lamp-smashing episode occurred only just before I came away, at the end of a day in which, as Ivy admitted, I had given up all work and devoted myself entirely to the task of keeping her happy ...

It is a great relief to be able to write to you without the fear that Ivy will condemn the letter.

In planning his escape Arthur compared himself to Defoe's traveller to the Moon, who did not go straight there from London, but first went to Germany, then to Russia, then to China, so that, to the reader, 'the final step from China to the moon seems little more than a crossing of the street.' His own object was to get free of Ivy for good, and Russia seemed an excellent first stepping-stone to that moon of happiness. For one thing you needed a passport to get there, which should hamper pursuit. Surreptitiously he provided himself with one, and then in late May went off to London, as far as Ivy knew. He took his second step by booking a passage on a cargo-boat bound for Copenhagen, and sent a letter to his mother, before boarding, in which he admitted only that he meant to spend three weeks in Copenhagen. On 31 May he smelt lilac coming off the Danish shore in a light breeze, and saw the green copper roof of Elsinore for a moment through the fog. It seemed an omen of renewal. He reached Copenhagen, and re-dedicated himself to Hans Christian Andersen: 'Some day I might yet learn to write tales that English children might overhear with pleasure, or had those years since 1909 put that kind of writing for ever out of my reach?' In mid-June he reached St Petersburg.

When Ivy discovered that he really had escaped she had a violent fit of hysterics, 'clawing and biting the dining-room cur-tains and screaming with tears and laughter', watched by her horrified little daughter.

A fitting coda to this most Strindbergian phase in Arthur's life was an adventure he had in Sweden on his leisurely journey east-wards. Strindberg himself had died the year before, but Arthur carried a message from his widow in London to his daughter in Stockholm.

I found the flat where she lived and rang the bell. The door was opened, one inch, on a chain. Suddenly the young woman who was looking warily out loosed the chain, opened the door, pulled me in, closed the door and bolted it, made me an ally without even asking who I was, and told me she was on the point of running away. As I was running away myself I could but sympathise. I helped with her packing. The bell rang. There was knocking at the door. We froze in silence. Steps sounded going down the stairs. Side by side, leaning out of the window, we saw a man, husband, fiancé, friend (I did not ask and was not told) come out on the pavement. The young woman watched to see which way he went, sent me to stop a cab and a few minutes later was hurrying to the railway station. I never met any of the Strindbergs again.

IV

Russia and War

I'm sick I didn't start romances earlier; the best world for stirring romance is a world in which nothing happens quite so stirring as the things in the romance. And in this world where things are happening everywhere that make our best romances read like fifty year old children's books, well, where are we?

ARTHUR RANSOME to his mother, 29 January 1916

In spite of everything, the Arthur Ransome who arrived in St Petersburg, the capital of the Russian Empire, on 14 June 1913 was still at heart the same ingenuous, eager boy that he had always been. Enthusiasm was less a function of his years than an aspect of his character. All the same, it is a little surprising, as well as delightful, to see how easily he was able to throw off the gloom of the recent past and plunge into the glorious new experiences that awaited him in Russia. He had no thought of any cloud over his future except the dread possibility that Ivy might pursue him. For she sent 'a wild furious letter' telling him to come home at once, which upset him greatly – for a time. But he was living in a 'calm Russian household, where there are no rows, no violent scenes', and where he could write in the open air, at a wooden table under tall pine trees, close to the Gulf of Finland, now and then hearing the guns from the island fortress of Kronstadt far away. He soon calmed down again. He referred Ivy to Sir George Lewis, and advised his mother to consult the solicitor herself, if Ivy pestered her.

The errant husband had fallen wonderfully lightly on his feet. He had been met at the Petersburg dockside by members of an

Anglo-Russian family, the Gellibrands, who had carried him off
to their dacha across the border at Terioki in Finland. There, the
Autobiography tells us, he discovered the white nights of the nearly
Arctic summer; heard nightingales all night long; tinkered at the
book on Stevenson; and, with the warm encouragement of his
hosts, began hastily to learn Russian. He was remarkably successful in doing so. In the *Autobiography* he states flatly, 'I have always
been very bad at languages', but whatever truth there is in the
assertion seems to be outweighed by the fact that, just as he had
made himself fluent in French in his critical years, when he visited
Paris regularly, so now he made himself fluent enough in Russian
to engage with absolute ease in conversations with Russians of all
types, including, eventually, the Bolshevik leaders and his second
wife. We may easily accept his disavowal of any great skill in
writing Russian; in assessing his modesty about his ability to speak
it we must remember that his standards of skill were high. He
denied that he was a good fisherman. He was not likely to claim
linguistic ability, having known a man, Harold Williams, who
had been able to speak forty-two of the languages and dialects of
the Russian Empire.

At any rate his method of learning a language was all his own.
He got hold of Russian children's reading primers, and worked
steadily through them, from those meant for five-year-olds to
those meant for children aged ten. He read the newspapers
systematically, with the aid of a dictionary, to improve his
vocabulary. Before long he was reading folk-tales, and selecting
ones he thought he might like to translate.

He stayed in Russia for three months. After Terioki he returned
to St Petersburg, and then paid a long visit to Estonia. He had
scarcely touched the true Russia (though he had been startled, on
his arrival, by the array of icons and candles in the booking-office
at the Finland Station in St Petersburg) but he had seen enough to
enchant him with the country and the people. Long after, he
remembered night-drives in horse-drawn carriages through vast
forests; the glitter of lanterns, 'multiplied by their reflections
where boys waist-deep were taking crayfish from the river
Embach'; and a students' feast at Dorpat University in Estonia.
The country was like a huge Coniston; the Russians seemed as
kindly as the Collingwoods. It was a wonderfully tonic holiday.

Life did not seem so enjoyable after he got back to London on
30 September. He stayed with Lascelles Abercrombie, but missed

Tabitha acutely, as he had all summer. Lascelles urged him to make a clean break and remove himself and his books for ever from Manor Farm; instead he was misguided enough to attempt a reconciliation with Ivy. He went back to Hatch, and the ill-suited pair struggled through another winter. Arthur did not let his wife distract him from work this time, though in March they went over to Paris for ten days, leaving Tabitha with her grandmother in Leeds. Before then Arthur had completed his rhyming version of *Aladdin*, a metaphysical fantasy called *Blue Treacle*, and a collection of translations of Caucasian fairy-stories. He had continued work on the Stevenson book, and written some miscellaneous pieces for magazines. He had also succumbed to a craze for photography, building himself a dark room and preparing lantern slides. But his relations with Ivy had not really improved, so he was miserable again; publishers were not encouraging; and when an unexpected chance to return to Russia appeared, he jumped at it. He was commissioned to write a guidebook to St Petersburg, and on 5 May 1914 started across Europe by way of Paris and Berlin. He arrived in St Petersburg on 13 May, with a horrible cold, but got to work on the guidebook at once, writing 1,200 words on his second day in the city.

The guidebook was finished in less than two months, but the war prevented its publication, and Arthur, who had never regarded it as a real book, eventually destroyed the manuscript. Its value to him was that it had made him free of St Petersburg, giving him the knowledge of it that was to be of the greatest possible use to him in 1917. He had enjoyed wearing out his boots on the business, drinking kvass and eating black bread in the buttery of the Alexander Nevsky monastery, and buying an icon of Nevsky:

(*To his mother, 23 May*[1]) I am going to burn a candle to him, because he is the patron of Petersburg, at least his relics are here, and I have pilgrimed to them, and he may help my book. It was very strange to see all the people kissing the floor and the carved silver box with the remains in them, and praying and crossing themselves and lighting candles. One old woman asked me to light a candle for her, because she was a very little old woman

---

[1] The pre-revolutionary Russian calendar was nearly two weeks behind that of the West, but since AR always used English dates, I shall do the same. The October Revolution hence becomes the November Revolution, and so on.

and could not reach so high. Monks, of course, all over the place.

He felt 'stupid and nervous' after the rough draft was complete, and his eyes hurt, but he and they rapidly recovered. 'I am mucking about in a cream coloured Russian tunic with a crimson belly-band of plaited cord, trying to pack my things in the most convenient way.' He was owed a holiday, he felt, and July was taken up entirely with tennis, billiards, swimming and, naturally, fishing.

Russia mobilised on 30 July. Ransome was as much surprised by the great catastrophe as anyone else; he was even incredulous, for a day or two, of the news that England had gone to war. There had been a feeling in the air like thunder, but he had connected it with the labour disturbances in St Petersburg, strikes and riots so violent that some people began to whisper once more the magic word, 'revolution'. A very different crisis had arrived. Arthur was present when the Tsar showed himself to the people on the balcony of the Winter Palace on 2 August. He saw an immense crowd on its knees outside the chapel of the Little House of Peter the Great: there was a miraculous icon inside, which had given Peter victory at the battle of Poltava. Candles were passed over the worshippers' shoulders to be lit by proxies, as it were, inside the chapel, which was only a few feet square. He noted with distaste the paroxysm of anti-German feeling that swept across the city, resulting in the looting of German-owned shops and the destruction of the German legation.

He was always singularly free of xenophobia, of racial or of class prejudice: one of nature's liberals. His attitude to the war was otherwise quite conventional. He wanted to do something for his country, though it was hard to decide what. His atrocious eyesight made him poor material for the army; besides, his piles were getting worse and worse. After consulting his friends he decided that he would be best employed as a newspaper correspondent in Russia; so on 18 August he left for England in search of an employer. It was the first of many dangerous journeys, but all went well. He was not on the steamer that was torpedoed or mined in the Gulf of Finland; the vessel he took from Christiania was not attacked by a squadron of German destroyers, nor blown up by a British minefield off Coquet Island. He landed at Hull on 24 August, and went straight to Hatch.

A strange interlude now began, which was to last for more than a year. Arthur found, as so many others have done in such times, that volunteers were not appreciated. He initiated what was to prove a stormy and complex relationship with the Foreign Office by approaching an old family friend, Francis Acland, now Parliamentary Under-Secretary for Foreign Affairs. By good luck Acland was in charge of the department responsible for press relations and propaganda. He quite agreed that Arthur would be useful in Russia, and encouraged him to seek newspaper work. But such work was simply not to be had. All the suitable papers had correspondents already. Arthur's offer of himself as a King's Messenger was declined. So the autumn passed much as usual. He lived at Hatch. He wrote articles on Russia for various periodicals, including the *New Statesman* and the liberal *New York World*; worked at his fairy-tales (he began *Old Peter's Russian Tales* on 14 November); and visited the Collingwoods.

So far as can be made out, his relations with Ivy were comparatively tranquil and friendly. The reason was absolutely in character – Arthur's character. He fished at Hatch as usual, and Ivy actually joined in. She made a night line, and the next day caught an eleven-ounce roach. 'Photographed said fish,' Arthur wrote in his diary. 'Incredible bother, forgivable because it was her first.' Indeed it was forgivable. Arthur was always happy, indeed anxious, to share his pleasures, and warmed to people who agreed to be his pupils. (In all this he was very like his father.) His proselytising tendency was roused to full activity by Ivy's display of interest in his favourite sport, and the pair angled amicably together for the rest of the season. On 17 October, for instance, 'I caught Ivy's supposed pike. It *was* a pike; and weighed 6 lb. 3½ oz.' He bought her a fishing-rod for a Christmas present.

He was still determined on a return to Russia, however, and when Acland got him a commission to write a history of the country he set off at once. He landed in Norway on Christmas Day, and was back in the city now called Petrograd (since 'Petersburg' sounded too German) on 30 December.

There was still no regular newspaper work for him, but his friend Harold Williams began to groom him for an opportunity, should one occur. Williams was probably the most influential person in Ransome's life at this time. He was another warm, erudite, encouraging father-figure like the Skald; another idealised version of Cyril Ransome. Arthur said of him, 'He was a very quiet man, unselfish, extraordinarily kind. I do not think it possible that he can ever have had an enemy.' He was a brilliant linguist, as I have already mentioned, and a dedicated savant, accepted as such in the most erudite circles of Russian intellectual life and holder of a doctorate from Munich. He earned his living as a journalist: in 1904 he had become the *Manchester Guardian*'s first full-time correspondent in a foreign capital. By 1915 he was the Russian correspondent of the *Daily Chronicle*. A New Zealander by birth, he knew Russia and the Russians as well as or better than any Englishman, and had married a Russian, the strong-willed Ariadna Vladimirovna Tyrkova, who was a fervent admirer of P. N. Miliukov, the leader of the Constitutional Democratic party, known as the Cadets. She was herself a leading figure in the Cadet inner councils: it was sometimes said of the party that there was only one man in it, and she was a woman. She was a talented writer, and kind to Arthur, but later turned bitterly against him when their political views diverged.

Williams thought that Arthur had the makings of a useful journalist, and partly with this in mind introduced him to a wide variety of circles in Petrograd society. He also thought that, whether for the sake of newspaper work or fairy-stories, it was high time that Ransome got to know more of Russia; and sent him off on his first visit to Moscow.

Ransome describes his stay there, which lasted from the Russian New Year until late March 1915, with his usual vivid clarity in the *Autobiography*; and there is a happy letter to his mother extant, in which he describes being taught to ski by the little girl at his lodgings, and speeding about the city by night in a sledge; but the most important thing that happened to him was a sudden rush of inspiration, which led him to begin writing his romance, *The Elixir of Life*.

His spirits had been rising for some time beforehand. On 4 February he reckoned that *Old Peter* was coming on very nicely ('I shall be able to write stories sooner or later'); that he had work appearing in both English and American papers, which should eventually pay for his Russian adventure; that *Aladdin* would be coming out at Christmas, and perhaps the Stevenson book too; and that the *Daily Mail* might be sending him to Warsaw. Two days afterwards he got up late and suddenly had an idea for a book-length yarn, a sort of by-product of the dialogue (now lost) between the philosopher and the homunculus. He turned the idea over for a fortnight, during which time he also fished through a hole in the ice under the walls of the Kremlin and sadly recorded in his diary that his health was rotten; then on 20 February, temporarily abandoning all other work (which at the moment chiefly meant *Old Peter*; we hear no more of the proposed history of Russia), he took the decisive plunge:

> (*Diary*) No letters. Spent the morning in writing out the idea of *Elixir of Life* in a twenty-chapter romance. Got the whole thing clear in my head during my afternoon journey to the P.O. Bought typewriting paper, and in the evening wrote half of the first chapter, six pages getting my hero flung out of a carriage and ordinary life onto the Great North Road. If I can get 40,000 words done in 2 weeks, I'll do it. The book should be 60,000 words.

For the next few weeks his diary records alternately the progress of his book and the almost equally rapid progress of his disease.

> (*6 March*) Piles dreadfully bad. Chapter XI. 5 pages.
> (*7 March*) Slouched. Read Wells. *Men in Moon*, and *Love and Mr Lewisham*. Lost a lot of gore.
> (*12 March*) Chapter XVI. 5 pages. Total 150. 45,000. 3/4 of the book. Buck up you lazy idiot and finish the wretched thing.

His conscience began to trouble him dreadfully. It is hard to see why, unless he felt he was enjoying himself too much, banging away at his romance when the world was in such agony and there was surely some less private work for him to do. On 26 March he returned to Petrograd to consult a father confessor, his friend Hugh Walpole the novelist, who was working with the Russian Red Cross. Arthur had watched him at work in Moscow and had been much impressed by the steady flow of his fictional output and the efficiency of his working methods. Walpole read the *Elixir*, all but complete, and was enthusiastic; so Arthur, his courage revived, went to Estonia to stay with his host of 1914, and polished off the business. By 22 April the finished work was in the hands of a professional typist.

It is an odd book, one about which it would be too easy to be wantonly unkind. Set in the eighteenth century, its affinities are with the works of Baroness Orczy and the sillier tales of Georgette Heyer rather than with serious literature, however slight. It describes how an insufferable young gentleman quarrels with his benevolent but peppery old uncle and is disowned by him; how the young man meets a Satanic philosopher, who has procured the secret of the elixir of life – an elixir that can be renewed only by murder – and who has a beauteous damsel in his clutches; how the young people fall in love and defeat the evil genius; and how they are reconciled with the peppery old uncle. The book is such complete tosh as to stifle any regret that Arthur destroyed so many of his prentice-works. The only thing of interest in this one is the character of the uncle, who is a distillation of the north country. His dream in life is to get his nephew to take up fishing: 'The chub are feeding well, and on dull days I have done well with trout. It is a sad pity you do not take to angling.' In a bold, cartoon-like way he has some vitality, and some touches of the later Ransome; but he is small reward for anyone who wades through *The Elixir*. The best that can be said is that the tale perhaps symbolises Ransome's struggle to find his own voice, and the closing phrases suggest that even so worthless a book has carried him some way nearer home:

> ... to hesitate between Lucretius and Vergil, and not knowing whether to take the philosopher or the poet from my pocket, to sit there in the dusk reading neither, and listening to the owls calling in the low wood under the fell.

Arthur's joy at finishing his first full-length work of fiction was heartfelt and abounding, and did not diminish in the following months, which was just as well, for troubles came upon him thick and fast. Money was getting dreadfully short. Appeals to Ivy for news about *Aladdin*, which she was supposed to be getting published, were fruitless: instead he got a bundle of alarmist letters and telegrams from his mother-in-law to the effect that Ivy and Tabitha were both at death's door. He suspected that this was simply one of the usual melodramas, but could not be sure. He was immensely relieved when his father-in-law wrote to assure him that Tabitha's illness did not warrant a return home. He volunteered a rare tribute to his wife:

> (*To his mother, 4 May*) Hatch must have been a pandemonium ... in the middle of it all, the poor little Babba. But there is one thing. Ivy, however mad, really does take every possible care

of the imptom, understands her thoroughly and couldn't be improved on as a nurse, if only she was herself fit.

Then news came of a relapse in another maddeningly vague and frightening telegram from Mrs Walker. 'If Mrs W. were sane the telegram would mean very bad news indeed,' he wrote grimly in his diary on 14 May; as it was, he did not know what to think. In his anxiety his head swelled up like a pumpkin until he had a reassuring and rational message from his mother. Meanwhile his piles were getting worse and worse. He was in no condition to emulate Williams, just back, tanned, cheerful and full of news, from the front.

(*To his mother, 20 May*) I've been counting up, and for more than a third of the time I've been here, I've been incapacitated either owing to my disease or flu or sore throats. It's as if I'd been ill every third day ... My dear Maw, I am ashamed of this dismal howl, but I post it because I really can't write another. Your battered son, Arthur.

The Williamses came to the rescue. They invited Arthur to pay a long visit to Ariadna Vladimirovna's family home, at Vergezha on the river Volkhov. There, in a big country house, Ransome could, with luck, recuperate, finish *Old Peter*, and sample Russian life as we know it in the works of Tolstoy, Turgenev and Chekhov. Arthur was delighted to accept, and profited mightily. The background of life was the horrible war, which created a 'slow, grinding unease', and his piles got no better; but work went well, the life was fascinating, 'now and then we were happy.'

(*To his mother, 15 June*) I celebrated the completion of the rough draft of the children's book by going down to the river and offering an artificial fly to a number of rising dace, with the result that I pulled them out one after another, and only stopped because I was driven indoors by the clouds of poisonous mosquitoes, who have made a most unholy mess of every visible part of me ... The flowers are coming out: I have lilac, narcissus, and lily of the valley on my table. Almost continuous rain. I've visited several very interesting villages, and talked with peasants even more delightful and witty than north of Englanders.

Messrs Jack postponed publication of *Old Peter* until 1916, which
was sickening; but Methuen had accepted *The Elixir* for immediate issue, though not on very generous terms. Never mind: he
had in the mean time the delightful talk of Vergezha, the white
nights, the fishing, and all the life of the river, down which huge
rafts of logs forever floated to market. The memory and joy of it
stayed with him to the end of his life; he soon forgot the anxiety
and constant pain.

At the time, the pain was clamorous, the weakness ever-
increasing; at last he had to have an operation (and was told when
it was over that without it he would have died). He had no particular forebodings, though he kept the news from Ivy, and wrote
to his mother: 'I shall think of you, all of you, when the actual
moment comes, and now I send you my very best love, and tell
you what you know already that I care for you much more than
for anybody else in the world.' Unfortunately he turned out to be
strongly resistant to cocaine, the best anaesthetic available; and
the ether which was substituted wore off half-way through the
operation, which had to be stopped while more was hastily
administered.

The operation was on 9 August. Three days afterwards he wrote
to Mrs Ransome: 'I have had a lively time and know more about
the nature of pain than I have ever known in my life before ... I
was 56 hours after the operation without sleep. They said it must
mean that writers are special beings with most anarchical nerves.
However all the worst they say is over now.' He said he was
cheerful, only very tired; nevertheless he was overcome by a
longing for home:

> I long for Leeds today with an overflowing desire. I want to
> have brandysnacks for tea, and eat them all, and to sit in a tram
> and see the smoke-cloud in the valley, and to smoke shag in the
> garden, and to hear Aunt Mat's voice laughing over the tele-
> phone, and to go fishing with Uncle John and no doubt catch
> grayling in trout-time and vice versa.

Gaily put; but even his exuberant fortitude was taxed by the
slow, painful progress of his convalescence. He left hospital on
25 August, sixteen days after the operation, but continued exceedingly weak for months. The Williamses took him into their flat,
but that was a mixed blessing. For opportunity knocked at last.

The Petrograd correspondent of the *Daily News* was even iller than Arthur, who, to spare Williams, took on the job of deputising for him. It was a curious début for a reporter.

> (*To his mother, 2 September*) I get headaches at once if I try to work ... I am no good as a journalist and never shall be. However after telegraphing I lie down, and the headache goes as soon as my blood is again evenly distributed. I have much less pain now. Really my only constraint is my extreme weakness, and utter inability to move about. However I can now move from one room to another of the flat successfully, and sometimes without the beastly headspinning that used to come if I merely sat up.

It was just as well that he had Harold Williams to take the cables to the telegraph office for him.

In these last weeks before he was sucked down entirely into the maelstrom of the war, his reviving spirits turned chiefly on the books he was going to write. Even in the first letter he wrote to his mother after the operation he was boasting of the historical romance on the fall of Novgorod that he meant to write next; and his horizons expanded euphorically from week to week. By the beginning of September he had five other works planned besides *Lord Novgorod the Great*, and apparently expected to write them with the speed and certainty of Hugh Walpole.

> (*To his mother, 2 September*) There's no end to them, all different, all glorious, all promising delicious months [of work] ... I feel on the very threshold of writing again, with all the freshness and eagerness I had when I first knew the Collingwoods. It's as if all the last ten years were simply preparation, and as if now were beginning a new wider and more various and independent work in which everything even the abominable unhappiness I've had to work through were going to be useful and precious as his metal to a craftsman. It's dreadfully exciting.

Edith Ransome may be forgiven if at this time she smiled and frowned and shook her head, remembering the child Arthur's grandiose plans to make a fortune from hawk-moths and Belgian hares. She told him that she enjoyed *The Elixir of Life*, the completion of which had so encouraged him. He replied, 'Lots of people will dismiss the book as sheer rot, I know. And it is sheer rot, God bless it, and the writing of sheer rot is the greatest sport on earth and I mean to do it again and again, D.V.'

God was not willing. The *Daily News* correspondent was not going to recover, and Arthur was offered his job. He decided to complete his convalescence in England, and negotiate with the *News* while there. His journey home, and sojourn there, were uneventful, except that the strain of living with Ivy brought on a recurrence of his headaches, which had previously gone away. He took the *News* post, and with his usual optimism said he was awfully pleased that '*this time* I really have got a job, and an interesting one. Also I have an assistant whom I can turn on to send telegrams in Petrograd while I am gallivanting about the country at the expense of the *Daily News*.' No doubt there would be slack times, when he could get on with his romances; and the salary would enable him to pay his debts, including the twenty pounds he had borrowed to cover the expenses of his operation.

On his return to Petrograd he found himself, for the first time since his marriage, part of a close-knit masculine world, that of the British correspondents; and for the first time since he abandoned publishing at the age of nineteen, he had a regular job. Both experiences suited him. He wrote to his mother, 'It does seem queer to be already in December. Having regular work to do makes the time go by astonishingly fast.' The journalists, many of whom he had already met, were happy to make him one of themselves, and to show him some of the trade's wrinkles – how to write telegraphese, for example. His health mended ('I am now a sturdy pink almost always') and in March 1916 he moved into a huge room on Glinka Street, 'fairly slopping over with gold light', with a friendly landlady. He found he enjoyed the pressures of a war correspondent's life:

(*To his mother, 6 March 1916*) The whole business of super-abundant work is ripping, especially now that I am beginning not to be so worried by the writing of my telegrams. I fairly charge out of bed, and start getting ahead while I make my tea and drink it, and after that it's hammer and tongs hammer and tongs. My only complaint is that I haven't time to do all I want.

Among the things he was less and less able to attend to were the romances and fairy-stories (though he did find an illustrator, Dmitri Mitrokhin, for *Old Peter*). There were few slack times. A crisis of fundamental importance was speedily developing, and it dominated his life, as it dominated that of his new associates.

Britain was fortunate in being represented in Russia at this juncture by a small group of remarkable men: among the diplomatists, Sir George Buchanan, the Ambassador, and Robert Bruce Lockhart, the Acting Consul-General at Moscow; among the journalists, Bernard Pares of the *Telegraph*; Harold Williams; and Morgan Philips Price, of the *Manchester Guardian*; on a limb of his own, William Peters, a young economist who was working, on a travelling Carnegie scholarship, in the Russian ministry of trade and industry. Britain was unfortunate in not knowing what to do with them. They were all in a false position. As Britons, their first concern was with the war; but as experts on Russia they were more and more aware that the country was taking a course towards revolution. Such advice and such information as they could get to London past the censors (or, in the case of the officials, past the filter of Whitehall routine and preoccupation) were futile, if addressed to the question of Russia's part in the war, for, as they well knew, it would probably take a miracle to keep Russia in the fight for much longer, a miracle which His Britannic Majesty's Government could not supply. They were equally futile if addressed to the question of the future state of Russian politics and society, for there was equally little that HMG could do about that, and nothing that it wanted to hear on the subject. The attack on Gallipoli having failed, and an overwhelming proportion of the available military material being earmarked for the approaching battle of the Somme, the Western allies' last chance to divert the course of Russian history had vanished, if it had ever existed.

Their common predicament drew the British together (except for Lockhart, somewhat isolated in Moscow). Arthur played his part in their friendships and dilemmas from the moment he took on the *Daily News* job.

The dreadful defeats which Russia had endured in 1914 and 1915 had left her especially vulnerable to German propaganda, which spared no effort to spread and deepen defeatism about the prospects of the Entente. British propaganda, by contrast, had been highly amateurish, a fact which had begun seriously to worry both the officials and the journalists. It was Arthur who managed to get something done about it. He thought that a strictly unofficial news agency 'might do good work by giving the Russian newspapers information about the western front': hard news from France would at least help to persuade the Russians that they were not alone in their sufferings. He went to Moscow to discuss the idea with Lockhart. The Consul-General was even younger than Arthur, an ambitious, talented, emotional, energetic man. He thought the scheme an excellent one, and, it seems likely, approved Arthur's other idea, that their common friend, Michael Lykiardopoulos ('Lyki') of the Moscow Arts Theatre, was the man to run the agency, on the grounds that he was energetic, with a talent for publicity, and that the Russians were likely to trust an office run by one of their countrymen. Arthur went back to Petrograd and on 22 January submitted his proposal, in writing, to the Embassy.

This contact with Sir George Buchanan was good for Arthur if not, in the long run, for anyone else. He was enduring another sharp attack of conscience about the war and went so far as to have a medical examination. The doctor gave him medicine for his piles, and told him that there was nothing to stop him joining up except his anaemia. Then an awful letter arrived from Ivy saying that she was having an affair with someone she had met through a lonely hearts advertisement, in her answer to which she had emphasised her love for her husband as well as her aristocratic descent. Probably the whole thing was one of her romances, but it was in doleful spirits that Arthur paid another visit to the Embassy on 1 February. However among the Ambassador's many virtues was that of knowing how to encourage his troops. He told Arthur that he was certainly not to enlist, that his work in Russia was much too valuable to be sacrificed, and that the British Government had approved the news agency scheme. There were no more crises of conscience.

The news agency was not a success. Its most valuable member by far was Harold Williams, who gradually became, in effect, the Ambassador's public relations officer as well as one of his closest advisers. For the rest, the organisation began by meeting almost surreptitiously in a small flat on the Morskaya, 'the street of furriers, flower shops, jewellers, expensive dress-makers and pretty ladies'. Its office was a small room 'where the best part of the furniture was a large bronze bedstead covered with a pink silk eider-down'.[2] For the simple purposes that Ransome and Lockhart had in mind this accommodation was sufficient: it was a quiet, pleasant place where Williams's friends could meet and compare notes and take decisions, and was known simply as the Anglo-Russian Bureau. The authorities had decided, against Arthur's views, to appoint an Englishman, Hugh Walpole, to head it. Walpole, who never really mastered Russian, could not be a very effective head (his biographer says regretfully that under him the office developed into something 'grievously like a joke') and Williams was no match for the paymasters, represented by Colonel Thornhill, the head of British intelligence in Russia. Thornhill had little use for subtlety or indirection; before long he had installed the Bureau, renamed the British Propaganda Office, in much grander premises near the Russian War Office, where Walpole had a staff of twelve, the atmosphere of an English club prevailed, and the utility to the war effort, or to Anglo-Russian understanding, was nil.

Lockhart rescued something of the original scheme: he ran a 'sub-office' in Moscow, headed by Lykiardopoulos, 'without any flourish of trumpets and without the knowledge of the outside world. In this way I was able to bring considerable influence to bear on the local newspapers without their feeling that they were being inundated with official propaganda.' So Arthur's initiative was not wholly unproductive.[3]

Unfortunately the business led to a breach with Hugh Walpole. Arthur's diary records a preliminary tiff on 30 March, which was made up the next day. Perhaps Walpole had heard that Ransome did not think him a suitable head of the Bureau. The big quarrel came on 1 June, by which time Walpole had certainly gathered that Ransome did not take the Bureau very seriously, for he had more or less said so in an article in the *Daily News*. He picked a quarrel with Arthur in the most childish way and lost his temper completely. Arthur did not, to his subsequent regret, for he felt that if he had, Walpole would have found it possible to make peace. As it was, all the efforts of Harold Williams and others to reconcile the two men failed. Arthur was more than willing ('as far as I was concerned there was no quarrel') but Walpole was not. The breach was not closed for sixteen years.

2 Ariadna Tyrkova-Williams, *Cheerful Giver*, p. 168.
3 R. H. Bruce Lockhart, *Memoirs of a British Agent*, p. 144.

A happier glimpse of Arthur's relations with his colleagues can be found in Sir Bernard Pares's memoirs. He says of this period:

> Ransome has always seemed to me one of the very few authors who can write such English that anyone must delight to read him. Once when I went up to his room he begged me to sit down and say nothing for some time. Then he explained ... he was trying to write a story of the time of Izaak Walton, with a lot of fishing in it, but without any plot or incident; and he had to take a long while to collect himself before he could put aside all the chaos around us.

This was *Piscator and his Phillida*, that Arthur described to his mother as his 'Roger de Coverley sort of book': he wrote at least 41,000 words of it, encouraged by Will Peters, but had increasing doubts. In the end he showed it to Harold Williams, and the diary tersely records the result:

> (*19 March*) Williams condemned *Piscator*.

No more is heard of the work.

Bernard Pares had a scheme to get Arthur appointed to a chair of Russian at Leeds University, which would have been a dramatically exact following in his father's footsteps; but that project too fell through. All talk of chairs was premature while the fighting continued.

Arthur visited the armies three times in 1916, getting as far as Bucharest when Romania entered the war, but perhaps the most important event of that year, for him, was the publication of *Old Peter's Russian Tales*, which occurred soon after he had sent the illustrations to Britain in the diplomatic bag. The book was a success from the first, has been more or less continuously in print ever since, and has today attained classic status. In the end it may outlast *Swallows and Amazons*. It was, in short, Arthur's first permanent success, and requires analysis.

The durability of the book must in the first place be attributed to the excellence of the tales themselves and to the imagination of the Russian people who conceived them: in this respect Ransome was right to describe himself as a mere editor. The stories appeal at all sorts of levels. Some of them are not only old, but universal in Indo-European culture: the story of the Golden Fish, for

example, is the same in all essentials and many details as the Grimm
story of the flounder and the fisherman. It is a story of profound
meaning. The climax is the terrible moment when the fisherman's
wife at last goes beyond the appointed bounds of human ambition.
In the Russian version, as reported by Ransome, the fish is slow to
obey the old man's last summons, and when it comes to him on
the crest of the storm it knows already what the last, monstrous
request will be. ' "What is it now?" says he, in a voice more terrible than the voice of the storm itself.' And when the poor old
fisherman replies, it answers not a word, but turns over and goes
down into the deep sea.

The other stories add up to a very various collection, full of the
usual episodes and characters of folklore: wicked stepmothers,
jealous sisters, envious brothers, tyrannous monarchs, witches,
giants, and magic of all kinds, usually associated with kindly birds
and beasts. Some of the tales are comic or satirical, others appeal
to a simple sense of the marvellous, and one or two ('The Golden
Fish', 'Sadko', 'Alenoushka') seem in their sadness to mean more
than they say: are couched in both kinetic and potential speech, to
use Ransome's terms. Above all, every story is subtly suffused with
the colour of the culture and country that produced it. The idiosyncratic Russian attitude to life, nature and society is what gives
the tales their most potent charm.

Such stories were bound to find their way into English, and
bound equally to establish themselves in that tongue; but Ransome
was perfectly right in supposing that a skilful editor was needed.
Other hands had tried the work before him, and had had nothing
like the impact of *Old Peter*. Arthur himself had had to learn by
trial and error what was required. His first efforts, a batch of
Caucasian tales, had been rejected by publishers, 'most fortunately', in the winter of 1913–14. But he was on the right track; he
had the practice of the Anansi tales behind him (and perhaps telling
stories to Tabitha had also helped); it was only delays caused by
the war, illness and *The Elixir of Life* that prevented him from
finishing and publishing *Old Peter* well before 1916.

Only examination in detail of one or more of the *Tales* could
do justice to their merits; but some general points may be made.
There is a new swiftness and economy of effect, and a newly energetic movement in the prose. No detail is superfluous. Ransome
also displays a new mastery in the framework of his book. It
would have been possible to present the stories without any con-

necting narrative; but their fascination would have been less, if only because they would have been harder to understand without the mediating voice and presence of Old Peter and his grand-children. Ransome explains, in the *Autobiography*,

> Direct translation is not the way to tell Russian stories to English children ... The Russian peasant storytellers, telling stories to each other, could count on a wide range of knowledge that their listeners, no matter how young, shared with them. Young English listeners knew nothing of the world that in Russia listeners and storytellers alike were able to take for granted. Continual explanation would have been as destructive of the tales as an endless series of asides.

So he left out almost all explanations within the tales themselves, reading as many variants of each story as he could find, and then laying them all aside 'while writing the story for myself'. But that still left the difficulty that the tales presupposed a society of which English readers would be ignorant. So the Ogre, the Imp and the Elf were transmuted into Old Peter, little Vanya and little Maroosia, sitting (mostly) in the hut in the forest before bed-time. Old Peter's voice is never missing: he is as omnipresent as Scheherazade in the *Arabian Nights*, and an equal artist. Sometimes the children interrupt him with comments or questions. In this way the Russia that Arthur loved is never forgotten. The book contains a charming sketch of the old peasant society. It is no more than a sketch, and a misleadingly bright-coloured one; the darker side of life in the Tsarist countryside is not even hinted at, and no one would guess, from *Old Peter*'s pages, that, even as the book was published, the world it described was disappearing for ever under the dreadful blows of war and revolution. Today that merely adds to its charm. We glimpse a lost world in which there are things to regret as well as things we may be glad are gone. The account of a village christening, at the very end of the book, seems, for instance, to have no other purpose than to bring peasant Russia vividly before the reader, in an almost anthropological belief that it was worth recording for its own sake.[4] It was an

---

4 cf. Kipling on the genesis of *Captains Courageous*: he wanted 'to catch and hold something of a rather beautiful localised American atmosphere that was already beginning to fade' when he wrote about the fishermen of Gloucester (*Something of Myself*, p. 131).

entirely characteristic undertaking of the mature Ransome, one that was to leave its mark on many later books.

Arthur meant to follow up *Old Peter* with at least one more volume of tales, but the engulfing storm of history now put an end to all such projects for many years. As 1916 wore on his letters home began to fill with ominous details, for example of rising prices, the result of growing shortages.

How much he knew of the real situation is hard to judge. Whether because of the censor, or enemy interception, or his pre-occupying work, or mere accident, his letters to his mother are unusually sparse at this time, his diary is unrevealing, and his telegrams were subject to editing by both Russian and English authority.

(*Diary, 19 September*) Telegram *DN* 1074 [words]. Much censored.

The *Autobiography* indicates that he saw enough of the sufferings of the soldiers to understand the anxiety of his friends in Petrograd as to the future. He knew that doubt was turning to something very like dismay among the Cadets, and Russian casualty lists were, appallingly, even larger than French or British ones. By the time he left for his annual visit to England at the end of October he was convinced that Russia was very near collapse. There are no allusions in his papers to the near-universal hostility to the incompetent Tsar and his wife; no accounts written at the time about what he thought of the ascendancy of Rasputin; but various remarks in post-revolutionary and post-war papers indicate that he noticed and disliked the 'profiteers' and their conspicuous consumption, which was such a prominent feature of life in wartime Petrograd. As a correspondent for the Liberal *Daily News* he began to be told things that would not be said to representatives of the *Morning Post* and *The Times*.

By the time he got home, on 3 November, he was ready to speak frankly to the Foreign Office, the more so as he had been well briefed by Will Peters. He predicted that there would be trouble sufficient to take Russia out of the war by the end of 1917. According to Peters there would be a revolt either in March or October, when food-shortages would be likeliest in Petrograd, a revolt which would either succeed or, if suppressed, give the Autocracy its excuse to withdraw from the war. Arthur seems to have thought the latter alternative the more likely. Furthermore, he took it for granted, and would for months to come, that it was right, as well as desirable from the British point of view, to keep Russia in the war if possible. The struggle against Germany still came first.

The prediction about March and October was a lucky one; it seems a shame to spoil it by pointing out that in 1917 the revolutions occurred either in February and October (Julian calendar) or March and November (Gregorian). But then Ransome's memory may have been at fault: Will Peters may have got it entirely right. Even if he did not, he did amazingly well. But Acland and the Foreign Office paid no attention. The censorship (headed by a notably stupid ex-colonial official called Swettenham) had made sure that no reports about the desperate military and political conditions of Russia had got into the British press, and this had made it much easier for Whitehall to ignore all the danger-signs. A wilful ignorance and complacency about Russian affairs were to be the dominant themes of British policy for at least the next five years; and neither Arthur nor anyone else, in spite of heartbreaking efforts, was ever to succeed in modifying them.

Arthur started back to Russia on 2 December, suffering once more from violent headaches, caused by a brief but thoroughly unsatisfactory visit to Ivy. He got back to Petrograd on 11 December and a few days later wrote gloomily to his mother: 'If it had not been for Coniston [to which he had escaped for a few days] I rather wish I had never come back to England ... You are wrong, of course, about my affairs ever straightening themselves out and becoming happy. However it's no good being bluer than one can help.' It was probably a relief to set out for the front again on 20 December.

The telegrams that he sent from the battle-zone are of interest on several counts. In the first place they illustrate excellently what the necessities of journalism were doing to his style:

Winter, late this year, has at last descended on the Russian front. The borders of snow-covered ice on either side of the Dvina are gradually spreading towards the middle of the river where little icebergs float in a steady procession. In ten days or less the river will be frozen over. Scouts are once more covering themselves in white overalls as even the palest colour shows up dark on the glittering snow under the light of rockets which the Germans send up continually, clearly afraid of Russian activity. Besides rapidly increasing motor transport there is a huge volume of horse traffic and wheeled carts, already being changed for sledges. Everywhere along the front I met long trains of sledges pulled by little shaggy horses driven by furcapped men in sheepskins. A new picturesque sight on the front are great bands of Khirgizes and Tartars from Tashkent brought from the far east for roadmaking and fortification. The Russian army is settling down cheerfully to the third winter campaign, better equipped, better organised and stronger than ever before, and fully conscious of its strength.

This is the Ransome style of later years in all but elegance. An eye for weather and telling details; carefully chosen adjectives but nevertheless entire plainness: these were excellent journalistic traits, which had always been latent in his prose, but were now absolutely required if he was to do his job adequately. The power of swift, lucid, precise reporting – kinetic prose that realises its potential by its very simplicity – now gained, was never to leave him.

His estimate that the Russian army was better equipped than ever before has been confirmed by historians; but his closing remarks are more striking for what they do not say than for anything else. The soldiers may have been cheerful and may have been conscious of their strength: that does not mean that they wanted to use it. Even more crucial, Ransome discovered, but could not, because of the censor, mention, that the army generally was convinced that it was being stabbed in the back by 'dark forces' – which meant the clique round the Tsar led by the German-born Tsaritsa and, above all, her idol, Rasputin. Incompetent leadership or pro-German intrigue, it was all one. Then on the night of 29–30 December Rasputin was murdered. A friendly general told Ransome the news the next day, and urged him to hurry back to Petrograd. He arrived on 2 January (Western calendar) and found the city coming slowly to the boil, 'like a pot of porridge'.

His telegrams for the next two months covered a variety of topics: the military news, which was not too bad for once; Russian reactions to Woodrow Wilson's peace speech of 21 January and to the breaking of relations between the United States and the Central Powers; the intricate politics of the struggle between the Duma (the feeble Russian parliament) and the Government.

But there is a ground-bass to his reports, in which one can hear revolution approaching:

(*18 January*) The general feeling here is of oppressive expectancy, and rumours come from Moscow of possible trouble on January 22, the anniversary of unfortunate Sunday 1905.

'Unfortunate Sunday' is of course a euphemism, used to avoid the censor's eye, for 'Bloody Sunday' – the day when the Cossacks, on orders from the Winter Palace, shot down Father Gapon's followers as they came to present a petition to the Tsar.

(*12 February*) It was officially announced today that eleven working men, members of the central Petrograd committee of mobilised industry, have been arrested. They are accused of belonging to the revolutionary parties and of using their position to provoke industrial unrest and setting before themselves the ultimate aim of turning Russia into a social democratic republic ... four other persons accused of carrying out their instructions in preparation for labour demonstrations were also arrested.

(*18 February*) There are only two subjects of conversation in Petrograd. What will happen when the Duma meets? and What is to be done about food? The war has made an unprecedented demand on the Russian railways which even in peace-time are barely adequate ... Half an hour in any big Russian railway-station would make it easy to understand the spectacle, at first sight strange, of Russia, the richest country in Europe, suffering from a lack of bread and wood, the two commodities which she was accustomed to export. That this is the case I can testify from my own experience, this being the sixth day that I have been unable to get bread for breakfast and the third on which through lack of wood for my stove I have considered myself lucky in possessing a kerosene lamp and a warm sheepskin coat in which I am now writing.

On 2 March he got a telegram from his editor urging him to cut down his messages to 'vital matters'. Unimpressed, he sent another long cable describing the meeting of the Duma that day, and indicating that not much could be expected of it: 'events have shown that brave words in the Duma are their own reward.' On

8 March he reported that the Tsar had refused to restore the vodka monopoly and thus (said the proclamation) had put an end to drunkenness in Russia for ever.

[*8 or 9 March*] A number of causes working together have brought the crisis momentarily to a head, though I do not personally believe there can be serious trouble while the Duma is sitting. A number of bakers' shops have been destroyed and at others the crowd seized bread from those who had succeeded in buying it. A crowd last night broke the windows of a factory because its workers refused to strike ... The feeling of the people is not hostile to the Cossacks though they instantly resented the action of a man who deliberately rode into a woman. For the most part the crowd is good-tempered and I still hope that serious conflict can be avoided. There has been very little firing so far.

(*10 March, 11 p.m.*) I spent today travelling about the town, finding much the same feeling as yesterday ... The causes of the crisis are vague. I have not personally seen any signs of real hunger but there is undoubted shortage due both to the lack of suitable organisation ... and to extraordinary demand, for example, lack of fodder means that over 40,000 horses are being partially fed on bread.

(*15 March*) The Revolution, which began in disorder deliberately provoked by the police and the old Ministry of the Interior, definitely began on 12 March when the first troops passed over to the side of the people.

V

Revolution

People interested in revolutions and revolutionaries will be shocked at my not being a revolutionary, and will not understand how one with a front seat at a revolution could be always thinking of books, and worst of all, books for children.

ARTHUR RANSOME, 1949

For two generations the Russian intelligentsia had predicted and yearned for the Revolution. The longing was acute in March 1917: even the liberal, Alexander Kerensky, declared in a Duma speech that 'the Tsar must be removed – by terrorist means if there are no others'. It had been easy enough to see, on the spot, that trouble was coming, even if the fact was invisible in London, or in Switzerland, where the leaders of the extreme Left endured their exile. There had even been a rehearsal of the situation in 1905, when the failed war with Japan had nearly overthrown the Tsarist regime. This time a greater disaster brought about the Tsar's abdication and the fall of the monarchy: no other Romanov could be induced to assume the crown, and none would have lasted long if he had. Yet the disappearance of the old order solved nothing. There was still an Eastern Front, more than 500 miles long: its nearest point was only 100 miles or so from Petrograd. The Germans were undefeated, and were preparing the destruction of Russia both on the battlefield and, through subversion, on the home front: soon a sealed train would be carrying Lenin from Switzerland to Finland, by courtesy of Hindenburg and Ludendorff. Nor did the March Revolution end the food shortages or the transport chaos which had largely brought it about. The collapse of all political authority left a hideously dangerous vacuum, which it was all too likely that authoritarians of either the Left or the Right would eventually fill. Russia might thus pay dearly for the longed-for catastrophe.

Until then it had not mattered to the world at large who was the Petrograd correspondent of the *Daily News*, nor all that much what he reported. Except for the brief local notoriety from which he had suffered during the Douglas case, Arthur's life had been that of an entirely private person. But now he was to be sucked into the central vortex of history and politics. He was to become notorious in many eyes; in others, distinguished. At times his private self was to be almost swamped, for all his struggling, by his public role; and the course of his life was to be changed for ever. And he was to incur as heavy a responsibility as any British overseas correspondent has ever borne.

Before following his adventures in the Revolution, it is as well to consider how adequately he was equipped to observe and interpret the great struggle. His experience as a war reporter had given him a valuable, if occasionally somewhat misleading, background. He had repeatedly travelled to the fighting front; he had visited the great Putilov munitions factory. He never forgot both the enormous military potential and the actual military weakness of Russia. For a time he hoped that the Revolution would re-animate the soldiers' fighting spirit, but it did not take him long to see that the fall of the Tsar initiated a process which ended by destroying the country's military effectiveness.

At the simplest level, that of straightforward chronicling, he was superbly endowed, and gave great satisfaction to his employers. The freshness of his response to life had not been dulled by age, and his now mature style enabled him to convey his personal vivacity even through the poor conductor of a news telegram:

(*13 March*) Tuesday. Having moved across Petrograd with the revolutionaries I now need move no further as the battle has come to me and my windows have the best possible view of the preparations for the storm of the prison which is next door on my right ... A yellow postal delivery car with a red flag and a machine-gun propped up in it ran out from my street, stopped a moment under the theatre, ran round behind it, and opened fire on the prison from the other side. The defenders replied, and while their attention was thus occupied people ran back to the deserted motor below my windows and put a machine-gun together on the side farthest from the prison. Then the car drove off and four men, with two students holding up the long ribbon of cartridges like a bridal train, carried the gun towards the prison.

Nor did Ransome lack energy and courage. He roamed Petrograd ceaselessly, reckless of life and limb, to find out what was going on, and came under fire more than once during the first days of the Revolution. He was by now so much at home among the Russians that he could see the Revolution through their eyes, feel it with their nerves and hearts. This gave his articles a special authenticity. They never seem to have been written by someone outside and above events. They never condescend.

A second undeniable advantage was Ransome's vast ignorance of politics. He was not a fool; but before 1914 it had been possible to live free of the sort of preoccupations we nowadays take for granted. He simply had no previous commitments to get in the way of perception. In this way he was much better endowed than most of the other British journalists in Russia. He remarked in his *Autobiography* that his fellow-correspondents had largely taken on the political colouring of the papers for which they wrote, whereas he retained his independent outlook; but he was too fond of some of those former colleagues to point out that their journalism was also influenced by their commitments to Russian political groups: Harold Williams to the Cadets, and later to the Whites; Soskice to Kerensky; Philips Price, eventually, to the Bolsheviks.

He could not do the impossible. A true revolution is so vast a phenomenon that no one, not even a man so well-placed as Arthur Ransome in 1917, can see more than a little of it. Neither was he well able to predict the long-term consequences of the Revolution. He was frequently taken by surprise. Had he concerned himself more with the long term he would have been a much less valuable journalist, and therefore a less valuable historical source. What the *Daily News* needed was detailed, accurate, intelligent reporting and analysis of events as they unfolded, and that is what it got, in strong clear Ransome prose.

He was not exactly unbiased. From first to last Ransome was pre-eminently concerned with Russo-British relations. The question he never ceased to ask was, how would events affect Britain, and how, therefore, should he report them? This preoccupation never

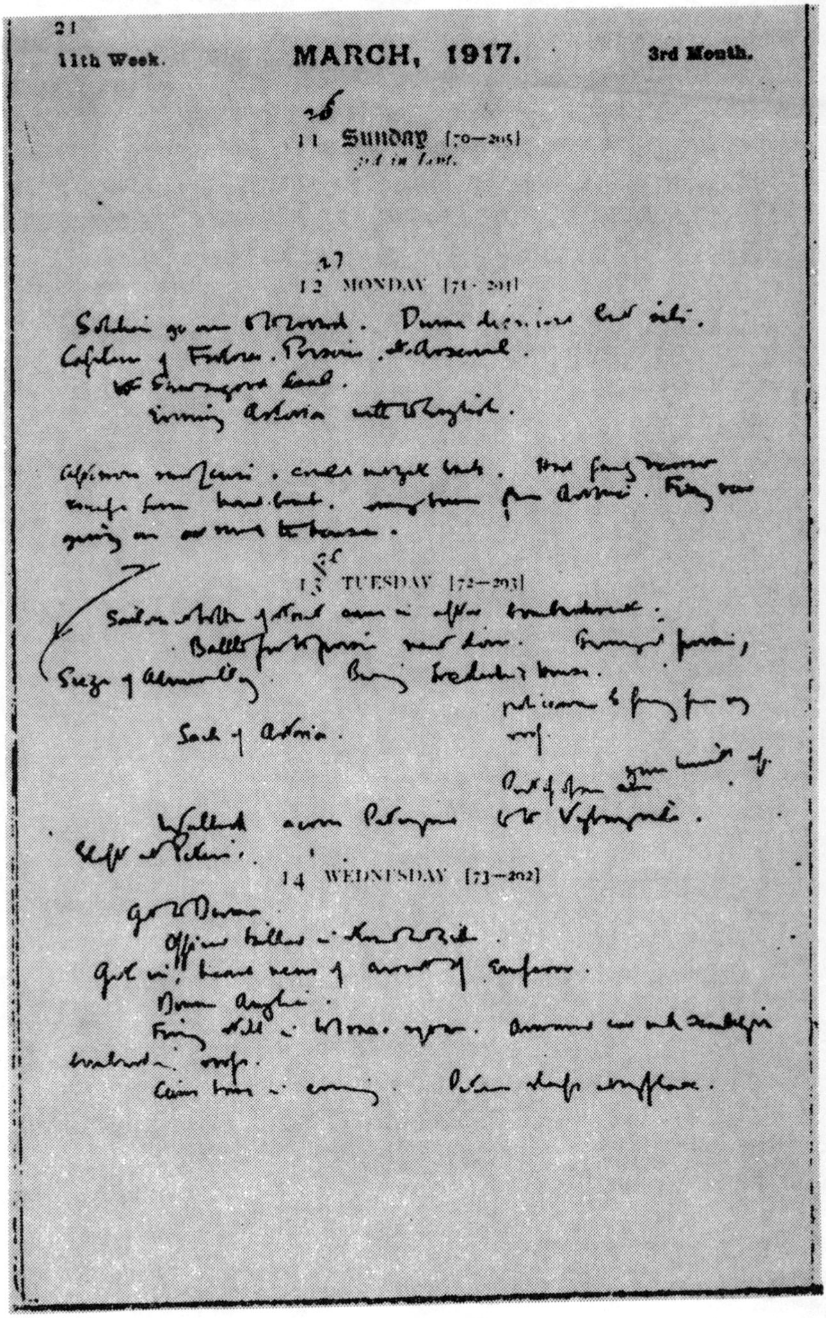
21
11th Week. MARCH, 1917. 3rd Month.

11 Sunday [70—295]
3rd in Lent.

12 MONDAY [71-294]

13 TUESDAY [72-293]

14 WEDNESDAY [73-292]

1 A page from Arthur Ransome's diary, 11–14 March 1917

led him to falsify occurrences; but it did colour both his perceptions and his writing, and readers in the late-twentieth century need to make allowances for it.

Finally, it should perhaps be stated unambiguously that he was, throughout, a Liberal, writing for Liberal papers; and that as the Revolution completed his political education, he became ever more firmly a man of the Left, though never a Communist or even a socialist. He was too much an English individualist for that.

All revolutions begin in an atmosphere of euphoria. Ransome's response to the overthrow of the Tsardom was ecstatic.

(*17 March*) This is far and away the greatest victory over Prussianism gained in this war. Germany will now have republican France as one neighbour and free Russia on the other side. Already Russian soldiers must be telling the Germans what they have done and asking when the Germans will do likewise ... only those who know how things were only a week ago can understand the enthusiasm of us who have seen a miracle take place before our eyes. We knew how Russia worked for the war in spite of her Government. We could not tell the truth. It is as if honesty had returned. As honest men we can only sing Nunc Dimittis. Russia has broken her chains and stands as the greatest free nation in Europe with republican France and liberal England. Nowhere outside Germany had Prussianism gone so far as it had here. Nowhere has it been so absolutely defeated ... Returning from the Duma today I met a steadily marching crowd singing an old peasant song. I thought at first it was a demonstration but I found that the men were new recruits called to the colours. And what colours? A red flag of revolution is flying over the Winter Palace where the Constituent Assembly will meet. The proud statue of Catherine the Great looks down on the Nevsky Prospect. Today she is holding a red flag in her hand ... The people themselves keep order. They wait in their turn for bread and wood and return marvelling: there are no police and yet the world goes on.
(*18 March*) Today the newspapers have reappeared and their tone and even their form is so joyful that it is hard to recognise them for the censor-ridden mute unhappy things of a week ago.

(*3 April*) Yesterday, lest things should be too solemn, deputations of *dvorniks* (yardmen or porters) presented a petition that in these times of freedom and equality their humiliating title of yardmen should be changed officially to that of house directors.

On 12 April he witnessed a grand reception for Catherine Breshko-Breshkovskaya, 'the granny of the Revolution', back from Siberia:

The little kindly old lady with nearly white hair and pink cheeks laughed and cried as she kissed them [the leaders and representatives]. At last she made a short speech urging that the Hohenzollerns should not be allowed to conquer what had been taken from the Romanovs. I have never seen such enthusiasm. Soldiers and sailors leapt from their places, rushed to the tribune and (in some cases kneeling before her) cried 'We have brought you from Siberia to Petrograd. Shall we not guard you? We have won freedom. We will keep it.' She gave away some roses from the bouquet with which she had been met at the station, and I saw a soldier who had only secured two petals wrap them up in paper while tears of excitement ran down his face.

And on the first of May he watched the celebrations from the same window from which he had watched the revolution in March:

I can hear the Marseillaise sung by thousands of voices away to the left. From the other side a procession is coming up from the great factories singing the special factory folk-songs which are, I believe, peculiar to Russia. Immediately below my window in the great square two processions are meeting. One of them includes a detachment from one of the regiments which first threw out the red flag in the days of revolution. The other procession, noticing this, breaks into wild cheering which spreads over the whole sea of people far away into the distance under the gold domes and cupolas of the old Russian Church. The soldiers wave their caps and shout in reply. In all directions as far as one can see red flags are waving above the dense crowd which leaves only just enough room for the perpetually passing processions. A long string of men and women walk along holding hands like an endless farandole. It is difficult to believe that this same square only six weeks ago witnessed the battle for the prison next door, which now, a picturesque ruin decorated with flags, makes a fit background for the rejoicing people.

When, he wondered, would there be such a May Day in Berlin?

But even in those first joyous days there was cause for anxiety, and a note of concern frequently breaks the tenor of the telegrams. Immediately after the fall of the Tsar there did not seem to be much reason to worry about the effect of the Revolution on the war and the Allied cause: the revolutionaries were soundly anti-Prussian. On 18 March Ransome reported that the newspapers were almost unanimous in supporting a vigorous continuation of the war. He saw a street orator, who talked of 'brother Germans', shouted down by the crowd. He went round to the offices of the Bolshevik newspaper, *Pravda*, which 'not unfairly' represented the views of labour. The soldiers, students and girls, all with red ribbons, whom he found there had a general air of 'extremism' but their programme was not so very extreme: 'they recognise that nothing can be settled until the meeting of the Constituent Assembly.' However he urged the British to bolster the pro-war party by giving every possible support to the Lvov ministry, which had been set up by the old imperial Duma as its last action. The business of this Provisional Government was to hold the country together while preparations were made for elections to a Constituent Assembly. Arthur had discovered that the Government had a rival.

The Petrograd Soviet of glorious memory, which had been the soul of the 1905 Revolution, had sprung to life again even before the birth of the Lvov cabinet. There was no time for proper elections to this council (soviet) of workers and soldiers: to start with, the members simply co-opted each other, but in a rough-and-ready way most of the factories and regiments in Petrograd were represented. Neither was there any clear demarcation of responsibility. The 1905 Soviet had organised demonstrations, distributed arms to striking workers, given them orders and kept them informed with printed bulletins. The new Soviet assumed that it would have at least equal authority, which meant that it was bound to come into collision with the Lvov Government, although Alexander Kerensky managed to be a leading member of both.

Arthur was working in his room in Glinka Street when he was

visited by a messenger who issued him with a pass admitting him to meetings of the Soviet. The workers had not forgotten a slight service which the correspondent of the *Daily News* had performed for the prisoners whose arrest he had reported on 12 February. The pass gave him the right to speak but not to vote. He used it only to listen. He went for the first time to a meeting of the 'Council of Workers' and Soldiers' Deputies'[1] on 19 March. By 30 March he had concluded that the soviets were the most important factor in the Revolution. The Petrograd Soviet already had 1,300 members, chosen by the factories and regiments in the capital, and he expected that when the first All-Russian Soviet met its decisions would be enormously important. 'To get a just idea of the situation,' he cabled on 1 April, 'it should never be forgotten that the Council of Soldiers' and Workers' Deputies enjoys practically decisive power in all questions which depend on the working class. Their daily newspaper has an actual circulation of over thirteen million.'

Ransome did not expect the new regime to abandon the old alliance. He expected the Germans to attack, and Russia to resist as never before, for defeat would mean the loss of her new liberty. He thought that the Revolution had confirmed the alliance, 'although I have heard regrets that in her public utterances England showed more anxiety over Russia's part in the war than rejoicing over the great victory of the democratic principles for which it is supposed we are fighting.' But the Soviet, Ransome soon realised, had somewhat different war-aims from those of the Lvov Government and, especially, from those supported by the Foreign Minister, Miliukov, an imperialist of the old school, who endorsed all the old Tsarist ambitions. Ransome, who had never shared the Williamses' idolatry of the Cadet leader (almost the only person mentioned with contempt in the *Autobiography*), felt it necessary to warn his English readers not to take Miliukov too seriously. The Cadets had been bypassed by a revolution which had been made without them. They represented a bourgeoisie which naturally wanted the Revolution to be purely institutional, not social.

1 This was what AR called the Soviet until after the Bolshevik Revolution. He also eschewed the word 'Bolshevik' for most of the same period. Presumably he wanted to spare readers of the *Daily News* the pain of mastering unfamiliar and possibly transient foreign terms. His word for Bolshevik was 'extremist'. The word actually meant 'member of the majority' (sc. of the Social Democratic party). 'Menshevik' meant 'member of the minority'.

'The revolutionaries, not without justification, believe they are willing to use the war and public patriotism to further this purely class desire' (13 April). So all in all the Soviets were right to maintain their independence, in order to watch over the interests of democracy.

Then there was Lenin. Ransome saw his triumphal arrival at the Finland Station, and saw him standing on the bonnet of an armoured car, making a speech as night gathered; but it was some time before he got his measure. At first, influenced no doubt by the story of the sealed train, Ransome seems to have thought Lenin a mere German agent, but not a very formidable one, even though he was urging the immediate conclusion of a peace without annexations. 'Lenin, while conducting this almost comic agitation, is housed in the palace of the ballerina Ksesinskaya and his proceedings are so exaggerated that they have the air of being comic opera' (22 April). All the same, Ransome was sufficiently worried about the growing unpopularity of Britain among the revolutionaries to send a telegram on 30 April explaining at length, for the first but by no means for the last time, how much damage was done to Anglo-Russian relations by such episodes as the refusal to allow delegates from the Independent Labour Party to visit Russia, and by articles in *The Times* denigrating the soviets and the Jews, who were said to be behind the Revolution.

This attempt to influence British opinion was one of several signs that Arthur was getting drawn into politics. Another was his plan to write a book about the Revolution (Dmitri Mitrokhin had produced a fine design for the dust-jacket). But he had not entirely surrendered to his fate. In a letter to his mother on 1 May he complained of being tired out, and of trouble with one of his kidneys. He looked forward to the time when, the war over (Will Peters thought by the end of September) and the book on the Revolution finished, he could get back to his original fairytales. Two days later the first of the great revolutionary crises erupted, and broke the March euphoria for ever.

It was Miliukov's fault. The Foreign Minister was one of those obtuse men, so peculiarly mischievous in times of crisis, who cannot resist any opportunity to be clever. His fundamental policy was defensible: he wished to protect Russia against both German invasion and Left dictatorship. He can even be forgiven for thinking that the two dangers were the same, or at least entailed each other: he was very nearly right. What cannot be forgiven are his actions, taken in the clear knowledge that most of his fellow countrymen had very different views and preoccupations. The popular cry was for peace as soon as possible; no annexations; war only in self-defence. Miliukov did not want peace until Austria and Germany had been defeated. He wanted to take Constantinople, Romania and Armenia, and assert Russian overlordship in Eastern Europe, so as to prevent any recurrence of the dreadful events of 1914, 1915 and 1916 (in this his policy strikingly resembled that adopted by Stalin during and after the Second World War). He hoped to raise a 'Liberty Loan' to sustain the Provisional Government and the Russian war effort; he even hoped to launch an offensive towards the shore of the Black Sea and the Bosphorus. Unfortunately, as Trotsky was to point out in his history of the Revolution, 'the plan fell through because of a mere detail: the refusal of the soldiers.' Miliukov's only hope for carrying out any of his plans was to remain in the Government and call in the aid of the Allies; or so he thought. But the Allies would give no help unless they thought that the Government was useful to them, and they might well not think this, since both the Government and the soviets were committed to a rejection of all domination of other peoples or seizure of foreign territory: in other words, they rejected the secret treaties of 1915, the provisions of which were generally guessed, which were supposed to cement the Entente by their plans to carve up half Europe. Miliukov had already embarrassed his colleagues by his open demand for Constantinople: Kerensky, the Minister of Justice, who was emerging as the strong man of the Government, had said publicly that in this matter Miliukov spoke only for himself. The Foreign Minister was next called on to send to the Allies a copy of the Government's manifesto of 9 April, which set out Russia's new policy. He did so; but he insisted on coupling it with a diplomatic Note whose language undercut the manifesto, and which amounted to a re-affirmation of Russia's traditional expansionist policy and a renewed commitment to the war. He sent off this document on 1 May, hoping that the Soviet would be taken in by its diplomatic circumlocutions. Instead the Note's publication on 2 May touched off huge and threatening demonstrations in the streets, while all the press to the left of the Cadets denounced the Note. After twelve days Miliukov was forced to resign.

This incident induced Ransome to come out openly against Miliukov and the Cadets:

(*16 May*) Miliukov, a wonderful leader in opposition, has been directly or indirectly the cause of all the more serious disputes which have arisen since the Revolution. After fighting nobly for 'a responsible ministry' he showed himself unwilling to be a responsible minister, and with his resignation there is a considerable clearing of the air.

He was forced to acknowledge that the 'Leninites' had made substantial gains in a few weeks: suddenly the streets were full of crowds shouting Bolshevik slogans. Competing cries of 'Down With Miliukov!' and 'Down With Lenin!' rent the air. But he still thought that real power lay elsewhere, with the Menshevik majority in the soviets.

Above all, though he was still not ready to admit, or even to conceive of, the existence of a gulf of incompatibility between the wishes and policies of the Russians and those of the Allies, he did begin to urge that the Russian programme *ought* to be that of the entire alliance, and to support with all his power the new coalition Government (still headed by Lvov, but in which Kerensky was more than ever the dominant figure). His telegram of 20 May set forth the position as he saw it, and displayed striking prescience:

The coalition Government has been formed with the single definite object of the salvation of Russia and of the Revolution which are threatened by a rising tide of anarchy, by disorganisation, indeed decomposition in the army, and by the continuance of a war which is beyond the country's strength. The main plank in the common platform of the coalition is a demand, not for a separate peace but for a general peace ... The whole energy of the coalition is directly or indirectly devoted to this aim. This is the aim put forward by Kerensky in his great effort to restore discipline in the army ... His task will be lightened the moment the Allies take the wind out of the sails of anti-Ally propaganda in the army by clearly expressing agreement with Russia. I do not think it an exaggeration to say that the coalition Government will stand or fall by the Allies' reply to its declaration. If the coalition is broken by failure in the main task it has set itself, it will have small chance of resisting attacks from the extremists who regard its very formation as a concession. If the coalition falls, then the biggest democracy in Europe may be

faced both by internal anarchy and by isolation from the West
... The next few weeks will decide the future both of Russian
democracy and of Anglo-Russian relations.

Events were to demonstrate the accuracy of this diagnosis, and
Ransome was undoubtedly right in pressing his information and
analysis on his editor, and through him, he hoped, on the War
Cabinet, on Parliament, and on British public opinion generally.
Had he been listened to he might have saved the Lloyd George
Government from blundering into a truly disastrous Russian
policy. But the obstacles in his way were much more formidable
than he realised. He might well assume that the Petrograd correspondent of the leading Liberal newspaper could have some
influence not only on his paper's policy but on his Government's.
At the least he must have supposed that with such a story to tell
he would be read attentively. Unfortunately this was a complete
miscalculation. If ministers read any paper it was *The Times*, which
was rapidly losing its way on the subject of Russia,[2] and would
soon be without a correspondent in Petrograd; and anyway, as
they ignored the excellent advice given them by the British
Ambassador, Sir George Buchanan, there is no reason to suppose
that even *The Times*, had it been better informed, would have
modified their outlook.

British official attitudes were marked by blandness and blind-
ness, and a refusal to take seriously any view but Westminster's.
Britain had been slow to understand the desperate need of the
Tsar's armies for weapons and ammunition, and had thus helped
to cause the military defeats which brought on the Revolution
and the collapse of Russia as an ally. In 1917, unable to accept the
fact that Russia could and would fight no more, Britain threw
away her one chance of establishing a friendly permanent Government. In part it was a matter of preoccupation. Hard as everyone
in Petrograd found it to realise (Arthur included), the tremendous
drama in which they were involved was only fitfully visible from
London and Paris, and seemed much less important than what was
happening on the Western Front: just as the sufferings in Flanders
were overlooked in Russia. Worse still, the Western Allies never
understood the significance of their own strategy. Their casualties
were so enormous that they overlooked the still greater sacrifices

2 It headlined its first report on the March Revolution, 'Win the War Movement'.

of the Russian people: some 2 million dead, 5 million wounded, 2.5 million prisoners. Rivers of blood, to what purpose? To relieve pressure on France and Britain. It never seems to have occurred to the high policy-makers that perhaps France and Britain ought to relieve the pressure on Russia, or at least to refrain from urging further offensives in the East. Even after the Revolution they meant to hold Russia to her commitments, in the name of the sanctity of treaties – in this case the treaty of September 1914, forbidding any signatory to seek a separate peace. Against these views Kerensky's policy and Ransome's reporting struggled in vain.

Even had that not been so, the Provisional Government was probably doomed, because of the Germans. Hindenburg and Ludendorff not only wanted a ceasefire on the Eastern Front, so that they could transfer their troops westward; they also wanted access to the vast material resources of Russia. So they kept up incessant pressure all through 1917. If the Russian army stood on the defensive, it would be attacked and beaten; if it tried an offensive itself, it would be counterattacked and beaten. In the mean time German agents were actively stirring up discontent behind the lines.

Finally, and most important of all, there was the question of the land and the nationalities. By the late spring the mass of peasants were stirring, moving to seize the acres which they farmed and believed they should therefore own. The peasant soldiers wanted to go home and get their share of the pickings. And on the fringes of the Russian Empire – in Finland, in the Ukraine – nationalist movements were arising. They might not go so far as to turn to the Germans for help, but they could no longer be depended on to support the Government in Petrograd.

This was the background against which Arthur would now be working. He had few or no illusions, except as to the practical utility of his efforts:

(*23 May*) Disorders in the country ... cannot be said to be growing fewer. Their characteristic in most cases is the seizure of land and the cutting down of forests. Country houses are being sacked. In one district the soldiers levied a tax in their own favour from rich oil-men and manufacturers, basing their demands on the ascertained profits of the unwilling tax-payers. Lynching is growing in frequency, of numbers of horse-thieves who as always get short shrift. Meanwhile fraternisation on the front continues, though stopped in some sections. The extremists continue to urge fraternisation as a means of 'forcing the bourgeois to end the war'. The extremists are in a minority among articulate Russians, but have disproportionate influences among what the Russians themselves call 'the dark masses', meaning by this the inarticulate, uneducated people on whose ignorance the agitators play in the most shameless manner, insisting always on the supposed distinction between the aims of the Allies and of the Russians.

He poured out his personal feelings in a long, rambling letter to his mother on 27 May. Ivy had written to say that Edward Thomas had been killed. 'It's pretty tough luck for poor incompetent Helen, but for Edward himself perhaps not. It's about four years or more since I saw him but I rather fancy he had a rotten time to look forward to after the war. He stayed with Ivy before going out.' Harold Macmillan had been badly wounded. Barbara Collingwood had written to say that she would be grey by the autumn: 'very likely when we do all meet again we shall be too old to write masterpieces or to enjoy anything except chimney corners and reminiscences.' He quite agreed that he was no good at politics, but what was he to do? He was extremely busy and extremely worried about developments in Petrograd, 'particularly with regard to proper understanding between Russia and England. I wish to goodness I had Geoff here, whose solid sense would be a mighty stand-by.' Perhaps he ought to go home, for accurate information would certainly be needed in London when the pending crisis broke, probably before the autumn.

Yet the old Arthur was still far from dead. The same letter announced that the long *Aladdin* poem had been revised and sent to the printer at last. He could take comfort from the coming of summer to Petrograd, though he felt like a truant whenever he caught himself enjoying the city's beauty; and

You don't know how often I look at your two pictures of the lake country which hang in front of my typewriter table above a mixed collection of Russian toys, and one each side of my ikon of Nicholas the miracle-worker who is decorated with a bit of heather from Peel Island.

The next few weeks brought the steady crumbling of the Provisional Government. The sailors at Kronstadt formed a soviet and rejected the Government's authority: they were never wholly brought to heel. Kerensky was preparing his offensive, for which, as Ransome bleakly observed, 'everything was ready except the will' (to *Daily News*, 29 May). The Bolsheviks in the Petrograd Soviet were beginning to show themselves impatient with the ordinary rules of debate. Brawling was beginning in the streets.

On 3 June the official Soviet paper published an appeal to socialist parties and trade unions throughout the world to send representatives to a conference at Stockholm on 28 June: the conference, it was hoped, might force the belligerent governments to state their war-aims and perhaps find ways of hastening the coming of peace. Arthur thoroughly approved: a joint Allied declaration of democratic war-aims would be of enormous assistance to the Kerensky Government. These sentiments did him no good with the arch-Conservative J. L. Garvin, editor of the *Observer*, for whom he had been writing articles. Garvin sent him 'a long and most excited telegram' defending the Allied policies with which the Russian socialists were so dissatisfied. 'This is of course unfortunate for us, but I can't alter it by telling lies about it, and pretending that all is for the best in this best of all possible worlds, so I think it quite possible that I shall have to stop being correspondent for the *Observer*.'

By pleasing contrast, his relations with the *Daily News* were excellent. On 8 May he had been able to send the editor, A. G. Gardiner, a telegram saying that 'The *News* attitude towards the recent troubles has given the greatest satisfaction here, your leader and comments being telegraphed from London and regarded even by the bourgeois press as the fairest estimate of the situation'. In return Gardiner showered him with congratulatory telegrams and letters, crowning all with a cheque for £50, 'I suppose to emphasise that he really means it.' He half-thought of returning the cheque with the comment that he did not take tips, but remembering that he belonged to the 'casual labouring proletariat' he decided to stick to it with appropriate joy. ''Enry Straker would have stuck to it, and grinned. Well, you should just see my grin.'[3]

He did not grin for long. He was too exhausted.

3 Enry Straker is the chauffeur in Shaw's *Man and Superman*.

(*To his mother, 16 June*) I fall asleep at once if I put my elbows on the table, so I work on a chair as far from the table as possible ... A Russian friend who takes the revolution rather more lightly than I am able to, brought along a concertina and left it here. I experimented on the thing. It was very difficult to play, but at last a tune came, and of course the tune was a particularly melancholy version of *Home, Sweet Home*!!!!!

Food was dear, bad and in short supply, so he was always hungry. He felt he had worked himself into 'a state near hysterical delirium'. He held on to his sanity by reading a story by Hans Christian Andersen every day. Mental ills, not to mention physical ones, were occasionally assuaged by fishing expeditions in the suburbs, where he caught roach; enough, on one occasion, to feed a family of eight at lunch.

Politics was the real source of his misery. 'One unfortunate thing happens after another.' The latest was Lloyd George's sabotage of the Stockholm conference: he had forbidden British socialists to visit either Petrograd or Stockholm.

We ought to have sent [Ramsay] MacDonald by express aeroplane the moment the revolution took place ... The coming of M. would let the Russians feel that England was not an actively hostile country ... Now, I think, it is too late. Half the Russian press is howling against England, and the other half calls us 'our splendid allies' which simply infuriates the first half.

So the Russian socialists were being driven into the arms of the Germans. Ransome had seen a car driving through Petrograd, from which were thrown anti-war pamphlets, addressed to the soldiers, in Russian and German.

Yet, 'if there had not been a revolution, things would have been worse.' At times he could still feel with joy that things had improved.

(*To* Daily News, *7 June*) Yesterday I met a big procession of Zionists singing Jewish hymns and bearing a blue-and-white banner with a Hebrew inscription. The Russians looked on with interest but without the slightest suggestion of hostility. Before the Revolution such a phenomenon would have seemed a miracle.

And he was moved by the arrival of deputies for the First All-Russian Congress of Workers' and Soldiers' Soviets.

(*To* Daily News, *14 June*) The Assembly will not meet in the Duma but in the enormous buildings of the Cadet Corps on Vasili Island. In these red-and-white buildings, which are only seven years younger than Petrograd itself, the deputies will not only meet but sleep. Hundreds and hundreds of beds with red blankets are arranged in rows and yesterday when I was there I saw crowds of deputies sitting on their beds talking like boys in a gigantic dormitory. Here and there a deputy, weary from his journey, snored under his red blanket. In one dormitory were the Cossacks, all together. Downstairs is a great refectory in the basement under a low ceiling where group after group of dusty soldiers sat drinking tea and emphasising their political views by thumping the heavy tables.

He found the tone of the Congress, when it opened, so encouraging that he even asserted that one thing was perfectly clear: 'Russia realises that a speedy end to the war can be obtained only by an offensive and ... is united in determination to fight against the forces of Germany both open and secret.' He was not impressed by a speech of Lenin's with a very different message, but his report of it is an unconsciously perceptive account of some of the great revolutionary's salient qualities. It appears to have been the first time that he had heard Lenin speak, apart from the glimpse of him at the Finland Station. The speech expressed the views of the extremists in, he thought, the clearest way:

(*To* Daily News, *19 June*) Thus although they are in a minority, he said 'our party does not refuse authority. It is ready at any minute to take authority in its own hands.' This statement was received with general laughter as also was his naif recipe for dealing with economic problems. 'Arrest a score or two of capitalists, keep them in the same conditions as those in which Nicholas Romanov lives and they will disclose to you all the clues and secrets of their enrichment. Capitalists must be arrested. Without this all your phrases will be empty words.'

He made a bid for the support of the separatists by declaring that Finland and the Ukraine should voluntarily separate from Russia if they liked, and as for the war said 'Advance at the present time means a prolongation of the imperialistic struggle.'

A few days later Lenin spoke again, causing Ransome to wonder at his 'strange tortuous mind': while still opposed to the 'imperialistic struggle', he now advocated war against all capitalists and war for the liberation of Asia.

Ransome approved of the Congress and its pro-Government majority; but he could not long blind himself to the real likelihoods in Russia: 'If starvation should come to Petrograd then no power on earth will prevent the collapse of whatever Government there may be.' And starvation was on the way. Food cost five times what it had before the war, and the distribution system of railways and canals was collapsing. A total stoppage of industry was threatened because of shortages of fuel and raw materials. There was a shortage of wood for winter firing, hence its price had swollen enormously. Many would be cold as well as hungry. Urged on by the Bolsheviks (Ransome reported) the workers were continually demanding enormous wage-increases of 100, 200 or even 300 per cent, which if granted would be wildly inflationary. Everywhere were Bolshevik agitators, acting to make things worse. To Ransome's mind only the moderate majority in the All-Russian Soviet stood between Russia and either reaction, which would certainly cause civil war, or a takeover by the Bolsheviks, 'who seem to regard Russia as a phoenix and the revolution as a fire in which to burn her in order that they may spoon-feed the new Russia from her earliest years' (it is perhaps a mark of his fatigue and ill-health – he was about to suffer his fourth attack of dysentery in six months – that he permitted himself such a spectacularly mixed metaphor). Perhaps worst of all was a sense of personal futility.

(*To his mother, 17 June*) I see the Anglo-Russian friendship, everything I've sweated at all these years, crumbling day by day, while Russia is being turned into a large helpless market ready for German goods and German influence and full of a dull resentment against England ... as far as I can judge from the newspapers that come out here, nobody at home realises at all how very serious the position is.

Despite himself, he filled his letters to his mother with political analysis, because he could think of nothing else ('It's incredible that there was ever a time when I was able to care twopence about writing books') and told her to pass on the information they contained to the Aclands – a desperate shot at influencing official perceptions, and not much good either, as Francis Acland had left the Foreign Office and Arthur's letters were now arriving in England months late. More and more, he felt he should go home to try and spread a little wisdom, or at least to keep the *Daily News* up to the mark – it seemed to have a faint inkling of what was going on, 'partly I suppose because of all that I told them when I came back a year ago'. But so much was happening in Petrograd that he did not dare to leave his post, which he regarded as that of a warder in a lunatic asylum: 'and I feel like a horribly observant warder who cannot help imitating the grimaces of the patients.'

The natural human need to hope, his love of Russia, and the fundamental buoyancy of his character made it hard for him to be consistently gloomy. During July and August he was even occasionally cheerful. A misleading calm settled over Petrograd for a few weeks, as Kerensky toiled to make his offensive a success. An uncomfortable feeling was abroad that there were parties or persons on the Right who would welcome a *coup d'état*, and the Bolsheviks made no secret of their own aspirations – which Ransome no longer treated lightly. He noticed that in their speeches Miliukov, for the Cadets, and Madame Kollontai, for the 'Leninites', both talked of 'our party' all the time rather than of their country. Good news came in of the offensive, which was commanded by General Kornilov, and in the Moscow municipal elections the Mensheviks held their own comfortably against both the Cadets and the Bolsheviks. The food problem in Petrograd grew worse. 'The sugar allowance has been reduced to two pounds per month ... A butcher in whose shop was found meat with maggots was shoved into a barrel and trundled up and down the street till rescued by the military.' Arthur felt free to worry chiefly about Anglo-Russian relations. On 30 June he had a long conversation with some moderate members of the Soviet executive committee, who told him plainly that even if they managed to keep things going until the meeting of the Constituent Assembly (which was supposed to occur in October) a separate peace after that would be inevitable, unless general peace negotiations had

begun: 'No power on earth will keep the Russian army in the
trenches this winter.' Although this accorded perfectly with his
own fears, Arthur did not report the conversation to his paper,
perhaps for fear of compromising his interlocutors. He also kept
to himself, or rather confided only to his mother, the good impression made on him by Arthur Henderson, just then visiting Russia.
(When Henderson got back to England and advocated allowing
British socialists to attend the Stockholm conference he was
promptly sacked from the War Cabinet.) English attitudes still
depressed or infuriated him. Now people were saying 'We must
count Russia out', as if she was a worn-out tool. 'Russia cannot be
counted out, except by people incapable of looking ahead. You
cannot count out the influence of 180 million people.' He was
getting nowhere with his book on the Revolution.

Suddenly the Provisional Government and the Soviet found
themselves under simultaneous attack from Right and Left. On
15 July the Cadet ministers resigned on a trumped-up pretext;
next day the sailors from Kronstadt and many Bolsheviks (acting
without Lenin's authority or even his knowledge: he was re-
cuperating from overstrain in Finland) rushed in a crowd to the
Tauride Palace, where the Soviet met, shouting 'Down with the
Provisional Government!' and 'All Power to the Soviets!' This
unplanned rehearsal of October was suppressed easily enough, but
it caused great alarm on the Nevsky Prospect:

(*To* Daily News, *17 July*) Things dropped by the bolting public
were taken into the Public Library, but not before daring
gleaners had found a harvest. I saw one respectable old lady
with great presence of mind grab up several goloshes which are
now almost unobtainable and make off with them ... the appearance of the town today is very curious. This was to have
been the first of three days of special agitation in favour of the
Liberty Loan, and the whole town is dotted with little orna-
mental platforms for intending orators. Thus at the corner of
the Nevsky Prospect is the model of a prow of a Viking ship.
Further up is a Chinese pagoda. In fact there is a whole series of
little oratories of fantastic design. But not one single speaker
has dared to mount them.

As was becoming habitual with him, Arthur blamed the Cadets
for provoking this crisis, not altogether fairly, although they were

the only ones who gained anything by it. Lenin had to go into
hiding, and Trotsky was briefly arrested, while the Provisional
Government felt it had no choice but to accept the terms laid
down by the Cadets. Of these the two main points were that
nothing must be done to legitimise the seizures of land by the
peasants which were now going on in most of Russia, and a
further postponement of the meeting of the Constituent Assembly.
The Cadets hoped that the delay would enable them to strengthen
their very weak position in the country at large: something might
turn up. Something did: despairing of the Soviets, which were
so easily swayed by the Right, Lenin laid it down that the Bolsheviks must now prepare to seize power by violence, in the name
of the proletariat.

Arthur's reactions to all this were, it seems, largely affected by
the partly-forged documents now published by the Government
which purported to prove that the Bolsheviks were nothing but
German agents. He preserved a certain scepticism about these
papers, but their message fitted in too well with his own apprehensions to be rejected. Then news began to come in of the failure
of the Kerensky offensive and the retreat of Kornilov on a wide
front. Arthur quickly decided that it was no coincidence that the
German counter-attack had come at the time of the riots in Petrograd, and of others in Kiev. A letter from his mother with news
of Tabitha, written on 17 July and arriving in Petrograd much
more promptly than usual, only briefly cheered him up: but he
had enough spirit left to deny that his daughter was growing
up plain. 'No. She's better than that. I'm very glad you liked
her.' But his mother, his daughter and England all seemed in
another, remote world, one with no understanding of Russia
at all.

You do not see the bones sticking through the skin of the horses
in the street. You do not have your porter's wife beg for a share
in your bread allowance because she cannot get enough to feed
her children. You do not go to a tearoom to have tea without
cakes, without bread, without butter, without milk, without
sugar, because there are none of these things. You do not pay
seven shillings and ninepence a pound for very second-rate
meat. You do not pay forty-eight shillings a pound for tobacco.
That is why those English newspapers which rail at the Russians
are criminally wrong.

Among all the other difficulties was the depletion of Arthur's financial resources by the price-rises. On 30 July he had to explain why he had let *The Times* scoop the *News* with reports of the participation of the British armoured-car squadron, under Commander Locker-Lampson, in the Kerensky offensive:

> (*30 July*) I am fully conscious that my recent telegrams are rotten like their author who telegraphed you weeks ago that he was pretty well dead after the continuous rush since the Revolution. Three days later I broke down with dysentery which has lasted till now, intermittently. Therefore I am working under extreme difficulties. I am unable to exist further on my present income in view of the quintuple prices. Unwant increase salary, but I think I should have a living allowance.

The *News*, fortunately, agreed.

He went to headquarters for a couple of days in early August, and was able to restore the credit of the *News* (it is to be hoped) by reporting a 'wonderful little fight' where the Locker-Lampson force carried off the day's honours. It made good, colourful reading. What makes it curious today is the assertion, in the same telegram, that 'the Russian army is coming to itself and is likely in the near future to prove to the enemy that his recent gains have been due not to skill or to strength but merely to the success of the extremist agitation among the ill-educated soldiery.' The fact that anyone so well-informed and realistic as Ransome could be taken in by official optimism in this way, at this stage of the war, shows how much he still wanted victory over Germany, how much the wish can be father to the telegram, and how much of an allowance we ought perhaps to make for all the other people – English, French, Russian; military and civilian – who deluded themselves so persistently about the army's ability and desire to carry on fighting.

He was facing the facts again in his next telegrams, reporting the endless small-minded squabbling of the parties; the renewed advance of the Germans in the south-west, gathering in the Galician harvest and pressing on to the Bessarabian cornfields; the continuing collapse of the Russian economy. He began to suggest that the only hope lay in Kerensky, 'passionate, ill, working on his nerves instead of his physical strength' (*7 August*), desperately trying to recreate national unity in the face of all this overwhelming misfortune. Through his friend Sergei Feodorovich Oldenburg, now a minister, Arthur got an exclusive interview with the great man.

(*14 August*) He was dressed in a khaki uniform without epaulettes and in brown leggings: a very different figure from the thin, anxious-looking young Labour member I used to watch with interest in the Duma before the Revolution. Revolution and responsibility have acted on him like a tonic. His face seems stronger, his hands less delicate. His whole figure as he sat there ... was one of energy and intellectual activity.

The subject of the Stockholm conference came up, and Kerensky denied emphatically that the Government was opposed to it: 'I have insisted again and again that any opposition offered to it by the Allied Governments is simply playing into the Germans' hands.' He gave Ransome permission to quote him, as well he might, seeing that the conference was one of the last cards left in his hand. Indeed the matter was so important to him that we may doubt if his arrival in Oldenburg's office just when the *Daily News* correspondent was visiting was accidental. Arthur put the case for the conference in several later telegrams. The Labour Party's vote in its favour had revived pro-British feelings, he said; to wreck the conference would greatly damage the Kerensky Government, and 'it is not to the interest of England that the coalition should be weakened which sets itself the task of keeping Russia united, of re-establishing the fighting strength of her army and of carrying her through economic difficulties of the most threatening kind.' True but wasted words. Ramsay MacDonald quoted his account of the interview in the House of Commons, but the French, terrified, after their army mutinies, of any contact with peace-seeking Germans, which might destroy what was left of French military morale, put pressure on the Prime Minister. Lloyd George consequently maintained his hostility to the conference; and British seamen had already, on the orders of their union, refused to transport any socialists to Stockholm.

An attack of dysentery meant that Arthur had to miss the first day of another conference, in Moscow, which Kerensky had summoned in the hope of broadening and strengthening support for his Government. Arthur did not think it much to miss. Although the Bolsheviks were excluded from the meeting their influence was rising in the Moscow factories because of a well-justified fear of the 'black ravens' of counter-revolution. Class opposition was the 'essential fact' of the whole struggle. 'That is the only compass which is of real help to anyone trying to find a way about these rocky waters in the fogs which are continually moving over them' (*25 August*). Kerensky gave one of his volcanic speeches, but in the atmosphere of the conference, where, as the Soviet newspaper *Izvestia* commented, 'morning coats, frock coats and starched shirts dominated over blouses', it did not succeed. When Arthur got to Moscow he was, characteristically, impressed by something quite different:

(*28 August*) At seven this morning deputies, who had only got to their beds at two after yesterday's session of the conference, were wakened by the sudden ringing out of the great bells in all Moscow's hundred churches. Then a thousand little bells broke in and the air throbbed with a long battle between the big bells and the little bells. Then at nine there rang out the famous bell-tower of Ivan the Great which solemnised by a peal the coronation of each Tsar. Solemn services in all the churches were followed by the march of the Cross (or church procession). 213 churches took part, each one contributing its gold-embroidered banners, its sacred ikons. In 22 columns of priests and acolytes in gorgeous robes the processions met at the huge white cathedral of the Saviour below the Kremlin close by the river. Then they all marched together to Red Square where they formed in close order an army of the Church in their red colouring and with their massed banners like some army of the distant past. Here, at the place of the skulls, famous for Peter the Great's execution of two thousand rebel guards, was a magnificent chanted service, after which the whole procession returned into the Kremlin through the famous gateway through which, by order of Alexei Mikhailovitch, no man may pass with covered head.

It was Arthur's last glimpse of the picturesque old Russia with which he had fallen in love in 1913.

More than ever he wanted to go home, and it began to look as if he might manage it. The *News* agreed that he was entitled to a holiday, and he badly needed one. He was due for a visit to the dentist, his nose had taken to bleeding whenever he wrote a telegram, and the recurrent dysentery had brought on a return of bleeding at his other end, 'which also is not cheerful, as it means my operation has gone to pot, which indeed was more or less to be expected'. He needed spiritual even more than physical renewal. He yearned to fish the Duddon once more, preferably while his mother and sister Joyce were holidaying there. 'This is the first year since I was nineteen in which I haven't a book coming out. I feel lost and wretched without one. *Aladdin* is all in print, but postponed ... However – ' and he broke into verse:

> Who cares for lack of printed books
> While there are fish in southern brooks?
> And who enforced oblivion recks
> With better fish in northern becks?

... I have any amount of dreams about the north. It's always the north, and I sometimes wake up in a most disgusted state at having to come back to breakfast and Petrograd and telegrams ... I don't think you can have any idea how homesick I actually am. At least, mountain-sick. I would not go so far as to say that I was sick for my own home.

On the contrary, he wanted news of his impending arrival to be kept secret from Ivy.

But I want to see Tabitha. I want to see you. I want to see the Collingwoods. And, inhuman beast that I am, almost more than any of these I´want to see the hills. I think of them all the time.

He was still catching fish – perch – to feed his porter's wife and her vast family; but what he wanted was to catch pike at Newby Bridge.

Eventually he got away, but before then the position of the Provisional Government had become desperate. It had succeeded in nothing, chiefly because this ostensibly democratic body could not bring itself to adopt the policies which the people passionately and overwhelmingly supported. To be sure, it had enormous problems, and none of the main forces in Russian life in 1917 gave it any help. The Bolsheviks valued the Government only because it prevented a right-wing military dictatorship; the Cadets, only because it kept out the Bolsheviks. The Allies had no use for a body which could not restore Russia as an effective belligerent; the Germans wanted to destroy it because it would not surrender. The peasants rejected it because of its shilly-shallying over the land question; the army, because it had insisted on the last, fatal, failed offensive. Above all, the knowledge that winter was approaching, that the economy was in ruins, and that peace was no nearer, exhibited to everyone Kerensky's futility. The Stockholm conference had been aborted by the joint action of the Allies, the Germans and the Bolsheviks. All that was left to Kerensky was his personal authority in the Soviet. Now that too was to be destroyed.

On 9 September Arthur, in common with the rest of Petrograd, learned that General Kornilov, the commander-in-chief, had been dismissed by Kerensky, and ordered to come to the capital; but that, instead of obeying, he had issued a manifesto of revolt, and was now moving on Petrograd with his army. For a moment it seemed that nothing could stop him: all the members of the Government had resigned except Kerensky himself, and there were no troops in Petrograd. But the news revived revolutionary *élan* and unity as nothing else could. Mensheviks, Bolsheviks and Social Revolutionaries came together, however briefly, to defend the Soviet; agitators were hastily dispatched to work on Kornilov's soldiers; railway-lines were torn up to hinder the army's advance; industrial workers were given arms – ominously, by the Bolsheviks' military organisation. The *coup*, although it had been in the making for weeks or months, had been most inefficiently planned; after three days of tension it collapsed. Kornilov was arrested, one of his generals committed suicide, and Kerensky was saved – for a while.

Ransome's comments on the business were shrewdly to the point. On 10 September he observed that the crisis was likely to intensify class feeling and to set the democracy in opposition to the bourgeoisie and the soldiers against their officers, 'which unfortunately I have had many occasions to point out as the inevitable end of agitation either on the extreme Right or on the extreme Left. These two extremes help each other, and their end is civil war.' Three days later he was able to report Kornilov's failure, but it did not cause him much joy. 'Equilibrium cannot be so easily restored, once shaken by an incident of this kind.' The affair had driven the Soviet to the Left. But civil war would inevitably have followed Kornilov's success. 'This should be understood in England.' The army would have been completely disorganised, 'to the advantage of Russia's enemies and ours'. The old warnings; but he was still preaching to deaf ears. Among the groups behind Kornilov, though Ransome did not know it, were the Allied governments. The British ambassador had kept clear of the business (except that he failed to do his duty and warn the head of what was, after all, a friendly government); but Knox, the military attaché, seems to have been one of the leading plotters. Buchanan and Knox covered their traces effectively enough not to be detected; *The Times* was less discreet. When news of the revolt reached London, it boomed forth a welcome: 'there must be an end of committees and debates, of councils of sham workmen and loafing soldiers, of talk about Utopia while the enemy are thundering at the gate.' When this gem reached Petrograd, Ransome cabled that it was having a very bad effect. 'Gorky's paper *New Life* prints the heading, PART OF FRENCH AND ENGLISH BOURGEOIS PRESS EXULTANTLY ACCLAIMS MUTINY OF KORNILOV.'

Still more serious was the news that next began to leak out, concerning Kerensky's own ambiguous relations with Kornilov. This has been, and still is, a matter of the sharpest historical controversy. But there can be no denying that the Bolsheviks, already restored to all the prestige and popularity they had enjoyed before the July days, thanks to their part in the resistance to Kornilov, made the most of the rumours and allegations. It all helped them to capture a majority on the Petrograd Soviet, and to increase their strength dramatically in the local elections at Moscow and elsewhere, and in the army. Another of the futile assemblies which characterised this stage of the Revolution, the so-called Democratic Conference, opened in Petrograd on 27 September. Arthur was there to watch Kerensky stand at bay:

(*To* Daily News, *27 September*) I was within a yard of Kerensky as he spoke, I watched the sweat come out on his forehead, I watched his mouth change as he faced now one, now another group of his opponents, and am still under the powerful impression of Kerensky's tremendous effort.

But he was not so spellbound as to miss the constant interruption from the Left; and although he thought that the weight of feeling within the assembly was favourable to Kerensky, 'this was not so

among the excited groups of disputants outside the theatre.' The
next day Kamenev spoke for the Bolsheviks, and was followed by
orators of the other parties. Once more Arthur's telegram showed
that he did not allow his feelings to mar his judgment:

(*28 September*) The Bolshevik[4] attitude was more clearly illustrated by the insults they threw at Kerensky, by the jeers or
applause with which they received statements of Russia's difficulties, than by the words of their official spokesmen. I watched
some of the interrupters closely. It was evident that they had
come prepared to interrupt. They alone at a moment of terrible
difficulty brought to the assembly the irresponsible nonchalance
of a debating society, sitting there smiling, indifferent to words
that to their speakers represented blood and tears. They sat
smiling, watching their opportunities and making use of them
with a unanimity that could only be the result of a concerted
plan. It is evident, however, that although the majority dis-
approve of the Bolsheviks, the moderate parties during the last
month have moved distinctly nearer to the Bolsheviks' political
position.

The agenda for debate suddenly seemed to be set by the Bolsheviks. Should all power be given to the soviets? Should all
bourgeois parties be excluded from the Government? Two days
later he cabled that 'The very air seems heavy with knowledge of
approaching danger', and, two days afterwards, that the Left was
preparing the ground for what amounted to a Bolshevik dictatorship.

Arthur did not stay to see the *dénouement* which his telegrams so
accurately foreshadowed. For one thing he did not think that it
would come before the meeting of the Constituent Assembly in
January. So on 9 October he left for Britain. He arrived in
Aberdeen on the 17th, and then went down to London, where he
'talked till I could talk no more'.

We know two of the people he talked to: Francis Hirst and his
associate Mary Agnes ('Molly') Hamilton. Hirst had been jockeyed
out of the editorship of *The Economist* the year before because of
his loathing of the war and, specifically, his opposition to conscription; since then he had started a new paper, *Common Sense*, a

4 This is the first telegram in which AR uses this word.

neo-Gladstonian rival to his old paper. His deliberations with Arthur were interrupted by the news of the Bolshevik seizure of power. Naturally, the *Daily News* employed Ransome to comment on the event, and he did so at sufficient length to show posterity the strengths and weaknesses of his understanding of Russian affairs at this point. He could not resist saying 'I told you so', however discreetly: 'The present situation has long been foreseen, and we are bound to say that the Allies are not blameless.' Western reactionaries had done all they could, most effectively, to undermine Kerensky: they 'may for the moment claim that they have been as successful in helping to make the Leninites triumphant in Russia as they have been in converting Ireland to the cause of Sinn Fein.'

> As to the attitude of the Bolsheviks towards the war and towards the Allies, it may be expressed in the formula (their own): 'We are opposed to separate peace with Imperialists of any nationality.' They do not want any peace which would leave Russia in the position of a sleeping partner of Germany. On the other hand, they are opposed to assisting what they regard as Imperialist war-aims on the part of ourselves. They will probably use their new position to press more insistently than their precursors for definition of Allied war-aims. If, however, we wish to force them into a more hostile attitude, and perhaps into a separate peace, we cannot do better than to follow the example of some of this morning's newspapers in loudly condemning what we do not understand.

(This last remark was probably a dig at *The Times*, which was sounding forth in its usual fashion.) For the rest, Arthur believed that the survival of the Bolshevik order would depend on the army, the hungry townsfolk, and the peasants; and that Poland, the Baltic states, Finland; and possibly the Ukraine, would break away. This was also the view expressed in a leading article in *Common Sense*, which stated his opinions precisely, and which he may even have written.

His further movements during this longed-for holiday are hard to trace. He saw his mother, and the Collingwoods, and, presumably, his longed-for north country; also, it seems likely, his brother and sisters. His diary, and the *Autobiography*, record that he went fishing at Fonthill and caught a perch weighing 3 lb. 2 oz.

This small if impressive item conceals the strangest episode of his idyllic break from the revolutionary storm. He went down to Hatch, no doubt because he wanted to see Tabitha, and perhaps because of his residual concern for Ivy; and to his surprise was happy. Some of his daughter's memories of him probably date from this visit, as does the charming photograph of the pair of them dancing in the lane outside Manor Farm. But he did not stay long (which was perhaps just as well) and Tabitha next saw him at King's Cross Station on the day he again left for Russia. She and her mother were given very little notice, and had a 'mad hectic rush' to get to London in time to see him off. 'Dor-Dor was in a long black full-skirted coat, belted, and a tall Cossack Astrakhan hat, and seemed put out that my mother had made such an effort.' Children can be acute: they can also be mistaken. Next day, as his wife and daughter went back to Wiltshire, Arthur was writing to his mother from the train:

> Got off all right. Tabitha was most extremely sweet, and Ivy was really very good indeed. I am not at all keen on this trip this time, and if I had been offered a job would have been very glad to stay in England for a time ... It was very melancholy last night, saying good-bye to Tabitha, who was a perfect darling, and nearly made me weep.

Had he stayed, it is unlikely that the good feeling between him and Ivy would have lasted. As it was, he had enjoyed for a few days being a family man again. The superstitious would suggest that all concerned had behaved so well because they had a premonition that it was for the last time.

Russia was his fate. Before leaving he had an interview with Lord Robert Cecil, a strongly right-wing Conservative, who had succeeded Francis Acland at the Foreign Office. Cecil must have had much on his mind that day (1 December) for it was that on which Lord Lansdowne published his famous Letter, recommending a negotiated peace much on the lines favoured by Hirst, who warmly welcomed the Letter in his paper. Nevertheless Cecil found what Ransome had to say 'very interesting', though it was no more than what he had told the *Daily News* and *Common Sense*. Cecil minuted the meeting: 'The only chance he could see of a lasting Government was in the formation of a Socialist Block, excluding the Bolsheviks, though he evidently did not think the

chance much worth having.' Cecil told him that he was unlikely
to be able to get back into Russia, and would probably find complete chaos if he did: and then what did he propose to do? (Just
like Grandfather in *Peter and the Wolf.*) But to help him on his
way he was given a diplomatic bag for delivery in Stockholm.
A few days later F. Rothstein, a Russian revolutionary working as
a translator in the War Office, gave him a letter of introduction
to his comrades, recommending Ransome as 'the only correspondent who informed the English public of events in Russia *honestly*'.
Thus doubly armed, Arthur set off on 5 December.

VI

Bolsheviks

Shouting in daily telegrams across the wires from Russia I feel I am shouting at a drunken man asleep in the road in front of a steam roller.

ARTHUR RANSOME, *The Truth About Russia*, 14 May 1918

The children of the British Minister to Sweden, Sir Esmé Howard, loved *Old Peter's Russian Tales*, and on this account, rather than because of Lord Robert Cecil's bag (which was delivered on 11 December), Arthur was lunched and dined most hospitably at the legation. He sang for his supper by telling Anansi stories. He enjoyed forgetting politics in this way, but his real business was to get into Russia if he could, and with this in view he set about pestering the Soviet emissary in Stockholm, V. V. Vorovsky.

Vorovsky was the first Bolshevik whom Arthur got to know informally. He made an excellent impression, as he was to do a month or so later on Lockhart. He was eventually to receive one of the two warmest tributes paid to individuals in the *Autobiography* (the other went to Harold Williams) as 'a much valued friend. I do not think that Vorovsky can ever have had a personal enemy.' However it was at present Arthur's duty to make Vorovsky's life a misery until he issued a visa for crossing the Russian frontier. Ransome had a revolution to report for his paper, and, as he explains in the *Autobiography*, was convinced not only that the place to watch such events was at their centre, but that it would take more than a few improvised armies to over-throw the Soviets, whose strength he had seen steadily growing since March. At length Vorovsky gave in. On 21 December

Arthur left Stockholm, and arrived in Petrograd after an unmemorable journey on Christmas Day.

He found a new city, 'grim, hungry, threatened by the hostility of the Germans without and the Allies within, the whole of the Civil Service on strike, armed patrols by little watchfires in the streets at night, occasional pitched battles to prevent the looting of wine stores by the soldiery, and almost daily touches of comic opera, inevitable with a Government of enthusiastic amateurs and Ministries staffed for the most part by young people who had never been inside a Government office before.' He noticed at once that the municipal services must have collapsed, for the city was nearly buried under snow. 'Sledging was like mountaineering. I remember being overturned, sledge and all, when my driver, greatly daring, tried to cross the valleys and mountain ranges from one side of the road to the other.' The city seemed to be quiet on the whole, and more orderly than it had been for months before the Bolshevik takeover. Arthur's first telegram to London would make much of this reassuring impression. It was not shared by Lockhart, who paints a different picture of Petrograd in his *Memoirs*. He described a city where the rich made merry by day while armed robbers ruled the streets after dark: 'desultory firing went on all through the night.'[1] Some things seemed unchanged. When Ransome arrived in Glinka Street the old porter asked his usual question: did Arthur think that peace was any nearer? In reality everything had changed, and it was Arthur's business to discover how by continuing the process, begun in his meetings with Vorovsky, of getting to know the Bolshevik leadership. He still hoped, besides, that he might do something for England in her continuing, desperate struggle. On 30 December he wrote to his mother:

Things here are such as to keep me frantically busy. I wish to goodness I had been able to get back before. It's too late to do very much good now; but there is a lot that must be done unless we are to throw up our hands and leave Russia to the Germans.

I am so busy seeing people that I am afraid my telegraphing is likely to suffer. Yesterday for example I saw in the course of the day something like eighteen or nineteen various folk, ranging from the present dictator of Russia to our ambassador

1 R. H. Bruce Lockhart, *Memoirs of a British Agent*, p. 225.

through pretty well every shade of contradictory Russian opinion.

The interview with the dictator took place in the Smolny Institute, the huge building, a former girls' school, from which the Bolsheviks had mounted their assault on power. At the end of a long corridor Arthur found a door, with a piece of paper fastened to it inscribed: 'People's Commissary for Foreign Affairs'.[2]

> Beside it stood a sentinel, who was a workman from the Red Guard in ordinary clothes, with a rifle and bandolier over his overcoat. In the anteroom one of Trotsky's secretaries, a young officer, told me that Trotsky was expecting me. On going into an inner room, unfurnished except for a writing-table, two chairs and a telephone, I found the man who in the name of the proletariat is practically the dictator of northern Russia. He has a striking head: a very broad forehead above lively eyes, fine-cut nose and mouth, and a small cavalier beard. Though I had heard him speak before, this was the first time I had seen him face to face. I got an impression of extreme efficiency and definite purpose. In spite of all that is said against him by his enemies I do not think he is the man to do anything except from the conviction that it is the best thing to be done for the revolutionary cause which he has at heart.

This careful portrait is a reminder of how little was then known of the Bolshevik leaders in the West. At the time of the November Revolution Ransome did not even know Lenin's real name, and neither Lenin nor Trotsky, nor any of the others, had known faces.

For the rest, Arthur pressed Trotsky to explain Bolshevik confidence that they could get decent peace-terms out of Germany. Trotsky replied, in effect, that the German proletariat would coerce the German ruling class. 'Every Government in Europe is feeling the pressure of democracy from below. The German attitude merely means that the German Government is wiser than most and more realistic.'

Events would soon show this blithe assertion to be entirely fallacious, but in the mean time it was splendid copy for the *Daily*

---

2 AR's translation of the Russian. The word 'Commissar' had not yet found its way into English.

News, and Arthur hurried off with it; but as he went in or out he found time to notice a 'tall jolly girl' among the crowd in Trotsky's anteroom. He did not have leisure to eat (as well as all the people he saw that day he had to read through the fourteen daily newspapers to which he now subscribed) and was very late in getting his telegrams written. As he had been back in Petrograd for four days, and had not yet sent off any messages, he was anxious to lose no more time; so he went in search of a censor to pass his dispatch. He hoped to find one in the official Commissariat for Foreign Affairs – not Trotsky's modest quarters, but one of the vast buildings which faced the Winter Palace. He was able to get inside without difficulty, and wandered the corridors unchallenged. At last he heard voices and entered a room where a few people were chatting. Among them was the tall girl from Smolny.

Ransome's *Autobiography* is a beautifully exact book. It is nowhere more true to life than in the account of this seemingly inconsequential meeting:

> She recognised me and when I explained that I wanted to find a censor to stamp my despatch, instead of remarking that it was long after office hours, she said she thought he was in the building ...
>
> 'Come along,' she said, 'perhaps he has some potatoes. Potatoes are the only thing we want. Come along.'
>
> We set off through the deserted Foreign Office. After long wanderings we were pulled up by a smell of cooking, or rather the smell of food burning.
>
> 'Quick, quick,' she said and knocked on a door, but without waiting for an answer we burst into a room where a little old man sat reading, while on a small table in the corner a primus roared under a coffee-pot; the room was full of a horrid smell. She seized the coffee-pot and tipped three potatoes out of it on to a sheet of official Foreign Office paper.
>
> 'Thank goodness! They've only just begun to brown. They're still edible,' said she. 'You must try not to let the water boil right out or there will soon be a hole burned through the bottom of your pot.'
>
> She introduced me to the old man and explained what I needed. He went off rather uncertainly to look for a rubber stamp with which to mark his willingness not to prevent the

sending of my telegram, and we went back to wait for him. Her sister was there. The old man came in and stamped my telegram. The two girls asked me to stay and drink a glass of tea. I said that now my telegram had been seen by the censor I had to go to the General Post Office to send it on its way. They told me to hurry up and come back. I did so.

Since Arthur's path had led him to so long a residence in Russia, it was probably inevitable that he would eventually fall in love with a Russian woman, after the deep bruises of his marriage to Ivy had faded. Perhaps his latest visit to England had restored Arthur's sexual self-confidence. He and Ivy had lived contentedly together, however briefly, and forgiven each other, however temporarily, and the sense of emotional bewilderment had burned off. It is even more likely that a couple of months of decent food and quiet sleep had restored his physical vigour, and his charm, and his propensity to fall in love. At any rate, he was immediately, helplessly bowled over by the first girl who took an interest in him; and she was equally attracted.

Her name was Evgenia Petrovna Shelepina. She was twenty-three years old. Little is known about her family and childhood: she was not one to live in the past, and in later years her English friends found it extremely difficult to get her to talk about her youth. At least it seems clear that her father was 'a very superior gardener for the Tsar'. According to her marriage certificate he was a Russian civil servant, a not contradictory piece of information. Perhaps she derived her well-attested passion for gardening from her father. On the evening when Arthur met her she was probably paying a call on the sister who was a typist in the Commissariat for Foreign Affairs. She herself had gone to work there as a typist before the November Revolution, and was one of the few who stayed at their posts after the Bolsheviks seized power. She thus publicly showed which side she was on. This commitment, and her natural ability, no doubt explain how she came to be Trotsky's personal secretary.

It could only have happened in a revolution, and perhaps not then if Trotsky had not been willing (in spite of his suspicious nature) to make use of non-Bolsheviks, as he would, for instance, in a few months' time, when he enlisted Tsarist officers to run the Red Army. Still, Evgenia would hardly have been able to keep her post (Trotsky took her with him when he left the Foreign

Office to become War Commissar) if she had not been, in Lock-hart's words, 'extremely able and tactful'. Nor, perhaps, if she had not been for a time more thoroughly committed to the Bolshevik cause than she would later admit.

Her vagueness about her past may eventually have become habitual. Originally it was deliberate. Between Trotsky's exile in 1927 and Stalin's death in 1953 there was everything to be said for obscuring her association with the great unperson. Her family still lived in Russia, and many people died in the Terror for lesser crimes than being related to someone who had once worked for Stalin's chief enemy. Even after 1953 it would have been prudent not to make oneself conspicuous unnecessarily.

In her later life she never displayed the slightest interest in politics. There is no reason to think she ever wanted to be involved in them. When she and Rupert Hart-Davis were preparing Arthur's *Autobiography* for publication she wrote him a series of letters in which she made a good many detailed comments on her life with Arthur. Her account of her political background is especially valuable:

> [Arthur] did not care in normal times one hoot for politics any more than I did, and it was only upheavals like the Revolution that stirred us up to taking sides. I have never been a communist or even a mild socialist but merely through starting reading the newspapers at the beginning of the war I gradually acquired a respect for the socialists and when for a short period between the first or Duma Revolution in March 1917 and the Bolshe-viks' takeover in October Russia enjoyed the real freedom of the press I was convinced that the Bolsheviks were the only party which had a chance to extricate Russia from the chaos into which the war, entered so irresponsibly into by the Tsarist Government, plunged the country.

But in revolutionary Russia events rather than individual choice determined the degree of one's commitment. Evgenia's place beside the Bolshevik leaders meant that, willy-nilly, she became a revolutionary and an embattled partisan in a savage civil war.

It took Arthur and her some time to come to terms. His work carried him repeatedly to the Smolny Institute; sometimes, after Evgenia, if she saw fit, had given out a bulletin on the day's news from Brest-Litovsk, where the Russo-German peace negotiations were proceeding, he would walk her home, or at least as far as the trams.

> Once, I remember, still after all these forty years, with a shiver of horror, the tramcar started before she had her foot on the step, and she was dragged, hanging on, along the track, lying on one of the lines so that if her grip had failed she would inevitably have been cut to pieces by the wheels [presumably somebody made the tram stop]. Those few horrible seconds during which she lay almost under an advancing wheel possibly determined both our lives. But it was not until long afterwards that we admitted anything of the kind to each other.

According to Evgenia, it was not until the summer. In the mean time they went on meeting.

We get glimpses of Evgenia, and of Arthur's courtship, in the memoirs of Edgar Sisson, who was officially the head of the American propaganda unit in Russia, but was busier as one of the numerous special agents whose activities made it impossible for anyone, German, Allied or Russian, socialist or capitalist, or Woodrow Wilson himself, to say with confidence what American policy was towards the Revolution, either generally, or at any particular juncture. (British policy was equally baffling, for the same reason.) Sisson was a professional journalist, and his writing is both vivid and detailed; but he had been trained in a bad school, and, though not a deliberate liar, except on really important matters, does not seem to have known at what point it became impermissible to touch up his stories. But he is often the only authority for what he describes, and his observations are too interesting, and in many cases too plausible, to be discounted entirely.

Sisson had arrived in Petrograd a month to the day before Arthur's return, and seems to have got to know Evgenia on his own account. He says the Americans called her 'the Big Girl' 'because she was a big girl'. On 30 December, the day after her first meeting with Arthur, there was to be a grand parade and demonstration in Petrograd. It had originally been planned in celebration of the Russo-German armistice, which had been signed on 15 December, and of the moderate peace-terms proposed by the Germans: Bolshevik diplomacy had seemed triumphant. Unhappily, in the last few days word had reached

Petrograd that the German High Command had interpreted the Bolshevik principle of 'no annexations' to mean that Poland, Lithuania and Courland (nowadays part of Latvia) could and would be stripped from Russia and added to the German Empire as satellite states. The Bolsheviks had not yet dared to release this news, and no doubt hoped that a cheerful parade on the workers' day off (30 December was a Sunday) would strengthen morale in advance of this bitter blow. Sisson wanted to see the parade and sent to Trotsky's office for a pass. He got one, and also the answer that Evgenia Petrovna Shelepina wanted to see the show without getting her feet wet.

> Anyone knowing her was bound to sympathise with her, for her tiny feet were the big girl's pride. She encased them in high-heeled and expensive shoes and refused to conceal them under the usual slip-on galoshes. Others might walk the ice but where Evgenia Petrovna went, she rode. An invitation went to her to do her riding this day under an American flag, and she accepted, sending back word that she would be an interpreter. This was humor, for she spoke only a few words of English. Her presence in the car, however, insured us of favors an interpreter could not have won with words. Alexis, the chauffeur, when he saw her enter the motor, straightened up with an air which said that with her in the car, he would drive through Red Guards as if he had Trotsky and Lenin behind him. And he did.

Perhaps those little feet and high-heeled shoes were to blame for the tram accident.

There is nothing to show that Arthur involved himself with the parade, Sisson, or Evgenia Petrovna on 30 December. He was writing to his mother, and seeing Trotsky again, which was to give him one of the biggest scoops of his journalistic career.

The Foreign Commissar had not been altogether frank on 29 December. His line then had been the one pursued by the Bolsheviks ever since they seized power and opened negotiations for peace: the news of successful socialist revolution in Russia would quickly touch off revolutions elsewhere, and the belligerent governments would be forced by popular pressure to come to the peace table. His chief hope lay in Germany. In all this he was not very wide of the mark. The Government of Austria-Hungary was indeed desperate for peace, seeing it as the only hope of preserving the Dual Monarchy; in Germany herself everyone was aware that the country was nearing the end of her strength. There was indeed pressure from below, and it would erupt in the autumn of 1918. But what the Bolsheviks needed was peace at once, if they were to satisfy the Russians and consolidate their own revolution. In the last week of December they reluctantly absorbed two bitter truths: that there was no immediate prospect of a German revolution to take the pressure off them, and that the German negotiators at Brest-Litovsk, well aware of the Bolshevik predicament, were prepared to take full advantage of it by imposing a victor's peace. To accept the German terms, after the proud boasts of October, would be contemptible and dangerous, for it might provoke an effective *coup* against the Bolsheviks, or even break their control of the soviets. To reject the terms would be to disappoint the Russian people, more insistent on immediate peace than ever, and to invite a German advance on Petrograd and Moscow that could not be effectively resisted. The Bolsheviks might fall, either way. The only thing to do was to play for time, and cast about for any other expedient. That meant the West. Accordingly, Trotsky on the 29th (presumably after he had seen Arthur) sent out a diplomatic Note begging the Entente Powers to agree to a general peace and, in case they did not, threatening them with a separate peace between Russia and Germany, and with revolution at home. But the Allies had never yet condescended to notice any of Trotsky's circulars. He could not depend on them to do so now, or to give any publicity to his views. Their official envoys were not allowed any direct dealings with him. Besides, like all the Bolshevik leaders, Trotsky was more at home dealing with journalists than diplomats. So New Year's Eve and New Year's Day found Arthur at Smolny again.

There he was given a carefully edited version of recent events. His briefing was equally carefully stage-managed. The news that the Russo-German negotiations, which had seemed so near success, had been suspended on 28 December was carefully withheld until certain other points had been made and transmitted to London (the Bolsheviks could, and I assume did, read all telegraphic traffic in and out of Petrograd). There was a real danger of a separate peace, he was told (it was perfectly true). Trotsky was doing his utmost to forestall this by stirring up revolution in Germany, through fraternisation at the front and the distribution of enormous quantities of incendiary newspapers in the German language (this was also true). But these devices might not work. If they did not, and presuming that the Allies did not want Russia to make a separate peace, the only way to avoid that dread eventuality was to turn the negotiations into a general peace conference. In other words, the Allies ought to go to Brest-Litovsk, as Trotsky had suggested in the interview on 29 December. Once Ransome had absorbed all this, he was told the startling news: the negotiations had been suspended on the question of Poland. They might not be resumed, because the Bolsheviks were taking a stern line with the Prussian militarists. The news would be announced in a couple of days' time. Now what (came the unspoken inquiry) would the Allied governments make of that?

Arthur accepted all this unquestioningly; and indeed the only major distortion was the concealment of the fact that the talks had been suspended only because the Bolshevik delegates, on discovering the full extent of German intransigence, had been utterly dumbfounded, and had fled back to Petrograd for instructions. The men at Smolny were tougher than their envoys. By 31 December Trotsky was already preparing to go to Brest-Litovsk himself (at Lenin's suggestion) to play out the game. In the mean time there was no harm in bluffing the West a little, through the medium of a friendly journalist. (Smolny played the same hand, at the same time, with the American, Raymond Robins.)

The result was two articles which made a profound impression in London when the *Daily News* published them on 1 and 2 January 1918. That of 1 January (written on 31 December) hammered home the point that a separate peace was the policy not of the Bolsheviks but of the German High Command, which wanted quiet in the East and access to Russian raw materials so that it could finally overcome the West:

> I am convinced that our only chance of defeating the German designs is to publish terms as near the Russian terms as possible, and by taking a peaceful hand in the proposed Conference to help at the same time the democratic movement in Germany and the Russians in forcing the German Government in the direction which it, partly under pressure from below and partly with a cunning view to the future, has had to take.

So Arthur added his voice to the chorus which at this moment was demanding a statement of war-aims from the Allied leaders: a chorus which would be answered when Lloyd George gave a speech on the subject on 5 January, and when Woodrow Wilson issued his famous Fourteen Points on the 8th. Like everyone in Russia Ransome had hoped for such a response ever since the March Revolution – and now it was coming, six months too late.

He also gave a warning against counting on an early Bolshevik collapse:

> Whatever party should be in power it would have to conclude peace, and M. Trotsky's manner of doing so is likely to do more damage to Germany than would be done by any more respectful and polite person in his place.

The article of 2 January used the announcement of the suspension of the negotiations to put in another good word for the Bolsheviks:

> I have private and reliable information [from Trotsky, of course] in regard to the breaking of peace negotiations which establishes beyond doubt the honesty of purpose of the Bolsheviks ... The Russian delegation, acting on the most unequivocal instructions from the Smolny Institute, took up an uncompromising attitude. They said self-determination was impossible until the last German soldier had left the country. Further, they jeered at the Germans, asking what they proposed to do. They asked whether they proposed to take Petrograd, feed three million starving folk, and disarm a revolutionary country where every worker had a rifle. They also asked what the Germans proposed to say to their own democracy, which protested a couple of months ago against the proposed annexation of Poland and Lithuania. They remarked that they were surprised that 'even Prussian Junkers had such audacity'.

A. G. Gardiner was greatly pleased by this performance of his Special Correspondent. He gave the story as dramatic a presentation on the front page as a sober Liberal paper could contrive:

PEACE NEGOTIATIONS BROKEN OFF
WHY THE RUSSIANS LEFT
German Attitude On Lithuania & Poland Leads To Break
BOLSHEVIKS' FIRM STAND ...

It was a great thing to have beaten Reuters and the other papers by forty-eight hours with such dramatic news. It was a great thing even to have got worthwhile news out of Petrograd: since the Bolshevik Revolution reliable information had been sparse, and convincing interpretation of events even sparser. Gardiner was not alone in feeling this. The War Cabinet read Ransome's dispatches eagerly. Since Sir George Buchanan had not been allowed to establish any serious contact with the Bolsheviks, British leaders were dependent on such stray crumbs of information as came their way. As it happened, the War Cabinet met on 2 January; the minutes show that they discussed the article of that day; but it is plain from the account of what was said that the article of the day before, devoted to Trotsky's intentions and desires, was even more on ministers' minds. In the light of the reports of Arthur Ransome, 'who is himself in full sympathy with the Bolshevik movement' (an inaccurate, and, in the light of later events, rather sinister remark),

> it was suggested that M. Trotsky was, perhaps, finding himself faced with an impossible situation involving a general peace at the expense of Russia, and that possibly Mr. Arthur Ransome's despatch was a signal that M. Trotsky would like to get into touch with the Allies with a view to extricating himself from his difficulties.[3]

Trotsky had achieved his wish to attract the attention of the West, but the almost wilful inversion of his message (which had stated plainly that the Bolsheviks were threatened with the consequences not of a general but a separate peace) in the minds of solemn English statesmen would have provoked him to rage, astonishment and scornful laughter. Another comment was that perhaps the Bolsheviks were looking for a way of extending their war on civilisation. The War Cabinet fluctuated between two ideas, both erroneous: either that the Bolsheviks were merely German agents, or that they were incompetent fanatics who could not last for more than a few weeks. Ministers were right, of course, to suspect that the picture Ransome painted was a little too good to be true; but their failure even to entertain the possibility that Trotsky

3 Cabinet minutes for 2 January 1918, from Michael Kettle, *The Allies and the Russian Collapse*, p. 178.

meant what he said illustrates their incompetence at forming a Russian policy. They could at least see the advantage in getting more information; so the Foreign Office was told to order Buchanan 'to get in touch with Arthur Ransome' (it would not occur to the Cabinet that such a pro-Bolshevik called at the Embassy almost every day) 'in order, if possible, to discover the precise meaning of his *Daily News* article, "and what M. Trotsky was aiming at".' Fortunately the Foreign Office knew its business, and had indeed already been considering the possibility of using Arthur as an intermediary. The telegram to Buchanan asked him to find out from Ransome whether Trotsky was really disillusioned about German desires for an acceptable peace. 'In any case it might be worth while to ask Trotsky what his definite peace proposals really are. We have always been ready for a very wide application of the principle of self-determination.'

Gardiner would not have been pleased had he known that there was already a tendency in high quarters to label his correspondent a Bolshevik. The articles in question give no warrant even for calling Arthur a fellow-traveller (had the phrase yet been current). But it must be remembered that he had gone the rounds during his autumn visit to London, talking at length. To men ignorant of the realities of Russia his willingness to make a case for the Bolsheviks might well seem like full sympathy with them, if not complete commitment. Furthermore, General Knox, the military attaché at Petrograd, was still reporting, and he had formed a decidedly hostile view of Arthur and his activities. A few months, or even weeks, later, and this misunderstanding would have led to complete rejection of anything which Ransome had to say, but for a moment in January events secured him a hearing. Trotsky's sudden interest in the West could not be overlooked even if it could not be understood; and British policy itself was still all too fluid. The forces working to drive the Entente and the Bolsheviks apart had not yet prevailed, though they were already doing much damage. Balfour, the Foreign Secretary, had announced himself, where Russia was concerned, 'a drifter by deliberate policy'. He did not contemplate extending diplomatic recognition to 'this crazy system', but he saw the sense of maintaining contact with it. Lloyd George went even further. Impressed by the virtual unanimity of the reports received from Petrograd before, during and after the Bolshevik Revolution, to the effect that Russia could and would fight no more, and that the only question before

Britain was how to minimise the ill-effects of this catastrophe, he seriously considered adopting the suggestion, made by both Buchanan and Knox, that Russia be released from her 1914 pledge not to make a separate peace. Unfortunately neither the French nor the Italian Governments would hear of such a concession (and in view of the impact it might have had on their own peoples, perhaps they were right). At least Lloyd George was sure that he was sensible in sending a special mission to Russia, headed by Robert Bruce Lockhart, to see what could be done.

Gardiner found out enough about these high deliberations to proclaim exultantly in his leading article on 3 January that 'the remarkable message from Mr. Arthur Ransome, the Petrograd correspondent of this paper, which appeared in our issue of yesterday, has been the all-absorbing theme of discussion in political circles.' Arthur himself soon got more direct evidence of the impact of his work. Obedient to instructions, Buchanan sent for him to ask him to sound Trotsky further. 'Col. Knox, our military attaché and a rabid interventionist, came into the room and broke into the conversation, addressing me, and saying "You ought to be shot!" The Ambassador quietly waved him away, and went on with what he was saying.'

Arthur did his duty, sought out Trotsky, and reported back to Buchanan. He also reported to the *Daily News* (without mentioning that his questions had been prompted by the Foreign Office) so that Balfour had his choice, on 7 January, of reading what Ransome had to say either in the morning, in the newspaper, in his own words, or in Sir George's telegraphed summary that afternoon:

(*6 January*) I had a hurried talk with M. Trotsky at the Smolny Institute just as, after a final consultation with the Russian members of the Peace Delegation, he was starting for Brest-Litovsk. He was leaving with the mistaken conviction that the Entente Governments wanted Germany to succeed in making an advantageous separate peace with Russia, so that, in guarding herself in the East, she might agree more willingly to surrender what the Allies want in the West ... He was under the impression that Mr. Lloyd George had made a statement that allowed such an interpretation. I assured him that he was mistaken, but he was difficult to convince. He said, 'That is the Allied policy.'

The same article conveys a sense of just how well Arthur was getting on with Trotsky at this period:

> I asked M. Trotsky what terms he actually hoped to get. He refused to be drawn, and said, laughing, 'If we were really logical we would declare war on England now for the sake of India, Egypt, and Ireland. You have read our peace declaration.' I protested that we made nothing out of India. He replied, 'Then give up being so altruistic. You English are the most Chauvinistic nation on earth without knowing it.' He laughed again, shook hands, and was off.

This incident was also the high point of Arthur's influence with his own Government. It led to nothing. Buchanan, whose health was breaking down, left Petrograd on 7 January, taking most of the Embassy staff with him; on his way home, in Norway, he encountered Lockhart, journeying to Russia. Lockhart's presence would make Arthur unnecessary as a go-between.

There was more to it than that. The little group in Petrograd, of which Buchanan had been the effective centre, was breaking up. Pares and Will Peters had left just before the November Revolution, Hugh Walpole just afterwards. Harold Williams remained, but in 1918 his relations with Arthur deteriorated sharply. Arthur could never bear to put the details down on paper, but it is clear enough what happened. As journalists, the two men had got hold of opposite ends of the truth. Ransome's attitude to the Bolsheviks in 1918 was certainly not unfriendly. He saw both the Bolsheviks and the soviets as the authentic expression of the deep longing for peace, bread and land of the Russian people, whose sufferings he felt deeply. Williams could not go so far. His knowledge of Russia and her people told him that she would have to leave the war; he and Arthur were also at one in urging that the Allies accept this and do their best to make things easy for the Russians. He telegraphed to his paper:

> We cannot contemptuously abandon a whole great people because of a temporary fit of madness ... Perhaps we shall have to part with Russia as a fighting Ally, but if we can show the Russian people that for the sake of the great battles we have fought together, for the great sacrifices we have all made to the common cause, we are prepared to continue our moral support,

then this greatest trial of the war will not be an unmitigated loss.

But after the arrest of some of the Cadet party leaders, and after the party itself was outlawed on 24 December (an incident never referred to by Ransome), Williams began to fear for his wife, Ariadna Vladimirovna. He was much depressed by the dreadful chaos into which the Revolution had plunged Russia. He came deeply to distrust the Bolsheviks, chiefly because they were strangling parliamentarianism in Russia and because they were opening the country's gates, as he thought, to the Germans. His temperament was, compared with Arthur's manic bounce, depressive, which made it easy for him to see the dark side of events. He did not lose his judgment; although he soon began to support Allied intervention he was utterly opposed to intervention by Japan (which the British Government was to spend much of 1918 trying to bring about) because he knew the antipathy of ordinary Russians to the Japanese. Rather, his negative view enabled him to make certain points which Ransome would not accept.

> The only Government in Russia is a peculiar tyranny whose hold is precarious, which has displayed no constructive ability whatever, which has only succeeded in throwing into the melting-pot all the political achievements of the civilization of the Russian Empire. This Government promises new and higher forms of civilization. So far we see no signs of them, we see only the wreckage of the old.

Arthur might have an answer to that. But no real answer could be made, then, or at any time before 1941, to Williams's sombre prophecy to Lockhart: 'Nothing will come of your mission. I've been to see Trotsky. He is one of the most evil men I have ever met. They want external peace for internal war. Remember my words, the Bolsheviks will fight no one except the Russians.' Holding such views, he was bound to break with Arthur politically; but it is hard to believe that the two men would have ceased to be friends, if it had not been for Ariadna Vladimirovna. In the eyes of this high-tempered patriot and politician Arthur was a traitor and an enemy. Arthur was equally shocked by her attitudes: when he heard the gentle Williams say, 'There has not been enough blood-letting', he knew whose influence to blame. Before the Williamses left for England in late March they had thrown off Ransome irreconcilably.

Arthur must have felt this loss acutely. He was not to find a close male friend to replace Williams until he met Ted Scott again. But he was not yet entirely destitute of English-speaking companions with whom he could discuss events in a way that was not possible with Russians. He needed people with whom he could keep fresh his sense of the Western point of view; people who could assure him that he was not going hopelessly in the wrong direction in his articles. Among those he could still turn to was Philips Price of the *Manchester Guardian*, who alone, of all British journalists, shared his perceptions, incurred the same difficulties, and occasionally enjoyed the same sort of triumphs. Price's great scoop had been the texts of the secret treaties, which the Bolsheviks had given him (while Arthur was still in England) and which the *Guardian*, alone among British newspapers, had printed in full. Price was a valued comrade. But he was not an entirely safe mentor. If Williams had swung sharply against the Bolsheviks, Price had swung sharply in their favour. He came of a line of radical MPs, would become himself a Labour MP, and easily adopted Leninism. He grew so indignant at the distortions of the British press that, by way of compensation, he sent the *Guardian* pure propaganda, abandoning not only his paper's Liberalism but also its tradition of impartially factual writing. As usually happens his colleagues saw through him, and his articles were discounted accordingly. Much the same fate was to befall Ransome: he was never committed to the same degree as Price, but this nuance escaped most people. The pair were written off together as dangerous Reds.

There were also the Americans. Arthur never seems to have had any close dealings with the US Embassy and military mission. Then and later he had a poor opinion of Sisson, and on his side Sisson suspected Arthur of being a British intelligence agent. In spite of these mutual reservations the two men saw each other regularly until Sisson left Petrograd for good on 3 March. Much more to Arthur's taste was Raymond Robins, titular colonel and head of the almost equally titular American Red Cross mission to Russia. Robins was another unofficial American agent. A self-made millionaire, former Progressive (he had chaired the party's convention at Chicago in 1916) and protégé of Theodore Roosevelt, he was a man of just the warm, inexhaustible exuberance to which Arthur so regularly responded enthusiastically. His character expressed itself perfectly in his celebrated appraisal of Trotsky: 'a four kind son of a bitch, but the greatest Jew since Christ. If the German General Staff bought Trotsky, they bought a lemon.' Furthermore, Robins, like his former chief William Boyce Thompson, who had recently returned to America to spread the word, believed that it was desirable and easy for the Allies to accept the Bolsheviks and work with them. He saw Lenin and his followers as the strongest bulwark against the Germans in Russia. It is no wonder that Ransome, who held exactly the same view, described him and Sisson to his mother as taking the most sensible line of all the foreigners in Petrograd. 'The people taking the maddest because the angriest view are the French.'

Yet Ransome's most important male friendship from now on was to be with one who was neither English-speaking nor Russian: Karl Radek, thanks to whom, even more than to Evgenia, he was to gain privileged status as an observer of the Bolshevik Revolution. He would have met Radek sooner rather than later in any case, for Trotsky had set up a Press Bureau at the Commissariat for Foreign Affairs and put Radek in charge of it. But matters were accelerated unexpectedly by the oddities of the two men's characters.

Arthur, fearing that his journey from Stockholm to Petrograd would be more perilous and difficult than it proved, had not liked to take more luggage with him than was absolutely necessary. So he had left behind a parcel of books and other items for the amiable Vorovsky to forward when there was an opportunity. In due course (we do not know the exact date, but it must have been on or only shortly before 5 January) the parcel arrived at the Commissariat for Foreign Affairs, and Radek impudently opened it. Inside were 'a Shakespeare, a folding chess-board and chessmen, and a mixed collection of books on elementary navigation, fishing, chess and folklore.' Radek was in his way a collector of human types, as Arthur was in his. He sent for the journalist with such an unlikely mix of interests and (it is to be guessed) found the man himself even more unlikely than his possessions. Arthur, for his part, instantly succumbed to the charm of the Bolshevik Puck (Lockhart's name for him). 'I found him a little, light-haired, spectacled, revolutionary goblin of incredible intelligence and vivacity. He was very ready to talk.' Arthur reacted as he always had and always would to such marked human individuality. He recognised Radek's type: 'Talking with him was for me like revisiting the Latin Quarter.' At one moment, lips and eyes compressed, face chilly, vast pipe exuding clouds of smoke, Radek would seem like a café intellectual who had just discovered that his *vis-à-vis* was unsound on phenomenology. At another, he would be taking a childish delight in, say, his revolver or his uniform, or teasing an indecisive Lettish rifleman by reciting 'To be or not to be'. He and Arthur were soon on the closest terms. Exuberance had met exuberance. Madame Radek worked in the Commissariat for Foreign Affairs, and was a friend of Evgenia. It perhaps also helped that Radek was not much less of a foreigner in Russia than was Arthur. A Polish-Austrian Jew by birth, he had joined Lenin in Switzerland and travelled on the sealed train, but had been refused admission to Russia because of his nationality. He had had to kick his heels in Finland until the October Revolution. He spoke Polish with a German accent, Russian with a Polish accent and French, says Ransome, 'with the greatest difficulty'. He could hold his tongue when necessary, but he delighted in being indiscreet – which made him a treasure to journalists. His friendship was altogether a wonderful piece of luck for Arthur. Not only did it give him entry to the innermost circles of Bolshevism – he would get to know all the leaders except, as he afterwards realised, Stalin – and enliven his telegrams (it is usually possible to tell when Radek is behind Arthur's reports) but several times it proved of the utmost value to him personally, possibly even saving him from prison or death.

Yet Arthur's close contact with the leadership did not guarantee that he would always see things as the Bolsheviks did. Looming over all else, for him as for everybody in Petrograd that January, was the question of peace or war; but for the Bolsheviks – those, at least, who commanded the party – the question of the survival of their regime, so intimately linked with the peace question, was ultimately even more important. Arthur did not yet see the full implications of that fact (for that matter, nobody did, except perhaps Lenin). Nevertheless he tended to accept Bolshevik statements at their face value: swallowing, for example, and regurgitating for the readers of the *Daily News* the false explanation given of the latest delay in the meeting of the Constituent Assembly. He reported that the nationalisation of the banks put a weapon almost more powerful than the guillotine in the hands of the Government, and that there would be a 'gradual leavening' of the Bolshevik ministry by men of other parties. Wishful thinking was nearly universal in Petrograd. Like almost everyone else Arthur wanted to believe that the Germans could be kept out of Russia and that some effective co-operation between the Allies and the Bolsheviks towards that end was possible. In early January he was seeing Trotsky almost every day. Under his influence, and that of Radek, and perhaps of Evgenia Petrovna, he wanted to believe that Trotsky's diplomacy was going to succeed.

On 13 January he telegraphed the *Daily News* that Trotsky had produced more open disagreement in Germany than any other diplomat during the war. Arthur had been led astray by facts and a strong personality. Trotsky believed that if he spun out the negotiations long enough, there would be a revolution in Germany; but if not, then Russia should simply lay down her arms, refuse to sign an ignoble peace, and dare the Germans to expose their brutality to the world by resuming their advance. Trotsky's amazing performance at Brest-Litovsk did indeed advertise German brutality; opinions were indeed sharply divided in the Reichstag as to what sort of a peace ought to be contrived, and the divisions were indeed made worse by the issue of Woodrow Wilson's Fourteen Points on 8 January (which Ransome welcomed as a help to Trotsky and 'the first Allied utterance that shows an imaginative understanding of the actual situation'). There was indeed a rupture at Brest-Litovsk when the Germans, all too literally, stuck to their guns; but those guns dominated the situation, as Lenin would soon be dinning into his comrades' reluctant ears, and to try to evade that fact, by whatever feats of revolutionary diplomacy, was simply to invite a worse treatment later on by the impatient victors.

Ransome also blundered in his discussion of the Constituent Assembly, for he saw it chiefly in terms of how it would affect the Russo-German negotiations, and this predisposed him to accept the Bolshevik rationale for destroying it. The Assembly, he said, or any Government it supported, would offer the German generals 'an antagonist infinitely less dangerous to them than M. Trotsky'. When at last the Assembly was about to meet, the Bolsheviks issued a declaration of their own policy, including complete nationalisation, immediate peace, and the announcement that the November Revolution had made the Assembly's mandate obsolete (since the elections to the Assembly were held *after* the

November Revolution, this last statement is not very acceptable).
Arthur commented:

> This indicates clearly the line of Bolshevik policy. In case the
> Assembly does not prove obedient they will probably look up
> Cromwell in English histories and learn what to do. From the
> rigid standpoint of theoretic democracy it is difficult to defend
> them. But the motives of the probable majority against them
> are neither idealistic nor patriotic. Bolshevik motives also have
> nothing to do with patriotism, but they have ideals, and the
> present struggle is really an attempt to force their ideals on the
> apathetic multitude.

All very well, but opponents of the Tsardom had dreamed for a
century of the glorious day when Russia would summon her Constituent Assembly to give the country the free institutions she
deserved. In 1917 it was universally assumed that a Constituent
Assembly would meet soon and enjoy the fullest political authority. This assumption turned out to be wrong. It was one of the
great tragedies of Russian history. For as a result of the November
Revolution, Russia was to be governed nominally by the soviets,
bodies that were solely class institutions: representatives of
workers, soldiers and peasants. All other groups were excluded;
and the real rulers were to be Lenin and his party. Lenin had never
pretended to be a parliamentarian. In the last resort his belief in
himself and his Bolsheviks rested on the conviction that they
alone understood the necessities of history, which could be realised
only through socialist revolution. In such a society the Constituent
Assembly could have no place, and Lenin was bound to suppress
it, for had it lingered it could only have operated as a feeble but
annoying challenge to the Soviet Government.

The surprising thing is that the Bolsheviks eventually allowed
the Assembly to meet on 18 January. Arthur spent the evening of
the 17th at the Commissariat for Foreign Affairs with Evgenia
Petrovna and Radek's wife, Rosa. On his way home he noticed
that leaflets were being distributed urging a demonstration the
following day in front of the Assembly. Next morning (his
birthday) he went with Sisson to the Foreign Office to collect
passes for admission to the Assembly from Evgenia. The men
found her and Rosa Radek huddled in furs against the cold,
although a fire was laid in the next room. They laughed at the

women for accepting their fate, and Arthur soon had a fire going for them (an act of skill for which Sisson would try to steal the credit in his memoirs). In return they got their passes. Rosa Radek said they would have a dull day of it; she herself meant to spend it beside the fire.

The day was not exactly dull. Arthur walked across the town to the Tauride Palace, noting that the sky was clearer than usual because lack of coal had closed down the factories and so put a stop to the smoking chimneys. About noon there was shooting, when various processions defied Bolshevik orders and tried to approach the Palace: 'In all about fifteen people were killed, about 100 wounded.' The Assembly was late in opening, so Arthur, feeling hungry, went to the Smolny Institute for some soup. He found Smolny bristling with guns and heavily garrisoned by Red Guards and Lettish soldiers; but no attack came.

In the early evening he was back at the Tauride Palace, where the opening session of the Assembly at last got under way. Arthur was still unimpressed. He found it 'ironic' that the Cadets had not been allowed to take their seats. The Assembly as a result was divided into two solid blocks differing very little as to policy, only as to the persons who should carry it out. He did not expect much to come from the collision of these blocks, and quoted approvingly a Bolshevik remark, 'What is the good of having a constituent assembly when the revolution is only beginning?' While the balloting for President went on he watched Lenin laughing and talking to Krylenko, the junior officer whom the Bolsheviks had sent to take over at Army headquarters from General Dukhonin after the Revolution, and who had tried, unsuccessfully and not very hard, to save Dukhonin from a lynching. He noticed that the galleries and boxes were packed with Bolshevik soldiers and sailors.

Red Guards and sailors were on duty throughout the building, and I was amused to observe a Red Guard on more than one occasion lean his rifle against the wall in order to be able more enthusiastically to applaud.

Ransome might have been less amused had he noticed the incident in which several of the 'guards' took to aiming their loaded rifles at the heads of non-Bolshevik speakers. Lenin had to order them to desist, on the grounds that the deputies enjoyed parliamentary immunity.

The Bolsheviks, who were in a minority, walked out, soon to be followed by their allies, the Left Social Revolutionaries (LSRs). Only the Mensheviks and Right Social Revolutionaries (RSRs) remained, and these, after passing various anti-Bolshevik resolutions, were at length forced out of the hall by the Red Guards. They were escorted to safety by the Bolsheviks and LSRs, for otherwise they would have been attacked by the soldiers and sailors.

Arthur watched all this without emotion; walking home he noticed that there were plenty of sledges about – a good sign, since when trouble was imminent they vanished from the streets. He was rather pleased when, next day, as he had predicted, the Assembly was dissolved. He emphasised the point that it could not have formed a government capable either of ruling Russia or of undertaking successful negotiations with the Allies or the Germans.

(*20 January*) The Soviets at least have real authority ... When opinion in the country really changes we shall find the character of the Soviets change. Until then a change in government is undesirable. Any *coup d'état* in Petrograd might be successful but it would be faced by Soviet opposition throughout the country, and the last state would be very much worse than the first. Telegrams from England laying stress on what is to be hoped from the Constituent Assembly suggest imperfect knowledge of the actual situation.

His view of the Revolution was still somewhat romantic, as was shown by his account of a meeting in a barracks addressed by Krylenko a few days later. In a riding school incongruously adorned with a Christmas tree and the remains of some theatrical scenery a crowd of soldiers was putty in the hands of the 'little, smiling, energetic, elderly man with a grey fur hat set jauntily on his head, and a military overcoat (of course without epaulettes)'. He reminded Arthur of a pirate king.

He must have been the smallest man in the room. I am sure he had the biggest revolver. But he had something else, some extraordinary power over his audience ... I have never heard

any orator listened to by a Russian audience with such absolute
attention as this little elderly ensign Krylenko, commander-in-
chief of the Russian army. He is a finished artist as an orator,
this little genius, who could hold an audience of simple Russian
soldiers breathlessly interested for an hour and a half while he
put before them the whole complex political situation.

Nobody mentioned General Dukhonin, but one of Krylenko's
themes was the murder of two prominent Cadets in hospital,
which had occurred four days previously. 'A blot on the revolution was that killing,' Arthur reports him as saying, 'that does not
mean there should be no killing in the revolution!' Fair enough:
Krylenko and his friends had their backs to the wall, civil war was
already beginning, he was rallying his troops. But Arthur did not
pause to discuss the role of violence in the Bolshevik Revolution,
or to consider where it might lead. He had no more than a perfunctory word of sorrow for the victims; he was quick to assert
the innocence of the Bolsheviks. There is nothing in him of the
emotional revulsion which the murder, and the suppression of the
Constituent Assembly, caused in, for example, Harold Williams.
In part this insensitivity may have been that of a big, cheerful man
who, whatever his experiences as a child, scarcely knew the meaning of personal fear. But he was not naturally callous. The truth
seems to have been that he was so caught up in the Bolshevik
drama that he became blind to some of its implications. It was a
phenomenon that was to become all too common in later years.

As soon as the Constituent Assembly was dead, the Third All-
Russian Congress of Soviets – the real revolutionary parliament –
took over the Tauride Palace. On 26 January Trotsky reported to
it on the peace negotiations. Arthur went to hear him, and in his
telegram once more demonstrated his romantic susceptibility to a
heroic personality:

(*28 January*) My position was immediately behind and above
the praesidium, looking down on Trotsky's muscular shoulders
and great head and the occasional gestures of his curiously small
hands. Beyond him was that sea of men: soldiers in green and
grey shirts, workers in collarless ones, or jerseys, others dressed
very much like British workmen, peasants in belted red shirts
and high top boots; all picked men, not elected for this assembly
alone but proved and tested in the local soviets that had chosen

them as delegates. And as I watched that amazing crowd, that filled the huge hall and packed the galleries, following point by point Trotsky's exposition of the international and inter-class situation and the policy of the Revolution I felt I would willingly give the rest of my life if it could be divided into minutes and given to men in England and France so that those of little faith who say that the Russian Revolution is discredited could share for one minute each that wonderful experience.[4]

Admiration for Trotsky and the soviets did not, however, quench the conscientious reporter's zeal to find out what was going on, nor his conviction that the Germans had to be conquered and that some sort of understanding between the Allies and the Bolsheviks was necessary if the conquest was to be achieved. By energetic investigation he began to get wind of the most genuinely dramatic events that were taking place in Petrograd in those stirring days; and what he found out he told his readers.

Trotsky had spun out the negotiations at Brest-Litovsk for longer than anyone else could have managed, but by 18 January the game was nearly up. He suspended the negotiations once more and returned to Petrograd to try to persuade Lenin to adopt his new tactic of a 'pedagogical exercise': that is, that at the right moment all further discussion with the Germans should be abandoned, and that the Bolsheviks should announce a policy of refusing either to fight or to sign an unjust treaty — 'no war, no peace'. This would finally demonstrate to the world that the Bolsheviks were not the tools of Germany; it might even persuade the German socialists and working class (who had remained deaf to Bolshevik calls for revolution) that the time had come to throw off their tyrants and rescue their Russian comrades. Meanwhile, in Petrograd, Bukharin and the group round him (which included Radek) were swinging over to the view that, since Germany was so merciless and so obdurate, there was nothing for it but to wage war against her. Of all the chiefs of the Bolsheviks only one stood out against both these imbecilities: Lenin. Further delay, Trotsky's

4 Oddly, exactly the same snapshot of Trotsky on this occasion is to be found in J. Wheeler-Bennett, *Brest-Litovsk*, p. 195, where the observer is said to be Lenin himself. Wheeler-Bennett gives no source for this passage, but it must derive, directly or indirectly, from AR. Wheeler-Bennett makes another unacknowledged raid on AR's article, and distorts it in the same way, on p. 259.

line, he saw to be useless: every day that passed would only encourage the German Supreme Command to put forward worse claims. It was more than useless to prate of fighting a revolutionary war, Bukharin's line: Russia's army had dissolved, and though the vast country might be defended by guerrilla warfare, the Bolshevik Government would fall. In the finest hour of his career Lenin set out to drive his colleagues to face the reality that he alone saw clearly and unafraid.

While the Soviet Congress sat, Ransome haunted the corridors of the Tauride Palace, and on 25 January came to the conclusion that

> the majority of the Bolsheviks, together with the allied party of Left Social Revolutionaries, are prepared, even in the present appalling circumstances, to take up Germany's challenge, to break off the negotiations finally and enter on a period of 'revolutionary defence'. I believe that the ultimate decision will lie with Trotsky, whose personal influence is enormous.

No mention of Lenin. The likeliest explanation is that even Radek (who had just been threatening Lenin with prison, to receive the dry reply, 'Some people indeed may go to prison; but if you will calculate the probabilities you will see that it is much more likely that I will send you than you me') – even Radek had curbed his tongue, and told Ransome very little of what was going on. It was far from desirable that the Germans and the world should know that the Bolsheviks were deeply divided or that the chief defeatist was the ruler of Russia himself. Yet in a way Ransome's report was correct: on 22 January Lenin, seeing that his own policy stood as yet no chance, and that Bukharin's was suicidal, threw his weight behind Trotsky, whose pedagogical proposal thereby carried the day. At the same time he extorted a promise from Trotsky that if this expedient failed, Trotsky would in no circumstances support the proposal of a revolutionary war. After this agreement, and the speech which Ransome so much admired, Trotsky went back to play out the bitter farce of Brest-Litovsk.

Another reason for Arthur's misreading of the situation may have been that he was seeing little or nothing of Lenin at this time. His contacts were all with Trotsky, Radek and Zorin, the President of the Revolutionary Tribunal. Zorin was the brother of Alexander Gumberg, Robins's chief assistant and interpreter, who had rapidly become one of Arthur's cronies.

In England and America, meanwhile, the dissolution of the Constituent Assembly, the repudiation by the Bolsheviks of the foreign debts of the Tsardom and the Provisional Government, even the fact that the negotiations with the Germans were still going on, had created a deplorable impression, which was not long in damaging Arthur's standing, especially as his telegrams were growing so rhapsodical. As early as 3 January American newspapers which were republishing his articles preceded them with a warning that he was an out-and-out Bolshevik sympathiser. More important was the consequence in England. From now on the temptation to dismiss Arthur's information and interpretation of events grew steadily more irresistible in official circles. Officialdom thus began to cut itself off from a first-rate source of light just when it could have been most valuable. For in essence Arthur had not changed, as some members of the Foreign Office, and diplomats on the spot such as Sir Francis Lindley, the *chargé d'affaires*, well realised. He wanted an understanding between his country and the Bolsheviks at least as much for England's sake as for Russia's; and he thought one ought to be possible, because even if the Germans did impose a victor's peace it would be worthless. Russia was too vast and chaotic to be any use to them. In this perception, which was also that of Lenin and Trotsky, he was perfectly right, as events were to prove. But in spite of all he and others could say the British Government moved deeper and deeper into muddle.

It was at this juncture that Robert Bruce Lockhart reached Petrograd. His journey from England had taken him more than a fortnight. During that time the conditions affecting his mission had radically changed. He had left London as a sort of unofficial ambassador to the Bolsheviks, charged by Lloyd George with seeing whether some form of co-operation could be worked out on the lines advocated by Arthur Ransome and others. With the backing of the Prime Minister, and confident in his own righteousness, Lockhart was sure that he could succeed. But by the time he arrived in Petrograd Lloyd George had handed over responsibility for him exclusively to Balfour. And although Balfour backed him sturdily against critics and competitors while his mission lasted, he backed alternative, incompatible missions too. The policy of drift thus turned insensibly into one of self-contradictory meddling in Russian affairs. It was obvious in Petrograd and Moscow that Britain could not rationally back both the Bolsheviks and their opponents; yet that is what Balfour, by refusing to choose, was attempting. His excuse was that he was ready to support any Russian group that was opposed to the Germans, including anti-Bolshevik forces among the Don Cossacks and in the Caucasus. This, he argued, showed that he was determined not to intervene in Russian affairs. He complained bitterly that Lockhart seemed unable to make his attitude clear to the Bolsheviks. With rather more reason Lockhart might have retorted that a muddled policy cannot be made clear, except by abandoning it. During February, March and April he persisted in his own policy, of Anglo-Bolshevik co-operation. He failed. Lenin had warned him he would, saying,

> So long ... as the German danger exists, I am prepared to risk a co-operation with the Allies, which should be temporarily advantageous to both of us. In the event of German aggression, I am willing to accept military support. At the same time I am quite convinced that your Government will never see things in this light. It is a reactionary Government. It will co-operate with the Russian reactionaries.

Lenin can seldom have made a more accurate prediction.

Lockhart, however, at the beginning of his mission, was full of hope, and was delighted to encounter Arthur Ransome again, who could be very useful to him. The two men began to meet almost daily, so that Arthur became, if not a member of the mission, yet, in its leader's eyes, something more than a visitor. Lockhart's *Memoirs* contain a pleasing sketch of Arthur at this time:

> Ransome was a Don Quixote with a walrus moustache, a sentimentalist, who could always be relied upon to champion the under-dog, and a visionary, whose imagination had been fired by the revolution. He was on excellent terms with the Bolsheviks and frequently brought us information of the greatest value. An incorrigible romanticist, who could spin a fairy-tale out of nothing, he was an amusing and good-natured companion. As an ardent fisherman who had written some charming sketches on angling, he made a warm appeal to my sympathy, and I championed him resolutely against the secret service idiots who later tried to denounce him as a Bolshevik agent.

For his part, Arthur was delighted to meet Lockhart again. The canny young Scot told him, not quite truthfully, that it was his articles which had induced the Government to send out the mission: 'It's your fault that we're here.' Flattered, Arthur did everything he could to help: introducing Lockhart to Robins and at least smoothing his way with Radek. Decades later Lockhart would write to him: 'I can still see you sitting with me and Radek and both of you, I think, smoking Naval tobacco which we got from Cromie.' Cromie, the naval attaché at the British Embassy, was making plans to keep the Russian Baltic fleet out of the hands of the Germans, should they ever take Petrograd. He too was a good friend of Arthur's.

During the first ten days of February Arthur continued to report on the Revolution: the decree disestablishing the Church, for example, and seizing all its property; or on the state of the food supply in Petrograd: 'In the district next to my own they were giving out half a pound of horseflesh to each child, but before evening the supply of horseflesh had run out.' But his prime concern was to try and bring about a more sympathetic attitude in England to the Bolsheviks. It was wrong to be put off by the revolutionaries' bad manners, he explained. Their insults to Germany and Austria were a form of propaganda. 'In order not to seem to be slaves of one capitalist group against another they must take a similar line with regard to us or sensibly weaken their position in the minds of the working classes of the Central Empires.' When the Bolsheviks announced their intention of sending one of their number, Petrov, to England, where he had previously been interned, Ransome exerted himself behind the scenes, at Lindley's request, to kill the idea; but in case it came off (it did not) he telegraphed to the *News* explaining that Petrov would not think of stirring up revolution in England, on the contrary, he was a warm admirer of British democracy and said so frequently at mass meetings. And a telegram about his cherished soviets goes far not only to illustrate his belief in the Bolsheviks, but also to explain it:

When the time comes for the Bolsheviks to follow their predecessors and resign power into the hands of another party, it will have come because of a real change of opinion in the country which will be reflected in the Soviets. The Soviets will survive them. In recognising the republic of Soviets as the

Government of Russia we should not be recognising any one party. We should be recognising the form of government which Russia has hammered out for herself by rule of thumb. It is a form of government especially suitable to a country of gigantic area of markedly differing races. It is a form of government which is not a new thing in Russia, but corresponds to older forms of Russian freedom.

Little attention would ever be paid to these telegrams, for on 10 February at Brest-Litovsk Trotsky made his planned declaration of 'no war, no peace': 'we cannot place the signature of the Russian Revolution under these conditions which bring with them oppression, misery and hate to millions of human beings.' He and Radek and the other Bolshevik representatives left for Petrograd in high good humour, for the Germans and Austrians had been staggered by such unheard-of behaviour; but since nobody knew what would happen next the Government took the precaution of shutting down the Petrograd telegraph office. It remained shut for more than a week, and although Arthur went to the Foreign Office as soon as the news of Trotsky's *démarche* reached him, even Evgenia Petrovna could do nothing for him. The story did not reach London, except through German channels, until the night of 17–18 February.

By then a second thunderbolt had fallen on Petrograd. On the morning of 16 February news reached Lenin that the Germans had denounced the armistice and would march again on the 18th. Trotsky was inclined to let them come: if they took Dvinsk, it would show the world how matters stood. Lenin would not allow such acquiescence: 'It's not a question of Dvinsk, but of the Revolution.' It took him more than forty-eight hours to win over his colleagues on the Central Committee of the Bolshevik party, but by midnight on the 18th the trick had been won and a telegram sent to General Hoffmann, whose troops were now moving relentlessly towards Petrograd, asking for a renewal of the armistice and for Germany's latest terms. The next morning, the 19th, *Pravda*, otherwise full of bellicose articles (there had been no time to scrap them), contained the news of the Bolshevik capitulation, and Lenin's article giving the reasons. Revolution was, he said, inevitable throughout Europe if the war continued, and it showed no signs of stopping; meanwhile it was Russia's duty to preserve her own revolution at all costs. Since she could fight no more, and further delay would only increase the penalty of defeat, peace must be made immediately. The rapid, grim advance of the Germans continued. Trotsky sounded Lockhart and Robins as to what help might come from the West if the Bolsheviks decided at last to resist. On 23 February the new terms reached Petrograd. They were exceedingly severe, and included a rigid timetable. They were to be accepted within forty-eight hours; Russian delegates must immediately return to Brest-Litovsk and there sign the peace treaty within three days; the treaty must be ratified within two weeks after that. Throughout the night of 23–4 February the Petrograd Soviet, first, and then the Central Executive Committee of the Congress of Soviets, wrangled and agonised in the Tauride Palace over what to do; but by morning the cold reason of Lenin had prevailed. That night a Bolshevik delegation set out once more for Brest-Litovsk.

It is possible to catch only glimpses of Arthur during these terrible days. The interruption of the telegraphic service between Petrograd and London, followed by a period of extreme confusion, meant that he got less copy to the *Daily News* than usual; and the file copies of his telegrams are largely missing. Nevertheless we know that on 13 February, when Trotsky reported on his *coup de théâtre* at Brest-Litovsk to the Central Committee, Radek made his own report to his friends Ransome and Gumberg with notable brilliance and humour. It seemed the description of a triumph. Ransome was with Radek in the Commissariat for Foreign Affairs on the night of 18 February while the telegram of capitulation was being sent. Radek, as an Austrian subject, was not allowed to vote among the Bolsheviks. Lenin was probably glad of an excuse to keep the eloquent little gadfly out of a crucial meeting where his tongue could do harm. Radek was full of fight. The German ultimatum of the 16th had not terrified him: he talked of compelling the Petrograd bourgeoisie to dig trenches for the defence of the city, and of forcing the Germans to fight the Revolution all the way to the Urals if need be. Arthur thought him sublime. Then came Lenin's article in *Pravda*, and the fact had to be faced that there were two points of view on the matter. Arthur again demonstrated his romanticism by sticking wholeheartedly to Radek, and swallowing his version of events complete. On 22 February he wrote to his mother to tell her that the Germans might well enter Petrograd, but she was not to worry about him (he had no very good reasons to offer why she should not). He went on, in the tone of a man facing the worst:

> Be good to Barbara.
> Under no circumstances is my book on the Revolution to be
> published without revision by me ... Goodnight my dear. I
> hope I shall see you again some time or other, though it looks
> as if I may have to go round the world to do it.

In the same letter he reported, on Radek's authority, that the
Bolsheviks were going to fight after all. But he overestimated the
influence of Radek, Bukharin (the real leader of the opposition)
and their followers. On the night of 23 February, the second
German ultimatum having arrived, Arthur went to the Tauride
Palace to hear the issue settled. As the night wore on it became
clear that the war faction was losing. For Lenin, who had come
as near to losing control of the Bolsheviks as he ever would, was
perforce showing what a superb parliamentary leader he could
have been if he had believed in parliaments. His wrath and scorn
and relish of battle were entirely missing. For days he had displayed unflinching courage, cold logic, massive patience and, what
probably counted as much as anything else, perpetual good humour. He spoke to the Petrograd Soviet, in one of the finest speeches
of his life, and left the meeting. Then Arthur saw him sitting with
his back against the wall,

> one leg crossed over the other, his arms folded across his chest,
> so confident in the rightness and compelling force of his opinions
> that he would not even take the trouble to hear what his oppon-
> ents had to say. His was the only cheerful figure in the hall and
> to look at his confident face was to know that the war party
> would be defeated.

This was perhaps the moment when Arthur unconsciously began
to shift his allegiance from Radek and Trotsky; in the mean time
he was utterly cast down. He heard Lenin address the Executive
Committee in another short, unanswerable speech which only
just half the meeting applauded. He watched the vote: 112 for
peace, 84 against, 22 abstaining. Then there was a roll-call vote.

(*24 February*) It was terrible to hear man after man who up to
the moment of the assembly had been working to prevent the

decision now, in dead voices, recording their votes for their party and against their conscience. Finally the declarations of the parties were read aloud from the tribune. The strongest of all in condemnation of the signing was written by Radek who, being an Austrian, could not vote. Then about six in the morning the assembly adjourned. There were no sledges. I walked across Petrograd in the cold dark winter dawn with a small group of Bolsheviks all but one of whom were convinced, like myself, that they had just connived at the death sentence on their revolution. We walked like convicts, and I could not force myself to realise that not quite a year ago on just such a winter's dawn I had walked those same streets in joy and confidence of the awakening Russian Revolution.

It is now clear that even, perhaps especially, from the revolutionary point of view Lenin was right and Radek was wrong (as Ransome would later remark himself).[5] So it is a little hard to enter into Arthur's anguish at this moment, and very easy to misunderstand it. He was moved, of course, by the distress of the brave men and women whom he had come to admire so much; and he had certainly absorbed a great deal of their outlook. But these were not the factors which made him so resistant to Lenin's logic. Underlying everything, for him, was the war. Arthur was in some respects an entirely representative Englishman in his attitude to the Russian Revolution; what set him apart were his better information, his warm liking for the Russian people, and his great common sense. Even these qualities had to take second place at times. Ever since March 1917 he had hoped that Russia, revitalised by revolution and democracy, would come to the rescue of England in her desperate struggle against Prussianism, that Moloch which had destroyed so many of his friends – Edward Thomas, Ivar Campbell, Dixon Scott – and would soon take his brother Geoffrey. He believed in his country's cause; he dreaded what a Russian surrender might do to it, as well as to Russia herself; he thought that the Bolsheviks were the only effective democrats, the only sincere anti-Germans in Russia; he respected them individually, and wanted them as allies; now it seemed as if he and they and their causes and their countries would all go down to ruin together.

5 Obituary of Lenin, *Manchester Guardian*, 23 January 1924.

Perhaps there was one last hope. He returned to the Tauride Palace in the evening, and met Philips Price there. A little later they were joined by Robins. The three of them agreed that maybe, if they could by their representations move the British and United States Governments to offer aid to the Bolsheviks, Russian belligerence would revive. 'The hatred of the Prussian military system knew no bounds now in Russia and some way must be found to turn it to the advantage of the Western Allies.' They all three resolved to try, oblivious of the fact that Lenin wanted a breathing-space for the Revolution, and would never agree to any pro-Allied developments which might provoke the Germans to renounce the treaty. For the Germans were on Russia's doorstep and the Allies were not.

Revolutionary events moved too fast to allow Arthur more than a moment for grief and the nurturing of new illusions. Since the German army was not to be trusted, and the German terms would draw the frontier dangerously near Petrograd, it had been decided to transfer the Government to Moscow, the capital of that old Muscovy to which, shorn of the Ukraine, Finland, Estonia, Livonia and Poland, the Russian Empire was so nearly reduced. Arthur as a result suddenly found himself helping to pack the Imperial archives for shipment. Nothing could be more symbolic of the almost complete chaos of affairs in Russia at that time. The man in charge of the operation was Mikhail Pokrovsky, the chief Bolshevik historian and a former delegate at Brest-Litovsk; he was also a leading associate of Radek. It would have been unthinkable, under Stalin, to give such a man such a task; still more astonishing is it that the only assistants he had were Madame Radek, 'a girl secretary' (presumably Evgenia Petrovna Shelepina) and a foreigner, Arthur. They worked like dogs for twenty hours at a stretch, Arthur and Pokrovsky somehow managing to repress their natural urge to read the documents instead of packing them. The papers were crated, and then it was found that there were no nails, no rope: a shopping expedition had to go in search of some. Then Arthur went back to his flat and collapsed into bed.

In the morning Lockhart knocked at his door. It was now 26 February; the American, French, Chinese and Japanese ambassadors, the British *chargé d'affaires*, Lindley, and all their staffs, fearing that Petrograd was about to fall to the Germans, were leaving that night. Lockhart, as he put it in his diary, meant to stay in Petrograd in all circumstances 'if the Bolsheviks can put up any show', until it was time to go to Moscow with Trotsky; but it might be necessary to have a bolt-hole, and he wanted Arthur to inspect Vologda, the little town, three hundred miles eastward along the railway to Siberia, where the American ambassador meant to establish himself. If a suitable building for the Lockhart mission could be found, Arthur was to claim it by flying a Union Jack (they got a suitable flag, a Pilot Jack, from one of the British ships trapped in the Neva). Robins was also going to Vologda, hitching his Red Cross wagon to the ambassador's train, and urged Arthur to join him. Arthur willingly agreed: it would be his first trip outside Petrograd since his return there. He packed; then he and Gumberg (whose compartment he was to share) found time to say good-bye to Sisson, who intended to leave Russia through Finland and was feverishly collecting documents, which he believed to be authentic, proving that Lenin and Trotsky were salaried spies in the service of the German General Staff. Fortunately for their peace of mind neither Arthur nor Gumberg knew of this activity.

The journey took twenty-four hours, and the train repeatedly jerked to a standstill, waking the sleepers. In the small hours of 28 February one of these sudden halts roused Arthur. He saw they were at a station, and soon found out that it was Vologda. The diplomatic coaches should have been uncoupled, but the stationmaster was proposing to send the complete train on to Siberia. Gumberg was able to bully the man into uncoupling the cars. After daybreak it was discovered that an earlier train, with half the American Embassy staff aboard, had gone right through Vologda; telegraphic messages had to be sent by an irate ambassador to get his men back. It was all too clear that they had not wanted to halt short of Vladivostok, or home. In later years Arthur came to think that they had some responsibility for the ambassador's own experience: an attempt had been made to hijack him to the east, which had been accidentally foiled by Arthur's wakefulness.

Vologda turned out to be a sleepy, pretty little place, comparatively untouched by war and revolution (even the ponies that drew the sleighs were well-fed, unlike the skeletal horses of Petrograd). Arthur liked it very much, but he soon realised he was wasting his time there. Behind him in the west the Brest-Litovsk treaty was at last being signed and the German advance on Petrograd was halted. Vologda might suit the Americans but it would be no use to Lockhart, who needed to stick close to the Government, and was certainly no use to a journalist who had to report events. Neither was it much use to Raymond Robins, who was hoping against hope that he could get a pledge for economic and military aid to the Bolsheviks out of the Allied Governments. He and Arthur (who, as we have seen, shared his hopes) were in their way as deluded as the War Cabinet in London: they clung, long after it was reasonable to do so, to the fancy that some sort of Eastern Front could be re-established to take pressure off the West, where a major German offensive was clearly imminent. Robins and Ransome decided to leave Vologda two days after arriving there, and would have done so but for an incident, some-what ridiculous, that nevertheless has so much significance for Arthur's story that it must be dwelt on.

The Bolshevik delegates reached Brest-Litovsk after a nerve-racking journey on the afternoon of 28 February. They met the Germans in plenary session the next day, and received the text of the proposed treaty for study. After looking over it the chief delegate, Karakhan, telegraphed to Lenin: 'As we expected, it was absolutely useless to discuss the peace terms. They are worse than the ultimatum ... We have decided to sign without discussion and leave at once.' Then he sent a second telegram: 'Send us a train to Toroshino near Pskov with an adequate number of guards.' Unfortunately the second telegram arrived in Smolny before the first. To the anxious men and women waiting there this sudden, imperious, unexplained demand for a train could only mean one thing: war. Lenin immediately sent off a telegram with the dread-ful news to 'the American Embassy, Vologda, attention Gumberg and Ransome' – an amazingly cool-headed and considerate action in the circumstances, even if it was chiefly prompted by the thought that now, at last, the Bolsheviks must turn for help to the Western Allies, and ought therefore to show attention to their representatives, agents and newsmen. At the same moment, and for the same reason, Trotsky was telegraphing to the local soviet at Murmansk, telling it to co-operate fully with the British naval force in the harbour there.

What no one had time to consider was that among those present at Smolny was Trotsky's secretary. She, in a remarkable display of initiative, added her own postscript to Lenin's telegram. Addressed to Arthur, it ran: 'As this means war, and consequently your immediate going further, I am sending my best wishes for a happy journey.' The first words created a fearful sensation in Vologda: as Ransome was to remark in his *Autobiography*, 'if some girl banging her typewriter in the Commissariat of Foreign Affairs could write "This means war", then war it must most certainly mean.' Robins decided to wait at Vologda for clarification, and Arthur, who could not get back to Petrograd without him, waited too, no doubt in some impatience. Fortunately the matter was soon cleared up, and the next day the return journey began.

It had been a storm in a teacup, and is treated as such in the *Autobiography*, no doubt because of Arthur's reluctance to display his feelings for Evgenia, and hers for him. Yet in the telegram Evgenia Petrovna gave herself away, although it was the last thing she wanted to do. She was too proud, too unsure of herself, and of him, either to ask him to come back to her in Petrograd or to admit, in so many words, that she wanted him to. She announced, for the world's benefit, that she assumed he would continue his journey with the fleeing Americans; and since he was a friend she wished him a pleasant journey. Yet Arthur would have had to be unusually dense, even for a man, not to have heard behind those cool, farewell words the note of need.

The second point is equally interesting. The telegram shows that at last Arthur (chastened by the Ivy experience) had learnt not to rush his fences with women. The telegram is not that of someone who knows exactly how her love is returned.

On 3 March, then, Robins hitched his coach to a train of fourteen cars of rifles and sailors, presumably coming from Archangel for the defence of Petrograd. In spite of this display of military vigour, the journey back gave Arthur plenty of evidence in support of Lenin's decision to make peace:

Every station was like an opened hive of grey bees, all drones, swarming over the lines and the platforms, packing themselves again into cattle-trucks, travelling on the buffers when there was no other room ... Every stopping-place smells like a vast latrine. Meanwhile other traffic is almost impossible. I believe myself it may be years before this new nomadic era ends and the de-mobilisation of the Russian army is concluded, and the grey sediment of aimless migration subsides. Yet even this is less dangerous than to have these millions ready to be driven, sacking, burning and destroying, in front of the advancing enemy, as happened last year.

However, as well as the wreck of the old army, Arthur noticed signs of the rise of a new one. Whenever the train stopped a guard of workmen in rough sheepskins and felt boots tumbled out and patrolled it with something more like keenness and discipline than he had seen since March 1917. This was not even the first time that he had reported on the beginnings of what was to become one of the three pillars of the Soviet state (the others being the Communist party and the secret police). On 10 February he had noticed a revolutionary eagerness to enlist. At that time the authorities were accepting only volunteers of guaranteed political convictions. The fact that only three weeks later old army officers were being recruited to train them shows how fast events were moving. Now Ransome reported, 'Until this army is formed, only a lunatic could expect Russia to do serious fighting.' The old army was useless, in fact the worst obstacle to a successful defence, offering 'good-tempered, indolent, passive resistance to any efforts to get the tracks clear for urgent traffic of war'. Arthur still remembered Will Peters's lessons. If Russia could not fight without efficient railways, still less could her cities eat while the Germans advanced. They were driving the Soviet power out of the Ukraine granary.

(*To* Daily News, *4 March*) This not only means corn supplies for Germany but also destroys what hope there was of getting that corn to starving northern Russia. The thousands who walk out along the roads and railways from Petrograd, and are willing to risk their lives travelling on roofs or buffers five hundred or a thousand miles and more, do so more for the sake of finding food than of escaping from Germans.

Since Arthur understood so well the conditions which made the ratification of the Brest-Litovsk treaty just about inevitable, it is a little surprising that he may have lent himself to the last-minute efforts of Raymond Robins to avert that very thing. Robins was still persuaded (in part because he did not understand Russia) that there was a real possibility of a military understanding between the Bolsheviks and the Allies. The early days of March were a period of frantic activity with him, and on the 8th he went back to

Vologda in his Red Cross coach, hoping to get some usable deed or document out of the American ambassador. Arthur went with him; perhaps to help; perhaps to keep informed; or perhaps just for the ride, since, when Robins left Vologda again, he travelled not back to Petrograd but to Moscow, where the Bolshevik Government was gathering.

Arthur benefited from his close association with the Lockhart mission and Robins: as a result he, like them, was housed in the Elite Hotel, the only one in Moscow which was still functioning. He dined, that first night, with a tobacco-merchant, but the occasion was depressing, the conversation being about equally pro-German and anti-Bolshevik. Next evening (12 March), on their way to send some telegrams from the post office, Arthur and Gumberg were stopped by some soldiers to be searched for weapons. 'Gumberg bolted, but was caught.' (Exactly the same thing happened the following day, when Arthur was out walking with Robins, except that Robins got away.) Looking in at the National Hotel, which housed the Government until the Kremlin was ready, Arthur had the pleasure of seeing Lenin sitting on his luggage in the hall, conducting his business surrounded by piles of 'unimaginable rags and tatters of baggage and bedding rolled in blankets, and every kind of tatterdemalion basket and battered trunk'. Lenin was 'calm as usual, fearless as usual, without any guard whatsoever in the old stronghold of Russian capitalism, which is his sworn enemy.'

Except for the second brush with the Red Guards 13 March was a day of brief, pure pleasure. First Arthur walked round the Kremlin wall, noting the blue-green reflections in the water between the blocks of ice in the river below the fortress. The crows were behaving like seagulls round the outlet of the Moscow drains; three men and a soldier were fishing through the ice. Then in the evening there was a cabaret at the hotel, showing that the old Moscow was not yet quite dead. There were dancers, singers, a gipsy choir. 'The only sign of the Revolution was that the whole staff of the kitchens came into the cabaret to enjoy the fun, cooks in their white caps and aprons, and the kitchenmaids with their shawls over their heads dressed for going home.'

It was back to business the next day, when the fourth All-Russian Assembly of the Soviets met in the evening, in the Hall of the Nobles in the Kremlin. The sole question before the assembly was that of the peace. A Left Social Revolutionary, Steinberg, the

Commissar for Justice, made a ferocious attack on Lenin, and Arthur looked about to see how the victim was taking it. He was much surprised to discover Lenin sitting on the floor close behind him, having come in late and found no chair. He was taking notes and smiling, 'now to himself, now to the grinning soldiers standing in that part of the hall. Although he was preparing his speech he was ready to be interrupted as often as anyone in the crowd wanted to shake his hand or worry him with a question.' Then he got up to answer Steinberg.

Ransome's comment on this occasion was perhaps the most suggestive observation he ever made about that extraordinary man. He emphasised the difference between Lenin and the other Bolshevik leaders in unexpected terms.

> He was the most Russian of them. Time and again, after listening to speeches which might have been made in any language in any country by men of any nationality I have been suddenly, as it were, brought back to Russia when this little urgent figure stepped to the tribune, stuck his thumbs in the armholes of his waistcoat, and mingled jest and argument in language that tasted of Russian tobacco and the life of the Russian peasantry. It was natural to him to talk of the principles of his international revolution in the language of the Volga peasants, and in his mouth political theory seemed in no way out of tune with the peasant proverbs that were characteristic of his speeches. At the Assembly which ratified the peace, for example, he suppressed Steinberg, who was asking questions, by remarking, to the general delight, 'One fool can ask more questions than ten wise men can answer.'

This passage throws a certain amount of light on Lenin: it makes it easy to understand why the Assembly approved the peace by a heavy majority. It throws far more light on Ransome himself. Like so many later pilgrims, he had found the sort of Lenin he wanted; and, like them, he mistook his rustic Lenin for the whole man.

The signature and acceptance of the Brest-Litovsk treaty came as a heavy blow to London, and turned many there against the Bolsheviks for good. Yet, ironically, all those Allied representatives closest to the Bolsheviks — Robins, Lockhart, Sadoul, Ransome — agreed that there had never been a better opportunity for some sort of collaboration. The difficulties were immense, not least being the morbid distrust of Westerners that was an almost universal characteristic of the Bolsheviks. But the Soviet Government had no confidence that the Germans would respect the treaty (and indeed it was promptly, flagrantly and repeatedly violated by both sides throughout its short life): the Bolsheviks might actually be forced to sue for Western military assistance. Worse still, from their point of view, was the spectre of Allied military intervention, growing larger and likelier every day. They were especially worried about the prospect of a Japanese landing at Vladivostok, for which there was strong support in England. If, by showing themselves co-operative to the Western representatives in Moscow, the Bolsheviks could ward off such an invasion, the effort, they thought, would be well worthwhile.

No such summary can be given of the attitudes of the Western Governments, or even of the British alone. As usual in diplomatic history, the French had the clearest idea of what they did and did not want; but clarity did not mean that their policy was sensible (it was automatically hostile to the Bolsheviks); and even the French descended into chaos from time to time. For example, their ambassador, Noulens, left Petrograd with the others on 28 February. He tried to leave Russia through Finland; failed; and spent several weeks fruitlessly moving about northern Russia before accepting defeat and turning up at Vologda. While he was circulating the French tone was largely set by Captain Jacques Sadoul, of the French military mission, who was ardently in favour of co-operation with the Bolsheviks.

British policy-making was pitifully incompetent. London was still undecided as to whether the Bolsheviks were German agents or not; just to be on the safe side, it supported both Lockhart's mission (which made sense only if Lenin and Trotsky were independent agents) and the Whites in southern Russia and Siberia (which made sense only if Lenin and Trotsky were Prussian tools). It also supported a secret-service operation about which, still, very little is known (Whitehall dreads to be caught in error even after sixty years) except that it was a dangerous embarrassment to Lockhart, who had to rescue it from the consequences of its repeated blunders. The War Office was strongly anti-Bolshevik and pro-intervention; the Foreign Office was united only in disliking the War Office's intrusions. The British Embassy at Vologda muddied counsel still further; and there were also the various consuls and military and naval commanders, scattered here and there, in the centre or on the periphery of Russia, all of whom exercised inevitable, but excessive, local autonomy. Finally, there was a plethora of rumour and misinformation (it was stubbornly believed, for example, that the Bolsheviks were arming German prisoners-of-war for use against the Allies) and a great shortage of accurate knowledge of Russian conditions, partly because they changed so rapidly. This made wise decisions exceedingly unlikely, if only because (let us be fair) there was no way in which Whitehall could recognise good advice when it arrived, either as articles in the *Daily News* or in dispatches from Lockhart.

The foregoing makes it clear how difficult a position Arthur was in. His information, to be sure, was incomplete, his perceptions not perfect; but both were infinitely better than anything available in London. He had seen at first hand the strength both of the soviets and of the party which had won control of them and, through them, of most of Russia. He knew quite well that the Bolshevik regime had the promise of permanence and that therefore, taking a long view, it was madness for the Allies to alienate it without grave need. That need, taking the short view, simply did not exist. It was Russian weakness which had brought about the Brest-Litovsk surrender, not German gold.

> Hostilities, military or political, will never actually cease until one or other [the Bolsheviks or Imperial Germany] is overthrown ... Nothing but the existence of the Soviet Government stands between Germany and the realisation of the grandiose dream of Mittel-Europa. The Soviet Government also has a grandiose dream of a European revolution which would make an end of militarism. Every step taken against the Soviets helps Germany. Russia is temporarily concluding a separate peace. If the Soviet power is overthrown that peace may be permanent. That peace and the Soviet power cannot long co-exist.

Time has amply vindicated these remarks. They were published in the *Daily News* on 14 March. On 20 March Ransome received a telegram from the *News* saying he must 'send shorter'. A. G. Gardiner, influenced, no doubt, by the atmosphere in official circles, was beginning to have reservations about his Special Correspondent. However, Arthur's serious difficulties in the months to come would be with the British authorities, not his editor. Yet if, during the rest of March, only one of the five telegrams which he sent was published, it was probably because on 21 March the long-awaited German offensive on the Western Front began. There was soon enough news from France to crowd everything else out of the war-shrunken English newspapers.

It was as well that Arthur had another concern to keep him cheerful, or at any rate lively. His diary begins to fill up with 'E.P.'. On 22 March they went for a drive together, and had a long talk about the beginning of the Bolshevik Revolution, for Arthur had resumed work on his history. He saw her twice in the next ten days or so, then on 2 April the diary records, 'E.P. telephoned in a very bad mood, tired out.' Two days later it was, 'E.P. very done up, and more barometrical than ever.'

She had as strong and stormy a temper, in her way, as Ivy in hers; but she had much to be short-tempered about, quite aside from the general insecurity of life in revolutionary Moscow, where opposition to the Bolsheviks was still vigorous in many quarters, and the great shortage of food. In the first place, Arthur was a married man, and he probably warned Evgenia that getting a divorce in England was not very easy. Then, he was English: if they stayed together, she might have to give up her country. Finally, there was all the extra strain imposed by Evgenia Petrovna's position with Trotsky. Not only was the job itself no sinecure, but (to judge from the usual Communist practice) she was probably required to report on her lover to the authorities, an unpleasant and alarming task, even though he was so reliable from the Bolshevik point of view.

Meanwhile Arthur had his work to do. He regarded it not simply as one of reporting the Russian Revolution for the *Daily News,* but of influencing opinion in England and America against the proposed Allied intervention. He had no sympathy with the view, already to be heard, that the Bolsheviks were a menace to civilisation and ought to be suppressed: he believed that the Russians should be left strictly alone to work out their destiny, which he thought was in good hands. However, this was as yet a subordinate consideration. His central point never varied: the purpose of intervention ought only to be to help defeat the Germans, and if attempted without Soviet approval it would have the opposite effect, and throw Lenin into the arms of Ludendorff. Yet on 6 March the British admiral at Murmansk had landed a

company of Royal Marines, and in the harbour at Vladivostok an
Allied squadron had gathered. The Japanese had landed two divisions in Korea. Nobody in Moscow knew what was going to
happen, but fears and suspicions were general. Ransome and
Lockhart worked closely together in their self-appointed mission
of building an understanding, and some sort of collaboration,
between the Bolsheviks and the British. They had not much time:
Germany would soon be sending an ambassador to Moscow, and
after that their task would be nearly impossible.

They were not helped by a speech delivered by the Foreign
Secretary, Arthur Balfour, on 20 March in which he expressed the
views then dominating Anglo-French counsels. Britain hoped for
a Japanese landing at Vladivostok, and he saw no reason why the
Bolsheviks should oppose it; indeed they should welcome it; the
Japanese were coming only to help the Russians. 'What Russians?'
asked Trotsky, to whom Arthur Ransome hurried on 22 March,
as soon as the text of the speech was available: obviously not the
Soviets, but rather the pro-German bourgeoisie. 'Do the Allies
not perceive that Japanese intervention now would ensure that
sooner or later German and Japanese interests would coincide in
direct opposition to the interests of the Allies?' Next Arthur
interviewed Lenin, who took exactly the same line:

> Which Russians? ... What can take the place of the Soviet
> power? The only power that can take its place is a bourgeois
> government. But the bourgeoisie in Russia has proved clearly
> enough that it can only remain in power with foreign help. If
> a bourgeois government, supported by outside help, should
> establish itself in power in Siberia, and Eastern Russia become
> lost to the Soviet, then in Western Russia the Soviet power
> would become weakened to such an extent, that it could hardly
> hold out for long; it would be followed by a bourgeois govern-
> ment, which would also need foreign help. The Power to give
> this help would, of course, not be England.

Arthur was so impressed by this statement that he induced Lenin
to type it out and write beneath the affirmation in his own hand:
'I confirm that I really said this in conversation with Ransome,
and I give permission for it to be printed, Lenin', with the date.
What next happened to this document is unclear. Probably Ransome gave it to Lockhart to use in his dispatches to Whitehall. It

was not printed until Lockhart brought out his *Memoirs* in 1932.[6] It had no effect in London; neither did another conversation Ransome had with Lenin at about this time, in which the Bolshevik leader said that so long as the English did not advance to Archangel, their presence at Murmansk might strengthen the Russians in resisting German demands, 'in that the Germans might feel that the Russians were not alone'. He could not say this publicly, indeed he might have to satisfy the Germans by making public protests, but he had no objection to Lockhart hearing his real views. Writing out this story years later Arthur commented bitterly, 'This statement of Lenin's was disregarded. We did advance to Archangel where, on the pretence of fighting non-existent Germans, we waged undeclared war against the Bolsheviks, who at the time were waging undeclared war against the Germans in the Ukraine.'

The ground was cracking and crumbling beneath Arthur. On the Western Front the greatest crisis of the war had erupted. So far as London was concerned, it seemed more and more necessary to distract the Germans in the East and, if possible, to raise an army against them: Red, White, Japanese, it did not matter. The Bolsheviks, meanwhile, were setting up the so-called 'Extraordinary Commission', or Cheka, the ancestor of the KGB. All non-socialist newspapers were silenced. All non-Bolshevik parties, except the LSRs, were driven from the soviets on the dubious grounds that they were counter-revolutionary. The seizure of private property, especially of industrial property, continued. Trotsky built up the new Red Army on an explicitly class-conscious basis – its nucleus consisted of industrial workers from Petrograd and Moscow – and re-introduced conscription. Bands of Red Guards were sent out into the countryside to coerce the peasants into giving up their stocks of grain to feed the cities. Anti-Bolshevik uprisings of various kinds began to erupt throughout Russia. Meanwhile the Germans and Austrians tried determinedly to make good their *de facto* annexation of the Ukraine, an effort which weakened them militarily and brought no compensating gains (peasants being as reluctant to send food to Vienna as to Moscow), while enormously increasing the misery of the Ukrainian people, who in desperation turned back towards the Soviets. In these circumstances it was all too easy for an English

6 R. H. Bruce Lockhart, *Memoirs of a British Agent*, facing p. 230.

correspondent to lose his way, the more so as neither letters nor newspapers from home were reaching him.

His articles covered a narrower and narrower range of topics. Gone were the vivid word-pictures: his last attempt at one described the second May Day of the Revolution in Moscow, when the towers of the Kremlin were garlanded in scarlet. Even that article turned into a bitter attack on the Church authorities for trying 'to use the superstitions of the people for counter-revolutionary ends'. (The *Daily News* did not print this passage.) He no longer even tried to be fair to the anti-Bolsheviks, or to report all the activities of the Soviet Government: nothing about the erosion of press freedom, for example, or the expulsion of the Mensheviks. Even when he narrated an occurrence which he had seen himself, his style had become dry. All these points are well illustrated by his account of the attack on the so-called Anarchists. These were not the peaceful followers of Prince Kropotkin but gangs of young people who had seized many of the palaces of the nobility in Moscow, turned them into fortresses, and from these bases carried out raids against society, the proceeds of which they used up in orgies. Their activities came home to Ransome and his friends when, at the end of March, they raided the American military mission. On 9 April they seized Raymond Robins's car, to his vast annoyance. The Bolsheviks too felt that matters had gone far enough. On the night of 11–12 April the Cheka mounted simultaneous attacks on twenty-seven Anarchist strongpoints, and carried them all, with much slaughter of the inmates. Dzerzhinsky, the head of the Cheka, sent round a car in the morning, in which Robins, Lockhart and Ransome, escorted by Dzerzhinsky's second-in-command, J. K. Peters, surveyed the battlefield. It provided Lockhart with one of the most memorable passages in his *Memoirs*, the climax of which shows Peters exhibiting the body of a young woman, shot down in the middle of a revel in the drawing-room of the House Gracheva:

> Her hair was dishevelled. She had been shot through the neck, and the blood had congealed in a sinister purple clump. She could not have been more than twenty. Peters shrugged his shoulders. 'Prostitutka,' he said. 'Perhaps it is for the best.'

Ransome did not mention this incident: his telegram was taken up with more material ruin:

I went round the various palaces and other buildings from which the Anarchists were dislodged. Some were badly smashed up. Pictures were ruined by bullet holes, and statuary lay about on the floor. Whole rooms were looted, valuable things being stolen by hooligans who attached themselves to the Anarchist groups. Doubtless the counter-revolutionaries are making use of the Anarchists. Among the weapons captured is a German machine-gun. The Soviet has finally shown itself capable of uprooting a movement which all previous Governments had not dared to touch.

And that is all. It is curious that a Liberal English journalist should exhibit even less compunction than a leading Chekist, and still more so that none of the English and Americans present on this guided tour seem to have questioned the brutal tactics used to defeat the Anarchists. 'Perhaps it is for the best.' A later age, with much frightful experience of urban sieges, adolescent terrorism and the methods of the Russian secret police, is unlikely to accept this proposition so easily.

In part the meagreness of Ransome's reporting in the spring and summer of 1918 must be attributed to the injunction 'send shorter', but the same cannot be said of the deterioration of his language, which by June was at times almost indistinguishable from that of the dreariest Communist propaganda. When Lenin announced the disastrous 'bread crusades', designed to set poor peasants against rich ones, which instead touched off a vast peasant rebellion that ensured a continuation of the general famine, Ransome was content merely to paraphrase his assertions: he did not question them. Isolated among the Bolsheviks, Arthur was insensibly coming to see the world through their eyes and to adopt their language. Philips Price well explains the process, which was afflicting him even more:

I was abandoning objectivity because it was now almost impossible to be objective. I was on a knife-edge and had to come down on one side or the other. To bring about conciliation and understanding between Soviet Russia and the Western Powers, as Colonel Robins, Arthur Ransome and I were trying to do, was becoming increasingly impossible ... I had been listening to the speeches of Lenin and Trotsky and reading articles in the Soviet press for so long that they were beginning to have an influence upon me. I talked about 'finance capital oligarchies, the proletariat and Imperialist blood-suckers in Germany and the Allied countries.' Looking back, I feel it was regrettable that I had not retained my objectivity and that I had forgotten how to write the English language as taught to me at Harrow.

In other ways Arthur did not fail in his professional duty. His ceaseless insistence that the Bolshevik-soviet movement was the only effective anti-German force in Russia can hardly be faulted, and his equal emphasis on the point that for the Allies to intervene against the Bolsheviks was to throw away the valuable friendship of Russia for years or decades, was even more prescient. Yet it was this very wisdom which made him the object of suspicion to the British censor, for by the summer the Government had decided on the policy he opposed: support for Japanese intervention at Vladivostok, and the dispatch of an expeditionary force to Murmansk and Archangel.

Nobody in Moscow knew much about this development. Even Lockhart, whose Government occasionally remembered that it ought to keep him informed, would in the end be taken by surprise when the Allies landed at Archangel on 4 August with a wholly inadequate force. From March to June, though hope was ebbing, it was still possible to think that the worst might not happen, or might be averted by vigorous action. In late April Robins decided to go back to Washington and make his case there. He and Arthur talked over the idea of a pamphlet setting out the situation as they saw it, but Arthur must have thought the notion had been dropped, for when, two days before his departure, Robins came to him (the Colonel not being a man of the written word, though a marvellously eloquent speaker) not a syllable had been drafted. So for once in his life Arthur had to write for publication knowing that not a sentence could be revised. He had only thirty-six hours for the job, and, starting at eight in the morning, writing steadily without sleep, finished at six o'clock in the evening of the next day. Ten thousand words were delivered to Robins just before he left.

The Truth about Russia was the first of Ransome's three pamphlets on the Russian Revolution, and is today much the rarest of them. It is of interest chiefly for what Radek had to say about its author in the preface he wrote for a Moscow-sponsored edition later that year ('He is a man with his eyes open, with a warm heart, without any prejudices, a man whose deep love for the masses and for all who were hurled into this war and its hellish misery, enabled him to understand Russia') and for what it tells us of Arthur's outlook in 1918. It does not seem to have had much impact, even on the Left, and its interpretation of the Revolution does not differ in any respect from that to be found in his *Daily News* articles. Ransome rather deprecated it to his mother as a thing done in too much of a hurry:

> (*21 May*) But, reading it over afterwards in copy, I think it gives a fair idea of the truth, and perhaps, when I revise it and expand it, will make a good sort of first chapter to my book of Portraits of the Revolution.[7] It beats the big drum a bit too much and there are too many trombones in it for my mother's refined taste, but the old Colonel who read parts of it while I was writing the rest, says it will hit Americans where they live, and that is what it was written for.

It contains one passage that shows how intensely romantic Ransome's attitude to the Revolution remained:

> Every true man is in some sort, until his youth dies and his eyes harden, the potential builder of a New Jerusalem. At some time or other, every one of us has dreamed of laying his brick in such a work. And even if this thing that is being builded here with tears and blood is not the golden city that we ourselves have dreamed, it is still a thing to the sympathetic understanding of which each one of us is bound by whatever he owes to his own youth.

Sometimes the 'trombones' can still startle:

> I love the real England, but I hate more than I hate anything on earth (except cowardice in looking at the truth) the intellectual sloth, the gross mental indolence that prevents the English from making an effort of imagination and realising how shameful will be their portion in history when the story of this last year in the biography of democracy comes to be written ... Shameful, foolish, and tragic beyond tears, for the toll will be paid in

7 Another item in the long list of AR's unwritten works.

English blood. English lads will die and English lads have died, not one or two, but hundreds of thousands, because their elders listen to men who think little things, and tell them little things, which are so terribly easy to repeat.

This is the authentic voice of 1918: the voice of Siegfried Sassoon, of Wilfred Owen, of Rudyard Kipling ('If any question why we died, Tell them, because our fathers lied'). The unusual thing is that here it is responding to the Russian Revolution, not to the Western Front. But to Arthur the logic was plain. The old fools who governed England had rejected the friendship of democratic Russia and driven her to make peace with Germany. This had strengthened the Prussians and would therefore prolong the slaughter on the Western Front. That January Geoffrey Ransome had been killed in France.

So much for Ransome the reporter. He was wrong and right, vigorous and productive. Yet the indications are that he was only a secondary incarnation, that spring and summer. The courtship of Evgenia Petrovna was going on enthusiastically, even though Arthur was often ill.

(*To his mother, 21 May*) My principal friends here are Radek and his wife, and two huge young women, Bolsheviks, as tall as Grenadiers, who prefer pistols to powder puffs, and swords to parasols ... One of them succeeded in extracting over a million poods of corn from the South under the very nose of the Germans, she at the time commanding an expedition of 300 wildly devoted sailormen.

This revolutionary heroine was Evgenia's sister Eraida (or Iraida, or Irka). Arthur was perhaps at times a little hard put to choose between 'the two EPs'; Evgenia was perhaps a little jealous. At any rate she lost no time in making herself as interesting as possible after this astonishing creature appeared on the scene. The very day after Eraida's return Evgenia told Arthur the sad story of her first love. She had got engaged to be married, and wrote to tell her mother. The next day she turned up at her mother's house herself, with the news that the young man had been killed in battle. Small wonder that she came to think the Tsar's war unjustifiable.

On 22 April Lockhart came in great agitation to Evgenia

Petrovna: the Bolsheviks proposed to install the new German ambassador, Count Mirbach, in the Elite Hotel, where Lockhart, Robins and Arthur all lodged. It was embarrassing; it was an insult; and Chicherin, the Foreign Commissar, could do nothing. Could Evgenia get hold of Trotsky? She could, and did, and he saved the day by ordering that the Germans should be sent elsewhere. Lockhart had triumphed, and, feeling that he owed it all to Evgenia Petrovna Shelepina, was eager to do her a favour in return.

Arthur was dazzled by these young Bolsheviks. On 14 May he left the Elite and went to live with the Radeks, Evgenia and others in what he later called 'a sort of Lunatic Commune' in a little Moscow palace, where they gave themselves indigestion by eating nothing but cheese. The experiment was not a success. At first Arthur was given a 'prison room', so dark that he could do no work. He felt rotten. On the day that he moved to a downstairs room Evgenia Petrovna was 'mad and sad'. Then she fell seriously ill. By 29 May she was beginning to recover, but 'the old freedom of talk has gone'. Arthur had moved out of the commune a week or so previously, after 'awful idiosyncratic rumpuses where temperament met resolute temperament and rent souls wailed and howled their woes'. He returned to the Elite, though he found it 'beastly expensive'.

On 28 May he sent a long illustrated letter to Tabitha, all about the sorrows of his life in Moscow: 'Dor-Dor wishes he and his Babba were lying in the long grass singing their songs and smoking.' It is the letter of a loyal husband and father. But some time that summer Ivy told Tabitha (now eight years old) that 'Dor-Dor' was not being good (not giving them enough money was the alleged offence) and asked her, should she divorce him?

> explaining to me what divorce was and meant. It was a terrible thought to me that she should do this, my Dor-Dor would not be a father any more. But she said yes, he would, and even perhaps come and see us sometimes, but that the court would compel him to provide for us.

Perhaps because of Tabitha's dismay, Ivy wrote to say that she would never agree to a divorce, so, as Evgenia tells it, 'after a lot of heart and conscience searching we decided that as we could not marry we shall live together without being legally married.' The weeks of heart-searching were not comfortable for either of them. Evgenia's temper was at times so bad that Arthur commented amazedly in his diary when she was in 'an odd mild mood'. He caught a snake for her in the woods, which pleased her very much ('E.P. much decenter than usual') but could not keep her in a good temper for ever. However at last the great decision was made:

> (19 June) Snake ate three frogs. Evgenia Petrovna unfriendly, very tired, agreed to go via land, if within ten days, although telephoned blue. Said sick of everything. So am I!!!!

This can only mean that on 19 June Evgenia accepted Arthur's plan to leave Russia. She stuck to it, even though the journey 'by land' was not to occur for more than a month and, even then, was to be extremely circuitous. So it is from this date that we should reckon their union, which was to last for nearly fifty years.

Arthur's wish to leave Russia was understandable. He told Lockhart that 'the show was over'; he meant that he expected the Bolsheviks soon to fall. He could no longer hope for Russo-British reconciliation, at any rate while the war with Germany lasted; and he may have felt that he could do more for that cause, now, outside Russia. In Moscow he was increasingly cut off from his editor, partly by the operations of the Soviet and British censors, but most of all by the suspension of the telegraphic link with England that followed the Allied occupation of Murmansk. He sent only seven telegrams in the whole of June, and only one in July. Radek arranged that messages from him and Price should be sent out by wireless, but that did not stop the British authorities intercepting and suppressing them. It is doubtful when Ransome and Price realised exactly what was happening, but they soon saw that they were doing little good. Price decided to stay on, but Arthur was longing to take Evgenia away on a honeymoon.

It was easier to plan to leave than to do it. Finland was swallowed up in civil war, and there was fighting all along the Trans-Siberian Railway between the Czech Legion and the Bolsheviks. The Germans still held the Ukraine. So time dragged by: a week, a fortnight. Then, on 6 July, Count Mirbach was assassinated by the LSRs, who followed up this exploit by an attempt to seize power from the Bolsheviks, or at any rate to force their way back into the Soviet Government. It was touch-and-go for a few hours, but

2 From a letter to Tabitha, 28 May 1918

DADDA IS BUSY EVERY DAY TRYING TO MAKE
IMPERIALISTS SEE SENSE

OBSERVE THE RAGS
ROWING UNDER THE
IMPERIALIST

THIS IS MEANT TO BE AS
MUCH LIKE A BARN DOOR AS
POSSIBLE. BUT THE IMPERIALIST
WONT SEE IT.

DEAR BABBA YOO MUST ASK MUMMUM TO EXPLAIN
THIS AND SHE WONT BE ABLE. NEVER MIND.
THAT IS BECAUSE SHE IS A GOOD MOMMUM WHAT
KNOWS ALL ABOUT WITCHES AND PUDDINGS AND
DUNKEYS AND BABBAS AND NOTHING WHATEVER ABOUT
POLITICS IF YOO WANT TO KNOW WHAT POLITICS
ARE DORDOR CAN TELL YOU. THEY ARE A KIND OF
PORRIDGE WHICH DORDOR HAS TO EAT THREE WHOLE
PLATESFUL EVERY DAY EVEN WHEN HE'D LIKE TO

3

BE FISHING OR PLAYING CATCH. POLITICS IS
WHAT KEEPS DORDOR IN RUSSIA AND MAKES
HIM SICK

the LSRs were no match for the Communists: soon they were utterly crushed.

The incident prodded Arthur into decisive action. He wrote out a three-page telegram on Mirbach's murder and sent it off, but the material never reached the *Daily News*, probably because the Bolsheviks stopped all foreign cables. It was the last straw, and Arthur did not try to telegraph again until he got out of Russia. Instead he went off to Vologda for the third time, on 10 July. For in the wake of Mirbach's assassination the Bolsheviks were unsure as to what would happen next: perhaps the LSRs would strike at the Allied ambassadors in their place of refuge. The envoys would be safer in Moscow, where (no doubt it was reckoned) they might also be useful hostages if Allied intervention were suddenly to take a more serious turn than the landing at Murmansk. Lenin sent Radek as his emissary to persuade the American ambassador, the French ambassador and the English *chargé d'affaires* to come to Moscow; and Radek took Arthur along, to act as his interpreter and to see fair play.

The mission failed, and a few days later the ambassadors left Russia by way of Archangel, shortly before the Allies landed there. In the story of Arthur's life the trip was important chiefly for the warning Lindley gave. Feeling at Murmansk was so high, said the *chargé d'affaires*, that if Ransome appeared there he would be shot. When Arthur got back to Moscow on 20 July he was in a sombre mood.

During his absence but with his knowledge (though not with Evgenia's) Lockhart had cabled the Foreign Office explaining that 'Trotsky's secretary, a Russian lady of great character and considerable charm', was anxious to leave Russia. She had been of great use to him, and he now asked authorisation for the Consul General to put her on Ransome's passport as his wife. 'I feel we have nothing to risk either from her or from Ransome who is now in favour of Allied intervention.' Even this last statement, which was either a complete misunderstanding of Arthur's attitude or a deliberate lie, failed to move the authorities. Yet Lockhart agreed with Arthur that should the Whites take Moscow, Evgenia's life would be in danger; and he knew (which Arthur did not) that an Allied landing in the north was imminent. The Whites might reach Moscow any day. The British would do little to protect the Bolshevik mistress of a notorious Red journalist. Arthur knew that he was as unpopular with the British in Moscow as with those at Murmansk: Lockhart always showed him the secret service reports denouncing him as a 'Bolshevik agent'. Lockhart himself regarded the reports as a joke, but there were those who differed (including the clownishly incompetent spy Sidney Reilly, who was to bring about Lockhart's own downfall). So a plot was concocted. Without permission from London, Lockhart issued a passport to Ransome on which Evgenia figured as his wife. In this the agent exceeded his powers, and anyway Evgenia was not Arthur's wife. It is probably just as well that the document was never used. But it made Arthur happier to have it.

At last the problem of getting Evgenia out of Russia was solved. Arthur's friend Vorovsky came to his help. He was about to return to Stockholm as the Soviet Government's minister to Sweden, and welcomed the chance of taking such an efficient and experienced secretary with him. Evgenia thought it was all a great fuss about nothing (and as Moscow never did fall to the enemy, she was right) but she went along with the men's plans, leaving for Berlin (with which Moscow was officially at peace) on 27 July, on her way to Stockholm.

Next, Arthur must leave himself. He had already laid his plans. While at Vologda he had got Lindley to agree that it would be as well for him to maintain his friendly links with the Bolsheviks, and he could hardly do that if he stayed in Russia after the intervention (now so clearly at hand) and refused to send anti-British dispatches over the Soviet radio. On the other hand if he made such broadcasts he would lose all credibility in England. Lindley approved of his trip to Stockholm and gave him letters to Sir Esmé Howard and to the Swedish representative in Petrograd to smooth his way. Next Arthur got the Bolsheviks to agree that he could be very useful in Stockholm as a distributor of news from Russia: they promised to send him all the documentation he could require. Better than that, they gave him the means to reach Stockholm. As an Englishman he could not travel openly across either Germany or Finland. Radek gave him credentials as a Soviet courier, and furnished a Lettish soldier to translate his Russian into, 'of all languages, English' for the benefit of the Germans when Arthur crossed their lines.

He was lucky with journeys. On this occasion, though he felt extremely nervous at Helsingfors (he attempted to solve three chess problems to steady his nerves, but could cope with only one) he passed into Sweden without difficulty, helped by the fact that

there was cholera in Petrograd: as he had calculated, this mini-
mised the zeal of the Finnish authorities to detain and examine the
travellers. Arthur reached Stockholm on 5 August. Evgenia did
not arrive until the 28th. Arthur does not describe his emotions
at their reunion, but Evgenia is forthright: 'Our ... setting up
house together in August 1918 was our honeymoon.' She meant
to enjoy it, and was very happy for the next few months. Arthur
admits only that he had 'an almost happy afternoon' two days
after she arrived. It was a perfectly characteristic one. On 30
August he and Captain Leighton, a young Englishman from the
Legation, sailed at Saltsjobaden in a small oak-built cutter. It was
the first time Arthur had been in such a boat since the war broke
out.

Meanwhile, in Russia, civil war was intensifying. News of the
Allied seizure of Archangel reached Moscow on 4 August; on the
5th two hundred French and British residents in the capital, including all the consular staffs of the two nations, were arrested
and imprisoned. On 31 August Lenin was badly wounded in a
nearly successful assassination attempt. The Red Terror began.
Peters arrested Lockhart. Arthur had returned across the border
just in time, thanks once more to Vorovsky, and to Radek.

VII

Lochinvar

So daring in love, and so dauntless in war

SIR WALTER SCOTT

Arthur's most pressing concern, on his arrival in Stockholm, was to re-establish himself in his job. During the past few months he had been more and more confined to the sidelines, largely unable to influence events or even to report them. Now was his chance to get into action again.

It was not easy. Britain was at war with the Bolsheviks, and the powers in Whitehall looked with extreme disfavour on the activities of Ransome and Price. There was a real risk that Arthur would not be allowed to function from Stockholm any more than he had lately been from Moscow. To get round this he sought out his old acquaintance Sir Esmé Howard and presented him with Lindley's letter. Howard was sufficiently impressed to send a series of telegrams to the Foreign Office making the point that although Ransome was now working completely on the Bolshevik side he might nevertheless be of great use, having such excellent sources, in gathering information for the British, so long as he was allowed to report from Stockholm. Ransome went along with this approach to the extent of writing at least two intelligence reports for the Foreign Office, which responded by agreeing that he might be allowed to stay.

That did not answer the central question, which was, should he be allowed to function as a correspondent? Back and forth went the plaintive memoranda. Gaselee, of the Foreign Office, thought that Ransome had been 'rather tiresome' at Petrograd, sending inflammatory Bolshevik messages; his telegrams ought now to be very carefully scrutinised by the Press Bureau and the Home Office to make sure that no Bolshevik opinions got loose, by this means, in Britain. Wardrop, the Consul-General in Moscow, warned that 'Radek's intimate friend, the sharer of his domestic hearth, Mr Arthur Ransome' would relay Radek's latest burst of anti-British invective to the *Daily News* unless stopped. Cook of the Press Bureau, answering Gaselee, complained that the War Office seemed to want to censor Ransome's telegrams not on military but on political grounds, and worried that the Bureau might 'get into difficulties' (i.e. Gardiner might raise a storm) 'if we stop Ransome too much.' In reply Gaselee, painfully astonished that he had not been understood, spelt out exactly how he proposed to make a cat's paw of Ransome and his editor:

I do not think that we should contemplate for a moment the course of telling the *Daily News* that Mr Ransome's telegrams will not be allowed through to them. That would defeat the very object which we have in view, which is to keep Mr Ransome at his post, because by being in touch with the Bolsheviks in Russia, he will probably be a valuable source of information. We must simply go on looking closely at the messages he sends, cutting out what is actually harmful, but still, I hope, leaving enough to make him go on sending messages, and his paper continue to keep him where he is.

Ransome cannot have known exactly what was going on, Howard being more discreet than Lockhart, but he had a shrewd idea, and to minimise the interference of the censors he eschewed in the coming months almost all mention of the intervention in his telegrams. It was just as well, as by October the Foreign Office was wondering whether to prosecute him and Price for offences under the Defence of the Realm Act (the notorious Dora) or even for high treason. There was gross inconsistency in this, for Arthur was shortly to be used in negotiations with the Bolsheviks, giving his services to his country in his usual straightforward fashion. In return he was insulted and harassed. But the episode makes entertaining reading nowadays, and well illustrates how entirely the Bolshevik Revolution had unnerved the British ruling class. All too plainly, Whitehall was more anxious about the effect that Bolshevik propaganda might have on opinion at home than about the possibility that the newspapers might compromise operations at Archangel and Murmansk.

Armed neutrality with the Government having been established, Arthur next found that he had some explaining to do to his editor. On 11 August, six days after his arrival, he sent Gardiner an immensely long letter, through the British Foreign Office, in which he gave a lively account of his escape from Russia, indicated what arrangements he had made for getting news, and discussed the present state of affairs. The letter crossed one to him, in which Gardiner said that he thought Stockholm was much the best place for Arthur at the moment, and then, in guarded language, indicated that he hoped Ransome would not embarrass the *News* by writing in too pro-Bolshevik and anti-interventionist a vein:

> The *Daily News* is committed, not to the theories of a party, but to the principles of the Revolution. It is the consolidation of the Revolution that should be the aim of the Allies and it follows that the touchstone of any intervention must be the consent of the general body of the people and not the interests of property or the manipulation of political currents against the sentiment of the nation. I am speaking in generalities, but I think you will understand what I have in mind and my purpose in writing.

The editor was rather at sea about Russia. A leading article of 13 August shows that he had lost sight of Ransome's basic insight, that the Bolsheviks were the most reliably anti-German force in Russia. Instead, Gardiner said he saw some merit in Lloyd George's view that Bolshevik rule was now based on force and terror alone, and that its effect was to rivet German domination on Russia. At the same time he thought that power was passing from the hands of Lenin and Trotsky, and hoped that they would be succeeded by forces 'disposed to stand for the idea of national self-assertion as against the exploitation of the country by Germany'.

After reading Arthur's letter Gardiner changed his tone. For one thing his correspondent quite agreed that, intervention being an accomplished fact, there could be no good in endlessly denouncing it: 'the thing to do is to see what can be done in the new conditions, regardless as to whether they are not worse than those one had hoped could be created.' For another, he showed that his journey to Stockholm had the support of the British authorities:

reassuring to an editor who did not want to drift too far into opposition. Then Arthur had reiterated his view that, although Allied intervention shut up the lion of German imperialism with the lamb of the Soviet Revolution, it was impossible for such an unnatural partnership to last very long: indeed, the Bolsheviks were already subverting it, for example by supporting partisan warfare in the Ukraine, and Germany would certainly suppress the revolutionary Government as soon as she was free to do so. 'There is such a lot to talk about that I can't help zigzagging into digressions. The main point is, what will happen, now that non-recognition and intervention are forcing the lamb into the rather unwilling jaws of the lion, who is not at all sure how good the lamb is going to be for his digestion.' Even if Germany did capture Moscow and overthrow the Bolsheviks, all would not be lost. 'It takes fewer people to disorganise a country than to run it', and the Bolsheviks, if driven underground, would be thoroughly effective saboteurs, as one of their leaders had told him: Germany would be unable to run a single train unguarded,

she will find factories breaking down, munition stores blowing up, workmen striking, peasants revolting, telegraphs and tele-phones going wrong, etc. etc. so that even if she does not try to steal bread, she will yet be forced to repressive measures which in their turn will create such resentment as the Ukrainian resentment.

The Brest peace and the subsequent behaviour of the Germans had generated widespread anti-German bitterness, and before the intervention at Archangel the Soviet ambassador in Berlin had repeatedly urged collaboration between Russia and England against German ambitions in the Ukraine and Turkistan (Arthur had seen some of his reports, no doubt thanks to Radek). The Soviets would certainly resist those ambitions, whatever England did, which could only be good news.

Gardiner replied to this in high feather:

I find your letter in spite of its very natural zig-zaggings pro-digiously illuminating. You cannot understand how befogged one gets at this end of things with all the perplexities and com-plexities of the Russian movement and it is immensely valuable to get them periodically elucidated, even if the elucidation comes, as it necessarily must come, after the situation dealt with had probably ceased to exist ... I hope that you will find time to let me have an occasional memorandum like the present one, on your more intimate views in regard to the situation.

Ransome had no more problems with his editor for several months.

The cabling resumed on 14 August. At first most of the telegrams concerned the civil war in Finland, in which one party, the Whites, fought to establish a German protectorate, while the other, the Reds, though nominally in alliance with the Bolsheviks, really depended for succour on the Allied force at Murmansk. Ransome, like most other people, had no idea how near Germany was to collapse, so, like many others, he was afraid that she might stage an attack on Murmansk and Russia through Finland. He wrote in this sense to his paper, thereby offering some justification for the Allied presence in the north. Some of his telegrams resumed the business of reporting and interpreting the Russian Revolution to the English. He told of food shortages in Moscow and Petrograd: an eighth of a pound was the daily bread allowance in Moscow, he said, 'and that was often not bread but a compound of straw'. Matters were even worse in Petrograd, where he had seen people dropping down in the streets and on railway stations from hunger-fostered diseases; nevertheless an anti-cholera campaign had been better organised than any such under the old order. 'This was largely due to the energy of Zinoviev, president of the Petrograd Commune, who by his success in that capacity has earned his inclusion in a triumvirate with Lenin and Trotsky.' He wrote of conditions in the countryside, once more palliating what was perhaps Lenin's most disastrous mistake:

A new phrase entered the revolutionary vocabulary, *kulak*, meaning 'tight fist' or 'rich peasant' and from that moment the revolutionary struggle reached the Russian peasantry ... hence the political significance of what were known as 'supply detachments' of armed workingmen and agitators who were sent out into the country districts with the double object of taking bread from the *kulaks* and showing the poorer peasantry that their interests and those of the *kulaks* were opposed and not identical.

However, even Arthur noticed that things did not go exactly according to plan:

> In many districts this policy was entirely successful. In others the *kulaks* succeeded in getting the poorer peasantry to resist what they represented as an attack on the peasantry as a whole. Colouring to this was often given by the misbehaviour of the 'supply detachments' which were often very difficult to control.

Readers of the *Daily News* were presumably more interested in the question of how events in Russia would affect the war, and Ransome devoted most of his space to this topic. He lost no opportunity of rubbing in the fact that the treaty of Brest-Litovsk had been ruinous for Russo–German relations: 'An observant German attached to the German embassy in Moscow remarked the other day "We Germans, by giving the Russians peace, seem to have succeeded in giving them what they never had before: a national spirit." '

Then came the news of the attempt on Lenin's life. Ransome wrote a long obituary of the victim, 'the most colossal dreamer that Russia has produced in our time', for use if necessary; and he added that the rumours that Lenin never moved without guards were

> absolutely false, both concerning him and Trotsky. Both Trotsky and Lenin laugh at the efforts of their assistants to protect them. Trotsky, for example, more than once, impatient after waiting for a motor, has set off on foot until pursued and captured by his harassed secretary.

Ransome was in a good position to learn such stories.

He played down Sverdlov's 'idiotic statement' that the Allies were behind the attack on Lenin: 'I do not think the accusation will have any serious results, and the suggestion of mass terror which accompanied it means nothing, because there can be no such thing unless the mass feels inclined to terrorize, which it does not.' This was one of Arthur's less fortunate observations. The assassination attempt was followed by the Red Terror, the September Massacres of the Russian Revolution. The Cheka descended on the gaols and murdered the political prisoners, without making any serious attempt to show that they had been involved in the affair. The Bolsheviks urged the soviets to purge the bourgeoisie with lynchings and hostage-takings. 'Not more than six hundred people were shot by the Moscow Cheka alone,' Peters was to record, as if this were moderation itself. Ransome would later spend much fruitless time trying to establish exactly the number and circumstances of the casualties.

He immediately, sadly, conceded that 'persuasion by assassination' had returned to Russia as a weapon of party politics.

> Political feeling runs far higher among the politicians than in the mass of the people, and each party is coming to the point when it considers all the others as the enemies of God and man. Whatever Government may be in power, its members will be subject to such attempts ... but in no case will assassination be the expression of the people's will. It will always be the expression of some small inner ring of determined politicians.

The position of the English in Russia, already delicate enough because of intervention, was now shattered. On 31 August, the day after Lenin's wounding, a mob, inspired by the Cheka, invaded the British Embassy building in Petrograd and murdered Captain Cromie, who was trying to defend it. Lockhart was arrested, released, and then, on 4 September, arrested again.

This news threw Arthur into frightful confusion. As ever he was not backward in doing what he could for his friends, his country and Anglo-Russian relations. At the suggestion of Captain Leighton he sent off a long telegram to Radek, pointing out the deplorable effect that Cromie's murder would have in England, warning him that the British Government would hold the Bolsheviks personally accountable, and urging the instant release of Lockhart and his staff, since otherwise the whole affair would confirm English official circles in their belief that the Bolsheviks were pro-German. Radek sent back what Arthur's *Autobiography* describes as a 'reassuring' message. Since it said that Lockhart was in prison and was not being shot only to avoid providing propaganda for 'Jingo', it is hard to imagine who, beside Arthur, can have been reassured. Radek was not in conciliatory mood. In this very month he composed a vitriolic attack on 'the Allied bandits' to stand as his introduction to a reissue of *The Truth about Russia*. In a later letter to Arthur he dismissed Lockhart as a 'little careerist', and poured scorn on Arthur's scepticism about the Red Terror: it would be very serious, he said.

Arthur's reassurance never went deep. At first he entirely disbelieved the allegations of a 'Lockhart Plot', and although he later had to admit (Lockhart admitted it himself) that his friends had been most indiscreet, nevertheless his scepticism was on the whole justified. But Lockhart was not really a problem. After the first few days' confinement his life was never in danger, and after a month of diplomatic wrangling he was released in exchange for Maxim Litvinov, who was at the same time set free from Brixton prison. The murder of Cromie was another matter. Arthur had known and liked him. He also respected Peters and Dzerzhinsky. On 5 September he sent a telegram in which, among other things, he described Peters as a person 'of scrupulous honesty, who during the Revolution made friends both among the English and the Americans in Russia'; next day he sent a tribute to Dzerzhinsky:

> He is a calm, cool-headed fanatic for the revolution with absolute trust in his own conscience and recognising no higher court. He has been much in prison where he was remarkable for his urgent desire to take upon himself unpleasant labour for other criminals such as cleaning cells and emptying slops. He has a theory of self-sacrifice in which one man has to take on himself the unpleasantness that would otherwise be shared by many. Hence his willingness to occupy his present position. He would not act in such a case as this, nor allow his subordinates to act, unless he was personally convinced that some such plot existed.

Arthur's only explanation of how it was that the noble Cromie could have been killed by the subordinates of the noble Dzerzhinsky was that the Bolsheviks had been misled by 'fabricators'.

It would not do. Cromie's murder caused a wave of passionate rage in the surviving diplomatic community in Russia, and in the Foreign Office in London. Arthur's propensity to make excuses for the assassins could not go unnoticed, and deepened the distrust in which he was held.

At this time Arthur himself became the object of some 'fabrication'. There survives in his papers an unsigned document (how it came into his hands is unknown), dated 11 September 1918. It is addressed from the American Consulate General in Moscow, a building which, since the rupture of Russo-American relations that followed the start of intervention, had been taken over by the Norwegian diplomatic mission. Some of Lockhart's staff were standing a siege there while the Cheka attempted to starve them out. Among them was Captain William Hicks, Lockhart's second-in-command. During his imprisonment he occupied himself by compiling this report, largely consisting of gossip about the Bolsheviks, but also making serious allegations against Arthur and Philips Price. Ransome, he said,

> has been in close and friendly relations with the Soviet leaders throughout but, in the month of June last promised Mr. Lockhart that if he would recommend H.M.G. to grant him a passport and obtain for him permission to live in Stockholm, he would occupy himself with the collecting of information concerning the Revolution only, and would entirely cease his propaganda work. [Indignant marginal note in Ransome's handwriting: 'Show this to Lockhart, who knows that every word is untrue.'] The passport was obtained entirely on Mr. Lockhart's recommendation. Our first doubts were raised when Mr. Ransome left Moscow without saying a word to us and when he already knew that our position was extremely dangerous. He had already told us that there was a party in the Soviet, headed by Radek, which wished to go to extreme lengths with us on account of our landing at Archangel. This was followed, almost immediately, by our first arrest and Ransome left while our fate was still undecided. [Ransome: 'Rubbish. I was already out of Russia.'] His influence with the Soviet was considerable and it appears to Mr Lockhart and myself that if he was too indifferent to exercise it on behalf of British subjects he does not deserve the protection of British Nationality. We are further informed that he is, in spite of his definite promise, continuing his propaganda work from Stockholm.

It is easy to see the real events behind their garbling in this document. One is the incident of Evgenia Petrovna's passport, and the 'propaganda work' referred to is presumably *The Truth about Russia* (this is the only evidence that it was ever noticed in official circles). Unfortunately Whitehall was in no position to detect the garbling. It may be that some well-placed friend – Leighton, perhaps – showed the document to Arthur for his comments. Perhaps his refutation found its way to high places. Yet it would not be surprising if the Foreign Office, taking into consideration Lockhart's telegrams, Arthur's journalism, his unquestionable intimacy with the Bolshevik leaders and the various other malignant reports that were received, came to the conclusion that Ransome was at best thoroughly tricky and at worst a committed Bolshevik. Such a view would have been inconceivable to anyone who really knew him, but there was no such person in the Office. When the Hicks allegations came to the notice of Lord Robert Cecil he ordered that steps be taken to see if criminal charges could be brought against Ransome and Price, and that their employers be told of the allegations.[1]

Stockholm, like any neutral capital on the edge of a great conflict, was full of spies and refugees, including a great many White Russians, which cannot have been comfortable for Evgenia. She and Arthur had found lodgings at Igelboda on the sea-approach to the city where there were waters in which Arthur could fish for pike. In spite of this amenity he was less happy than she was. He always responded magnificently to a crisis, but in day-to-day living the anxiety which his childhood had implanted caused him to fret excessively over trifles, or over problems about which nothing could be done. He was dependent on England for money and the right sort of tobacco, and they were both slow in coming through. The outcome of the war and of the Revolution were still obscure to him. Evgenia's position was anomalous: what would happen to her if the Swedes turned against the Bolsheviks, or if a White regime were established in Moscow? A long stream of English visitors came to the house, many of whom attacked Arthur for his Bolshevik sympathies, and probably looked askance at the Red with whom he was living. Fortunately Evgenia as yet spoke little English and understood none (she would soon pick it up) and was oblivious of what was said.

Arthur got on with his telegrams, fished when he could, and occasionally tried to refresh his mind by working at a sequel to *Old Peter*. He completed only a handful of fresh stories. Some of them got into the magazines, but only one, 'The Soldier and Death', ever reached book form in his lifetime, in 1920. It is a more grim and witty tale than anything in *Old Peter*, and in mood

---

1 The Director of Public Prosecutions said that no grounds for prosecution existed.

is not very far from Stravinsky's *Soldier's Tale*, with which it has several details in common.

It was a comfort to be getting letters from his family and friends in England once more. Yet they too required explanations, which led him to be wholly explicit about his attitude to the Revolution as he had not been in even his frankest telegrams.

(*To his mother, 2 October, Stockholm*) I've had letters from Barbara, who says that the Skald is vigorously anti-Bolshevik, and prepared to have a free fight with me on the subject. Well, I've only met about three likeable Bolsheviks myself, and they mostly likeable because of something extraneous to their Bolshevism, Radek, for instance, who knows Shakespeare better than I do, and is prepared to talk brilliantly on anything under the sun, and is full of admiration for British Imperialism, which he hates at the same time. No one who knows Radek can dislike him, and certainly no Englishman could dislike him who had ever heard him describe how in Trafalgar Square he was suddenly enlightened, like Saint Paul, and, a small comic figure he must have been, looking up at the stone lions, wished he could have been an imperialist and an English imperialist, if only he had not had the misfortune to be born a Pole and a Bolshevik.

Most of them, however, are not human figures like that at all. They are a pigheaded, narrowminded set of energetic lunatics, energetic like as if they were possessed by seven devils apiece, and each one of them capable of getting through the amount of work that would be done by twenty ordinary Russians.

None the less I sympathise with them very much, because in Russia they took on a job that would have broken any other Russians, and, of course, will eventually break them. Also, such an infernal number of lies are told about them by the other and more incompetent Russians, that I am driven to be more pro them than I otherwise should be. Also, I think that we could have made much better use of them, if only we had not allowed ourselves to take other Russians at their face value, and the Bolsheviks at the value set upon them by their enemies ...

I think the Soviet form of government a most ingenious combination of central directive with local autonomy admirably suited to Russia, and I think that the natural course of things would have allowed the extremist character of its inception to mellow into something of a very satisfactory kind. As it is, it is being forced to fight, and therefore is likely to become more instead of less excessive.

He was still sceptical about the reports of a Red Terror, finding such horrors possible but not probable, 'and I cannot telegraph them as facts'. He was appalled to see the score of injury and hate rising 'between the two peoples I belong to and care for most', and he made a most prescient observation:

One thing is quite clear; that we and the Germans together are hammering into the Russian people (by seizing their land and cutting off their food supplies in the East) such a hatred of every kind of foreigner that it is quite possible that the little handful of Internationalists who made the Soviet Revolution may find that they have on their hands one of the most Nationalist nations in the world.

This exposition of his views seems harmless enough today; but on reflection Arthur decided not to send it, probably because it might be stopped by the censor. Instead he wrote another version of the letter, confining himself to family matters and to a description of his life in Stockholm.

(*To his mother, 2 October, second version*) I do wish I could come home and see you and my beloved Tabitha. I simply long to see that blessed brat. And thanks to the way things have turned out, I think it will be ages before I can.

And I am getting so tired of work. Here it's harder in a way even than it was in Russia, because I have another language to deal with for all ordinary news, and I am setting myself to know as much about what happens in Moscow as if I were there, which means far more careful work over printed stuff than was necessary on the spot. I get all the papers published in Moscow, and a good lot of the Petrograd ones, and masses of pamphlets, and I get up at 7.30 and never get to bed before 12.30, and, literally, am at it the whole day long ... With much love, your busy and unpopular son.

He mentioned neither Evgenia nor Ivy to his mother, nor was he to do so while he remained in Stockholm. As to politics, he remained as certain as ever that the Allied intervention in Russia was a fearful mistake. It was not the right time for the British Legation, following up its earlier contacts (and presumably not taking London alarms very seriously), to approach him with a view to obtaining his services as a spy. Yet that is apparently what occurred on 27 September. The actual diary entry reads simply: 'Wyatt made his proposal', but the typed, somewhat written-up version made when Arthur was preparing his *Autobiography* reads: 'One Wyatt made his silly proposal allegedly on behalf of F.O.' It is difficult to imagine what this can mean except that he was asked in some way to exploit his Bolshevik contacts while acting as a paid intelligence agent for the British Government – exactly what many Bolsheviks must have suspected him of doing anyway. To be sure, Arthur had already, unpaid, passed on intelligence to HMG and acted as an unofficial intermediary; but it is clear that Wyatt had gone beyond the line.

Where Arthur drew that line is nevertheless far from clear. The war was at last visibly coming to an end: on 7 October the Scandinavian papers were full of peace news. But the Russian crisis continued, so did British involvement in it, so did Arthur's sense of duty to his country. The head of the Foreign Office intelligence network in Stockholm, who also had close contacts with MI6, was Clifford Sharp, the editor of the *New Statesman*. No doubt Arthur, as an occasional contributor to that paper, had met Sharp before, in London; yet even if they had previously known each other only on paper it was inevitable that they should see a fair amount of each other in Stockholm, for they were fairly close politically, above all on the matter of Russia. Both during Sharp's wartime absence and after his return the *New Statesman* advocated a conciliatory attitude to the Bolsheviks. However it does not appear that the two men actually had much contact until early October, when Lockhart, fresh from incarceration in the Kremlin, arrived in Stockholm on his way home. Arthur met him and his party at the railway station, and later reported that Lockhart's first words were, 'You know, in spite of everything I am still against intervention.' According to Lockhart, Arthur was 'very worried about his fate and still more about his girl.' There is no need to doubt the superficial accuracy of these observations, but they seem more revealing of the state of mind of their authors than of their subjects. Lockhart, the architect of a discredited policy, had every reason to expect a chilly reception in London, and had left an adored mistress behind him in Moscow; Arthur, as we shall see, was getting more and more fretful about the Allied intervention and his own position in regard to it.

He and Lockhart would soon be on opposite sides of the political fence, though their personal relations would always remain excellent. In the mean time their meeting was useful to Arthur, not only because it enabled him to learn more about the so-called 'Lockhart Plot', the alleged details of which the Soviet Government was blaring forth to the world, but because it forced him at last to admit the occurrence of the Red Terror. On 9 October he telegraphed to the *Daily News* about the childish ferocity of the Bolsheviks. After giving an account of Lockhart's experiences, he went on:

Ferocious is not too strong a word to describe the treatment of some of the [British] prisoners, who starved of course, like the rest of Moscow, but were compelled while starving to live in damp cells together with criminals suffering from filthy diseases ... With regard to the effect abroad, the utter childishness of their calculations is shown by the treatment of Corporal Miller, a member of the British Labour Party though of Polish origin. Before the war he worked at Pontefract. Miller was first arrested at the British Consulate, but while he was arrested, sitting in a room together with a few very careless guards, Miller, seeing that he was unobserved, slipped quietly upstairs and hid, I believe under a bed, in one of the upper rooms of the labyrinthine old house which long ago was a hunting lodge of Ivan the Terrible. Later he made his way out and escaped over the garden wall. When he was finally seized he was taken before Peters who asked him what were his politics? Miller replied that his paper was the *Daily News*. 'That Radical paper?' said Peters. Miller told him he was a member of the Labour Party. 'They are worse than our Right Social Revolutionaries,' said Peters, in whose eyes of course Ramsay MacDonald is something of a Tory, and he sent poor Miller off to prison. Miller describes the room in the prison from which people were taken off to be shot – thirty in ten days ... On the wall was a list of prisoners who had written their names, many of the executed were among them ... At the bottom of the list Miller wrote 'Here Miller, member of the British Labour Party, completed his education in Soviet socialism.'

Ransome received further enlightenment when Major Wardwell of the American Red Cross arrived in Stockholm from Russia. He had news of the English prisoners captured on the Archangel front, and painted a graphic picture of starvation in Petrograd and Moscow. Arthur asked him about 'the truth of the mass terror'. Wardwell replied that the mass of the people seemed to take no interest in events, but that the terror was real enough. It was probably worst in the provinces, but

> The thing that made the most terrible impression on me was the indifference of the young girls in the Extraordinary Commission. They seemed absolutely unaware that they were dealing with human lives. Relatives would come in to enquire from one, then another, the fate of the prisoners. A young girl would turn up a ledger as if consulting an account and reply 'Shot' or 'Unknown' with the most utter disregard of the effect on the unfortunate questioner. Sometimes in the outer room of the Extraordinary Commission half a dozen persons would be in hysterics at once. It seemed that these girls had lost sight of humanity altogether. For them the prisoners were counter-revolutionaries, not human beings.

Wardwell said that the Cheka was not under proper control, and that Peters, though an honest man in himself, was dangerous as an institution.

Arthur listened to all this in growing dismay, and in particular anxiety for a colleague, Marsden of the *Morning Post*. He was one of the Englishmen who had been arrested at the same time as Lockhart. Not all had yet been released. Most of these prisoners were of military age, and if liberated might theoretically have been conscripted into the Allied anti-Bolshevik forces; but Marsden was too old. On his own responsibility Arthur sent a telegram to Moscow asking for his release, and then told the *Daily News* what he had done.

He was not the man to neglect any channel. He did not much mind whether he influenced British public opinion or the British Government, or both. The important thing was not to miss an opportunity. So his diary shows him lunching with Clifford Sharp the day after Lockhart left Stockholm; and no doubt the two men saw each other on occasions not recorded in the diary (which is scrappy for this period). Arthur's character was in his favour here. It was impossible for anyone who met him to distrust him for long; and then, it is in the nature of intelligence services to try to make use of all who come their way. MI6 and Arthur, in short, were each trying to exploit the other; but whereas MI6 was not very clear as to what it wanted or expected from the association, Arthur knew exactly what he hoped to achieve: the alteration of policy by means of information.

Yet it is no wonder that he was growing very sick of his position.

(*To his mother, 12 October*) How I do long to be quit of revolutions ... I would so like to have a couple of months to spend on a new children's book. Children go on and on. The sight of them was the one thing that made me bear up when in woe these last few months. Revolts may come revolts may go, but brats go on for ever. And, I would like to do a perfectly stunning brat book ... Barbara gave me some good advice, when I left England last year, not to let myself get drawn into politics but to stick to my tales. For my own sake, materially speaking, I wish I had followed it. But, as an honest man, I could not, and there is an end of it.

He meant that he had hoped, through his reporting, to help avert a war between England and the Bolsheviks; now he hoped that he might help bring the actual war to an end. News of Bolshevik atrocities was not encouraging, even though he believed that the atrocities were ultimately caused by the Allied invasion ('Terror depends on terror in the executioner as well as on terror in the executed'). He began to wonder if cabling from Stockholm was really the best way of explaining the Russian Revolution to the British people.

(*To his mother, 27 October*) I have no personal news, except that I may very likely be seceding from the *Daily News*. Temporarily at any rate. You see the position is too jolly difficult. I am quite sure I am right about Russia, and that time will prove it, as indeed, it is already proving it in the north. But to write what I think at the present moment would do harm rather than good.

At least, so I judge. I therefore rather want to be able to shut up publicly while continuing to keep watch on events in Russia and report on them privately, at any rate until events prove clearly whether I was right or wrong. It's a tough job anyhow, having an opinion which is only held by about two other people. The only satisfaction is that the other two folk, one of whom, the Frenchman, I do not know, are the only other two foreigners who got as near the inside of Soviet affairs as I did myself. I mean by that that we three have a real right to our opinion ... [2]

Also I am most unholy tired. And I can't stop and take a holiday ... If I were to let go for a fortnight I'd never get hold again without going back. Which latter, of course, I awfully desire ... I watch the steamers leaving Stockholm, and slipping out at night through the long line of low rocky lake country hillocks that leads to the Baltic and so to Russia, and a good lump of me gets as far as my throat in an effort to follow them.

To cold common sense it might be hard to see what Arthur found so attractive in the thought of a return to starving, war-torn Bolshevik Russia. In Stockholm he had work to do, Evgenia was with him, and he could retreat to England if necessary. But Arthur's attitude to Russia was anything but coldly sensible. The sentimental streak which Lockhart had noticed now predominated. After he took up with Evgenia he seems to have felt as if he had assumed a second nationality; but his main feeling, indeed his passionate belief, was that the people of Russia, the peasants and the industrial workers, Old Peter and Young Ivan, had taken control of their destiny; that the Soviet Government was *their* Government, the Revolution *their* Revolution; he identified himself wholly with their cause, and wanted to go back to record their victory and, perhaps, contribute to it.

Being Arthur, and in a difficult position, he could not easily make up his mind to any course of action. The question of Evgenia's future was a distracting worry. All was well so long as she could stay in Stockholm, but the pressure on the Swedish Government was intense, and at any moment Vorovsky and his mission might be ordered out of the country. Evgenia might have to go with them, since it was far from clear that Arthur would be

2 The Frenchman was Jacques Sadoul. The third foreigner was presumably Philips Price.

allowed to take her to England, even if she agreed to go there.
Then there was the pressure of his private wishes. However hard-
worked he was at Stockholm, his life there was much more normal
than it had been in Russia, and, inevitably, his literary ambitions
began to revive. Not that he had much hope of them. He told his
mother:

> I doubt if I shall ever write again. The dear good wild mad
> practical impractical credulous suspicious purblind clearsighted
> infernally energetic Bolsheviks fondly imagine that I am writing
> their history. I fondly imagined I should write it myself. But,
> as a matter of fact, I have not written one line of that said history
> since I got to Stockholm. I have written masses of notes, but
> that is all I have time for. And as for sustained writing, as for
> English prose, on which once I rather fancied myself, it's gone
> for good. I am more than ever convinced that I am finished *qua*
> writer, and as I have no intention of setting up as a politician,
> my ambitions are getting smaller every day, and are practically
> circumscribed by a cottage in the country, a trout stream, and
> some winter pike fishing. Russia has broken stouter hearts than
> mine.

Even his faith in the Revolution tottered as he pondered the
significance of the Cheka. He did not realise — and never was to do
so — that the Cheka owed much of its power, energy and criminal-
ity directly to Lenin's will. He began to expect a crisis of legitimacy,
a struggle between the Bolshevik Government and its creature.
'If the Extraordinary Commission wins in that struggle it will be
impossible for the Revolution to hope to recover a normal pulse.'
The Cheka had already inflicted great damage on the cause. Its
excesses were wrong in themselves, they alienated foreign public
opinion, they seemed to be creating a Government within the
Government. The Cheka seemed to be under no control but its
own, and, having its own troops, might even resist a Government
attempt to curb it. Arthur tried to persuade himself and his readers
that the solutions to the problems of Soviet Russia's internal and
external policies were one and the same:

> Many of the same moderates who wish to curtail the sinister
> liberty of the Extraordinary Commission are looking ahead,

and would welcome any chance of finding a *modus vivendi* with
the Allies. They reason that if the war ends, so does the need for
an Eastern Front, and that the Allies, finding that the population
as a whole is unwilling to take arms against the Soviets, will
not be anxious to undertake the occupation of a hostile country.

He reported that Litvinov had passed through Stockholm on his
way to Petrograd, and had promised to do his utmost to secure
the release of Marsden and of Rennet, Arthur's predecessor as
Daily News correspondent. But for someone who hoped to foster
Anglo-Russian understanding, these were paltry pickings, and
there was little prospect of better.

The world war ended with the armistice of 11 November, but
the Allied intervention in Russia, to widespread bafflement, went
on. Many arguments were offered, at the time and later, within
and without the bureaucracies and cabinets, as to why this was.
One favourite explanation was that the Allies were bound in
honour to support the anti-Bolshevik forces which they had encouraged; another was that unless the Allies maintained a presence
in the East, a dangerous Russo-German alliance would arise to
threaten the peace of the world – whether an alliance between a
revolutionary Russia and a revolutionary Germany, or between
two restored reactionary regimes, did not matter. The real reason
seems to have been that Allied, and especially British, forces were
so thoroughly committed to intervention that they could not be
withdrawn without loss of face and military difficulty. In other
words, the intervention would continue because it had started.
The impression of muddle and short-sightedness is reinforced by
the declarations made at the time by Balfour, who had a genius
for spreading darkness over any subject he examined. Lockhart's
sensible contention that there was no viable middle course between all-out war with the Bolsheviks and coming to terms with
them was not the sort of thing that Balfour ever listened to.

If the end of the war robbed the interventionists of the best
justification for their policy, it did the same for those who advocated withdrawal. Ransome had always argued that the Bolsheviks
were worth supporting because they were the most effective anti-
German force in Russia; now it did not matter what their attitude
to Germany was.

He went on writing his telegrams, filling them with speculation
about the prospects of a Bolshevik revolution in Germany, but he

felt more than ever that such activity was no longer useful. So he wavered between going home and returning to Moscow.

(*To his mother, 12 November*) I do most awfully want to come home. This last year has had such a lot in it, of such a brain-tearing, heart-wearing, and latterly heart-breaking kind, that I feel I have been away from home for a very long time indeed. And, as you know, a year ago when I was in town, it was such a hectic Russian period that I was really mostly in Petrograd. It seems at least five years since I was really solidly with both feet in England.

The *Daily News* sent me some tobacco, including four blocks of black plug, guaranteed to kill at ten yards. I cut up some, stuffed it in a clay pipe and at the first puff I was back at home drinking beer with Lascelles Abercrombie in the Hark to Melody by Haverthwaite. Then I was talking to the charcoal burners who used to bake clay pipes for me in the wood above Coniston. Then I was in a good old stinking Furness Railway third-class carriage with a lot of miners going oop Millom way. It's no good; the Russian Revolution has failed utterly in alter-ing me personally. And once I get a little peace and quiet, and get my sketch of the development of the Revolution written, I shall write FINIS and fetch politics a good boost with a boot in the latter parts, and return with no regrets whatever to pen, ink, tobacco, fishing and the lake country.

What seems to have been nagging him most was the undertaking he had given to the Bolsheviks to write a history of the Revolu-tion. They had promised to let him back into Russia whenever he wanted to come for purposes of research; but how could he go back to Russia while his country was at war with her? How could he find the time and the energy to write a book while he had to file telegrams?

At the very end of November Litvinov returned to Stockholm. The Soviet Government had started a 'peace offensive' at the beginning of the month, and Stockholm, the only capital where the Bolsheviks could have direct contact with the outside world, was its most important theatre. Litvinov was officially no more than a commercial attaché, but the day after his arrival he sought out Arthur as his best means of disseminating the news that he was, in fact, fully empowered to open negotiations with England.

This was Arthur's best opportunity for the past eleven months to influence British policy. He sent off a telegram at once:

(*30 November*) In Moscow he [Litvinov] personally visited the British prisoners, and reports that there is one Englishman in prison in Petrograd, in Moscow about twelve including naval and some army officers captured in the north, and persons implicated in the alleged conspiracy. They told him that conditions were much improved, they were satisfied but complained of boredom. They receive parcels freely. The interned English of military age have been released. They are freely walking about Moscow. Litvinov had promised to communicate with the prisoners' relatives, but the list of addresses was in his diplomatic valise which was seized by the Finns ... He said, 'We want peace. We do not know what the Allies want from us, but we are prepared to make concessions on all questions except those concerning internal affairs. The immediate payment of our debts is impossible, but a moratorium might be arranged, with a compromise such as commercial concessions.'

Arthur also seems to have acted as Litvinov's intermediary with the British Legation. Not only did he pass on the points made in his telegram, but also the information that the Bolsheviks were prepared to give compensation for the murder of Cromie, and that Litvinov wanted to be put in direct communication with some members of the Legation.

These messages provoked a lively discussion within the British Government, but the Imperial War Cabinet was still too deeply divided to come to any agreement on the Russian question. Some, such as Curzon and Churchill, favoured a greatly strengthened intervention; others, above all Lloyd George, leant towards a hands-off policy. Since no choice could be made, the contradictory policy of drift favoured by Balfour continued to prevail: for the time being the intervention would go on, but it would not be reinforced; no contact would be made with the Bolsheviks, and pious protestations against any idea of taking sides in the Russian civil war would still contradict the plain facts. The only difference that emerged was that the Foreign Office was no longer quite sure that the Bolshevik regime was certain to fall. When, in the middle of December, Arthur told the Legation that Litvinov now had definite proposals to make, the Cabinet was at first interested, but the Foreign Office (or perhaps only Balfour) dallied, the French protested, and the opportunity was lost.

More important for Arthur's personal future were the unmistakable signs of a change in British public opinion. No longer distracted by the war with Germany, people were beginning to notice that sizeable British forces were deployed all round the edges of the former Russian Empire, apparently for the purpose of fighting the Bolsheviks. On 7 December the *Daily News* carried its first leading article on Russia since August, demanding an explanation of Government policy in Russia and an end to the censorship of foreign cables. The *Manchester Guardian* had issued much the same demand a fortnight earlier, and ministers were getting plenty of other signals that doubts about their Russian policy were spreading. To soothe this uneasiness the Secretary for War, Lord Milner, issued an open letter which was published in all the newspapers on 19 December, explaining that it would be abominable, dishonourable and inhumane to abandon the White Russians, whom Britain had encouraged to take up arms against the Bolsheviks. This did not silence the critics. Even the *Daily Telegraph* remarked that 'The country is entitled to more information than that ... We have at present a war on our hands in Russia such as would have filled the newspapers at any normal time; and the nation is entitled to know how the war is going, and what end to it is contemplated by the Government.'

Inevitably the same circumstances that brought out the critics of the Government brought out its friends, especially as Lloyd George had called a snap election and a virulent campaign was in progress. Even Arthur's mother was sceptical about his views, though she conceded that he had the courage of his opinions (he retorted, 'My dear Maw, of course I have'). More serious were Gardiner's recurring doubts, which centred on the Red Terror. He must have asked Arthur some definite questions, and furnished him with some figures from other sources, because in the 30 November telegram Arthur, basing himself on Litvinov, was happy to report that, according to the Cheka, 'only' 400 people had been killed in Moscow, of whom 40 per cent were robbers or other criminals and 30 per cent had been tools of the old order, such as members of the secret police. Things had been worse in Petrograd because the local authority had got out of control. This apologia did not satisfy the shrewd editor. Another letter provoked Arthur to write a thorough-going self-vindication:

(*10 December*) Point 1. I told Litvinov that the *Daily News* had trustworthy evidence from other sources putting the number of executions much higher. He said, 'It is quite impossible. The figures I gave you were taken from the books of the Extraordinary Commission, and there can be no better sources. Perhaps the *Daily News* figures refer to the whole of Russia, whereas mine referred to Moscow.'

Point 2. Impartiality. My definition of impartiality is, partiality for the truth. The thing which has made it so difficult for me not to let a spirit of partisanship get into my wires is the knowledge that they had to meet an overwhelming bulk of partisan statements on the other side.

Gardiner really must beware of Russian refugees. Revolution had made them untruthful and wildly credulous. How many times had Lenin and Trotsky fled? How many times had Petrograd been burnt or captured by the Germans? The flood of misrepresentation had only one purpose, hidden or open: 'to get us committed in Russia'.

I do think I have earned a right to my opinion. I contradicted everybody about the coming of the Revolution, and I was right. Early last year I said it was idle to watch the Duma and the Provisional Government, because the future would be decided not by them but by the soviets who had the real power. I was right. I got howled at by everybody for saying that the Cadets were playing with the Germans. Well everybody now knows Miliukov's history during the last six months. My point is, that if my telegrams have been partial, they have been partial for the truth. And now, again, I am perfectly content to disagree with everybody, and perfectly convinced that within the year the position will be clearer and my judgment vindicated.

That's a pretty conceited thing to say. But when so much is at stake it would be cowardly to pretend to take another view for the sake of temporal comfort.

This vigorous self-confidence no doubt satisfied Gardiner – by the end of the month, influenced by Arthur's dispatches about Litvinov, the editor was demanding direct negotiations with the Bolsheviks – but there was still the *Morning Post*. The Harmsworth press was in full cry against the Bolsheviks; and Lloyd

George had engineered a *coup* by which the *Daily Chronicle* had become the mere mouthpiece of the Coalition. Arthur felt depressingly isolated.

(*To his mother, 4 December*) I rather gather from what friends in England tell me, that I have earned an unpopularity as colossal as it is undeserved. Malevolent devils seem to be inventing all kinds of lies about me. That, however, can't be helped, and lies however flourishing for a time in the long run defeat their own ends. I should be more worried about them if I were a politician.

But he was a writer, and consoled himself with a volume of Mrs Ewing's stories for children.

Years later Evgenia recalled Christmas 1918 as very happy; but the trap was closing on her and on Arthur. Anti-Bolshevik pressure on the Swedes, both from the Allied Governments and from White Russian refugees, was steadily increasing, and Arthur had for weeks foreseen what the result was likely to be. First Litvinov's diplomatic privileges were sharply curtailed; then he was requested to leave Sweden by a certain date; then Vorovsky too was told to go, with all his subordinates – including, of course, Evgenia Petrovna Shelepina.

Evgenia's attitude was straightforward.

Arthur was very upset at my going back to Moscow from where he extracted me only such a short time ago – it never occurred to me to do anything else while all the others went home. But the Swedes expelled him too for good measure.

A thing, she adds, which he liked to keep dark in later years.

It is not surprising that Arthur could not lightly contemplate Evgenia's return to a starving city which might fall to White attack at any moment; nor that he resolved to go with her. The *Autobiography* says nothing about these considerations.

It seemed obvious to me that by going to England I should be sacrificing the extraordinary position I had built up for myself in personal relations with the Bolsheviks. At the same time if England were to be at war with Russia, if Intervention was to go on, my position would be impossible and useless. I put the onus of decision on the Foreign Office.

The Foreign Office meant Clifford Sharp – in other words, the intelligence services. Through Sharp the word arrived that it would be worth while for Arthur to go. He uses a curious phrase in this connection: 'I felt I had no right to refuse'. Perhaps he means that it was still his patriotic duty to help the Government of his country in time of war. Or perhaps he felt he owed a return for the permission he had just been given to take Evgenia to England if he wanted to (if so, he paid dearly, because the permission was soon withdrawn). It is even possible that he looked on himself as being, in some sense, under orders. After all, he had co-operated with the Foreign Office and looked to it for instructions and advice ever since 1914. Whatever he meant, it is still more curious that he says nothing about Evgenia's attitude, which might well have been the deciding factor. Forgetfulness is not a likely explanation. Perhaps he had no intention of submitting to Evgenia's decisions. Had the Foreign Office advised against a return to Russia, he might have invoked the permission for her entry to Britain and tried to make her take advantage of it. If he had done so, there would probably have been a terrible row, and it is doubtful if he would have got the better of it. Evgenia had made up her mind.

An unexpected hitch arose at the last moment: the Bolsheviks strongly objected to allowing Arthur back into Russia (and when later he met Trotsky in Moscow it became sadly clear that at least one leading Bolshevik was inclined to think that he was a capitalist spy). Bruce Lockhart, most unintentionally, rescued him from this embarrassment. On 14 January, in London, Lockhart gave a lecture on Russian affairs, defending the Government's policy. Somebody brought up Arthur's views: Lockhart replied that as Ransome had been out of Russia for six months he had no right to speak of conditions there. A lady in the audience (it was Mrs Maurice Macmillan, the mother of Daniel and Harold) protested strongly at this, and the meeting broke up in confusion. Providentially, the *Morning Post* carried a full report, which reached Stockholm. Litvinov, who was by now a firm friend (he had found Arthur's *Daily News* reports invaluable during his imprisonment in Brixton), used the article to make the point to Moscow that only if Arthur was again admitted to Russia could he maintain his usefulness as a corrective to the interventionists. The argument was accepted; and so on 30 January 1919 Arthur was one of the party which left Stockholm by sea for Finland; from which in turn they crossed into Russia on 3 February.

It is not altogether clear what Arthur meant to achieve by this journey. Partly, of course, he just wanted to be with Evgenia. Partly he had his history of the Revolution to prepare, through interviews and the further collection of documents. Partly, as he states explicitly in his journal of the trip, he was gathering material for a report to the Foreign Office. And as we have seen, the idea had already crossed his mind of seceding from the *Daily News*: perhaps the idea of issuing a pamphlet had crossed it too. The Bolsheviks were sympathetic to all these projects, except perhaps the last, for it was as the famous, the notorious Special Correspondent of the *News* that he was welcomed in Petrograd and Moscow.

He was helped by the company he kept. He cemented his friendship with Litvinov during a chess tournament which was started on the boat from Stockholm to Finland. Arthur came second after a lucky win over Litvinov, whom he readily admitted to be a better player. On their first morning in Petrograd (4 February) the two men and Evgenia took the tram to the Smolny Institute and received a warm welcome. Nothing seemed changed, except that there was now a horrible statue of Karl Marx outside the entrance, and the building was less crowded than in its heroic days. Presently Arthur found himself having dinner with the Petrograd Commissars, among whom was an old colleague of Evgenia's from the Commissariat of War. Zinoviev was also there. He had always distrusted Arthur, but now, on hearing of his expulsion by the Swedes, was vastly amused and became 'quite decently friendly'. In fact he was pressing in his offers of access to materials in Petrograd for Arthur's history. It was a fair beginning to what turned into a very successful visit.

While it lasted, Arthur was to be always hungry and usually cold (on 4 March he had to put snow on his nose to prevent frostbite). On the night of 4 February he took the train to Moscow, where he stayed until 14 March. For someone wishing to study the developing Soviet state it was good to be there during a lull in the civil war, when the Bolsheviks were victorious on all fronts. The Allies, increasingly half-hearted about intervention, had invited all the Russian factions to a conference on Prinkipo Island in the Sea of Marmora. Nothing came of the invitation since the Whites, deeply disheartened by this evidence of Allied willingness to treat with the Reds, refused. The Bolsheviks, who had accepted, were correspondingly encouraged. Approaches were also made to

Moscow by what was left of the Second Socialist International, but the Bolsheviks rebuffed them and in early March launched the Third International. They thus initiated the formal division between Communists and Socialists which has lasted to the present day.

Arthur took note of all these developments, but his main concern lay elsewhere. He wanted to understand the day-to-day workings of the Soviet state. He went from one Commissariat to another, interviewing the head of each about his or her plans and problems. He hoped in this way to gather information which would convince his readers, as he was convinced himself, that the Soviet state had come to stay (barring the accidents of civil war) since it was based on the needs and wishes of the Russian people and was making a serious attempt to satisfy them. He also hoped that he would be able to blot out the caricature of the Bolshevik leaders as so many pantomime demons by showing them for what he believed them to be: normal human beings, remarkable only for their devotion and their energy.

By the beginning of March he had accumulated more than enough material and began to think of returning to the West, though he was not very sure how he would do it. The Swedish frontier, he supposed, was closed to him[3] and he might find the same was true of the Finnish. The problem was solved by the arrival in Moscow of yet another unofficial American mission, headed by William C. Bullitt and Lincoln Steffens, the celebrated muck-raking journalist. Allied policy and procedures with regard to Russia were as confused as ever. French, British, Japanese and American troops were all operating on Russian soil, but Winston Churchill's proposals of large-scale intervention to bring down the Bolsheviks had just been firmly rejected at the Paris peace conference. It seemed reasonable to Woodrow Wilson to explore the alternative policy, of reaching an understanding with Moscow, even though such a policy was bitterly disliked by the French Government and the British Conservative Party. Lloyd George, unofficially, agreed. So Bullitt (characterised by George Kennan as 'twenty-eight years old, liberal in his views, brilliant, inexperienced, and greatly excited')[4] was sent to Russia. He reached

---

3 Actually, the Swedes made no difficulty, either on his voyage home or on his return journey in October.
4 George F. Kennan, *Russia and the West*, p. 126.

Moscow on 11 March and instantly sent for Arthur, whose work and views were well known to him through the syndication of his *Daily News* articles in the *New York Times* until the summer of 1918 (when, Arthur believed, the returning American Ambassador to Russia had put a stop to them). Bullitt was full of gossip about the attitude to Arthur in official circles, indicating that it had chiefly been American allegations of his untrustworthiness which had caused his difficulties in Sweden, and revealing that a cable had ordered the American Embassy in Stockholm to prevent Ransome, even though he was English, from leaving the country. Arthur listened to all this gloomily. Perhaps as a legacy of *Douglas v. Ransome*, or because of the anxious streak in his temperament, he was always inclined, when in trouble, to see himself as the victim of general hostility. When Bullitt assured him that he had a great many friends in America he could stand it no longer.

> I replied that so far, as a result of my sticking to the truth about Russia, I had met none but enemies, and very bitter ones at that, and told him that for more than six months every Englishman I met, with the exception of one, treated me as a traitor, and that I knew that I owed that to reports spread about me by Americans. He said that if I only knew it, I had many who contended that America got the truth about Russia mostly from my work ... I was very tired and perhaps more bitter than I should have been.

This outburst did no harm: by the next day Arthur was on excellent terms with the Americans, and enjoyed listening to Bullitt's further gossip, this time about the peace conference, which Arthur decided was being wrecked by the French. He, in turn, must have been useful as a guide to conditions and individuals in Moscow. Bullitt's discussions went well, and he left Moscow on 14 March with a set of Bolshevik peace proposals in his pocket. Arthur travelled with him.

It was a light-hearted party. Bullitt was sure that President Wilson and the conference would accept Lenin's terms, for they were, on the face of it, most reasonable. The other members of his group had been deeply impressed by what they had seen in Moscow: Steffens was to remark when he got back to Paris, 'I have been over into the future, and it works.' As for Arthur, he had accumulated a large store of papers, notes and memories to serve as the basis for future work; he was on better terms than ever with the Bolsheviks (Lenin had been friendliness itself, which had induced Trotsky to swallow his suspicions of Arthur as a 'Chauvinist Imperialist' and shake hands); he had left Evgenia with her mother and sister and a new job (in the Commissariat of Education); he did not anticipate any difficulty in getting back to Russia. So he was in ebullient form, and enjoyed his long conversations with the Americans as they tried to digest their experience. According to Steffens's *Autobiography* he blended literary and revolutionary criticism, saying and showing that after Russia Shakespeare looked different, and, unlike some other authors, still true.

Bullitt thought that Lenin's proposals meant the end of intervention; he also thought that the views of a journalist of Arthur's standing, with such privileged access to the Bolshevik leadership, would be of real value in persuading officials and public alike that such a change of policy was correct. Ransome quite agreed with him, but they were both wrong. Trouble might have started in Finland: orders were out to intercept Arthur and clap him into a Finnish jail, lest he bring his inconvenient information and opinions to England; but the Finns were not expecting him to travel as a member of the Bullitt party and thus overlooked his transit across their territory. So nothing happened until Arthur got to King's Cross station on 25 March, where he was met unexpectedly by a plain-clothes policeman who summoned him forthwith to Scotland Yard. It was a curious welcome to the country Arthur had not seen for sixteen months.

Leaving Bullitt and Steffens to travel on to Paris and their own disappointment (Woodrow Wilson refused to see Bullitt, Lloyd George disavowed him in the House of Commons, the Soviet proposals went unanswered) Arthur followed his captor to the Yard, where he was received by the head of the Special Branch, Sir Basil Thomson.

THOMSON (looking extremely grim): Now, I want to know just what your politics are.

RANSOME: Fishing.

THOMSON (staring): Just what do you mean by that?

Arthur told him: how he wanted intervention to end so that he could get back to his favourite sport ('We are very near the beginning of the season'). Perhaps Sir Basil was a fisherman himself. At any rate, it did not take Arthur long to convince the policeman that he was an honest man, and soon he was in full flood, explaining why he thought intervention was a disastrous mistake. He was interrupted when the Foreign Office telephoned to warn Sir Basil that Arthur Ransome would be landing at Newcastle the next day. Arthur realised that this interest in his movements was anything but flattering: it seems to have struck him for the first time that Whitehall might be less welcoming than in the past. When at last he took his leave of Thomson he was invited to return in the morning to complete the conversation. He duly turned up, and after that Thomson was a friend, which turned out to be just as well.

For this auspiciously farcical beginning had increasingly unpleasant and worrying sequels. Official Allied policy had swung into a new pattern of contradictions: troops were to be withdrawn from Archangel and the east, but until they actually left they were to be reinforced and resupplied, and generous material aid was to be given to the White Russian forces in their attempt to overthrow the Bolsheviks. This was bad enough from Arthur's point of view; the execution of the policy was worse. The Foreign Office and the War Office were full of eager supporters of the anti-Communist crusade and they were anxious to do whatever they could to prevent the anti-interventionist case from being put to the British public. They had reason for their anxiety: in March British soldiers had mutinied because demobilisation was so slow. In June the Labour Party's annual conference would threaten a general strike against intervention. The Foreign Office was busy preparing a White Paper on Bolshevik atrocities, ironically enough, in response to a suggestion by Basil Thomson. It was full of reckless and implausible lies, which Arthur was well equipped to refute. He knew that the Bolsheviks were not busy turning churches into brothels. Yet he was hardly prepared for the chilly reception he met at the Foreign Office when, after finishing his conversations at Scotland Yard, he presented himself there. Gone were the lofty days when he was received by Francis Acland and Lord Robert Cecil: now he was allowed to see no one but a 'temporary clerk'. He paid two visits, then the young official let fall a revealing remark: 'Perhaps you do not realise that we could damn you with the Left if we let it be known that you have been working with us.' Arthur was unimpressed by the threat, but it may have given him an idea. At any rate he left the Foreign Office and sought out George Lansbury, whom he had met once before (probably through his friend Molly Hamilton). If the Government could not be moved against intervention, perhaps the Opposition might be.

Before Arthur could commit himself full-time to the business for which he had returned to England he had to attend to his private concerns. His mother had recently had an eye operation, from which she was recovering in Kent. He stayed with her on his first night. Three days later he went down to Hatch.

His last contact with Ivy had been a 'perfectly beastly' letter that had arrived in Stockholm just before his journey to Moscow. He cannot have looked forward to the reunion, but he wanted to be with Tabitha. So he stayed at least three nights. It must have been a difficult meeting for everyone. Tabitha was nearly nine years old. Arthur was very glad to see her again. He gave her her first fishing-rod, and showed her how to use it, on the Little Nadder, and at Slapton Sands, where he took her and her mother. He taught her to be silent, and not to let her shadow fall on the water, and made her thread her own worms. Unfortunately Tabitha did not really take to fishing. She caught only minnows, and at Slapton Arthur caught an outsize pike, which had to be beaten to death by the boatman, who, not being very competent, took a horribly long time over it. Besides, Tabitha was now old enough to notice things and sense atmosphere – she had always been perceptive. In her memoir she writes that she saw that her parents were quarrelling; that her mother was unhappy and her father cross. Before long Arthur went back to London. Ivy had not relented on the question of a divorce.

By 7 April Arthur had made up his mind what to do with his Russian material. He lunched with Clifford Sharp, now back at the *New Statesman* and in no mood to co-operate with the Foreign Office, having learned all too much about White atrocities on a brief visit to Finland. He would soon be publishing two articles by Ransome. After this, Arthur made an agreement with the publisher Stanley Unwin to write a pamphlet on Russian affairs, about 150 pages long. He would deliver it as quickly as possible, and Unwin would print it as cheaply as he could, in vast quantity. The next day Arthur left for his mother's house in Leeds, which was being looked after by two maids. They could look after Arthur too as he worked against the clock. In tandem with the pamphlet he would be writing a report destined, without much hope, but out of an abiding sense of duty, for the Foreign Office.

Working flat out, Arthur produced his pamphlet in nineteen days, dictating from his loose-leaf notebook to a shorthand typist. He averaged two thousand words a day. He allowed himself and the typist two short breaks for refreshment. On 12 April he took a walk over the country from Bolton to Ilkley. A week later he travelled up to Coniston to stay with the Collingwoods for a couple of nights ('Caught trout below boathouse on Woodcock Orange'). He also went to Manchester, presumably by invitation, to visit C. P. Scott, the editor of the *Manchester Guardian*. Otherwise he kept hard at it.

Two extracts from the work in progress were published in the *Daily News*. It was Ransome's last appearance in that paper. A. G. Gardiner's opposition to Lloyd George and the Coalition was as unrelenting as ever, but his proprietors, the Cadbury family, had had enough. In May the editor was dismissed. The *News* rallied to the Coalition, and therefore to its foreign policy, including intervention. If Arthur wished to continue to write on Russian affairs he would have to find another paper.[5]

Six Weeks in Russia in 1919 was published on 12 June. According to its author it had enormous sales, even though it was only one among many more or less ephemeral works on the Russian Revolution then appearing. Some of its success was undoubtedly due to the fact that most of the other tracts were ferociously anti-Bolshevik; more, to the widespread anxiety about British policy in Russia. No one thought it fair that British conscripts, most of whom had been promised rapid demobilisation once the war with Germany was over, should still be fighting for the hazy objectives which were all that the politicians, themselves uncertain and at odds, could lay before them. The clear message of Arthur's book was that a peaceful understanding with the Bolsheviks was possible and desirable, and although such a policy was still quite outside the Cabinet's vision it had enormous appeal to the Left. Furthermore, Ransome's portrait of Lenin and his associates as

---

5 To judge by his victories over *The Economist*, the *Chronicle* and the *Daily News*, Lloyd George was one of the most effective enemies of the independent British press that it has ever encountered.

sympathetic human beings, and rather impressive ones too, was as he had hoped a convincing corrective of the hobgoblin fictions put out by the Right: as late as January 1920 the *Morning Post* would be asserting that Lenin was not in fact Lenin at all, but a secret organisation run by revolutionary Jews plotting the destruction of the world. There was a danger in this, and in due course it claimed its victims: opinion on the Left, as it came to see how thoroughly it had been bamboozled in 1917 and 1918, began to disbelieve almost everything that was said against the Bolsheviks, thus exposing itself to the equally fantastic lies that Stalin put out in the 1930s. But Ransome was hardly to blame for that. His little book may stand in his record as one of his worthiest achievements. It told an important truth at a time when it was badly needed, like John Reed's *Ten Days That Shook the World*, which was also published in 1919.

A comparison with Reed's book brings out very clearly the merits and limits of Ransome's. *Ten Days* is understandably the more famous work. It has an incomparable dramatic subject: the actual Bolshevik seizure of power in 1917. It is much longer than *Six Weeks*, and more ambitious. Reed makes a serious attempt to explain the causes of the February and October Revolutions, and to set out the history of the Russian political parties. He also prints a vast number of illustrative documents, enabling readers to sample for themselves something of the revolutionary mentalities and programmes. As an eyewitness who was also a practised journalist Reed was able to bring many great scenes to life: Trotsky consigning the Mensheviks and Social Revolutionaries to 'the garbage-heap of history', Lenin announcing, 'We shall now proceed to construct the Socialist order!' and being greeted by an 'overwhelming human roar'. *Ten Days*, in short, is a book that richly deserves its status as a classic.

Yet if *Six Weeks* is not of similar stature, it remains extremely valuable as a supplementary eyewitness account of a later phase of the Revolution. Ransome's Bolsheviks have been in power for fifteen months; he shows them actually at work constructing 'the Socialist order' and grappling with practical problems (food, transport) in the middle of a terrible civil war and under the pressure of blockade and invasion. Then, Ransome knows the men themselves so much better than does Reed. He is able to write of them with the casual insight of long and close acquaintance, whereas to Reed they are always heroic figures at a slight distance (which may be why Lenin so heartily endorsed *Ten Days* but at first disapproved of *Six Weeks*, and why it was not published in Russia until 1924, the year of his death). Furthermore, Ransome is the better writer of the two. Not only does he avoid, with seeming effortlessness, all the repulsive clusters of initials and awkward transliterations ('Tsay-ee-kah' is the worst) with which Reed litters his text, he writes with a vivid clarity and economy beyond Reed's powers. They bring his story magically to life. Ransome had already exhibited this ability in *Old Peter* and in much of his *Daily News* reporting, and was to do so again, to much greater effect, in later works; here it adds undeniable distinction to his pamphlet.

Reed and Ransome, then, supplement each other. Their works were to have a somewhat similar post-publication history. After huge initial success each became an embarrassment to the Left, because the authors took it for granted that the second chief of the Revolution was Trotsky; neither mentioned Stalin. For years the two books vanished from sight. *Ten Days* long ago re-established itself (helped by the fact that it is now out of copyright), although the most available English text, that of Penguin Books, still carries bothered little footnotes correcting Reed with references to a 1926 Communist publication, *The Errors of Trotskyism*. *Six Weeks* has not been republished since the 1920s. Its author was never in the least ashamed of it, but so long as Stalin was alive he did not want to risk any action which might endanger Evgenia's relations; and after 1953 he was too much taken up with other concerns, and too old, to bother to republish such an ancient work.

To be sure, the book has faults. One which must surely strike any reader today (though it will not surprise those who know Ransome's *Daily News* articles) is the pervasive sentimentalising of Lenin:

> Walking home from the Kremlin, I tried to think of any other man of his calibre who had had a similar joyous temperament. I could think of none. This little, bald-headed, wrinkled man, who tilts his chair this way and that, laughing over one thing or another, ready any minute to give serious advice to any who interrupt him to ask for it, advice so well reasoned that it is to his followers far more compelling than any command, every one of his wrinkles is a wrinkle of laughter, not of worry.

This picture of the great Bolshevik is accurate as far as it goes, but it does not go nearly far enough. Ransome not only fails to mention, but he does not even seem to know about, the other side of Lenin – the side so memorably set out in the equally unbalanced portrayal by Solzhenitsyn, *Lenin in Zurich*.

Six Weeks is undeniably a work of propaganda. This fact is especially striking if one compares the published version with the notes on which it was based. Not everything in *Six Weeks* is to be found in the manuscript 'Journal of a month in Russia': for instance, Lenin's celebrated verdict on Bernard Shaw, 'a good man fallen among Fabians', appears only in print. Some of the omissions were presumably dictated by the need to keep the book short. Some other matter must have been omitted because it was too explosive: Krylenko, for instance, showed Ransome papers which proved that Lockhart had indeed been involved, if only as paymaster, in some sort of anti-Soviet intrigue. Ransome cannot have wanted to be accused of betraying Government secrets or of hampering Government plans: at the very least, such accusations would distract attention from the real purpose of his pamphlet.

The same can hardly be said of the suppression of a long and revealing conversation with J. K. Peters. This occurred on 8 February, after Lenin had sent Arthur a letter requiring all Commissariats to give him any help he needed in gathering information for his history.[6] The first use that Arthur made of this privilege was to cross-examine the second-in-command of the Cheka.

I told him he and his terror had been the best card in the hands of the counter-revolutionaries abroad. 'You know perfectly well,' said Peters, 'that we are against the death penalty, but there are times when it is necessary to be hard to prevent worse things.' He said 520 persons have been shot in Moscow, and he promised to try and get definite figures for me for all Russia. In Moscow a very large proportion were criminals. 'For more than two months,' he said, 'we have not had to shoot anybody till just lately when there has been an outbreak of robbery. We have now shot eight robbers, and we posted up the fact at every street corner, and there will be no more robbery. I have now got such a terrible name', he added smiling, 'that if I put up a

6 This letter, in Lenin's hand, is preserved in the Brotherton Collection, Leeds.

notice that people will be dealt with severely, that is enough, and there is no need to shoot anyone.'

This chilling sketch of a Grand Inquisitor was reinforced by a document prepared for Peters's own use, showing exactly how many Cheka executions had occurred in twenty-seven provinces.

Such information, Arthur must have felt, had no place in a work designed to put the Bolsheviks in a good light: the truth may have been less lurid than the allegations put about by the Whites, but it was quite bad enough. Ransome never published it. Similar considerations might have induced him to tamper with, or omit, a speech by Felix Dzerzhinsky. Dzerzhinsky was explaining the future status of the Cheka (theoretically, it was to become a mere auxiliary of the Revolutionary Tribunals and lose the power of summary execution):

> Its business would be to hand offenders, such as Soviet officials who were habitually late (here there was a laugh, the only sign throughout his speech that Dzerzhinsky was holding the attention of his audience), over to the Revolutionary Tribunal, which would try them and, should their guilt be proved, put them in concentration camps to learn to work.

Arthur also noted unconsciously the beginnings of another Soviet practice with a long future:

> I did not see Spiridonova, because on February 11, the very day on which I had an appointment with her, the Communists arrested her, on the ground that her agitation was dangerous and anarchist in tendency, fomenting discontent without a programme for its satisfaction. Having a great respect for her honesty, they were hard put to it to know what to do with her, and she was finally sentenced to be sent for a year to a home for neurasthenics, 'where she would be able to read and write and recover her normality.'

When all criticisms have been made, *Six Weeks* remains a valuable historical testimony. Arthur made no claims for the book as a work of art ('it is far too incomplete to allow me to call it a Journal') but it nevertheless foreshadows the next phase of his purely literary achievements. Using the skills developed in four years of daily journalism, he was able to compile a wonderfully convincing and interesting log of his journey to Russia; good practice for the day, not long ahead, when he would start the log of his ship *Racundra*.

The report on which Arthur had worked simultaneously with *Six Weeks* vanished into the Foreign Office and was heard of no more. It could have no effect on official thought. There were many conflicting opinions in Whitehall, but no one was willing to contemplate, what Arthur took for granted, that the Bolshevik state had come to stay, and would sooner or later reassert its claim to all the old lands of the Tsars, and to be received as a full member, on equal terms, of the community of nations.

There was some excuse for this neglect of Ransome's arguments, for in the summer of 1919 the White cause was at its zenith. Admiral Kolchak's advance to the Volga had been checked at the end of April, but the 'Supreme Ruler' still held Siberia. In May General Judenitch threatened Petrograd, and General Denikin resoundingly defeated the Tenth Red Army in the south. In June he captured Kharkov, and in July ordered an advance on Moscow itself. It seemed clear to many that the fall of the Reds, so often prophesied, was at last about to occur.

Arthur began to worry desperately about Evgenia. He knew enough about White atrocities (Peters had shown him photographs of Red Army corpses, some with their noses cut off) to be sure that she could expect no mercy if the anti-Bolshevik forces captured the capital. In March it had seemed impossible that they might: the front was a thousand miles away from Moscow. By May the ring was closing, or so it appeared.

Arthur snatched at every expedient that offered. He enlisted Lockhart's help in getting the Foreign Office to confirm Evgenia's right of entry to Britain, and hoped that the excuse that he needed her to help him with his history of the Revolution would be good enough to persuade the Bolsheviks to let her go. He found a Coalition Liberal MP, Lt-Col. Lestrange Malone, who agreed to travel to Russia to see conditions there for himself. Arthur gave him a letter for Evgenia, and hoped that he would bring her back with him, but she thought it best to stay where she was. Furthermore, Malone came back an enthusiastic convert to Bolshevism, and joined the Left wing of the Labour Party; so his trip did nothing to weaken official, Conservative, Coalition support for inter-

Edith Ransome, Arthur's mother

Cyril Ransome, Arthur's father

Arthur in his House XV at Rugby. He is in the back row on the right. Ted Scott is sitting at the end of the front row on the left

Ivy and Tabitha at Manor Farm, Hatch, *c.* 1913

Arthur and Ivy outside the Law Courts at the conclusion of the Douglas case, 1913

Arthur Ransome in old age

Arthur and Evgenia at Hill Top, September 1960

vention and the Whites: Malone's views were dismissed as those of an eccentric.

If Evgenia could not be got out of Russia, might Arthur get in? The Foreign Office thought not. At this time it was part of British policy to maintain a strict blockade, which involved refusing passports for journeys to Russia, and cutting the Bolsheviks off, as much as possible, from mails and from telegraphic communications with the rest of the world. There was no reason to make an exception for Arthur Ransome, though he raged that it was 'blazing madness' not to have someone in Russia capable of getting first-hand news at the top and not from underground.

He was to remember that summer as the most miserable of his life. He fished desperately, in an attempt to distract his mind. The Collingwoods were a great support, especially Dora and her husband, Ernest Altounyan, whom she had married in 1915. Arthur had known Altounyan for ten or eleven years – ever since, a schoolboy friend of Robin Collingwood, he had turned up at Lane Head and adopted the family as enthusiastically as Arthur himself. He had seemed a rival, and Arthur, jealously, thought him 'quite unnecessary'. Half-Irish and half-Armenian, he was like Arthur in more ways than one, an energetic, abounding person of many interests (among other things he was a poet who would one day be published by Virginia Woolf), though he outdid Ransome in pertinacity: in later years Dora told her children that she had only accepted him at last – on a railway journey – because she was worn out with refusing. Arthur soon forgave Ernest his good fortune.

In 1917 Arthur had been cheered in Petrograd by the news that a baby girl had been born (at first called Barbara Harriet, then Taqui) who, according to her aunt Barbara, seemed to be angry about something or other and howled like a Turk. Now, in an even gloomier year, Ernest encouraged Arthur by going fishing with him, and by taking him on an expedition to Southampton to look at a boat which was for sale. On the same trip they went together to Hatch for a few days, where no doubt Altounyan acted as a buffer between husband and wife, as Daniel Macmillan had done during the Douglas trial. Arthur also spent some weekends fishing in Hampshire with Francis Hirst. Through Molly Hamilton he met leading Liberals and Labour Party members such as Ramsay MacDonald, and hammered home his critique of Government policy. But he was getting no nearer to Evgenia, and the White armies were.

Help came from Manchester. C. P. Scott had been having enormous difficulties with the Russian correspondents of the *Guardian*. Philips Price had moved to Berlin the previous winter. Various unsatisfactory substitutes had been used. W. T. Goode had got into Russia and interviewed Lenin, but then nothing more was heard of him (when he reappeared in October Scott was outraged to discover that he had been kidnapped at Reval by a British destroyer which carried him off to Sheerness, and that his papers had been rifled). Scott read *Six Weeks* when it appeared and liked it. He sent for Arthur again and invited him to become the regular Russian correspondent of his paper. Arthur was delighted to accept, even more because Scott would be a powerful ally in the quest to rescue Evgenia than because the *Guardian* was a splendid paper for which to write. He also welcomed a new source of regular income, for he had been living on his savings, such as they were, since his return from Moscow, and had had to refuse Ivy's request for an increased allowance.

The Foreign Office continued to make difficulties, but at last, with the help of Sir Basil Thomson, Arthur obtained his passport and visas, and was able to set out for the Baltic once more. Thomson hinted that it would be as well to get out of England quickly, before the Foreign Office interfered again. It proved unexpectedly difficult. A coal strike began, and there were no trains from London to Newcastle, the port of embarkation. Arthur hurled himself and his typewriter successfully across a widening gap of water on to a coastal steamer sailing from the Thames to the Tyne. At Newcastle he found that the Norwegian packet, bound for Bergen, could get no coal for the voyage because of the strike. But Arthur's luck had turned. The Norwegian captain had promised his wife to be home for their wedding anniversary and, after much cogitation, agreed to sail for Bergen using the coal dust and rubbish of his ballast for fuel. Soot blackened everything, but Arthur did not care. From Bergen he took the train to Christiania, and then on to Stockholm, where he arrived on 2 October. Next day he wrote to his mother in something like his former high spirits: 'I have not a regret in my mind whatever happens. I know I must go, I want to go, and whatever happens it cannot be worse than my own self-reproaches if I had avoided going. So that's that.' Clearly Mrs Ransome now knew all about Evgenia.

From Stockholm Arthur travelled to Reval in Estonia. Reval was not obviously the best place from which to reach Moscow:

the fighting front of Reds and Whites was in the way. At the northern end Judenitch was again threatening Petrograd, whose defences were being hastily organised by Trotsky. However, Arthur was well aware that the Estonians, who held the middle section of the line, were more than ready to make peace with the Bolsheviks. They were sick of the war, and only the Bolsheviks were making dependable promises to respect the independence of Estonia, Latvia and Lithuania. A victory for Judenitch might be as unpleasant for the Estonians as his defeat, for either might entail re-annexation. When Arthur presented himself to the Estonian Foreign Minister, asking for assistance in crossing the line, he was greeted as a messenger from God. The Minister, A. Piip, was willing to do all he could to help Arthur, if he would agree to carry word to the Bolsheviks that Estonia would accept any suggestion for an armistice and was ready to begin peace negotiations at once. The Estonians did not dare to entrust this message to paper, lest it fall into the wrong hands; Judenitch and the French must not know what they were doing. If the Bolsheviks would give a pass to Arthur, ostensibly to further his private business, he would be the ideal emissary. Arthur naturally accepted this proposition. Unfortunately Moscow did not. Arthur had fallen out of favour again, and was flatly refused permission to cross the front.

He was not to be put off. He scribbled a telegram for Piip to send when he was well on his way, 'RANSOME ALREADY LEFT FOR MOSCOW', and departed for the front. Next morning saw him walking eastwards across open country towards the Russian trenches. He carried his bag in one hand, his typewriter in the other, and his pipe, emitting clouds of smoke, in his teeth. It burnt his tongue, but he kept it going, for he reckoned that no one was going to shoot a man strolling along in as unconcerned and peaceable a frame of mind as the smoke signalled. Presently he saw ahead of him half a dozen soldiers, 'their rifles pointing in a direction I deplored'. He carried on, reached the trench, was seized, and threatened with death as a spy. They gave him a glass of tea, and he was able to convince them that though they could always execute him, he had urgent business with Lenin, and if a mistake was made that could not be put right they would regret it. Better leave it to battalion headquarters. So instead of shooting they apologised for tea made out of cherry-leaves. Arthur assessed their morale. The doubts he had felt in England about Bolshevik prospects vanished. He told them that Judenitch was at Gatchina, thirty miles south of Petrograd. 'If he takes Petrograd that means another three months to the war before we turn him out,' said the young officer.

The same sort of scene was played out at battalion headquarters before Arthur was conveyed to Moscow under arrest. His escort was a single soldier who let him call at the Commissariat for Foreign Affairs on arrival. Arthur walked into Litvinov's office to find him reading the telegram from Piip, and the journey back to Moscow was thus triumphantly completed. Before long Arthur and Evgenia were reunited. They celebrated with a feast of potato-cakes and Horlick's Malted Milk Tablets.

The next business had to be the return to Reval. It seems that the Bolsheviks, though welcoming Piip's overture, were as dis-inclined to trust ordinary channels as the Estonians. Once more Arthur was to act as messenger. Evgenia went with him.

Discussing the *Autobiography*'s account of this episode in a letter to Rupert Hart-Davis in 1974, Evgenia was emphatic that she had not been rescued:

You must not use the word *escape* for the title of Chapter XXXV, for the best of all reasons, that he would never have used it himself because neither of us considered it as such. We were separated by circumstances without any means of com-munication for months – so we naturally were happy to be to-gether again and for Arthur it was a tremendous relief because he thought of me as being in mortal danger. As for myself, until we got to Reval and saw Arthur's maps marking the position of White Army troops as practically surrounding Moscow, I did not realise how ignorant and unconscious of the true position we, inside this circle, were. But this only made me ashamed of myself and quite prepared to be despised by all my friends, who were as openly as myself on the side of Bolsheviks at the time, for running away from common danger in pursuit of personal happiness.

She pooh-poohed the risks they ran:

The crossing of 'No man's land' in both directions was a very dangerous (dramatic, foolish?) as well as picturesque performance of Arthur's but we have certainly been as close or closer to death together when sailing later on.

Since both Arthur and Evgenia now expected Moscow to hold out, there was no need to run away. But Arthur had to return to Reval. Evgenia decided to share his danger, in exactly the spirit in which he had come to share hers. Off they went together.

What followed showed the usefulness of studying folk tales. They teach one how to behave. Arthur and Evgenia left the Russian lines behind them, and three times were challenged, as in a folk tale. The first test was at a farmhouse in No Man's Land where Arthur burned all the papers given him by the Reds and Evgenia made tea with their travelling kettle. The men of the farm looked on Arthur's proceedings with deep disfavour, and were all for hanging him out of hand (they did not want to be found giving shelter to a Bolshevik spy) or at least detaining him and Evgenia as hostages; but Evgenia courteously offered the tea-kettle as a present to the farmer's wife, and she persuaded the men to let them go forward. The second test came when they were overtaken by a troop of Lettish irregulars. By good fortune Arthur was wearing an old Tsarist officer's greatcoat and a grey fur hat. As the leading horseman came up he turned round and shouted, 'Have you got an officer with you?' 'No.' 'Are you going to Marienhausen?' 'Exactly so, Excellency.' 'On with you and tell them I am coming.' Away went the horsemen, and when Arthur's little party, consisting of a luggage cart led by a phlegmatic boy, in which Evgenia perched, and Arthur stumping alongside, reached Marienhausen, a guard of honour had turned out. It was even more disreputable in appearance than Arthur. Gravely he passed along a motley line of irregulars, armed with fowling-pieces, rifles and pitchforks, and answered their salute. The corporal in command found the travellers good quarters for the night. Next morning at half-past six they set off again, once more saluted by the pitchforks and the miscellaneous guns and the corporal (the only real soldier among the lot).

The third challenge was the most amazing of all. Ahead of them appeared a long column of White cavalry. As it came up,

it seemed to me that there was something familiar in the look of the young officer in command. I stared at him. He stared at me. He suddenly shot forward, pulled up his horse, and exclaimed, 'What luck! Now we can have that other game of chess! We were on the point of stopping anyhow.'

I had last met that young officer at Tarnopol in Galicia, when we had played a really memorable game of chess, in which, at a moment when he had obviously been winning, I had been fortunate enough to bring off a smothered mate. Nothing is more galling than such an ending to a game that has seemed won, and he had at once demanded his revenge. We had been interrupted even while we were setting up the pieces and had never met again until now. It never for a moment occurred to him that I had not as much right as himself to be where we were.

So while the soldiers had their soup, Arthur and the officer played their game. The officer won. When he found that Arthur was bound for Reval he gave him a chit for his general; and the result was that they ended the journey in high style, rolling down to Reval in the general's own railway car. At Reval Arthur reported to Mr Piip, and soon an armistice had been arranged between Estonia and the Bolsheviks. By the end of October the Red Army was advancing on all fronts; by the end of the year the Bolsheviks were in control of all Russia.

In the mean time Arthur had collapsed under the sudden cessation of strain. He went down with stomach pains 'and a sharp attack of something like brain-fever'. Evgenia pulled him through. Against enormous odds, they had won the chance of a new life.

VIII

Racundra

I telegraphed, because it was my duty; I write, because it is my pleasure.

ARTHUR RANSOME's translation of Rémy de Gourmont,

A Night in the Luxembourg

Arthur had become a journalist only because he thought it was his duty in time of war. Now the war was over, but he was still a reporter. Happily for him the *Manchester Guardian* was a very different paper from the *Daily News*. Work no longer consisted of incessant telegrams, commonly of no more than five hundred words each. The *Guardian*, with that rather disdainful attitude to hot news which then distinguished it, really preferred Arthur to write intermittent, lengthy, reflective pieces. Perhaps he needed the change after so many years of hurried telegraphese, though he was now exposed to the opposite danger of wordiness, which he did not always avoid. He was not required to be in daily contact with his subject. C. P. Scott readily agreed to his covering Moscow from Reval. There was at least one good reason: it freed him from the clutches of the Soviet censor. So for the next few years Arthur and Evgenia lived in the Baltic states (first in Estonia, then in Latvia). Arthur made frequent forays into Russia, and wrote his articles when he got home. The rest of his time was his own.

One of the first things he did in this new leisure was to buy a boat. He had never before been able to apply himself sufficiently to sailing: it had come into his life too shortly before his marriage to Ivy, and then there had been the interruption of the war. Evgenia knew nothing of the art. But she was brave and adventurous, and from the rock of Reval an incomparably tempting view of water stretched northwards to the Baltic. Arthur could not rest until, in the spring of 1920, he bought a little ship which, for good reason, he and Evgenia christened *Slug*. They had a wonderful time tumbling in and out of her (it was about now that Arthur nicknamed Evgenia 'Topsy': in revenge she called him 'Charlie', after Chaplin) as Evgenia learned to sail and Arthur learned navigation.

Evgenia was also learning English, and she was discovering her lover's peace-time character. Sometimes he would agonise over romances which, as in the old days, never got much farther than their beginnings. It is understandable that Arthur's creative ambitions began to revive, but curious that they still drove him up the same blind alley, as if everything which had happened since *The Elixir of Life* had been irrelevant to his literary development. Sometimes he would agonise over his *Guardian* articles. When it all became too much for him, off he would go with Evgenia in *Slug* to picnic on one or another small Baltic island amid clouds of mosquitoes and clouds of smoke from the fire lit to keep the insects away. Photographs and drawings surviving from that period still convey a sense of the complete happiness which they then enjoyed together.

In 1920 his long poem *Aladdin* came out at last, and in the same year he published *The Soldier and Death*. The latter was one of Ransome's finest achievements, but Arthur seems to have felt that he had exhausted the *Old Peter* vein. On 1 February he told his mother, 'It's a nice little thing, but I very much doubt if I shall write any more in that kind. I have too much else to write before I can settle down again to writing merely jollities.'

As for *Aladdin*, it was issued with sumptuous sub-Beardsley illustrations of the sort that automatically start one looking (unsuccessfully in this case) for concealed phalluses. The pantomime verse swings along, though it does not scan properly, as Ransome acknowledges in his rhyming dedication to Lascelles Abercrombie. By its very nature, the book could lead to nothing, not even large sales, and the wonder must be that Arthur ever thought it worth writing.

The time had not yet come for a full-time return to imaginative literature. Russia, though Arthur told Mrs Ransome he was sick of it, still dominated his thoughts. But the project of a full-length history of the Revolution received what turned out to be a mortal blow. So hurried and preoccupied had been his comings and goings for a year or two that it was not until April 1920 that he was able to revisit his old Petrograd lodgings in Glinka Street. The Communists had got there before him.

(*19 April, Reval*) The infernal idiots had made a search there. They found my collection of newspapers, every copy of every paper issued in Petrograd from February 1917 to February 1918, an absolutely priceless and irreplaceable collection which I had intended for the British Museum. THEY BURNT THE LOT amid the protests of my old landlady, who, however, succeeded in saving my favourite fishing rod, a few pictures and my Turkish coffee mill. Boots, felt winter boots, the files of my old telegrams, cameras, practically everything of value stolen. I was very angry for a moment when I heard it, and saw my bare and ruined room, and then I grinned a deep and solid grin. It is after all just that I as a bourgeois should suffer like the rest, and now at least I have the necessary feeling for the chapter on that subject in my history. I had such contempt for the Russian bourgeois that I had difficulty in thinking of him without impatience, and found it hard to take him seriously when he complained of losing his piano and what not. I despise him as much as before, but in describing his mental state after the Revolution I have now the best of subjective material. Devil take it. I forgive them for stealing my boots, which were no doubt wanted for the army, but to burn that collection of papers, to destroy such material for the chronicle of their own revolution, and to BURN it (if they had collared it for their own archives I should not have cared a damn) – but to burn it – Forty thousand million dancing devils with pink tails and purple stomach aches.

All historians, especially all those who know the value of the Croker collection of French Revolutionary pamphlets in the British Museum, must sympathise with Arthur in this disaster, though it is nice to think that the landlady saved the fishing-rod which had procured her so many meals in 1917. Its owner's reaction must not be misunderstood. A casual reading might suggest that he had at last gone over completely to Bolshevism, but more probably his contempt for the Russian bourgeois was based on a simple feeling that in a time of crisis, with universal starvation and the collapse of industrial society just round the corner, it was unworthy to lament the loss of a piano. There is plenty of evidence that many Russian bourgeois gave way to this unworthy if natural impulse. Arthur's remarks, in short, were more the outcome of his sympathy with proletarian and peasant Russians than of Communist theories of class.

As the letter implies, Arthur did not at once give up the historical project. But as it also tells us, he had something else to do first:

> I have done a lot of work in Moscow, and collected material for a small book on the economic crisis and the means being taken for dealing with it, which should be pretty useful to everybody if I can get it written in time. I shall probably go into the country with my good Evgenia, and write like blazes for the next six weeks, not bothering about telegrams.

He did not stick to this resolution: the next telegram to the *Manchester Guardian* was dated 13 May; but a lot of the material which he eventually put into *The Crisis in Russia* appeared in his *Guardian* articles that year, so it may be presumed that he was working at the 'small book' (it is really a pamphlet) fairly steadily during the early summer. He was ill with what he called 'rheumatic flu' during July and early August; in the middle of the latter month he had to travel to Minsk to cover the Russo–Polish peace negotiations, which in the event were aborted by the Polish counterattack that drove the Red Army off Polish soil. Arthur's account of this crisis never saw the light because in late August a three-week printers' strike began, which kept the *Manchester Guardian* out of circulation until 20 September. A further handicap to authorship was that proofs of the pamphlet had to travel to Reval and back. So *The Crisis* did not appear until 1921, which accounts for some chronological confusions: readers of the pamphlet need to remember that most of the time, when Ransome writes 'this year' and 'last year' he means 1920 and 1919.

Little needs to be said of *The Crisis* in the way of criticism. It is very much the mixture as before. Ransome's virtues and faults as a reporter of Soviet Russia are the same as ever. He paints a devastating picture of the economic problems facing post-war, post-civil-war, post-Revolutionary Russia. The Bolsheviks could not have described their own difficulties better. Ransome is equally precise and intelligible in describing Bolshevik remedies and the reasoning behind them. His romanticism still powerfully shapes his interpretation: 'We are witnessing in Russia the first stages of a titanic struggle, with on one side all the forces of nature leading to an inevitable collapse of civilization, and on the other nothing but the incalculable force of human will.' It does not stop him reporting a strikingly accurate prophecy made by Rykov, then the President of the Supreme Council of Public Economy. Opposing excessive reliance on 'bourgeois specialists' Rykov said, 'There is a possibility of so constructing a State that in it there will be a ruling caste consisting chiefly of administrative engineers, technicians, etc.; that is, we should get a form of State economy based on a small group of a ruling caste whose privilege in this case would be the management of the workers and peasants.'

On the other hand Ransome still makes excuses for the Bolsheviks. For instance, he acknowledges that the Cheka is cruel, capricious, universally feared, even by Communists. Yet he pleads in mitigation, 'Without this police force with its spies, its prisons and its troops, the difficulties of the Dictatorship would be increased by every kind of disorder, and the chaos, which I still fear may come, would have begun long ago.' (Soon he would justify the suppression of the Kronstadt mutineers.) He still believed the Bolsheviks to be in the main men and women of good will who could be trusted with the immense power they were accumulating, and trusted, too, to give it up when called on to do so. So he accepted at face value all the justifications they offered for their burgeoning tyranny. When he questioned Trotsky about the system of labour conscription, including the issue of labour books ('a kind of industrial passport') and the enforcement of industrial discipline by the sanctions of the criminal code, saying that as an Englishman he would find such measures intolerable if applied to himself, the answer was: 'You would now. But you would not if you had been through a revolution, and seen your country in such a state that only the united, concentrated effort of everybody could possibly re-establish it. That is the position here. Everybody knows the position and that there is no other way.' Ransome accepted this. A final quotation shows his limitations even more devastatingly: 'I have never met a Russian who could be prevented from saying whatever he liked whenever he liked, by any threats or dangers whatever.'

The Crisis is of limited literary interest. Its plan offers little scope for Ransome's humour and humanity. Only in the account of Radek's visit to a conference at Jaroslavl, which is based on a diary, does the vivid reporting look back to the *Daily News* articles and forward to *Racundra's First Cruise*.

Published by Allen & Unwin, *The Crisis* was deliberately planned as a sequel to *Six Weeks*. It did not have anything like the impact of the earlier work, and probably could not have done. The end of the civil war and intervention had been the signal for a stream of visitors to pour into Soviet Russia, so that Arthur was no longer a unique witness: for example, Unwin also published Bertrand Russell's *The Theory and Practice of Bolshevism*. Delays in getting into print did not help either: H. G. Wells visited Petrograd and Moscow in September 1920 and hurried out his *Russia in the Shadows*, which Arthur praised, even though it covered much the same ground that he did himself: 'I think on the whole it is easily the most lifelike sketch of the affair that has been done,' he told his mother. But the eclipse of his own work was undeserved, for on the whole it is a much more solid piece than *Six Weeks*, though it has less charm. It has a much weightier thesis to put forward, and argues it with greater power. Part of this may be attributed to the influence of Will Peters, to whom the book is dedicated: he had turned up again as a member of the British mission which was seeking to normalise trade relations between Britain and Russia. Yet the book is Ransome's alone. It may stand as his last word on Russia and the Bolsheviks, since after 1921 the pull of his life's other concerns gradually became irresistible.

Circumstances still forced Arthur to write on Russia. The *Guardian* sent him there frequently until 1928. He wrote a series of powerful articles on the terrible famine of 1921 (which did not come as a surprise to the author of *The Crisis*). He had his living to earn, and had to do what his paper told him, the more so as he and Evgenia felt some unease about arriving in England as an unmarried couple. Ivy was as recalcitrant as ever about a divorce, and so they had to stay in the Baltic, where money could be earned and no one questioned their status. However Arthur refused to surrender to his fate. His concerns were less and less political; Russia vanished from his letters to his mother. And though his diaries were as sketchy as ever, when, as occasionally happened, they expanded a little, the subject was never politics. The sailing craze had him in its grip.

In the spring of 1921 he was looking for a replacement for *Slug*.

(*21 March, Reval*) Inspected a little boat with Captain Jackson.

Bought little boat for £25, of which paid £10. Named little boat *Kittiwake* from picture of said gull in Coward's *British Birds*.

(*23 March*) Believe we are swindled about the ballast.

(*13 April*) *Kittiwake* fearfully topheavy and heels over violently even with 2 reefs down.

(*15 April*) In the evening went and fell in love with Mr. Eggers, with the probable result that we shall have a boat built by him. The enthusiasm of the fellow when he is talking of a possible boat simply carries me off my feet and hundreds of pounds out of my depth. He proposes a perfect boat to go anywhere single-handed with every kind of tweak. Talked it over with Evgenia who herself is bowled over by Eggers. She too votes for getting his boat.

(*21 April*) Evgenia says she can live until April 21, 1923 with no new clothes?!!!!

(*4 May*) Dinghy arrived. Complete failure.

This was the dinghy made, for lack of any other builders, by a coffin-maker. In the *Autobiography* Ransome says it was a triangular box 'looking like the bows of a boat sawn off square by the first thwart. There never was such a boat for capsizing.' The entry goes on:

> Evgenia refuses even to try it, or to be rowed in it, or to take it with us. So it may be regarded as 11,000 wasted Esthonian matches, and we are still without a dinghy and should be starting. [*In Evgenia's hand:*] Evgenia herself is a complete failure. [*In Arthur's hand:*] Only partial.

Eggers, the boatbuilder, was clearly a remarkable man, and the effect of a summer's cruising in the unsatisfactory *Kittiwake* (among other deficiencies, her bunks seemed uncomfortably narrow to the two large lovers) made the idea of building a boat of their own more and more alluring. In August they moved to Riga, where there was a functioning boatyard (Eggers had lost his own during the war). Arthur was able to replace the triangular coffin with a properly-made dinghy for sailing and fishing on the Stint See, a large lake just outside Riga, on the shores of which, in the village of Kaiserwald, he and Evgenia set up house. This so encouraged him that he commissioned plans from Eggers, showed them to the boatbuilder, who said they would present no difficulties, and signed a contract for the building of a large, roomy, handy vessel. It was far from clear how she could be paid for, but in later years Arthur commented that this commission was one of the few wise things he had done in his life, for it got him back to his proper trade of writing.

In the mean time it got him back to England, where he talked about possible commissions with his former schoolfellow E. T., or Ted, Scott (the son of C.P.), who was beginning to take over the day-to-day running of the *Manchester Guardian* from his father, though the formidable old man remained in nominal, and sometimes tiresomely actual, command. He spent a night with his mother in Leeds, saw Barbara in London, and had an unproductive meeting with Ivy. He gave her a large cheque, which did not stop her trying to get more out of Edith Ransome as soon as Arthur's back was turned. He was in Riga in time for Christmas, mulling over the idea of a book about the Baltic. The first chapter, 'The Ship and the Man', was written on New Year's Day, and soon afterwards was published in the *Guardian*; but it got no further for the time being.

At times during the rest of the year he must have wondered if the new boat would be finished either. In *The Picts and the Martyrs* Captain Flint's nieces quote him to the effect that the only boatbuilder who ever finished a job on time was Noah, who knew he would be drowned if he didn't. It was an aphorism based on the maddening experience of 1922.

(*To his mother, 29 March 1922*) My boat for this year is getting ready for the water. You will be pleased to hear she is twice the size of last year's, a huge creature, thirty feet long and about twelve feet broad so that it will take a miracle to upset her ... Her name is to be *Racundra*. But it's lucky I brought so much stuff with me from England for her, because it is extremely hard to get anything here ... I suppose some time in May we shall be afloat. Now there is still snow, and the lake is frozen solid and shows no sign of melting. Carts and horses drive across it. Sledges rather.

(*27 April*) The boat in which I shall cruise will not be ready for sea for another month, which is most annoying, as we shall lose about three weeks of good weather ... it is maddening about her not being ready, when we have been howling at the

man, and tinkering and hammering has been going on all
winter. However, when she is ready, she will be a really stout
ship, and it will be our own fault if accidents occur. I have
taken the compass down to be fitted in a good place aft of the
mizen mast and in front of the steering well. Her appearance
when ready will be something like this:

(*8 June*) We are still wrestling with difficulties here in getting
ready for sea. The boat itself is nearly ready, and we are busy
with mattresses and things of that kind. But nothing on earth
will induce the swine who is alleged to be doing some metal
work for the mast to deliver the goods, ordered about three
months ago. However, the tiny little motor I am sticking in to
push us along in calms is now being installed, though I admit
it looks rather toylike, its propellor looking rather like a little
brass flower attached to the big hull of the *Racundra*. You will
be pleased to hear that I have persuaded the old man who looks
after our dinghy to come with us on the first trip to Reval. He
is very ancient (sailed with Lady Brassey in the *Sunbeam* about
the time that I was born) but very efficient, and highly entertaining.

This was the original of Peter Duck, and old Simon in *Coot Club*,
and the Ancient Mariner of *Racundra's First Cruise*. He was thus
one of Arthur's most important friends, the source of much of the
warm, unsnobbish humanity of his best books. His name was
Captain Sehmel, but Arthur scarcely ever uses it. Instead he makes
him immortal under his pseudonyms.

He wants to sail to England with me next year. He is quite the best sailor in these parts, and I shall be glad to have him if only to pick up hints from him, to polish up what, hitherto, I have been finding out for myself. I think I can now safely say that on Midsummer Day I shall be able to date a letter to you from on board the *Racundra*.

(*Diary, 26 June*) Boat ready in two months. Two men only working on her.

(*14 July*) Lehnert definitely promises *Racundra* for Aug. 3.

(*3 August*) Boat not ready.

At one point in this saga of disappointment, on 28 July, when *Racundra* was at last afloat, the workers in the boatyard by stratagem got Arthur and Lehnert, the boatbuilder, to sit side by side on a wooden bench 'which they had decked with beanflowers stolen from a neighbouring garden and lifted us, full of mutual hatred, shoulder high.' This comic moment did not soothe Arthur's feelings. On 5 August he kidnapped the still-unfinished vessel and took her to the Yacht Club, where after a fortnight's desperate labour she was more or less ready for sea. On 20 August she set out for Reval, Arthur Ransome, owner, in command, with, for crew, Sehmel and Evgenia. She returned to her home port on the Stint See on 26 September.

Arthur had kept a log of the voyage, and the idea of expanding it into a full-length book must have suggested itself early. No journalist likes to waste good copy. At any rate, within three days of the return, he was hard at work on what became *Racundra's First Cruise*. Fresh from the voyage, he was full of confidence:

(*To his mother, 2 October*) In the way of writing I did pretty well, and came home with eighty photographs (sixty of which I still have to develop) and over 30,000 words written of my first little sailing book. I want to make it sixty thousand altogether, that's the same length as *Bohemia*, and I think that when I have revised the stuff I wrote while actually sailing and worked in the material I collected last year, I should have a pretty jolly little book ... It's a huge joy really doing a non-political book at last. And in fact it is almost violently non-political, so complete a contrast is it to the things I have had to do during the last few years. I feel almost like starting author again, and somehow think that this will be a sort of breaking of the ice.

Parts of it at any rate I think you'll like, though parts of it may seem too technical. At the same time I do not want to leave them out, for I expect the book will be read quite considerably by people like me, and I rejoice in detailed accounts of other people's navigation of difficult bits. The worst trouble is that there are three several storms in it while at sea, and several which are dodged in harbour, and though the storms were S.E., N.E., S.W. and N.W. and so had each his quite special character, yet even for a sailing book there seems to be a blessed sight too much wind. There are also calms and one beastly fog, besides several days of simply jolly sailing. On the whole it gives a pretty good all round picture of autumn sailing in the Baltic, enough perhaps for the escape from the particular to the general which is essential for a good book.

He hoped to go to England as soon as *Racundra* had been laid up for the winter and finish the book there, but the *Guardian* sent him to Moscow instead. He stayed for a month, working at the *Cruise* (as I shall call the book, to distinguish it from the boat) in the intervals of journalism. Then back to Riga in early November, and at last, in December, to England. In London he met Ivy, and she agreed to divorce him. He began to look forward to giving up Russian journalism and to bringing Evgenia home. That was good enough, and then on a visit to the Collingwoods' winter quarters at Barmouth he showed the Skald the *Cruise* manuscript. Mr Collingwood was enthusiastic: 'You've got a book there ready-made.' Much encouraged, Arthur returned to Riga for Christmas, and pressed ahead with his writing. By 16 January the first draft was ready, except for the chapter on Reval, which dissatisfied him, as indeed the book itself was beginning to.

(*To his mother, 16 January*) I feel that it betrays the process of learning how to write it, and that only the second half, when I have more or less caught the trick of this kind of anecdotal narrative is really up to scratch ... I daresay there will be found some few lunatics of my own kind who will like it. And I have learnt a lot from doing it about how to deal with the next.
(*20 January*) It has, in parts, a certain pleasantness. In parts, however, I do not much care for it and find it rather dull ... Nobody will read it, of course, but I shall be glad to have copies of it to give to one or two folk.

This natural displeasure with the work in hand was to complicate the writing of almost all his later books.

He next went back to Moscow for another month, to make a study of post-Revolutionary literature and theatre. While he was there the house at Riga burnt down. Evgenia was wakened by the cat, and got out in time, having grabbed a dress but not much else. By the time the fire brigade arrived almost everything was gone. 'We have lost all the things belonging to the boat,' Arthur reported to his mother before leaving Moscow, 'sails, ropes, every single thing, all the tackle that was stored for safety! ... Evgenia was taken in by some strangers living in the same street ... She says that what was not burnt was stolen in the general excitement of the fire.'

Back at Riga, he found that Evgenia had stood the shock nobly, though she went down with a frightful cold, but the material loss was if possible even worse than he had thought. He walked grimly about in the frozen ruins of their house and found two boat shackles, the twisted bottom of his beloved cabin-lamp, and a bit of iron rigging: that was all. Even *Racundra*'s tiller was gone.

(*To his mother, 24 February*) What was not burnt was stolen by the fire brigade, who even saved camera-cases, from which the cameras had miraculously disappeared, and were actually seen by a neighbour smashing open the sextant-box with a hatchet and breaking the sextant in doing so after it had been saved undamaged from the wreck.

Only the hull of *Racundra*, safe in her shed, was left to them. Apart from the high cost of replacing everything, it looked as if it would take so long that there would probably be no sailing, and no sequel to the *Cruise*, in the summer. Arthur resigned himself to a year of journalism rather than of imaginative writing, and in late March travelled to Manchester to get commissions from his paper. But first he made a hasty translation of a short novel, *A Week*, by Iury Libedinsky, which had recently appeared in Moscow. It was a pot-boiling undertaking, no doubt, prompted by the need to get some ready cash as soon as possible, but Arthur thought very highly of the original as a specimen of post-Revolutionary writing, and in his introduction elaborated some of the ideas he had expressed to Lincoln Steffens and in *Six Weeks*:

What the Revolution did, at once, was to revise all former literature. Everything with which one was familiar now looked new and different, under a red light. *Samson and Delilah* became, suddenly, a revolutionary opera with the very spirit of the streets of Petrograd brought on the stage. Tchekhov became an antiquary ... Even I, a stranger in the gates of the Revolution, found that I was reading Milton with new eyes, and seeing in a quite unaccustomed perspective Hazlitt, Coleridge, Wordsworth, Southey; it was as if this new Revolution threw fresh lights and shadows on those men who had all been profoundly affected by the revolution of their day.

Unfortunately the book did badly in both England and America, and later on Libedinsky himself joined the Communists and became a characteristic party-line hack. The next Russian work that Ransome translated dealt exclusively with fishing.

On 15 March Arthur finished the rough draft of *A Week* and left Riga for England. The diary does not say so, but presumably he saw his mother. Then he went to Manchester, and to Lanehead. He found the life there unchanged, though Mrs Collingwood had been ill.

(*To his mother, 29 March*) Lovely weather here. I fished yesterday in the lake and caught, on fly, one large minnow. Today I am taking Barbara to Ulverston on her way to London, and then am going to fish up the Crake, when I hope I may do a little better, but the water is dead low, and very clear and bright, like August water. We picked daffodils, masses of them, in the woods behind Grizedale. The garden is full of flowers, and the birds are nesting. Last night I heard three different kinds of owls ... we went up the fell behind the house, and looked across to Helvellyn and the Langdales, just a few dabs of snow left on Helvellyn, like white Spring lambs.

... Mrs Collingwood is really much better, and walks about and is now in the garden knitting for her grandchildren, who are expected in bulk in the Spring.

Then he went back to Manchester, where plans were made for the year's reporting, and where the Scotts agreed to give Arthur an annual retaining fee rather than piece-rates. This was a great relief: he would now have a regular income for the first time since he left the *Daily News*; it was also, perhaps, something of a surprise, for as Evgenia remarked years later to Rupert Hart-Davis, the *Manchester Guardian*, though liberal-minded, was never liberal-handed – 'if there is such a word.'

Otherwise matters went on as usual. Riga in late April, Moscow in early May; where Arthur walked into the last of his diplomatic crises.

Russo-British relations, though continually fluctuating, had improved out of all recognition since 1919: a trade agreement had been signed in 1921, and the current of events was clearly making for full British recognition of the Soviet Government. On the day that Arthur reached Moscow this benign process was suddenly interrupted. The so-called 'Curzon ultimatum' arrived. This was an insulting Note from the British Foreign Secretary to the Russian Government, which the British representative was instructed to deliver to the Foreign Commissariat, but not to discuss in any way. If events were allowed to take their course the Russians would reply as angrily as Curzon expected, diplomatic and commercial relations would be totally ruptured, and there might even be a renewal of the war of intervention.

Fortunately the British head of mission, Robert Hodgson, a good friend of Arthur's, took the same view of the business as he did: that whatever was true of Curzon, the British Government as a whole certainly did not desire a rupture. Arthur had talk after talk with Chicherin and Litvinov, trying to persuade them of this view ('I have seldom drunk so much tea in the Kremlin in so short a time') but nothing would serve except a meeting with Hodgson, who, fortunately, was ready to defy his instructions and talk to Litvinov if an accidental meeting could be contrived. With Arthur acting as an intermediary, this was soon arranged, and, reassured, the Russians sent a soothing answer to London which ended the immediate crisis. In the autumn the Conservatives fell from power and were replaced by the Labour Party, under Ramsay Mac-Donald, who soon recognised the Communists as the Government of Russia.

In the mean time the summer found Arthur back on the Baltic, sailing *Racundra*. On 6 July the author's copies of *Cruise* arrived. It was a handsome volume, with a fine photograph of the Ancient Mariner on the dust-jacket, and an intelligent blurb:

No sailing man but will be interested in this account of autumn cruising in the Eastern Baltic. The publishers, whose ignorance of sailing is extensive, found that this misfortune or privilege in no way prevented their enjoyment of the human interest of the book and of a world in which it is not only possible, but easy, to forget that politics exist.

Arthur was pleased:

(*To his mother, 11 July, Riga*) Unwin has made really quite a nice book of it, and I am full of joy over my new baby, my first non-political book since the war. I fear it will get slanged by my political enemies just the same. But that cannot be helped. Let's hope somebody will find something nice in it. The American publisher writes enthusiastically about it, so I have hopes of the Yanks, though very little at home.

Whatever his enemies did, his friends at least were helpful. The *Guardian* printed a long and enthusiastic review, alluding to Ransome as 'a skilled navigator in the troubled waters of European policy', praising *Racundra* to the skies, and looking forward to hearing more of her in due course. There were a dozen other favourable notices, so that even Arthur dared to hope for adequate English sales: 'I cannot help having a sort of feeling that it may find its way.' It did; it became a yachting classic, and was to be reissued in three different editions before Arthur's death.

Racundra's First Cruise is the first 'Arthur Ransome book': the first work, that is, in which all Ransome's qualities as an author are successfully displayed in characteristic combination. As such it requires more than passing notice.

It was an experiment in a well-established *genre*, in which Arthur had read widely. He thought that Joshua Slocum's *Sailing Alone Around the World* was the best sailing book ever written, but even closer to his heart, I fancy, were the works of E. F. Knight. Knight was the author of what became Dick Callum's bible, *Sailing*. He also wrote three notable cruise books, including *The Falcon on the Baltic* (the western end of that sea, not Arthur's Finnish and Russian waters). He was a journalist, who covered the Boer War for *The Times*; a prodigious walker; a man who spent a week among the Communards of Lyons in 1871 ('despite their views which were detestable to a born Tory like myself, they were I found a very decent lot of fellows') and one who went on

a treasure-hunting voyage across the Atlantic to the West Indies
(a tale that lay behind several of John Masefield's fictions as well
as *Peter Duck*). In his introduction to the Mariners Library edition
of *The Falcon on the Baltic* Ransome remarks, 'Grown-up people (if
those who love sailing ever grow up, which I doubt) are like
children in taking particular pleasure in stories that tell of adventures that might happen, with luck, to themselves.' This is the
author of the *Swallow* books speaking; he is stating a truth which
he hit on long before he wrote it down, and one of his purposes
in writing the *Cruise*. He wanted to please other yachtsmen, who
might make, or consider making, or only dream of a voyage in
the upper Baltic. Hence the careful particulars about lights, currents, winds and harbours; hence the book's excellent charts.
Ransome knew quite well what the book's potential public was
like, because he was part of it. He even remembered what more
professional sailors, who were less professional authors, often
forgot, that many of his readers would be, on many matters,
ignoramuses. This, he explains, is why he gives all the details of
swinging his ship at Helsingfors: an early example of one of his
greatest literary skills, his ability to describe, not only clearly but
enthrallingly, the driest of technicalities to the least informed of
laymen.

Yet Ransome remained too acute a critic to rely for success
exclusively on nautical information and the sailing public's passion
for the sea. He wanted to please as many people as possible
(*Racundra* had to be paid for, after all) and re-establish himself as
a non-political writer. Since the cruise book is only a special sort
of travel book – sailors cannot be always at sea, and if they write
books must describe the ports where they revictual – it can, skil-
fully handled, appeal to the sort of people who enjoy travel books,
as well as to those who enjoy sailing; and Arthur saw to it that his
Cruise should do so. It needed some extra appeal, for the actual
voyage of *Racundra*, however windy, was a somewhat tame affair.
'There were no wrecks, and nobody drownded': *Racundra* proved
beautifully seaworthy and marvellously comfortable; Arthur, to
his own surprise, made no mistakes in navigation; the worst that
happened was a steadily contrary wind at the end of the cruise,
which detained *Racundra* at Werder when her crew were eager to
run for home across the Gulf of Riga.

But Arthur and Evgenia had gone ashore whenever they could,
as *Racundra* sauntered through the Estonian islands. Ransome had

something to record about all of them, for those which he did not visit this year he had gone to the year before, in *Kittiwake*. 'The Ship and the Man' was incorporated in the *Cruise*, taking its place easily enough as one of the dozen or so odd little human encounters through which Ransome brought to life the places where they occurred. His first landfall, for example, was the island of Runö in the Gulf of Riga. There he found an astonishing society of seal-hunters, Swedes who were scarcely ever visited except by strays like *Racundra* and who used words that in Sweden had become archaic. In effect they were primitive communists.

> These men, perhaps better than any other European except the Laplanders, continue into our times the life their forebears lived in the Middle Ages and earlier. Steam has meant nothing to them except a visit from the steamboat once a year. The Iron Age brought them knives and iron boat-fastenings (though even now they often build without). A flint-lock gun, a Japanese rifle, that rare treasure of a Newmarket cap: what are these but trifles? They could kill seals and cover their heads without these things. One thing of real value to them dropped from civilisation ... and they brought it to me in its box and opened its dark magic with proper reverence. It was an old dry compass from a maker in Wapping, taken, no doubt, from some ship wrecked fifty years ago on the rocky western shores of their island.

The first readers of the *Cruise* must have been struck by the extraordinary degree to which the little Baltic communities visited by *Racundra* had survived the war and the Revolution unscathed (though few were as unmarked as Runö); today we can only be glad that they were described with such careful sympathy before the even greater storms to come.

Even in 1922 politics could not be kept out entirely. Arthur noted a dispute among the fishermen of Dago as to whether it was patriotic for newly-free Estonians to speak to foreigners in any save the native language (particularly if the alternative was Russian, the tongue of oppression), but the *Cruise* was avowedly a book of escape. Ransome rigorously excluded all speculation about the present or future of the Baltic States. He was more and more engaged in an attempt to break free from the net in which the First World War had caught him and to become, at last, the sort of man he had always wanted to be. It was a quest which baffled and at times irritated many of his male journalist friends; his women friends, such as Molly Hamilton and Barbara Collingwood, seem to have been much more encouraging.

The omission of politics left a gap which needed to be filled by art: organisation, style, characterisation. By the time Ransome had finished, the *Cruise* was half-way to being a work of fiction.

The form of the book was dictated by the tradition of cruise-books and by circumstances: it was to be a written-up version of the log which Arthur had kept of the voyage. The same process had produced *Six Weeks* and part of *The Crisis in Russia*, but the revision was more elaborate than in the earlier examples. Style was a much more important contribution. Ransome's was now mature, like the author himself, and in its cheerful directness reflected his character. The years of journalism had burnt away his youthful preciosity and sentimentality. Arthur had learnt never to waste a word and to aim always at absolute clarity: traits which might have damaged a dealer in shot-silk such as Virginia Woolf, but which were admirably suited to Ransome's concerns. Through journalism he had purged himself of the Nineties, yet kept some of the most valuable skills he had learned from his long study of Nineties writers and their French masters. The *Cruise* benefited. The following passage could have been written only by someone formerly immersed in Flaubert, the Goncourts and Zola:

We walked out of this village of Storaby together with three mottled cows, driven by a woman with a handkerchief on her head of red, orange and white, a deep rich green skirt and a bodice of bright purple, flaming like a tulip. As we walked we were joined by other women and other cows, until at last there was a considerable herd, driven by four women with long sticks over an open space of moorland, green grass and swamp, with grey rocks showing through the turf. Fields on either hand were enclosed with stone walls built without mortar, like our walls in Lancashire and Westmorland, but lower, because the stones are round, sea-worn boulders and harder to fit together than the flat slates at home. Presently we broke away from our companions and made for the woods to get out of the wind and find a place for dinner. The woods were even wetter than the open country, carpeted with moss that squelched under our feet. They were not the pinewoods of the mainland, but birch-woods, and under their silver stems, wherever the ground was not a morass, were lilies of the valley. Near the far edge of the woods we stopped and cooked our dinner under the shadow of a great rock on a good fire of birch, which is the best of all trees for the fire that is in it.

It is like a painting by a member of the Barbizon school.

No style, however clean and vivid, will suffice to save a book from triviality. As a last enhancement Ransome relies on his ability to draw interesting sketches of character. He depends comparatively little on his chance encounters with memorable strangers like the seal-hunters. The strength of the *Cruise*, next only to its seamanship, lies in its portrayal of the Ancient Mariner, the Master, the Cook and *Racundra* herself. Here the fictional instinct, so long misdirected, began to sense that it was near home, and to make itself effective at last.

Little need be said about the Ancient Mariner, the old sailor from the *Thermopylae*, with a white beard and a head as bald as Arthur's now was. 'Sometimes on board he wore a crimson stocking-cap with a tassel, when he looked like a gnome, a pixy or a fairy cobbler. If Queen Mab went to sea she could not find a fitter mariner.' He is a beguiling character, whose memories of the great days of the clipper ships and whose attitude of respectful scepticism towards the Master, with his fussy taste for accurate compasses and sextant readings, help to enrich the book with history and quiet humour. The whole theme was to be exploited again, on a larger scale, in *Peter Duck*. Neither need much be said of the Master, though the whole of the *Cruise* is in a way a self-portrait, fuller than anything else Ransome undertook before the *Autobiography*, and in a reticent, subtle way somewhat more convincing than the later book, if only because it invariably sets its author in a slightly comic light.

The third of us was *Racundra*'s 'master and owner,' who writes these words even now with the swelling pride that he felt when he first saw them on the ship's papers handed to him on departure by the Lettish Customs Office. 'Master and Owner of *Racundra*.' Does any man need a prouder title or description? In moments of humiliation, those are the words that I shall whisper to myself for comfort. I ask no others on my grave.

We share his joy when at last, for the first time not on paper and not in dreams, 'I had the little ship alone in my hands in a night of velvet dark below and stars above, pushing steadily along into unknown waters.' We share his anxiety when he has to make difficult decisions about navigation at night, aided only by half a dozen obsolescent charts, a faulty compass and the gloomy prognostications of the Ancient Mariner. We share his vexation when, tacking laboriously down the channel between Wormso and the Nukke Peninsula, he has to watch more than twenty sail running free in the opposite direction. These emotional ups and downs of the Master help to bring the voyage alive.

The portrait of *Racundra*'s Cook ought perhaps to be called a caricature. Evgenia is presented as a dervish of pots and pans.

We saw her throughout the day in a cloud of cooking, and the steersman at night, looking down the companion, saw always busy hands cleaning obstinate aluminium, and he who rested on his bunk heard, as he turned in comfortable sleep, the chink of crockery and the splash of washing up. The Primuses roared continually, like the blast furnaces in Northern England. And we, relentless and without shame, called continually for food. Of the three of us, the Cook, without a doubt, was the one who worked her passage.

This was one way of dealing with the problem of Evgenia's status. Leave out her name, give no explanations, exhibit her as a cook, and every reader without inside information will assume that she is legally as well as in fact your wife.

As the book goes on, traits of the real Evgenia begin to modify the caricature. On the way to Reval they run into a night of storm, and *Racundra* loses her mainsail. The Cook struggles up the companion-way with a sandwich.

COOK (real inquiry in her voice): Are we going to be drowned before morning?
MASTER: Why?
COOK: Because I have two Thermos flasks full of hot coffee. If we are, we may as well drink them both. If not, I'll keep one till tomorrow.

They drink one Thermos and eat the sandwiches, the storm seems more enjoyable, and Evgenia falls asleep in the middle of a laugh.

'She was tired out, and when the next big splash woke her, I sent her below to lie down, knowing that there would be plenty of work for her in the morning, whereas there was nothing she could well do at the moment. I do not believe she has forgiven me yet.' Some time later there is a calm, and the Cook is urgent that the engine should be used, angry when it does not work, and unappeased when she is not allowed to throw it overboard. 'However, when a breath of wind came diffidently down to us from the N. and we got steerage way again, she relented and gave us luncheon on deck.' Towards the end of the voyage she collapses, in part because of the fumes of raw tobacco which Arthur, little more considerate than in the days of Ivy, is drying over the cabin lamp. It becomes clear that Evgenia is companionable, courageous, long-suffering, warm-hearted and rather warm-tempered too (he could have said more about that). It says much for the character of her marriage that Arthur was free to paint such a frank, if slight, sketch of her.

The true heroine of the story is *Racundra* herself. 'Good little ship', 'stout little ship', says the Master of 'the modest, the admirable *Racundra*'. It is essential, in a cruise book, to convey the character of your vessel; Arthur does so admirably. Perhaps his only literary mistake was to put his description of *Racundra* in an appendix instead of in chapter two, where it belongs; but when at last they appear, the details of the boat's beam and draught, sails and other furnishings, even the 'simple and efficient closet' on the starboard side, are as interesting as snapshots of an old friend. For Ransome takes infinite pains over the personality of his ship, telling how although she would not stay during the night of storm after her mainsail gaff was broken, she wore out the night on the open sea, enjoying herself breasting the huge waves, as her skipper, three-quarters asleep, kept her up into the wind; how she was expected to do her best when beating against the wind down the narrow, shallow Nukke Channel, knew it, and responded ('There was a toughish wind too, and that always suits her'); how she disgraced herself by rolling abominably in the Moon Sound, although her owners had previously boasted that she never did such a thing; how there is a lucky stone from Coniston 'and the friendliest house in England' (Lanehead, of course) on her cabin wall. How on the last, weird, exciting night of the cruise, when in darkness they flew south across the Gulf of Riga towards a lee-shore, *Racundra* comforted her helmsman:

She ran so steadily, steered so easily, was so much less flustered than her 'master and owner' when, glancing back, he saw the horizon, apparently only a few yards off, rise astern like a white-topped mountain, up and up and up, and nearer and nearer, till it seemed that it must overwhelm her in its majestic rush. But *Racundra* kept quietly on her path, rose as the huge wave reached her, dropped down its mighty back, and was running still while the horizon heaved itself again behind her for another effort.

This personification of a thing of wood and rope may seem at best doubtfully legitimate, at worst childish. In fact it is deeply truthful. *Racundra* was not a mere machine, but an idea realised. Her good traits and her limitations were alike the results of the long ponderings of Otto Eggers and the enthusiasm of Arthur Ransome. When he was aboard her Arthur escaped indeed from the everyday trammels that kept him from his proper path through life. No wonder the *Cruise* is a love story.

It was a rich achievement, boding more to come; but no account of *Racundra*'s second cruise ever appeared. This was not for lack of enthusiasm on the part of the publishers. The first *Cruise* sold very well, and Unwin readily agreed to a sequel. The Master, the Ancient Mariner and the Cook seem to have spent most of the summer of 1923 afloat. In July, in the Gulf of Riga, they saw a waterspout, 'a solid column of water between sea and black cloud, like a long indiarubber tube, that twisted and twisted and finally broke, a wonderful but rather awful sight. The Ancient said he had never seen one except in storms in the tropics.' A late venture to the islands off the Finnish coast suggested that material for a new book might well be gathered from those waters. But the weather was dispiriting: they were buffeted for five days by rain and a contrary south-west wind. Arthur fell for a time a little out of love with *Racundra*: she was most awfully slow, he told his mother, and very bad against the wind.[1] He decided to put off the project until the following year. It was never revived.

Arthur was always curiously unrealistic about his literary plans. It was not simply that he had more ideas than time in which to carry them out; as he found early in 1923, when he considered

---

1 If *Racundra* was slow, it was AR's fault. He had deliberately rigged her so that she could always be sailed single-handed. Her second owner, Mr Adlard Coles, found her 'woefully under-canvassed', and replaced her gaff rig with Bermudan.

writing a book of Moscow sketches, which he would have done delightfully. He was also bad at cutting his losses. On 23 August he wrote to his mother that Methuen had agreed to take a book on Hazlitt,

> as I have been urging them to do these last seven, no these last nine years [it was actually a project that he had first considered in 1910]. It is to be a book of the same length and general design as the *Wilde*, and to have lots of small word-portraits of Hazlitt's friends and an account of the way in which the French Revolution affected literary England, all of which ought to be infernally interesting. Their agreement, I am sure, is entirely owing to the way in which *Racundra* has been reviewed, which really has encouraged me as well as my publishers to feel that I have made a fresh start in real writing.

It is difficult to believe that this ancient notion had much life left in it, although it is easy to see why Arthur was attracted by the idea of writing about the literary impact of the French Revolution. Anyway, external circumstances slowly settled the matter, beginning with the news that in July the first stage of Ivy's divorce of Arthur had been completed.

He had grumbled to his mother, earlier that month, about the way in which the business was hanging fire. 'She has planted another winter out here on me and I never thought I should get through the last. However as the Ancient Mariner keeps saying, "What must a be must a be." ' Arthur missed his friends. He was always hoping that Robin Collingwood or Ernest Altounyan or one of the Scotts would come out for a voyage in *Racundra*, but they never did. Evgenia had other distresses. The voyage to Helsingfors on 22 August was the first day of real summer sailing they had ever enjoyed in *Racundra*, but that evening the weather turned wild again, blowing and raining. It was too much for her. Arthur's diary records:

> The Cook says there is no point in living in *Racundra*, that only children are glad to live in a ship, that there is nothing to see, nothing to write about, that she is sick of wind and rain and living in a small cabin; that I grow worse with age, and that proper authors live at home and write books out of their heads.

Arthur was well-placed to adjust to these heretical views, having just made the agreement about Hazlitt, but for the moment there was nothing to be done. The divorce would not become absolute for some months, and until then they went on as usual. Arthur spent the last days of September in Moscow, and the second half of October in England.

(*To his mother, 12 September*) I hope to stay for a month, working in the Brit. Museum and collecting a packing case full of my books for Hazlitt. I hear very good news about *Racundra*'s sales, but it's hard to judge by inexpert reports. However, I get letters from all sorts of people about the book and the boat, and that is always an extremely good sign. I am bitterly sorry that I have not got another such book for next year. However, I must make shift without, and shall do my best to get Hazlitt done in time for publication next autumn.

It is not clear whether he collected the packing-case of books, but it seems certain that he did not fill it from his own library, which was still at Hatch. There is no record of a journey to Wiltshire. He may have made inquiries, which in turn may have given Ivy a vengeful notion.

The position of abandoned wife was hardly a dignified one, and that of a divorced one (even if innocent) would be barely respectable, and Ivy, who was as snobbish as ever, did not enjoy her invidious situation, though she managed to remain on good terms with the local gentry. Her financial position is obscure. Arthur believed that she had delayed the divorce so long because otherwise her father might have altered his will: certainly proceedings followed hard upon Mr Walker's death. His disappearance may not have made his daughter any richer, as Mrs Walker was still alive. According to Evgenia, Arthur sent back a third of his income, but Ivy may have felt that this was not a particularly generous provision for his wife and daughter. These considerations do not go to the heart of the matter. For the rest of her life Ivy seems to have been torn between a genuine wish to make friends with Arthur again and a wish to hurt him. In her better moments she no doubt realised how badly she had failed him. She still needed him, especially now that her father was dead, for emotional support and worldly advice; he had been the most important man in her life, and was her daughter's father; she was still capable of responding to his charm. At other times she remembered how he had failed her. She was humiliated and jealous at the thought of Evgenia; the role of martyr was as attractive as ever. It was in this latter frame of mind that she approached the concluding stage of the divorce.

As the law then stood, a petitioner might secure a decree nisi, meaning that the courts would make no objection to a separation; but for the divorce to become absolute the petitioner would have to give his or her explicit consent some months after the nisi award. This procedure gave ample opportunity for extortion. Since Arthur's income was still small and uncertain, Ivy, if she wanted to be paid for agreeing to an absolute divorce, could only make a levy on his goods; and that, principally, meant the books, since with the exception of a few pieces of Ransome family furniture they were the only belongings which Arthur was likely to want to take away from her. Distraint of the books would not be economically very advantageous, though the library was a fine collection; but it would hurt Arthur, who had assembled them so lovingly, and Ivy may have thought that it might ruin him as an author, since in the days when they had lived together almost everything he published derived, in one way or another, from books. Arthur and Evgenia always believed that this last was Ivy's chief motive. In the spring of 1924 her solicitors made it plain to Arthur that unless he resigned his library to her, Ivy would not complete the divorce.

It was some time before Arthur realised what she meant to do to him. He got news of what he called a 'frantically bad' divorce settlement at Riga in December, but next month found him staying in Moscow with Will Peters, and writing to Evgenia (he always put 'Mrs Ransome' on the envelopes) in his usual high spirits.

(*19 January*) My fortieth birthday passed quite calmly and un-noticed, and the world looks just the same. At least I can't see any difference though I have tried hard ...

Last night I caught the first rat. Peters and Dunya had tried a lot of times, but the rats just ate their baits and went off laughing, and every night there was the most terrible row. The night before last I think the rats had a sort of Yacht Club dance. They threw portmanteaus about and I thought I heard them throw the servant out of bed, but she says they didn't. Anyway it was decided to have another shot at them. So I set the trap myself with my well known skill, and at a quarter to six off went the trap and there was the first. Peters came in this morning. I told him. 'I don't believe it,' said he. Mrs Peters: 'I don't believe it.' Dunya: 'Nye ... e ... et.' Triumphal production of bloody rat ... I am appointed rat catcher in ordinary.

I have spoken to Dunya about the little pig for your mother and she says there are plenty on the market, so she will buy one today or tomorrow, and I will duly present it.

It was a sorrowful time for the Shelepin family, for Iraida's baby sickened and died. Arthur wrote at length to Evgenia about this loss, but another death that month, that of Lenin, meant much more to him. It happened on 21 January.

I walked sadly through the wintry streets, thinking of my talks with him, thinking that I should never again see him edging his chair round the table in little jerks while he argued, remembering him speaking in the old Soviet in Petrograd, delightedly observing that the Revolution had outlasted the seventy days of the Commune and was now fairly to be called a revolution and not a revolt, imperturbably forcing his opponents to face plain facts, and giving them the time to take in those facts while he sat quietly writing in a notebook until he felt he had given them long enough, when, as he had expected, plain facts had brought most of his opponents round to agree with him. I walked through the streets and saw that people were weeping as they walked. Lenin was dead.

The account of Lenin's funeral which he sent to the *Guardian* was equally elegiac in tone:

Only a few besides members of the Central Executive Committee and the Diplomatic Corps were allowed into the Hall of Trade Unions to witness the last ceremony there. A few had arrived when I got there. In the middle of the hall, under the tall palms, the body of Lenin, in dull khaki, lay on a crimson catafalque guarded by a group of his old comrades. From time to time the guard was changed. All the guard stood motionless, some looking straight before them as on parade, others unable to turn their faces from the pale, sleeping face of their dead leader. Dzerzhinsky, in a brown leather coat, stood with bent head like a Franciscan monk. Stalin stood with arms folded, iron like his name. Bukharin, beside him, was still for once, like a figure carved in wax. Revolutionary banners hung on the walls, and among them in white letters on black were the words, 'Ilich is dead; his work lives.'

Gradually the hall filled with Communists, all in ordinary working clothes. Only in the group of diplomats, where beside Mr. Hodgson and Mr. Peters were men of almost every nationality, were there clothes that in any way reminded one of ordinary funerals. Here and there about the hall a summer lightning of white fire for the benefit of the kinematograph operators brilliantly lit up the white faces of bearded peasants in sheepskin coats, leather-jacketed workmen, and dull khaki uniforms.

Suddenly a stir ran through the hall, and all stiffened to immobility. Mrs. Lenin was standing by the bier looking at Lenin's face, calm, dry-eyed, as if unconscious that he and she were not alone in the room. There was absolute silence; then funeral music, a requiem followed by the International, after which, when the orchestra had finished, a revolutionary dirge was sung by all in the hall, while soldiers, even outside the hall and in the passages, stood at attention. I had a curious feeling that I was present at the founding of a new religion.

Arthur was present a few days later at another ceremony which, if possible, meant even more to him: when Hodgson presented the official Note to Chicherin in which the British Government formally recognised the Soviets as the *de jure* Government of Russia. 'It was a very happy day for me. "My war", which had lasted for more than five years after the Armistice of 1918, was over. I was free to struggle back as best I could to my proper job.'

(*To Evgenia, 3 February, Moscow*) I am illish and not fit to go out ... And you, poor Top, having an awful time with your dentist. Never mind how much your teeth cost. Have them done the best possible way. It will be much cheaper in the long run. Also if you have bad teeth your famous profile will be spoilt and your front view will be even worse than it is ... You do not really mean gold teeth. Gold teeth look perfectly awful and, in England at any rate, are only worn by Jew immigrants.

What you must have are teeth like mine, and the very best you can get, or, perhaps even better, teeth built on your old ones, what is called bridging. These stay in your mouth all the time. But I am inclined to think that my sort is the best ... I wish you were here. I would ask you to come in at once, but it would be silly as I must go to England anyway to deal with the divorce business and settle up about the blood money that I am to pay.

In mid-February Arthur returned briefly to Riga, and then set out for England. The vessel got trapped in the ice off the Swedish coast. Rescued from that adventure, he reached home and found, as he had expected, that Ivy's solicitors were holding up the decree until they had induced Arthur to agree to the money settlement they wanted. He put in a counter-proposal, and while waiting for an answer went up to Coniston.

(*To Evgenia, postmark 3 March, London*) It was really most beautiful. The high mountains were covered with snow and there was a dusting of snow over the lower ones, like a silver veil over the dark rocks, with a very blue sky, and the trees ruddy and dark purple. The lake was like black ink. Then I went across the lake to the village in the old dinghy, and bought some tobacco, and heard owls in the woods on the way back ... I drove to Windermere station this morning to come back to London, about ten miles over the hills, with perfectly gorgeous views every few yards, one after another of the mountains towering up, some with clouds about their heads and others quite clear against the sky. In the valley there was a little thin cat-ice on the lake, but only round the edges, and the little steamer was puffing up the lake as usual. I wish you could see it.

... The old Collingwoods are, I fear, getting very old indeed. He went for a little walk in the evening and got tired at once because Barbara and I walked too fast, and only a year or two ago he used to walk everybody off their feet and I well remember having almost to run to keep up with him. And he himself thinks he is finished, which is awful. But in his brain he is as fine as ever, and has done a lovely little history of the lake district with pictures by himself, which will be out in a few months. Robin also has a book just coming out, and I saw the proofs but they were very much too clever for me, and I could not make anything of them at all except that they made me very sleepy.

In London Arthur began to enjoy the sensation of being a successful author.

(*To Evgenia, 6 March*) I have been to the Cruising Association rooms, where there is a really fine collection of books on sailing, including *Racundra*!!!!!!!! I learnt there that several people are intending to sail to Riga and Reval this year because of the good time had in those parts by the Cook and me!!!!!! I only wish I had a photograph of the Cook's feet on the way back from Helsingfors. [Evgenia had a way of sticking out her feet in anger, when boats were becalmed and engines wouldn't start and husbands were unsatisfactory.] However as I haven't and as everybody seems to think that we were all in a permanent state of joy, unperturbed by weather or motor and full of mutual admiration and affection, I don't undeceive them and everyone who has a boat is dreaming of landing on Runö and visiting the harbour of Heltermaa.

... Most of the photographs we took in the garden when the shutter went wrong are quite useless. A few however are very good. There is a really lovely one of you. Anyone who did not know would think that you were really beautiful. Profile perfect, and a smile that would melt Spitzbergen. The very gentlest, sweetest creature! I look an ass in mine, so that's all right.

(*10 March*) I wish I did know for certain what we are going to be doing ... Only one thing is quite certain and that is that whatever happens we shall spend enough of the summer in *Racundra* to get another book. People are still buying the first *Racundra* ... Tell me what you think of the idea of trying a boy's book. I think it would be rather fun. In general I am digging round trying to make sure of driblets of money from enough sources to make it possible for us to scrape along in England, just going to Russia when necessary.

He had an unsatisfactory interview with the *Guardian* directors (in other words, the tribe of Scotts) when they refused to continue his retaining fee beyond the end of March. And he had an equally painful session at the dentist. Evgenia was sorely missed.

(*14 March*) It is a whole month today since I left you and I miss your ugly mug and even your horrid temper. I wish to goodness you were here to come to the Boat Show with me tomorrow. I wish to goodness we could go for one of our walks round our rooms at home and ostrich dance to show we don't really mind being unemployed. Generally I am very miserable not to have you about. Further I am very nervous because in an effort to get the divorce thing settled I have asked for an interview with Wiltshire. And that always keeps me in a fearful state of terror till it is over. Altogether I very much lack your large comfortable presence.

(*15 March*) My dearest old Top, I was so awfully glad to get your nice long letter ... I got it last night when I had come home from town extremely miserable after getting an awful letter from Wiltshire in which she says that all she is going to let me have of my things is my father's gun and my writing desk. She is not going to give up any of my books ... I shall be leaving England either this Friday or, if the Wiltshire business shows signs of getting done, Friday week. I should think it worth while to stay if I were really going to be able to get it finished up and to come out actually free to make discreet love to a certain young woman in Riga and ask her what she thinks of me as a possible husband.

I spent the whole day at the Boat Show today with Barbara, having a special press ticket from the *M.G.* A huge pile of *Racundra* was on sale and you would have been much amused. The show was interesting but it made me feel that we are jolly lucky to have got such a stout lump of a boat as *Racundra* so cheap. Not one of the boats shown, though some of them were much bigger, had anything like her cabin. I wouldn't care to live in any one of them unless alone, certainly not with anything less than an angel as a sailor and an archangel as a cook. Anybody with stiff white feet would make one of those boats impossible in five minutes, while in *Racundra* one can rub along for weeks with storms inside as well as out. Plenty of room for cyclone and anticyclone.

(*17 March*) Alas, it is quite clear already that I shall have to give up my books. I comfort myself by remembering that I needed no books for writing *Racundra* or the Fairy Stories, and generally I dare say that we shall be able to rub along without them. Though that does not lessen my woe at losing the books which

I have collected ever since I was a little boy. Still, the main thing is to get free from that appalling woman.

Francis, Joyce's eldest brat, tried to pull out some of his hair today to give me, and as in spite of tugging it would not come out, crawled to me across the floor and bravely offered his woolly head for me to take what I wanted. He saw that my need was greater than his. But it was extremely nice of him.

(*21 March*) My dearest Jenny, You are very good not to curse me for being so long. I am now getting cursed by the *M.G.* for not starting. And I simply can't start leaving all the legal business in such an awful unfinished mess. My solicitor, with whom I had tea yesterday, is a charming person but with a brain like a frozen potato. Everything I say to him gets all the point blunted before ever it reaches the other side. And the other side are claiming so much that it won't be worth while for me to do any work for the sake of trying to save money for writing afterwards. Their last move is to threaten not to have the decree made absolute at all. If they stick to that and insist that I shall agree to their full demands, I shall simply agree and then bring them to reason by coming back to England and earning no money. If we are very careful, we could, I think, manage three or even four years living simply on what we have plus what I should be able to earn by writing in England ... My new teeth hurt like anything.

(*22 March*) I comfort myself in the middle of all this beastliness by thinking of the good old Topsy who however cross and sulky she sometimes may be is really made up of solid comfortable decency and with whom I always feel as if I were in a comfortable harbour able to laugh at whatever beastly wind may be blowing outside. Good old Topsy. Wicked plump Topsy who will presently get back a very thin and worn out worried Charles ... If only I could write stories, we should be all right.

There were occasional alleviations of his misery.

(*23 March*) My dear, The appalling and terrifying Cruising Club interview is over. A lot of people were there and I was as shy as a very small schoolboy, ridiculously, childishly shy. I sweated all over inside my clothes. But it passed off all right and the master and owner of *Racundra* is going to be put up for membership by the Commodore himself, Sir Arthur Underhill, and by a member of the Committee of very high standing, so unless something untoward occurs I should get in at the very next vacancy ... Of course some swine may raise objections about politics and so on, but I hardly think so against the recommendation of the Commodore. So that's that. I got outside and shook myself and breathed heavily and am slowly recovering my normal confidence.

Evgenia gave him support from afar.

(*25 March*) I was just writing to Leslie when your next letter arrived, and such an awfully nice one. Don't you be a fool, 'not considering that you are worth so much.' You are worth a very great deal more than that. You have made the whole difference in my life, and books and money are only THINGS. Life matters ten times as much as all that and no one in the world has got such a jolly good dear decent wife as I have. So that's that. And no more rubbish on that subject please. The corners of my mouth are turned up almost to my eyes, and generally your letter made me feel I don't care a damn about anybody or anything except your good old self.

And there was a rather flattering political episode.

(*27 March*) I spent all yesterday afternoon with the Prime Minister [MacDonald]. I went to Downing Street at two thirty, and we talked there, and then went across to the House of Commons and continued. Then came question time in the house and I was let into the Distinguished!!!!! Strangers' Gallery and watched, and afterwards continued the discussion in the Prime Minister's room. It was incredibly interesting, much the most interesting thing I have seen for years. But if anything were needed to decide me that on no account would I ever stand for Parliament, yesterday afternoon was enough. It's not for me, but I much enjoyed watching other people at it, and wished you could have been there too ... The P.M. was very jolly and asked me to send in more reports on the general state of things out there. So that is all right.

At last he got his release.

(*9 April*) My dearly Beloved old Madam, All clear at last. I signed documents yesterday. Today at one, we exchanged documents with the other side, and on Monday, mechanically, the thing becomes absolute ... I am tired completely out but feel a sort of undercurrent of hope and the feeling that now at last we can make a fresh start ... TELL SEHMEL TO VARNISH THE FISHING BOAT AND PUT IT IN THE WATER! MAKE HIM GET IT READY AT ONCE SO THAT IT HAS TIME TO DRY.

There the matter officially ended. Arthur hurried back to Evgenia, and two days later they set off for Reval, to prepare *Racundra* for the summer, and to get married, which they did at the British Consulate on 8 May. Edith Ransome, who had already promised that as soon as they were established in England she would give them many of the books from her own house to start a new library, now wrote the kindest possible letter to Evgenia, welcoming her into the family. On 10 May *Racundra* was in the water and soon they were cruising in her. Arthur bought an accordion, presumably out of sheer lightness of heart. In June they were off on a month's visit to Moscow (the last which Evgenia was to pay for almost fifty years). It was a happy summer and a good beginning.

But the past cannot so easily be obliterated. It is striking that in all Arthur's letters about the divorce he never mentions Tabitha. Yet she was part of him, and very much part of the story. Her interests were as much affected by the divorce as anyone else's. The extreme bitterness between her parents was bound to injure her.

She was now fourteen, and had scarcely seen Arthur for five years. Her individuality was beginning to emerge: for instance, she had become deeply religious, which would draw her away from her father (on the other hand, she inherited his passion for walking). She might have grown away from her mother too, but it was not allowed. Ivy had even less intention of letting Arthur have a share in Tabitha than of letting him have his books. She read every letter which Tabitha received, and every one that she wrote. Sometimes she drafted the girl's letters to her father herself, handing each over for fair copying with the instruction, 'Just alter it a little bit to sound more like you.' Tabitha's *Reminiscences* add:

my mother never actually said anything against my father. She always maintained that he was charming, but then she would add some little thing which made me think differently. This was built up over the years, and gradually I almost grew to dislike him, and what letters I wrote became stilted and never natural. Whatever he did, or said, or wrote, I saw the wrong side of it.

This statement is unhappily confirmed by such letters as survive. And these letters in turn made an unfortunate impression at the other end, perhaps particularly on Evgenia, who soon came to think that Tabitha was a party to her mother's plots, and shared her mother's character, especially her untruthfulness. In these circumstances it would have been wonderful if father and daughter had remained friends. As it was they did not, to their mutual loss.

The breach was long in opening. One day, a year or two after Arthur's permanent return to England, when Tabitha was sixteen or seventeen, he suddenly wrote asking her to meet him in Salisbury and go for a walk.

It was autumn and the russet leaves were on the ground, and orange and bronze still on the trees. I went, and there was Dor-Dor tall and erect as ever, beaming with smiles, and we enjoyed our autumnal walk, around a race course I think, and talked of this and that, almost naturally, without my mother's supervision. Afterwards he gave me tea at the Cadena in the square ... He insisted I ate a cream and strawberry pastry sandwich. For years afterwards my father would talk to me of our happy walk at Salisbury.

At about the same period, when Arthur and Evgenia had settled near Windermere, they invited Tabitha to come for a sailing holiday.

My mother, on hearing this, absolutely forbade it, saying, 'No, your father will drown you. Make an excuse and say you can't go.' ... to tell a young girl that her father had only invited her for a holiday in order to drown her must have made a deep impression on me, for I always believed every word she said ... Looking back, I think I had very little chance of being the friendly daughter I might have been.

Arthur had long ago faced the fact that his flight from Ivy entailed the loss of Tabitha, for he not only dreaded the rows that would have attended any attempt to enjoy what today would be called equal access, but believed that it was important for Tabitha to belong entirely to one parent (since they could not all live together) and not be the object of cat-and-dog fighting. He stuck nobly to this perception, but its emotional cost to him may perhaps be assessed from the persistence, passion and unreasonableness with which he threw himself into the battle of the books, which would preoccupy him until after Ivy's death.

However much Arthur valued his library, he had got along quite well without it since 1915. The books are never mentioned in his surviving papers until they become a bone of contention at the time of the divorce. Then they began to acquire a fearful symbolic value. There can be no doubt that Arthur was bitterly hurt by Ivy's behaviour, which he thought at first was dictated by greed. No doubt he suddenly realised how much the books meant to him. 'A writer's library is part of himself,' he later commented; the loss of his books was the hardest but one personal blow he ever experienced – the other, worse, blow being the death of Ted Scott. But he hoped that when Ivy came to her senses and realised how useless the books were to her, she would hand them over. He met her in January 1929, ostensibly to discuss some minor problems about the payment of alimony, but really to negotiate about the books. The meeting was unsatisfactory. Arthur did get an undertaking from Ivy to give up one or two thousand volumes, but by this time they were so far apart that they were incapable of carrying out such an agreement. She let fall malicious remarks to the effect that she was not the only person who thought he could no longer write (it was now six years since the *Cruise* – journalism did not count); but she swore that it had not occurred to her that Arthur's career would be affected by the loss of his library. Arthur replied that the two things were connected: he could not write the sort of books he wanted to (perhaps he was still thinking of the Hazlitt project) without the library. He was never going to see that Ivy had unintentionally done him a good service by forcing him to rely on his imagination rather than his reading; nor did he know that in two months' time he would be starting *Swallows and Amazons*. When Ivy got home she persuaded herself that all she need do for the time being was to send some specially wanted volumes and some papers: some Santayana, that is, and as many of Arthur's pre-1914 diaries as she could find. He was miserable and furious with disappointment, the more so because he had been so confident that the books were going to arrive that he had laid on a lorry to bring them from the station to his house. This was characteristically unrealistic. He never asked himself how Ivy was going to pack the books and pay for their transportation: she must perform her act of atonement unaided. Besides, Tabitha was ill in the spring, and later in the year Ivy cracked her ankle. It is really not very surprising that the lorry was never called into service.

If that were all, Ivy might deserve sympathy. But she could not resist dragging in Tabitha, either to shelter behind or, more likely, because here was a golden opportunity to divide father and daughter. After her return to Hatch she drafted a cruel letter for Tabitha to copy and sign in the usual way. It protested against the proposed removal of the library, and asserted that Arthur would never be able to write any more books. This was bound to distress Arthur, as was a later letter which does not survive, though his comment on it does. Tabitha was apparently made to report that she and Ivy were 'rearranging' the books. Arthur protested in a draft letter (perhaps he did not send any version of it):

> Does she not realise the cruelty of saying such a thing to a man who spent the first thirty years of his life in collecting these books, to a man who is continually in need of them. There are not many daughters who would be happy to take their father's library while he is still alive.

Relations between father and daughter never recovered from this episode, though for years to come first one and then the other made earnest attempts to bridge the gulf: attempts which always went astray. It was all too sadly like the story of the crane and the heron in *Old Peter's Russian Tales*.

IX

Pastoral

My diary records events in the shortest and most useless form for the writer of an autobiography ... For the year 1926 I find entries like: Feb. 25: London. March 3: Larches in bud. March 6: First daffodils. April 20: Swallows in the garden. April 24: Sheep broke in and ate our lupins. May 15: Eight trout in the Crake. Manchester, wrote a leader. July 30: Salmon (9 lb.) at Winderwath, and so on – merely pastoral.

ARTHUR RANSOME, *Autobiography*

It is a relief to turn from the bitter wreckage of Arthur's first marriage to the cheerful progress of his second.

The *Manchester Guardian* accepted that Arthur had had enough of living in eastern Europe: he was allowed to come home, though Ted Scott was firm that he would have to live in or near Manchester, not a city of which Arthur was very fond. But it was enough to return, even if not in *Racundra*. For the time being the idea of sailing her to England was given up – presumably Arthur was not sure he could find her suitable quarters. She was laid up to winter at Riga, where Captain Schmel could keep an eye on her. In November the Ransomes set out for England. They left Riga and *Racundra* with considerable regret, which would have been no doubt much enhanced had they known that they were never to sail her again.

They reached London Bridge on 19 November, and were made welcome by Molly Hamilton. During the next few days Arthur celebrated his reunion with his friends by playing billiards with John Scott, dining at the Hirsts', and introducing Evgenia to everyone, including, of course, his family. Evgenia found Edith and Joyce distinctly stiff and formal at first (no doubt they were shy) but circumstances soon threw them together, and they all became true friends, 'especially mother'. The *Guardian* sent Arthur to Egypt for two months. Evgenia went to stay at Kemsing with her mother-in-law. Arthur worried about how she was getting on, alone on her first visit to England among numerous strangers, 'after being always alone with me'. He soon heard: his mother sent him a letter that made him howl with laughter.

(*To his mother, 13 January 1925*) Your second sentence 'Evgenia was getting savage' called up a very vivid picture and I know that it takes the hand of a practised tamer to deal with it. I laughed and am still laughing, with much affection both for her and you. I am glad my letter arrived in time. She evidently enjoyed Christmas with you very much and wrote a most jolly account of it ... Thank you very much for looking after my much beloved old Madam. I am so glad that she got on well with Cecily. And I think you realise too her solid goodness that is really only emphasised by her streaks of intolerance.

The *Guardian* was greatly pleased with Arthur's Egyptian reporting, but he himself got little out of the trip except one or two new friendships. Real life began again after his return to England on 18 February. He and Evgenia started to house-hunt at once. They wanted something in the Lake District, of course. It was the country of Arthur's heart, within convenient distance of Manchester – not too far, not too close (Arthur already dreaded the possibility that he might be drawn into the day-to-day routine of his newspaper). It was the Collingwood country: Evgenia and that family had taken to each other warmly, to Arthur's great relief and joy. On 2 March they travelled to Windermere, where they had heard that a cottage was for sale. Next day they visited it, and bought it at once.

(*To his mother, 5 March*) We have found the cottage, on very high ground but sheltered from the north, overlooking the whole valley of the Winster. From the terrace in front of the house you can see Arnside and a strip of sea under the Knott. Away to the left you can see Ingleborough, and from the fell just behind the house you can see Ambleside, and all the Lake hills. The house is called Low Ludderburn and is marked on the Ordnance maps.

It contains two rooms on the ground floor, plus scullery hole. Two rooms upstairs. A lean-to in bad repair, capable of being turned into a first-rate kitchen. A huge two-storey barn in first-rate condition, stone built, at present with stables below, and the top part which has a double door opening on the road is used to put up a Morris Cowley. Water from a Roman well just behind the house, our title deeds giving us the right to lay a pipe from it to the house. A lot of apples, damsons, gooseberries, raspberries, currants, and the whole orchard white with snowdrops and daffodils just coming.

Blemishes. Very low beams in the rooms. A good deal to be done to make it really nice. But it is a stout place (walls two feet six thick) and livable in at once, uncomfortably, while capable of being pulled about and turned into an almost perfect place, bit by bit.

They asked £650 but the owner in the absence of the agent came down to £550. Freehold, with 1¾ acres, including a tiny scrap of wood, and a jolly rough garden, a terrace jutting out of the hillside and the orchard sloping beneath it. It is the best *site* from the point of view of having a good view in the whole district, and will consequently most certainly go up in value, as building spreads beyond Storrs ... There is not room in it for much furniture.

A postscript from Evgenia shows that she was equally enthusiastic:

My dear Mother, we are so overcome by finding ourselves in possession of the loveliest spot in the whole of the Lake District with a very small house that wants a lot of doing to it to make it really nice and comfortable, that we can't write coherently about it and we hope you will forgive this very short letter.

Not much needs to be added to this evocation of Low Ludderburn (so called because there is another house, High Ludderburn, a little further up the fell). It has changed very little in half a century. The orchard is still white with snowdrops in February and golden with wild daffodils in March; white violets grow in every crack of the terrace; the view over to Whitebarrow Scar is as stupendous as ever. The ceilings are still low (they bothered both Arthur and Evgenia). Such improvements as the present owners have introduced – running water and electricity chief among them, and a magnificent fireplace of three slate monoliths in one of the sitting-rooms – have been most tactfully done. This is still the house that the Ransomes inhabited.

They made some alterations themselves, which decisively affected the character of the place. Evgenia saw at once that the big barn offered enormous scope for an ingenious hand. The doors on to the road in the upper storey were replaced by a fireplace; a solid new floor was put in; and a large window facing White-barrow. Arthur thus acquired the best workroom he was ever to have. And Evgenia, in whom a passion for horticulture had steadily strengthened since they started putting in bulbs and seeds at Kaiserwald, had a garden.

Unfortunately the purchase of Ludderburn entailed the sale of *Racundra*. It is hard to believe that anything other than financial considerations would have induced Arthur to sell his peerless vessel and finally give up his dream of sailing her to England; while buying and altering his house had made a large hole in his savings. *Racundra* was advertised in *Yachting Monthly*. Adlard Coles, already a promising writer on sailing, took the bait, and on 4 July Arthur agreed to sell *Racundra* for two hundred guineas. He was in Riga by this time, and wrote long letters to Mr Coles full of helpful advice and introductions to useful people in Riga, including the Ancient Mariner, for he himself would have left before Mr Coles could get there. The agreement between the two men had one curious detail: Coles had to agree not to use the name *Racundra* in the book he was planning about his voyage from Riga to England. In the book that eventually emerged, *Close Hauled*, she was named *Annette II*, and the truth about the identity of the two boats did not leak out for thirty years, though it is obvious to anyone who happens to compare *Close Hauled* with *Racundra's First Cruise*. It is difficult to fathom Arthur's motives: had he allowed Coles to use the boat's true name the sales of *Close Hauled* might well have helped those of *Racundra's First Cruise*. Maybe he feared that Mr Coles would make a botch of his book; or did not want him to exploit a market which Arthur had created; or (perhaps the most likely) did not want to advertise his treachery in selling the boat of which he had boasted so much.

At any rate, *Racundra* came to no harm: in 1982 she was still afloat, though now based in the far waters of the West Indies.

Her former master was not so lucky. Two hundred guineas was no doubt a fair price for what Adlard Coles bought; it scarcely

covered what Arthur Ransome sold, which was more than his
dream-boat. The *Racundra* years had been ones of steady good
health: the sea and sea-breezes seem to have been sovereign for his
ulcer. The moment he became a landlubber again he began to go
downhill. The Lake District did not altogether suit Evgenia,
either. She found it much too rainy for comfort. Arthur recorded
in his diary that he accepted Coles's offer with some doubt; it is
a pity he over-rode his reluctance. But, as was to be shown again
and again in his later life, he had a genius for making bad bargains.

Meanwhile he and Evgenia were utterly happy at Low Ludderburn. The big workroom was a particular joy. It is impossible to
paint an absolutely accurate picture of Arthur's arrangements
there, but an approximation is possible, and may be fortified by
details of what we know about his dispositions in later dwellings.

Books accumulated freely, as in the days before 1913. There
was a big work-table with an 'Aladdin' oil-lamp on it (such
lamps were then common in houses without electricity) and a
comfortable armchair, a present from his mother, between it and
the fire. On a little table close at hand was a portable Victorian
desk, also a present from Edith Ransome. Arthur would sit in the
chair ploughing through all the newspapers that he had to read in
the line of duty; sometimes Evgenia would look in and collapse
into it with a sigh of relief at getting off what she at least once
called her 'threadmill'. The work-table never resembled the clean
desk of a businessman. The blotter was businesslike, perhaps, with
its smart AR stamped on one of the corners. There was also a tin
of pen-nibs, because he never used a fountain-pen; a typewriter,
because he did use that; seal and sealing wax, for parcels; mapping
pen and pencils, in a china tray, for drawing (a special anti-roll
device, necessary in those days before chamfering, was a Turk's
Head knot tied in string about the waist of each pencil); an antique
Russian ink-well; an ash-tray, also Russian, carved out of wood
in the shape of a duck with a hole in its back; a black cat, for luck:
a little one of plaster, bought in Egypt, reproducing an ancient
figurine; a lucky stone from the top of Coniston Old Man – perhaps the same that once adorned *Racundra*'s cabin. All this testified
to Ransome's need, like that of other professional writers, to have
the comfort of pet gadgets and objects round him as he worked,
things to play with when stuck for a phrase or a thought. But the
effect is as well of a small boy surrounded by his toys. There were
also: two dismountable miniature candlesticks, which had been

very useful in unlighted railway carriages on his Russian travels; a miniature telescope; a 'bun' penny; a George III penny; a pocket compass. Over the years other items accumulated, if not on the work-table, then on nearby walls and shelves – pictures, and presents from admirers. Finally, on his mother's death, he inherited his father's desk, a handsome, plain mahogany affair that he used for the rest of his life. But it was never at Low Ludderburn, and in practice Arthur found it too small for him: so his work spilled over on to several small side-tables.

Fishing was also given its due. One of Arthur's angling cronies, Major Birkett, gave him leave to fish all the upper part of the river Winster which flowed along the valley below Ludderburn; another, Colonel Kelsall, helped him to do so. Kelsall lived across the valley at Barkbooth, a house which, like Low Ludderburn, lacked a telephone. So a signalling system was devised by means of which the two fishermen could concert plans. Black wooden shapes – triangles, squares, diamonds – were hoisted against the walls of whitewashed Ludderburn; white ones against the dark grey stones of Kelsall's barn. Urgent messages flared across the valley: HAVE YOU ANY WORMS? and are remembered in the neighbourhood to this day. If possible, Kelsall enjoyed the business even more boyishly than Arthur. He observed strict military security with his signal book. As Arthur observed, 'the fish never had a chance of learning beforehand what was planned for them.' The signals eventually found their way into *Winter Holiday*.

Kelsall also had two small sons, Desmond and Richard (or Dick). Arthur found them excellent playfellows, and some of their adventures together also sowed seed. For instance, when Dick was about six, Arthur took Desmond, a keen angler, fishing on the Winster. Dick was indifferent to the sport, but, not to be left out, joined the party, and while the two experts sought for trout with little success, landed a half-pounder with an ash stick, black thread and a bent pin. Arthur sent him a card of congratulations on landing 'the best fish of the season, so far. My best was only 7 inches. Perhaps they like thread.' A year or two later, inspired by voyages in the Ransomes' boat on Windermere, the young Kelsalls fitted a sail, made out of an old sheet, and a mast (a ten-foot bamboo sweet-pea support) to their Triang pedal car. Arthur arrived in time for the test runs, and joined in with whoops of joy. The boys greatly enjoyed his company. He used to give children's parties in the barn at Ludderburn, at which he played the accordion, sang sea shanties and told Anansi stories. Evgenia was just as welcome. She had a wonderful sense of humour, they thought, and though they could not help noticing her heavy Russian accent they admired her splendid command of English. She used to help Mrs Kelsall with the *Guardian* crossword. What impressed them most was her strength. 'She introduced us children to a Russian game like skittles but played with large logs. The ease with which she could pick up a log and throw it at the set pieces amazed us.'

Life at Ludderburn would have been impossible for the Ransomes without a car, so they bought what Arthur called 'a perambulating biscuit tin' and promptly collided with a wall at Hartbarrow Farm where they were staying while their cottage was made ready. The biscuit tin survived, and gave them easy access to the lake, where, if they could not hope to find, let alone afford, a worthy successor to *Racundra*, at least they could sail in dinghies. The car also made it possible to sample all the good fishing rivers in the region, and to visit friends: the Collingwoods at Lanehead, and Barbara, who had recently married an old friend, Oscar Gnosspelius, and some farther afield, for instance Philips Price, now re-established at his family house in Gloucestershire. Price's daughter, Tania Rose, well remembers Arthur's first arrival in September 1928. Price was in the fields, Arthur was unexpected, Mrs Price welcomed him excitedly as an old friend. She was so certain that she was preparing a pleasant surprise for her husband that she hid Arthur behind the drawing-room curtain, and when Price came in drew it back suddenly, to reveal a beaming Ransome, arms thrown wide.

Arthur had now got pretty much what he had always wanted, and a bit more: he bought a gun, and occasionally bagged rabbits or pheasants which strayed on to his property. Evgenia learned to enjoy walking up and down steep hills. But there were drawbacks. For one thing, Arthur's ulcer began to give trouble and would eventually prostrate him completely before a cure was found. That would not happen for some years; in the mean time he had to earn his bread and butter; and that meant the *Guardian*. The workroom, it seemed, was to be used for cranking out leading articles on Russia and Egypt, not for what, in his heart of hearts, Arthur still believed was his vocation, the writing of stories.

He loved the *Guardian* in many ways, and Ted Scott in particular. Scott was a man whom everybody liked, though sometimes (for example, with Malcolm Muggeridge) pity for his position, chained under his father, almost outweighed affection. He was quiet, considerate, earnest and solidly sensible – an excellent counterweight to someone so volatile as Arthur. Arthur enjoyed fussing over Ted. He too disapproved of the way in which old C. P. Scott hung on to power, adding to the weight on his over-conscientious son's shoulders, and constantly looked about for ways of diverting his friend. He never thought much of golf, and drew rude pictures of the sport in his letters to Ted ('AN AWFUL GAME'): for it left the editor free to worry about the paper while tramping round a course. Now if Ted could be induced to take up fishing, or sailing ... meanwhile, he went down with flu, and was overwhelmed with advice on what to read while in bed: 'HAVE YOU EVER READ MONTAIGNE?' Ted protested mildly against this concern for his literary education.

(*To E. T. Scott, 7 February 1929*) Blow your literary education. I never gave it a thought anyhow. What I did and do think is something quite different, and that is that I never knew a man who had managed in the course of a life as long (within a month or two) as my own to evade so many forms of enjoyment. A natural dislike of waste prods me to prod you.

Scott bore up under the prodding with good humour, but from time to time he put Arthur in his place. When Ransome wrote an unsatisfactory notice of Bernard Pares's memoirs – Arthur was deeply vexed by a few passing inaccurate references to himself, and devoted most of his space to correcting them – Scott published it, but told Arthur plainly why it would not do:

I really think you allowed your obsession with the personal aspect of Pares's book to spoil the review. I don't think I should have printed it from anybody else, and if your name didn't carry it to some extent, not even from you. You could have done all that was necessary in a sentence and then reviewed the book – which you have not done.

There were not many people from whom Arthur was ready to accept such straight talking. Fortunately it was not often necessary. Scott had a deep respect for Arthur's skill as a reporter, particularly for his ability to visit a foreign country and quickly get the hang of its politics. This admiration was at times highly inconvenient: Evgenia passed her second Christmas in England, like her first, without her husband, whom the *Guardian* had sent at that season to China. This experience was rather more productive than the trip to Egypt. It led to the last of Arthur's political books, *The Chinese Puzzle*, published in 1927; and, years later, gave him the idea and the raw material of one of his best children's books. Arthur hugely enjoyed himself in China. He visited his old aunt, Deaconess Edith Ransome, still labouring as a missionary in Peking: she was delighted to see him again, and wrote to tell his mother so, adding: 'I hope his hair will grow before he sees you. He had it cut by a Japanese barber, who shaved his head till he looked like a Buddhist priest!!' She may not have realised that the Japanese barber was only completing the work of nature.

Arthur was full of dread that C. P. Scott would send him away for a third Christmas. As it turned out, the old man stayed his hand, and so on 31 December 1927 Arthur and Evgenia were able to initiate what became a tradition: they climbed up Ludderburn Hill at midnight and listened to the church bells ringing in the New Year. The bells were almost certainly those of Crosthwaite, but Arthur, influenced perhaps by his friend Gordon Bottomley's poem, always said they were the bells of Cartmel. He never explained how, if so, they reached his fellside through, round or over the noble bulk of Gummer's How. Then the news arrived of Trotsky's fall and exile, and CPS sent Arthur off on what proved to be his last visit to Moscow. He was there throughout February 1928, seeing Litvinov and Chicherin and being entertained by Chinese exiles (led by Madame Sun Yat Sen); but the diary entries are ominous: they show that he was ill during at least half his stay. His ulcer was getting out of control.

Ted Scott knew that there was more to Arthur than his reporting skill, and joined with a will in the search for acceptable ways of combining Low Ludderburn with a job on the *Guardian*. Arthur was being groomed for the literary editorship against the day, not too distant, when Allan Monkhouse would retire; in the mean time he must be kept happy. Besides, ever since the *Cruise* it had been clear that Ransome could write fascinatingly on anything he chose. He would enliven the pages of the paper on any topic. So when he said that the *Guardian* wasn't doing enough for fishermen, Scott jumped at the opportunity. He offered Arthur a regular column to fill with what material he liked, on fishing or similar subjects. Arthur was delighted.

(*To his mother, 2 April 1925*) My job is to include a fortnightly or possibly weekly article on the fishing in the whole district north of Manchester, and such events in the Lake District as the Grasmere Sports, Grasmere plays, hound trails, hunting articles etc., which I am to deal with in my own way and make as jolly a feature of the paper as I can. It will be great fun, and if I manage to knock out a fairly original and picturesque method in these things, they will be naturally unwilling to send me out of England more than they can help ... I think the arrangement is pretty well ideal, as a transition at any rate, and I think that as it will mean a lot of open air in pursuit of things that I am interested in anyway, it will mean a very jolly life in itself.

The result was 'Rod and Line', a column which could have appeared in no other paper than the *Guardian*. It flourished for a few years, and was dropped when the author had exhausted the vein. Arthur always under-rated these articles. At first they were welcome as an excuse for an orgy of fishing in every river or pond of the lake country and several outside it, but in the end the thought of the articles he would have to write began to spoil his pleasure in angling. He enjoyed his fishing much more once he had given up the column, and dismissed as mere journalism the volume which collected some of the pieces. In fact it contained some of his best writing, and has never been without friends.[1] It is at least clear that, if book reviews and leading articles are added to the account, the *Guardian* got its money's worth (£300 p.a. and piece-rates).

It was 'Rod and Line' which took him down to Gloucestershire in 1928. Philips Price had told him of a pond near his house which was full of easily-caught tench, and Arthur, the trout season being nearly over, and thinking he should do his duty by as many fish as possible, went down to have a try at it. Unfortunately it turned out that Price, ignorant that fish have their close seasons as much as game, had caught his tench in May; and since then ducks had devoured all the green weeds which, according to a seventeenth-century writer, tench love exceedingly. Arthur fished the pond

---

1 In 1982 it was used as the basis for a charming little television series on Channel 4, in which the actor and angler Sir Michael Hordern recited AR's words in voice-over while the screen showed him fishing the rivers mentioned in the book, and re-enacting some of the incidents described.

for two days and caught nothing but eels. He expressed his views on the whole business both in 'Rod and Line' and in Price's visitors' book:

Where is the man who'd use a cartridge
In April on a sitting partridge?
Where is the man who finds it pleasant
To shoot the bantling July pheasant
And where the man who blithely kills
Grouse in the time of daffodils?
O Philips Price! Did you not blench
To catch and eat a Maytime tench?
What wonder that a spell was thrown
When such a monstrous deed was done?
The affronted tench have gone for good.
Ducks undisturbed eat all the food.
The angler watching by the shore
Shall see the great fish roll no more
And Price's guests come late to meals
Bringing not tench but wriggling EELS!

Price was not going to submit silently to such rhyming. He wrote beneath:

Where is the man with knowledge slender
Who sought a crow's nest in November?
And where the boy who climbed a larch
To rob a magpie's nest in March?
Oh Arthur Ransome! You amaze
Me at your ken of Nature's ways;
For who has seen, when daffodil
Our meadows deck o'er dale and hill
A partridge sitting in *April*!!!

The next visit to Taynton was not so cheerful. The pond was given up as a bad job, so Arthur was provided with a packet of sandwiches and dropped at a nearby river for the day. Unfortunately he was also provided with a companion, Tania, Price's daughter, who was about nine years old. Tania had charge of the sandwiches and served Arthur his lunch; but he didn't speak to her all day, from ten in the morning to five in the afternoon. The poor thing was sick all that night. It was unlike Arthur to be so unimaginative, not to say selfishly bad-mannered; and perhaps a hint was dropped. For next time he turned up he taught Tania and her brother Peter to fish in the despised pond. Still it is not surprising that Tania formed the impression that he was a with-drawn, silent, broody person, and was astonished as well as pleased when, on getting to know him again in the 1950s, she found him rosy, beaming and talkative.

Matters went better with Dick Scott, Ted's son. Arthur en-thused him over fishing for trout with worms, and taught him how to do it. His way of doing so throws some light on his blunder with Tania.

> He never actually and directly taught me at all. That was not his method. He took me frequently to watch himself fishing. He was not of course a jokey man even with children. In fact I believe he behaved exactly the same with children as with adults. And he was a serious man who did not moderate his seriousness for the benefit of children. He was also one of the few adults in whose presence it seemed perfectly natural and acceptable to remain silent if one had nothing to say, and to accept readily his own silence. I occasionally drove up to his Windermere cottage from Manchester with him – aged be-tween 12 and 14 – and there was certainly no chatter – little conversation. Although he had particularly sparkling, almost glinting eyes and a formidable moustache he was not intimidat-ing to the young – but neither would they ever have presumed with him.

Behind Arthur's behaviour in these encounters may have lain the memory of how his father tried to drive him into fishing. Arthur was not going to make the same mistake. Children were free to watch him, if they liked; if not, they were equally free to go and find loaches, or catch trout with black thread. His mistake was in forgetting that some children were bound to dislike this treatment as much as he had disliked Cyril Ransome's.

Richard Scott has warm memories of Arthur Ransome, but he knew quite well that the Scott who mattered was his father. At bottom Ted was as fond of Arthur as Arthur was of him. They were complementary characters, and as such the editor really needed his employee's moral support. Scott was lonely in 'the corridor', surrounded by men who were his father's appointees, not his; men alert for signs that he was unequal to the legacy of CPS. He had to guard his tongue, yet he badly needed a confidant. Arthur, who never passed as many as two consecutive nights in Manchester if he could help it, was perfect in the role. 'When I came to Cross Street to write a leader, and went to spend the night at Ted's he could say any mortal thing he felt like saying, knowing that it was like dropping a letter down a disused mineshaft. By six o'clock in the evening of the next day when he had to meet "the corridor" again, I should be back in the hills.' In these conditions the friendship ripened steadily, becoming an ever more essential part of Arthur's pleasant life.

But nothing seemed to bring any nearer the writing of books worthy of the Ludderburn workroom.

X

Swallows and Amazons

'I will make, if possible, a book that a child shall understand, yet a man will feel some temptation to peruse should he chance to take it up.' – Walter Scott's Diary, June 10, 1827, about his plans for writing stories from Scottish history for little Johnnie Lockhart. I have always thought this a perfect description of the books I should like to have written.

ARTHUR RANSOME, undated memorandum

In April 1928 Ernest and Dora Altounyan came back from Syria for a long stay at Bank Ground Farm below Lanehead. By now they had five children: Taqui, Susie, Mavis (known as Titty), Roger and Brigit. The family lived most of the time in Aleppo, where Ernest and his father ran a hospital; but they visited Coniston every few years. A surviving photograph shows three of the children sailing as passengers with their aunt Barbara on the lake in 1923. By 1928 they were deemed old enough to learn to sail for themselves.

As far as the children knew at first, what happened immediately after their arrival was simply a characteristic piece of their father's impulsive, enthusiastic generosity. While the others were unpacking he went off to Walney Island, by Barrow-in-Furness, and came back with two rather heavy fourteen-foot dinghies. These were to be the children's boats for the rest of the season. But one of them was to become Arthur Ransome's property when the Altounyans returned to Aleppo: the business had been concerted between the two men beforehand, and Arthur had paid his share. He also took a hand, naturally enough, in teaching the children to use their vessels. He stood on the end of the Lanehead jetty and scolded them affectionately if they behaved like 'duffers'.

It is easy to misrepresent his general attitude to children. All his surviving friends remember occasions when he displayed an unmistakable aversion to infant company. But he was always interested in anyone who wanted to learn something from him. It is perhaps Malcolm Muggeridge who, in his memoirs, states the truth most precisely.

> Ransome never seemed to care much for children, which may well be a necessary qualification for writing successfully about and for them. Most adults like children because they are different from them; a child-like adult like Ransome dislikes them and is bored by them, precisely because he *is* like them. For that very reason, he can understand their games and attitudes as an adult cannot, and so his writings interest them.[1]

Mr Muggeridge had several opportunities to observe Arthur fishing, and like others saw him do it in silence and with solemnity – 'the beautiful solemnity of a child, though one with a large soup-strainer moustache sprouting out of a rubicund face.'

So it is not really surprising that Arthur enjoyed playing with the Altounyans. They had several recommendations. Not only did they want to learn something he loved to teach, it was a pastime they could share with him afterwards – by racing the dinghies, for example, or sailing to Peel Island for a picnic tea. Then, they were part-Collingwoods. And he had too acute and generous a sense of character not to respond to their individuality, once a ripening acquaintance began to make them properly known to him. He had met them before. In 1924 Taqui, the eldest, had flatteringly remarked, 'Not all uncles are ugly. Uncle Arthur is pretty. So is Uncle Robin,' and the observation, passed on by Barbara, had been proudly set down in Arthur's diary. Now they all began to get to know each other really well. Arthur thought the children charming, in part, perhaps, because of their slight touch of Eastern exoticism.

He was also delighted to have a ship of his own again, even if she was on loan to others for a while. The question was, which of the two little boats from Walney would become his in due course? One they named the *Swallow*, after the old Collingwood dinghy of long ago, and the other *Mavis* (Victorian for song-thrush) to show

1 *The Green Stick*, pp. 178–9.

that she was a sister-ship and perhaps in compliment to Titty. *Mavis* had a centreboard, and was somewhat the better sailer; but *Swallow* was the one they all came to love most. She was fast and steady and her brown sail gave her character, as did her deep keel. Arthur loved her as much as the children did, and in the generosity of their hearts they decided to give up *Swallow* to him. *Mavis* they kept in the family, and she is sailed on Coniston Water by Roger Altounyan to this day.

It was an idyllic summer. Work for the *Guardian* was not unbearably demanding. The only real shadow on life was Arthur's wretched health. He was falling ill at shorter and shorter intervals because of his ulcer, and was displaying an alarming tendency to come out in lumps (perhaps because he had a grumbling appendix). None of this was enough to kill a resurgence of his creative energies. At some point he wrote two yachting yarns, rather in the manner of Rudyard Kipling, which were published next year in the *Pall Mall Magazine*: they are companion pieces to *Racundra's First Cruise*, and one of them, 'The Unofficial Side', is interesting as the only fictional use Ransome ever made of the Russian Revolution. He began to make plans for collecting some of the 'Rod and Line' papers into a book. He saw two little girls in red caps playing on the shores of Coniston, and idly began to consider how they might be put into a story. In the autumn he agreed to write a short play about Aladdin for performance at Peggy Scott's school in Manchester. Peggy was Ted's young daughter, and appeared in the play as the Slave of the Lamp. Arthur and Ted watched it together; according to the playwright they agreed that it was 'pretty bad'. 'All the same,' Ted added, 'it's no good thinking you won't go on doing this kind of thing.' And the audience laughed in the right places: even the teachers.

Then work and winter closed in together. *Swallow* was laid up on 17 December. Arthur hoped he could now devote himself to writing a story but 'every day or two there is some new tiny bit of a job that has to be done, one thing after another, and all these little things, which cannot be helped when you work for a daily newspaper, make book-writing proper almost hopeless.' The 'Rod and Line' book didn't count, since it was only a collection of articles. Arthur began to feel that he would never again write a true book. His immediate future seemed so restless. He and Evgenia would have to move about a lot between late December and early January, going to London as well as to Manchester, and there was talk of the *Guardian* sending him to South America after that. This proved to be a false alarm, but he still had a great deal to do when he got back to Ludderburn on 12 January 1929. He was not pleased when Ernest Altounyan announced his intention of calling on the 19th. Arthur was busy going through old copies of the *Guardian* to select material for *Rod and Line*; he and Evgenia had scarcely got over a three-night stay by Dick Scott, who had left on the 16th. Nervous, probably irritable, at the idea of turbulent children creating untidiness in the workroom, Arthur said that Ernest would be welcome, but he must come *alone*. On the appointed day a car drew up outside the big stone pillars that form the entrance to Low Ludderburn, and Arthur, from his window, was indignant to see children getting out. He hurried down into the yard with anything but hospitable intentions, and there were Susie and Titty coming towards him, each holding a large and handsome red Turkish slipper and uttering cries of 'Many Happy Returns'. It had been Arthur's birthday the day before; his friends had remembered, if he had not; the slippers were his present. Ernest soon felt it safe to emerge from hiding (no doubt he was lurking behind one of the pillars), for Arthur was delighted, and ashamed of his earlier grumpiness.

He was deeply touched by this attention from the youngest members of the family that meant so much to him; touched in ways he could never quite explain, though he often tried to do so.[2] Some defence fell, and the Altounyans walked into his affections as directly as their elders had done twenty-five years before. He felt for them all the more because only three days after the gift-giving they had to leave *Swallow* and the lakes for the dust of the East. Then and there (perhaps as he was trying on 'the handsomest slippers that anyone ever saw') it occurred to him to write a book about *Swallow* that they could read when they were far away among the sands, the camels and the mosquitoes (Arthur seems to have imagined Syria as totally arid). It would be some

2 The story of the origins of *Swallows and Amazons* has been often told, in versions of varying accuracy. AR wrote at least three different accounts at different stages of his life; Evgenia wrote others; the Altounyans have given their own testimonies. AR's versions contradict each other in important points; those of Evgenia are thoroughly untrustworthy. Contemporary documents (e.g. AR's diary) provide some measure of control, and bear out several of the Altounyan recollections. Of AR's versions it is clear that the earliest (1930: 'A Letter to a Friend') is the most accurate.

compensation to them, perhaps. He said nothing about the idea, either on the 19th, or when he went to see the children off at Windermere station. His life had been littered with projects that came to nothing. Best to keep quiet about this one in case it too proved abortive.

It seems likely that originally he had in mind a book modelled on *Racundra's First Cruise*, in which the boat would be the central character. There were obvious difficulties in carrying out this scheme. *Swallow* was a much simpler boat than *Racundra*, if no less beloved, and messing about on Coniston or Windermere lacked the drama and the narrative possibilities provided by the voyage on the Baltic. But Arthur soon settled that the book, if written at all, would centre on the *Swallow* and her actual crew; which was just the pattern of the *Cruise*.

He mulled over these points without, so far as can be gathered, any great sense of urgency. There were other things to think of. It was a very cold winter. The rainwater tank froze, so did the spring up the fell: the Ransomes had to draw all their water from the lower well, which meant lugging full buckets uphill. They watched skaters on Windermere at Bowness, walked across the ice from the steamer pier to the Hell Hole, and round a boat called *Maid Marion* that was frozen in. The frost lasted until early March. There were such crowds out to enjoy the ice that the roads were as choked and dusty as in summertime. It was a moment for semi-hibernation. Arthur did not object. His summer tale was forming in his mind. His only anxiety was that years of discursive journalism might have made him incapable of planning and carrying out a coherent narrative. He was afraid to start writing.

The Scotts, very involuntarily, gave him a prod. The *Manchester Guardian* was losing Sprigge, its Berlin correspondent, it was soon going to lose its Saturday essayist, before long it would need a new literary editor. Ransome, already designated for the last of these jobs, was just the man, they thought, for the other two as well. On 20 February CPS sent for him to Manchester, and asked him to be ready to go to Berlin at the end of April; a year or eighteen months later he could return and be literary editor. Arthur said he knew no German, but Scott brushed the point aside: he had learned Russian easily enough, hadn't he? Arthur saw the prison shades gathering round him again, and returned to Ludderburn in gloom. The shades deepened on 2 March when Scott gave Arthur lunch and offered him an enormous salary: approximately £1,100 *per annum*. They became pitch-black on 18 March, when CPS sent a telegram: 'Sprigge left Berlin. Will you go there as soon as possible?' Fortunately Arthur and Evgenia had already talked the whole thing through, and she, admirably, had agreed with his wish to have done with political journalism for good. It squared with her own tastes – she was far too caught up in the progress of the Ludderburn garden to want to leave for a city – but it was nevertheless courageous and loyal to accept Arthur's decision to resign from the *Guardian* with effect from 19 June; for after that date they would have no sure income at all. Arthur went to Manchester at once and gave notice.

Swallow was a comfort. On 13 March they had gone to look at her in her winter shed. On 24 March they got her into the water for the first time and sailed down Windermere to the Storrs Hall pier, where they ate tea, and then had a fine sail back in the dusk, although there was very little wind. Robin Collingwood liked sailing in a calm because he could be alone with his deepest, most creative thought; now Arthur got the same benefit. He thought about his voyages in *Swallow* with the Altounyans; and the days when he had first known Dora and Ernest; and days before that; and making camp for tea on Peel Island. He thought about the girls in red caps. ' ... before I got home I had the beginning of the book in my head and I took a sheet of paper and began to put down some of the things that happened.'

He had settled three important related points, which determined the development of the story, and much else besides. First, it was to *be* a story: only fiction could give the book the shape and impetus it needed. Second, since Arthur was in no position to neglect any idea which might bring in money, he had to think of possible customers, and do something about the over-supply of girls in the Altounyan family. What would have been quite all right for a private audience would not do for a public one. So Taqui was replaced by the boy called John. Thirdly, since the essence of the book was to be an attempt to catch the joys of boats, lakes and islands, and joys have first to be felt as discoveries, the story must be one of exploration, a sort of modern *Thorstein of the Mere*: the children would come to the shores of the lake, find *Swallow*, and then an island, and then go exploring further. And like all explorers they would meet adventures: pirates; savages.

Arthur began to write, and found he was doing so with extraordinary speed and certainty, as if he were Hugh Walpole. No writing had ever made him so happy.

> I used to hate everything else I had to do (except fishing and sailing) and I used to get away into my room in the top of the old barn (putting cement to keep the rain out drove the owls away, but you'll be glad to hear they went no further than the biggest of the yew-trees, and one of them, calling at night, made his contribution to the book). Up in the old barn I used to wonder what was going to happen and how, and while I was writing things came tapping out on the paper that used to make me get up and walk about and chuckle as if someone were telling me a story instead of me writing one for other people.

He wrote the story continuously (which was not his later practice) until he reached what became chapter 24, carried along on the wave of creative gusto. At night he would take the manuscript to his bedroom, so that he could reach out his hand and touch its cover as it lay beside him in the dark (a piece of magic like dipping that same hand in Coniston). This urgency, this artistic certainty and delight, surprised the author, but need not surprise anyone else. By no blundering process of trial and error, but by the natural growth of his skill and spirit, he had evolved to the point where he could at last achieve the original form which he needed to fulfil his ambitions. He had wanted to write stories for children since his early youth. He had reflected endlessly on the art of narration. The years of journalism, little though he thanked them, had given his style lucidity, flexibility and strength. They had also cleared his mind on matters of value: had confirmed his commitment to the world of the imagination, not that of action. Finally, he had a vision, a burden of feeling and memory to discharge: for the deepest psychological reasons the world of childhood on the waters of Coniston and Windermere was full of significance. Writing about it would enable him to act out a profound personal drama, and thus be free. The process by which he came to write *Swallows and Amazons* was, in short, perfectly logical, though the accidental played its part. The materials had all been assembled, but they might have waited over-long for the detonating spark. It was most fortunate that the Altounyans decided to make him a present of those slippers.

By 5 April (that is, nearly a fortnight after he started) he had written just over fifty pages, and decided that it was time to consult a publisher: much though he was enjoying himself, money was too short to allow him to continue with *Swallows and Amazons* if there was no market for it. Fortunately he was already in touch with Jonathan Cape, the outstanding publisher of his generation. In 1926 Molly Hamilton had tried unsuccessfully to interest Cape in the unpublished fantasy *Blue Treacle*. Then Cape had approached Arthur with a view to issuing *Racundra's First Cruise* in his Traveller's Library. Arthur had agreed, and so, foolishly, had Allen & Unwin. Or rather it was foolish of them to let Arthur slip between their fingers entirely, as he was about to do. Perhaps they despaired of his money-making capacity, for of the five books he had published with them only the *Cruise* can have made a respectable profit, and the last, *The Chinese Puzzle*, had fallen totally flat. Meanwhile, at a party of Molly Hamilton's, Jonathan Cape was suggesting to Arthur that it was time he 'put together' some books to support him in his old age. He thought of Ransome as an essayist. It was this meeting that started Arthur selecting and arranging his 'Rod and Line' articles, and now he went to London with the completed typescript in one hand, so to speak, and in the other a paper setting out the title and chapter-headings of *Swallows and Amazons*. He also took his precious fifty pages with him, but he showed them only to Molly Hamilton, who liked them enormously and by her enthusiasm greatly encouraged him. Cape offered material tokens of support. He agreed to publish *Rod and Line* and, after Arthur had told him something of *Swallows*, that too, for an advance of a hundred pounds. 'But it's the essays we want.' He never got them.

In high feather, his smouldering anxiety quenched for a while, Arthur worked steadily at his story, interrupted only briefly by the proofs of *Rod and Line*, until the middle of June. He had hoped to finish *Swallows and Amazons* by 8 May, but the book kept on growing under his hand. When at last it was three-quarters done in rough draft he felt he could take a short holiday, and on 21 June, two days after his notice to the *Guardian* expired, he went down to Hampshire and Francis Hirst for some fishing on the Meon. Hirst, while in London, had been telephoned by the *Guardian* in search of Arthur, but it was the weekend, so when Arthur was told he simply went on fishing and playing chess with Hirst in usual tranquillity. Early in the following week he contacted Ted

Scott and heard the news: CPS had retired at last. Arthur hurried back to Manchester where he, Ted and Ted's brother John celebrated the new era with champagne in the editor's room. Arthur rejoiced wholeheartedly in his friend's fair prospects. The snag was that his own escape from the *Guardian* would now have to be postponed indefinitely. Ted Scott had never resigned himself to letting Arthur go, and probably never did: a few months later he was writing to a colleague, 'I am rather cross with him ... he has some stupid notion of a personal career.' Now he begged Arthur to start writing Saturday essays for him as soon as possible. Arthur could not refuse; besides, both he and Scott thought the essays would be easy work. They were quite wrong. He had a dreadful time thinking of subjects, spent three days drafting and polishing each one, and, worst of all, had to abandon *Swallows and Amazons* half-way through his revision of the complete rough draft. The strain of producing fishing articles had been nothing compared to what he now went through.

It was at this point that *Rod and Line*, the collection of those same fishing articles, was published. To the non-angler fishing can seem a singularly cruel sport and it is difficult to understand how a humane man like Arthur – one, furthermore, who was an enthusiastic bird-watcher and cat-lover, and a brilliant student of the habits of fish – could apply himself so incessantly to emptying ponds, streams and rivers of their most interesting denizens by making them bite on hooks. Ransome confronts this difficulty in his essay 'Back To The Stone Age?', a comment upon an attack by Graham Wallas.

The fisherman engages in an activity that allows him to shed the centuries as a dog shakes off water and to recapture not his own youth merely but the youth of the world ... There is no hostility in this contest. The trout chasing minnows or picking flies from the surface of the stream is contesting with Nature in the same way as the fisherman chasing trout ... The truth, I think, is, that we resume 'paleolithic life' not because of any preference for any past age but to seek a relationship with Nature which is valuable in any age ... the good fisherman is always engaged in an active exercise of his imagination. He is the fish he catches. He, as that fish, feels the currents in the pool and pushes his way to shelter in a pocket of still water. The fish that go into his creel are so many testimonials to his right reading of nature. The power of vision that he develops while fishing persists when the rod is in its case. The fisherman knows what is happening in the river when he is not there. As the rain pours down on autumn streets, he is conscious, as he buttons his coat about his neck, of the fish running up the Eden from the Solway Firth. The pavements are soft grass under his feet, the stone walls of the houses are no prison for him and through the roar of the towns he can hear running water.

This plea, adequate to its object or not, was put forward in complete sincerity. Every page of *Rod and Line* demonstrates, in luminous prose, its author's knowledge of his subject; and the book is full of humour, humanity and lore, not only piscatorial but also historical, geographical and social. Like any good sporting book, *Rod and Line* deeply enriches the reader's awareness of country matters, particularly, as it happens, English country matters (salmon-fishing in Scotland was mostly reserved for a later collection). At the end comes the bonus of a long essay on Aksakov. Large chunks of translation surrounded by stretches of commentary, it is as beguiling an introduction to angling in Russia and to the man whom Ransome calls 'the first and most delightful of Russian writers on fishing' as could be conceived. It may be taken as Ransome's gracious farewell to the country with which he had been so deeply involved. Except for a batch of obituaries (of Bukharin, Kamenev and Rykov) which the *Guardian* suddenly needed in 1936, he never published anything about Russia again.

Arthur laboured at Saturday articles until the early autumn, while *Swallows and Amazons* gathered dust. His health was getting worse and worse. He ought to have seen a doctor, but did not. Instead Ted Scott, who seems to have recognised that Arthur's bother about the articles was doing him physical as well as mental harm, sent him at the end of November to cover a general election in Egypt. He saw him off at the dockside and assured him that there was no need to worry about the articles until his return: Ivor Brown was standing in. Arthur's body and soul always improved at sea, and now they were not seriously cast down even after rough weather off Portugal emptied the water-cistern over his pillow two nights running. He started work on *Swallows and Amazons* again and was soon vastly enjoying himself. He wrote to his mother from Cairo on 13 December:

I got here last night still with an awful cold, made much worse by my low-necked dress as a dowager at the fancy dress ball on board ship. I was a good dowager (took you as a model, but improved on your outfit by adding a lace cap and black mittens).

A few days later he reported to Ted Scott on an exercise in talent-spotting. He had been asked to take a look at a young Englishman in Cairo who had sent one or two articles to the *Guardian*:

(*15 December*) Calls himself Labour but considers Labour better served by the *M.G.* than by its own representatives. Wants to write. Has a congenital interest in politics ... I asked him how long it took him to write the sort of articles he has been sending us. He said he never has time to give more than a morning to doing an article. Concealing my respect behind a pompous manner, I did not let him know that I considered him one of the heavenborn ... I led the conversation to the subject of journalism in general and asked him if he had ever thought of going into a newspaper office. He did not express the revolted horror that I should have felt at his age at such a suggestion. He wondered if by doing that sort of thing he would be able to earn 400 or 500 a year. He is extreeeeeemly young, but decidedly nice in feel, altogether unlike some other rabbits whose diseased livers and swollen spleens affect the corridor atmosphere. I think he is the sort of lad you would find it refreshing to have about, and one who, as his articles show, has a natural instinct for the *M.G.* attitude ... The feel of the fellow is thoroughly simple, eager and pleasant, and free from any kind of intellectual cockiness, while at the same time he is extremely clever and has crammed a lot of experience into his 26 years.

And so Malcolm Muggeridge joined the *Guardian*. Arthur was especially pleased about this because Muggeridge could do much of the work that would otherwise fall upon himself. He was as determined as ever not to be put in a hutch on the corridor.

Mr Muggeridge was grateful to Arthur for getting him a trial period on the paper: he says so in his memoirs. However he also lets his pessimistic irony have free play:

He was carelessly dressed in unseasonable tweeds, and wore a large, loosely tied coloured tie of the kind favoured in those days by middle-brow aesthetes of the C. E. Montague – J. C. Squire variety. As I came to realise subsequently, he was in a sense the epitome of all *Manchester Guardian* writers: amateurish, literary, opinionated, conceited, eccentric; immediately recognisable in any gathering of journalists, however large, by virtue of a certain self-righteousness of expression and bearing; the firm mouth and chin saying that news is sacred, the bright left eye, that comment is free. His great glamour in my eyes was that he had witnessed the Russian Revolution, and known and talked with Lenin, Trotsky and the other leaders in the flesh. It all made him, to me, more remarkable than if he had actually been present at the Crucifixion, or accompanied Moses when he received the Ten Commandments carved on stone at God's hands. When he told me that he had actually played chess with Lenin, who proved to be rather a poor player, and with Litvinov, a much better one, I inwardly genuflected.

He did not tell Arthur that he had never actually read the paper he admired so much. But Arthur was no more deceived than he was himself about his suitability for a position on its staff.

Arthur enjoyed his renewed bout with Egyptian politics, which he did not take at all seriously, but his health was no better. He told Scott, in the letter of 15 December,

> The weather here is vile, cold and raining. Furness is ill at his cottage outside Cairo. I am ill in my room in a *pension* inside Cairo. The telephone is at the other end of about three corridors, and all sorts of Ahmins and Mohammads are ringing up to tell me how wrong each other's views are. What a life.

In these conditions the revision of *Swallows and Amazons* went on swimmingly.

He came back to England resolved to have a month to himself in which to complete work on the story. He found waiting for him all sorts of invitations from various publishers (one of them offered him a thousand pounds to translate *And Quiet Flows the Don*), and an offer from Ted Scott of a job as leader-writer. Arthur was immensely touched by his friend's persistence, and his attempt to understand Arthur's point of view, and poured out his heart in a long letter. He had never wanted to be a journalist, he said. He had set out to be a writer of quite another sort. Then his first marriage and the Revolution had gradually thrown him off course, but he never lost hope of getting back to his proper job.

> Coming into the office is going to mean writing nothing but leaders, and possibly writing more of them than I can write well. It means that I shall have definitely turned my back on my original object, an object I still think the one which, but for the obstacles produced by my own folly in my first marriage, I am more or less capable of attaining ... With all this there comes also a sort of feeling that I may be too late, that I may have been defeated already, and that the publishers who are still ready, it seems, to give me any chance I want are mistaken in thinking that I could take a chance if I had one. Not a pleasant idea at all, but the fact sticks out large and prominent, that I simply cannot produce more than a certain amount in a week and that I find it almost impossible to get on with a book when I am busy with something else as well.

A week later he screwed himself up to make a definitive refusal. He hated to let Ted down, but saw no alternative. He was always willing to help in an emergency, and would continue to freelance, but a salaried place in the corridor – No.

> Supposing the position were reversed and I were inviting you to leave the *Guardian* and join me in some kind of freelancing. The shifting of aim would not be more violent than in me becoming a regular leader-writer. I hope to get a letter from you to say that you don't feel that I am being a pig in refusing.

It was all very firm, but Arthur had been equally firm a year previously. We may doubt if it would have been the last word on the subject had *Swallows and Amazons* failed. Arthur knew that everything turned on the book. In April, while Evgenia was taking a cure at Malvern, he went to London with his precious manuscript and in an agony of reluctance handed it over to G. Wren Howard, of Jonathan Cape. Then he fussed and fretted and bothered his friends all through the summer until publication day. The book meant so much to him. He would not be able to bear a rejection. He could hardly bear to expose it to the risk of one.

There was no rejection. First came good news from Syria. The Altounyans had known nothing of the enterprise, and cheerful letters had revealed that the country was not so arid as Arthur had imagined: there was a lake in the hills where they sailed regularly. They might not particularly care to be reminded of colder waters, and what would their parents think? Particularly Dora.

I thought of tigresses defending their young. And yet, in a way, they were my children too, at least the ones in the book were, and the other ones, outside the book, had always counted me as a bit of their family. At last I persuaded the publisher to let me have a very early copy of the book, so early that it had a misprint in it that is in none of the later copies, so early that I was able to send it out to Syria nearly three weeks before the book was published. And then I went fishing as hard as I could, trying to forget about it.

Taqui Altounyan has described the arrival of the book in Aleppo:

One morning a parcel arrived and we crowded round my mother as she cut the string. It was a book called *Swallows and Amazons* – about travel in South America? – By Arthur Ransome. My mother turned the pages while we breathed down her neck. 'Susan' ... well, that was quite a common name, 'Roger' – ... a queer coincidence ... TITTY ... There were our names and the story must surely be about us! Even the name of the boat was *Swallow*, the same as our boat. My mother then turned to the dedication and read out 'To the six for whom it was written in exchange for a pair of slippers.' That really settled it ... We were very excited at being put in a book but I was disappointed that my name was not there ... Titty and Roger were very true to life, Susie we thought a little too good. We all wrote to say how pleased we were and Uncle Arthur wrote back relieved, 'because some people, when put in books, might feel like butterflies stuck on pins.'

Arthur was so gratified that he wanted to sit down right away and start another book for them.

Publication day was 21 July. The book was widely and kindly reviewed, by some not altogether distinterested persons: Molly

Hamilton in *Time and Tide*, Malcolm Muggeridge in the *Manchester Guardian*, and Sylvia Lynd, to whom Arthur had once proposed marriage, in the *News Chronicle*, the successor to his old paper, the *Daily News*. However the book did not need to rely on anything but its merits. It was praised in the *Daily Telegraph*, the *Daily Herald* and the *Church Times*. It was slow to sell, taking two years to earn its advance, but it was a *succes d'estime*, and the publishers were decently eager for a sequel.

Swallows was not a book to take the world by storm. Neither was it as easy to launch an original children's story as it had been in E. Nesbit's day. The *Pall Mall Magazine*, in whose pages the Bastable family had first appeared, and which had lasted long enough to publish Arthur's two short stories in 1929, did not survive into 1930. It was not the only such victim of the rise of radio and the cinema. But it is clear enough in retrospect that the slow initial progress of the Walker family was no lasting disadvantage. The friends they made were devoted, and spread the news. The really striking thing is that within three or four years of their début the tales of their adventures were universally accepted as classics of children's literature.

It is easy enough to find superficial reasons for Ransome's great success with *Swallows and Amazons* and its successors. There had been hundreds of school stories since *Tom Brown*, but no one had thought to write holiday stories. It was a gloriously obvious idea, once discovered, a fresh appeal to the half-innocent egoism of the young: they liked to see their schooldays dignified and romanticised in fiction, and were naturally responsive to the same treatment of their holidays. Any professional writer who hit on the formula – and Ransome was exactly that – was bound to succeed in such an undertaking, and a generation of writers, following in Ransome's steps, also profited. But their work never had the enormous popularity of the *Swallow* books, and now is almost wholly forgotten.

Ransome's strengths as a writer were not easily duplicated. They were too deeply involved with his personal history. Proust's dictum that the self which lives in time and the self which writes are not the same would not have appealed to Arthur Ransome, the stout admirer of Sainte-Beuve. But the self of his books is plainly cooler, shrewder, more intelligent, more patient, more good-humoured, more worldly wise, than the Arthur of life. Perhaps Proust did not go far enough. Perhaps he should have said that the self which writes is *better* than the self of time. At any rate it was so with Arthur. His happiness in writing *Swallows and Amazons* both relaxed and stimulated him, bringing into play powers he scarcely knew he had, and putting all disabling self-consciousness to sleep.

Why was he so happy? Perhaps it was because the invention of John enabled him to put his own young self into the tale. For the Walkers are not simply the Altounyans in light disguise, even in *Swallows and Amazons*, where the fit is designedly closest. There are mysteries about them, of which their surname is the greatest: it was that of Arthur's first wife. Perhaps Arthur unconsciously hoped that there was some magic in using the name which would draw Tabitha, a half-Walker, back to him. But whatever the explanation, the choice can hardly have been accidental (Arthur nowhere attempts to explain it). Neither was the substitution of a boy for a girl as the eldest child. Arthur had been the eldest himself. Through the substitution he was able to depict himself as he must at times quite passionately have wanted to be: reliable, unimaginative, good-hearted, skilled in all practical matters, and on entirely harmonious terms with his parents. 'BETTER DROWNED THAN DUFFERS: IF NOT DUFFERS WON'T DROWN': John's father's telegram is famous. John's comment is enormously significant: 'Daddy knows we aren't duffers.' It was something that the boy Arthur could never have said to himself with any confidence; yet how much he had wanted to! Now, in fiction, all could be arranged.

So Arthur gave to himself, as well as to the Altounyans, the absolutely cloudless Lakeland childhood that he desired; and thus assured, his imagination was free to rampage. He knew just what the book ought to be. He did not live to encounter that marvellously self-serving critical doctrine according to which the only subject of art is art and even such works as *Emma* are concerned chiefly with their own writing; but his tale comes close to exemplifying it. As early as 1906 he had published an essay on books and children, in poor old *Temple Bar*, in which he had laid down what children's literature ought to be; and *Swallows and Amazons* perfectly illustrates his doctrine. The essence of the child, he held, is its imagination, the way in which, left to itself and not withered by obtuse or manipulative adults, 'it adopts any material at hand, and weaves for itself a web of imaginative life', building the world again into a splendid pageantry: and all without ever (or hardly ever) blurring its sense of the actual. Such a child is Titty, the most richly-conceived of all his characters.

> "I wonder," she said, "if the man on the houseboat has his family with him."
> "He's all alone," said Roger.
> "He's probably a retired pirate," said Titty.

And a retired pirate he remains for the series, nicknamed Captain Flint, after Long John Silver's commander, even though he is soon revealed as Nancy and Peggy's Uncle Jim.

Yet Ransome held that the most important exemplar of this principle would not be one or more of the characters in a tale, but the author himself. 'The good children's books have an easily recognisable hallmark. They are written by children' – children such as Nathanael Hawthorne, Charles Kingsley and Rudyard Kipling. For Ransome, the glorious thing about *Swallows and Amazons* was that it liberated the child in himself. Utterly committed to what he was doing, he felt free, for example, to take liberties with the Furness geography: so that Peel Island of Coniston and Blake Holme of Windermere could merge to become Wild Cat Island; so that the Old Man of Coniston (Kanchenjunga) could look across the lake to Bowness-on-Windermere (Rio); so that Silver Holme (Cormorant Island) and Belle Isle (Long Island) and Allen Tarn (the Octopus Lagoon) and Bank Ground Farm (Holly Howe) could all, as it were, rub shoulders; and so that the old *Gondola*, which he had loved so much as a child, could be moored as a houseboat in a bay of his composite lake, and be inhabited by a bald, fat man, busy writing a book, and hostile to children: Ransome's daytime self, the self he was escaping from; Captain Flint, the unrecognised *alter ego* of Captain John.

Swallows and Amazons, then, is full of symbolic meaning; its plot recapitulates several of the most important dramas of its author's life, and beautifully resolves them. Children do not bother their heads about such considerations. They find, instead, that someone is playing a fascinating game in the book's pages. Of the early reviewers Malcolm Muggeridge was the one who saw this clearest:

> The explorers in *Swallows and Amazons* are supplied with milk by a farmer only thinly disguised as one of the less hostile

natives, and buy their lemonade over the counter – a fact which does not at all prevent it from becoming vitriolic grog. That is to say, the book is the very stuff of play. It is make-believe such as all children have indulged in: even children who have not been so fortunate as to have a lake and a boat and an island but only a backyard amongst the semis of Suburbia.

And once they are drawn into the game, they will perforce learn about many things: not just the joys of sailing and camping, and the particular skills which Ransome was so good at describing, but the charm of the human comedy – Ransome's humour is quieter than that of E. Nesbit, but just as firmly grounded on observation and a love of character – and increasingly, as they read and re-read all the books, a vision of nature and society which may colour their outlook for the rest of their lives. How it is done must remain, in the end, a secret between children and the author; but an adult may suggest that it could not have been done at all for a generation to which reading was less important than it was to the children of the 1930s and 1940s. Ransome is able to assume that children take their reading seriously and are not daunted by demands on their attention, intelligence and vocabulary.

Arthur looked forward to the book's appearance with the utmost eagerness:

> (*To his mother, 4 July*) I feel quite childish about it, bursting to see the brute and feel it. I haven't been so eager to see a new book since *Racundra* was done. Well I remember the excitement of the parcel arriving in Riga. The only other book of which I can remember the actual arrival of the first copies is *The Souls of the Streets*, at Gunter Grove. Funny, isn't it, to be as much of a baby about it at 46 as I was at 20. Perhaps it's because nowadays I get so very little chance of doing books at all.

But his physical symptoms were becoming too acute to be ignored any longer. Intestinal discomfort, frequently turning into sharp pain, was now continual; there were bouts of vomiting; sudden unexpected fainting-fits. He was horribly tired, 'for no reason at all'. The glands in his armpits were swollen. The day after *Swallows and Amazons* at last appeared the specialist whom he was consulting, Danvers Atkinson, diagnosed duodenal or gastric ulcers, told him that a long cure was necessary, and ordered him to give up smoking.

What followed displayed the devotion of Arthur's friends. Molly Hamilton was off to America on a lecture-tour, so she let the Ransomes have her London flat for two months. Everybody else rallied round and came to visit repeatedly as soon as Arthur was strong enough: Ivor Brown, Ric Eddison, Lascelles Abercrombie. Desperately weak to start with, half-starved and filled with medicines, Arthur nevertheless began to enjoy himself as soon as the pain wore off: he liked life seeming, as he said, 'a tune played with finger-tips on a spinet instead of with a fist on a grand piano.' He liked the visitors, loved Sylvia Lynd's warm review of *Swallows*, and was overwhelmed when Lascelles Abercrombie dedicated his long poem, *The Sale of St Francis*, to him. He lay on a divan and wrote three articles about Hazlitt for the *Guardian* to commemorate that writer's centenary, reassured his mother about his progress ('I am allowed to have some toast on condition that I chew it till it's like cream. You have no idea how LOVELY toast tastes after five weeks of olive oil and bismuth. Tomorrow we shall see if I suffer any ill effects from this ORGY') and looked forward to a little float-fishing when he was released. In October he and Evgenia set out for the North. Arthur was very cheerful, in spite of chilly weather and the fact that he was to continue on a diet for six months more. The ulcers were said to be healing nicely, and the doctor had told him to take a holiday and keep in the open air as much as possible. 'He says that I may do crosswords!!!!!!' Then on 1 November came the news that *Swallows and Amazons* was to be published in America by Lippincott's, which would bring in at least $600.

He overdid things, although his doctor had told him that his internal troubles probably originated from his refusal to lead a quiet life for long enough after his operation in 1915. Subsequent events suggest that Dr Atkinson was on the wrong track about Arthur. So it is hard to blame him for going after sea-trout and salmon at Levenfoot (he caught chiefly pike) and for starting on a new *Swallow* story. He planned to devote a whole book to one of the adventures that his children imagined (he had sketched one in chapter 30 of *Swallows and Amazons*), thus again illustrating the delight and value of fantasy. He packed them off for a winter holiday in Norfolk on a wherry with Captain Flint, and set them to spinning a yarn about treasure and piracy on the high seas.

Then the ulcer began to act up again, and Dr Atkinson told him that once more he would have to go through the milk, bismuth and bed routine.

Fortunately he had the sense to seek a second opinion, and got one worth having. Dr Forest Smith put him on yet another milk diet, but nevertheless told him to eat a lot – 'the nearer you get to fifteen stone the better' – and to avoid all food and drink which had been in contact with aluminium. This gave Evgenia a new object in life: many a hostess was going to remember with a shudder Mrs Ransome's descent on her kitchen to make sure that her husband was not going to be poisoned; and the treatment worked. Arthur, whose weight had got down to as little as ten and a half stone, began to make a solid recovery, and before long wore the round and rosy appearance that was to be his for the rest of his life. Queen Mary bought a copy of *Swallows*: Arthur hoped that would boost sales. Cape and Lippincott were both eager for a sequel. Arthur was in very good spirits by New Year's Eve. 'Heard the bells at midnight with great difficulty. We went up the hill to listen for them. A wild duck and an owl were also awake.' Evgenia's diary entry was in a different vein: 'What a shame! Forgot that there is not a drop of wine or spirits of any kind in the house, so can't drink the New Year in. We shall be very very sober all through 1931.'

Since Arthur's diet forbade him all alcohol for the time being, this prophecy probably came truer than most. 1931 was one of those years when much progress is made, but is invisible at the time. Arthur was still suffering agonies from his ulcers, although he felt, and the doctor confirmed, that they were slowly getting better. Money was a problem. Arthur still wrote occasional pieces for the *Guardian*, on literary or other topics, but the slump was hitting Manchester and its newspapers hard, and Ted Scott had little work for him. He and Evgenia lived off their savings and the occasional money-present from Edith Ransome. By March *Swallows and Amazons* had sold 1,656 copies. Wren Howard regarded this as satisfactory. Arthur did not. 'Until I can get into the 3,000 sales, there will be small chance of making a living out of books. Once you get among the people who sell 3,000 regularly things are all right, and you have only to hold your mouth open for windfalls. But I doubt if I shall ever be among these lucky ones.'

Nevertheless he was pressing ahead with a sequel to *Swallows*.

He had abandoned the pirate story for the time being. The opening had dissatisfied him (a certain self-consciousness in it was to survive into the published first chapter of *Peter Duck*). More important, the last pages of *Swallows and Amazons* had looked forward emphatically to a sequel describing the next lake holiday. Both writer and readers would feel cheated without it. And if the tale were postponed until after the appearance of *Peter Duck*, would it not go stale? So Arthur started *Swallowdale*, but showed his flair for narrative surprise by contradicting expectations: for most of the book the Swallows are shorebound by the loss of their ship, and the Amazons are even more completely frustrated by the presence of their Great-Aunt. When the adventurers are at last reunited on Wild Cat Island the book ends.

Swallowdale is the longest of Ransome's children's books. It is also, in one respect, the most audacious: it has almost nothing that can be described as a plot. The most dramatic incidents are the holing of *Swallow* and the spraining of Roger's ankle. Nowhere else was Ransome to escape so entirely all need for the suspension of disbelief (even *Swallows and Amazons* had featured a burglary). The author stakes everything on his ability to make the absolutely commonplace fascinating by his imagination and the imaginative use of language. Sometimes the imagination gets a little out of hand: Titty, in her agitation over her fancied murder of the Great-Aunt, seems at times in need of a strait-jacket. But on the whole the book succeeds as a sunny enchantment. The lake ceases to be the unknown ocean of the first story, instead taking on its true character as a mere among the English fells. The farm-folk, who were purely background figures in *Swallows*, now appear more solid. Even the Amazons gain credibility as figures at home in the Furness world. One passage in particular shows how Ransome has extended his range and thereby increased his appeal. Nancy is telling the southern children about the sports of the North:

> She told the Swallows of the great hound-trails of the district, of the guides races where the young men row in boats across the lake, race up to the top of a big hill and down again each to his boat, and so back. She told them of the sheep-dog trials, where the sheep-dogs gather sheep, pen them in a field, take one sheep from among the others, and all at no more than a sign or a whistle from the shepherd. Then she was back again talking of the hound-trails, of the white specks flying through

the heather, dropping down through the bracken on the steep hillside, getting larger and larger, until at last with the whole world yelling itself hoarse the winning hounds come loping into the sports field and the hound-trail is over ... Nancy was still in full cry, when the chorus of hound noises far away in the valley swelled out very loud and urgent and then came suddenly to an end.

'They're off,' she shouted. 'Come on.'

Ransome was to make use of this effect repeatedly in later books, in some of which, indeed, it became a dominant theme.

He worked steadily at *Swallowdale* through the spring and summer of 1931. At the beginning of May there was a break of a week. Ted Scott had yielded at last to Arthur's exhortations and taken a cabin yacht on the Broads: he invited the Ransomes to come with him and teach him how to sail her.

(*To his mother, 5 May*) The whole cruise was a great success. I got a bad whack on the head, from the boom, which depressed me for a day and a half, Genia[3] came a terrible cropper on a cinder path and cut her knees and hand most horribly, which depressed her for about half an hour, Ted Scott fell overboard but scrambled aboard again after a struggle which depressed him for about half an hour, and Dick Scott fell overboard and couldn't get back but wallowed ashore and out on a muddy bank, caked from head to foot, which depressed him quite a lot but cheered his father very much indeed, as Dick had been jeering at his father's misfortune ... Ted picked up the sailing in no time, and went back to Manchester looking better than I've ever seen him look.

Such joyful notes were comparatively rare. In January and February there had been talk of selling Ludderburn, partly no doubt to raise some money, but chiefly because Genia was beginning to find it too tiring to run. Arthur could not be much help (the doctor had forbidden him to lift anything heavy). Edith Ransome lamented Genia's aversion to servants: 'they so soon learn to do just what they are told and she need only be about 2 or 3 hours in a day.' Arthur was not above presenting his wife's solitary toil as a martyrdom imposed by poverty when

3 As AR and all their friends now called Evgenia.

he needed to resist Ivy's clamour for more money (she was already getting more than the agreed share of his income) but in fact it was Genia's choice, and she stuck to it to her dying day. Anyway they could not yet bear to part with Ludderburn.

(*To his mother, 25 January*) It had been a wild week up here, so they say, and we found a good many boughs on the ground, saving trouble in collecting firewood. But just as we arrived, there was a bit of sunshine and it looked so lovely that we both felt that we could never really leave it. Genia soon had three heaters and two fires going in the house (which was surprisingly dry) and we got to bed in proper time in a cottage that was already in complete going order. The snowdrops are just beginning. We will send you some presently.

Writing was not quite such a pleasure this year as last. Tabitha sent a tactless letter in March, saying that she hadn't been able to get past chapter 12 of *Swallows and Amazons*, which for a little quite crushed her father's spirits; and *Swallowdale* did not satisfy him when complete, or so he told his mother. This probably meant that it also did not satisfy Genia. She was never pleased with Arthur's books at the time of their writing. The most recent one was always unworthy of him, and a falling-off from the last. Arthur was, invariably, dreadfully depressed by this attitude. He needed encouragement and appreciation at least as much as other writers do, and even if he had not it was cruel to be so dismissive of so much hard labour. In the *Autobiography* Arthur was to thank his wife for her 'relentlessly honest criticism', and since she was highly intelligent as well as voluble, opinionated and obstinate, her criticisms of detail were often useful. From time to time she made valuable suggestions. But she was not the only woman who did that for Arthur. Where she was unique was in persistently belittling his work and decrying whatever project he had in hand. In the end she prematurely ended his writing career. Perhaps she was unconsciously envious of it.

The anxieties of 1931 proved to have been misleading. There was no dreadful physical collapse as in the year before; Ludderburn remained the Ransomes' home; *Swallows and Amazons* continued to make friends, and was issued in an edition illustrated by Clifford Webb; to Arthur's vast surprise Wren Howard liked *Swallowdale* better than its predecessor. The book was published on 26 October and was well received ('If there is a nicer book this side of *Treasure Island* I have missed it,' said the *Observer*). Its appearance led to a fresh burst of letters from Aleppo. The children were still enthusiastic, but they were growing up fast: Taqui was sixteen. They wrote, 'Why don't you come and see what we are really like?' Their father, eternally energetic and optimistic, was sure that the Altounyan hospital was just the place to be cured of ulcers. Arthur, not a patient man by nature (in *Rod and Line* he argued that the patience of fishermen was entirely legendary: anglers were too incessantly busy to need that particular virtue), was getting very tired of the slow processes of his treatment, and was ready to believe Ernest's promises. Genia had always wanted to eat oranges straight off the tree. They had just enough money to cover the cost of the trip. In short, they let themselves be tempted, and in early January 1932 were off to the East. Ted Scott said goodbye to them at Salford Docks; he and Arthur talked to the last minute about sailing. Ted had decided to buy a dinghy like *Swallow* so that he and Dick could sail on Windermere with Arthur and Genia. Arthur knew of just the right boat, one that was unsinkable because fitted with air-tanks. They would have great times together when the Ransomes got back.

Sea voyages were always good for Arthur's insides. He put it down to the air, but it seems at least as likely that the cause was the absence of worry. Unable to affect events, suspended between his ports of embarkation and arrival, there was nothing to fret about; he could look at the waves, enjoy the movement of the ship, relax effortlessly, and grow fat. 'Life on shipboard is extremely soporific and leaves one with absolutely nothing to say,' he reported to his mother on 20 January. After describing some of his fellow-passengers, and drawing caricatures of them on a blank side of writing-paper, he could only report that he had done no work, though he had taken a lot of notes from a copy of the *Channel Pilot* (they were to be invaluable in the writing of *Peter Duck*); express envy of the fluency of an Italian writing at the next table; and sign off. It was a letter buoyant with restored health.

The voyage across the Mediterranean had just the right amount and variety of excitement: a bad storm off Malta, interesting ports of call, and an agreeable ship, the *Scottish Prince*. At Alexandria they shifted to a coastal steamer which wandered about from Port Said to Cyprus (where Genia picked her orange and Arthur caught a large speckled chameleon) to Tripoli to Alexandretta.

Some of our luggage

3 The voyage to Aleppo, from a letter to his mother, 20 January 1932

(*To his mother, 3 February*) Here after a bit we saw a boat coming off entirely full of Ernest and his family. We then had a tremendous long drive up into the mountains and through the pass called the Syrian Gates, a terrifying affair, twisting round hairpin bends above precipitous drops, and through wild villages in the hills, and then down on to the plain of Antioch, a lovely place, with the great Sea of Antioch and mountains all round it, and in the flat plain three great rivers, like the rivers of Norfolk, running through reedy banks. This is where we shall be sailing in little boats. Here we met Turcomans and Kurds and Armenians, all in their primitive dress, absolutely untouched by any civilisation whatever, except the fine road across the plain, which the French are making really very good indeed. Then leaving the plain we climbed up again. This time through desert stony hills without one particle of vegetation, though all over the place there were colossal ruins built with huge stones, so that at some time in the very distant past there must have been whole towns living there. We saw the tents of the nomads. Towards evening we saw Aleppo, a magnificent citadel like the castle of Edinburgh, rising up among low hills covered with ploughed land ...

Ernest and Dora are in good form, and the children are as good as usual, but I must say it seems a little queer now after two years of living with them all in *S. and A.* and *Swallowdale*, to meet them once more as actual human beings running about. My lot somehow seem to me the solider, but Ernest's are very nice, and eager to know 'what is going to happen to us next?' They have, of course, adopted Genia completely.

The visit began extremely well. The Ransomes had brought a present with them: a new dinghy, built at Pin Mill on the Orwell. It was a magnificent gift, not in the least what might have been expected from a man so constantly insisting on his poverty as Arthur. Perhaps he worried as much too much about money as he did about everything else. The splendour of the present perhaps also demonstrates how important the Altounyans were to him at this period. The dinghy was named *Peter Duck*, in honour of the book that Arthur was planning, and was promptly taken to Amouk Lake. Taqui Altounyan records:

We launched her at the farm into the blue waters and the water-lilies. The varnished planks glittered in the sunshine, and the creamy sails flapped out for the first time, and the silky shining ropes took their first strain. The little walnut shell built at Pin Mill ... threaded its way through exotic eastern waters, avoiding submerged buffaloes, racing with piratical-looking Arab boys poling their *kayaks*.

Arthur was soon installed in Dora's room at the top of the house, overlooking the Turkish cemetery, and there between early February and mid-April he wrote just over three hundred pages of *Peter Duck*. He worked in the mornings, descending when the dinner-gong sounded.

We pounced on him: 'How many pages?', and he held up fingers to show. Usually it was three or five, on bad days, two, or even one. 'ONE' he would say with a wry look, and 'Genia says it is awful.' He wrote carefully and slowly, thinking it all out before he put it down, and he hardly altered anything afterwards. After lunch he read us what he had written, and we always liked it and tried to cheer him up because he kept saying he was sure it was a failure.

Since *Peter Duck* was ostensibly the Swallows' and Amazons' own fantasy story about themselves, it seemed a good idea to illustrate it with their own pictures. As a relaxation from writing Arthur set about preparing these. Titty helped him. 'She is most comically like her imaginary self. Ditto Roger. The others have rather shot up with the years.' Dora Altounyan, daughter of painters and an accomplished artist herself, was doubtful about Arthur's efforts.

> She thought the figures rather stiff. He usually shirked drawing faces and got over that difficulty with back views of shaggy heads of hair or large hats — but he was meticulous in drawing endless graded lines in Indian ink for fog scenes. We used to tell him he put one of them in every book on purpose. He enjoyed doing the insides of caves too, because this meant great washes of black ink, and the figures needed only to be silhouettes.

Life was not all writing, drawing and sailing. Arthur fished for cat-fish and listened to stories about the brigands who infested the countryside. He played tennis with the children every day, and was proud to report to his mother that after a fortnight he was beginning to hold his own against them. He went on excursions to antique sites. He sat by the fire in the spring evenings telling Anansi stories or singing ballads in a fine voice. (He seemed to Taqui to be like a small boy yearning to go on a spree, but Genia kept him firmly in check.) And in his letters home he boasted about the hot weather — 'hotter already than ever we have had it at Ludderburn in midsummer.'

Yet the heat in the end was his undoing. Ernest Altounyan's treatment for ulcers was no improvement on Forest Smith's, and since Arthur also had to be inoculated against typhoid, he was actually rather worse off, for he felt sick, 'headachy and boneachy', with a swollen arm. Genia was also inoculated, without ill result, and Ernest was unsympathetically delighted, in the way of doctors, that Arthur's dose had so palpably 'taken'. There was the filthy bismuth: he drank it with so strong an expression of horror and loathing that he always had an audience for the feat. The heat grew abominably oppressive, and Arthur gloomily computed the number of diseases he now risked catching: malaria, ophthalmia, smallpox. And could he be sure that his food was not being cooked in aluminium? All this, and the normal neurosis of composition, made him despond frightfully over *Peter Duck*:

> (*To his mother, 17 March*) I remember I was pretty sick with *Swallowdale* this time last year, and got reconciled to most of it later on. But the new thing is much more difficult. The only thing in it that is much pleasure to me so far is the development of the characters of Peter Duck and Captain Flint. And, of course, my red-haired boy is rather a lark, and a useful change from the others. But, I fear people who like the other two books will be horribly disappointed to find this one so different. Still I daresay they'll forgive some of the strangeness on account of having the same set of children in it.
>
> ... I am beginning to hanker very badly after Ludderburn but I shan't start from here until I have got the whole rough draft done, anyhow. Unless, of course, the heat gets altogether unbearable.

On 22 March Dora took to her bed with a temperature, and Arthur was dismayed to be told by Titty that her complaint was indeed malaria. On the 29th he had a row with Ernest, presumably about the risk of disease, and the next day Genia had the same, only worse. A fortnight later they fled. Arthur's health was clearly worsening, the book was in difficulties ('the remaining 100 pages or so need a lot of spirit and jump, and, at the moment, I haven't got any') and they had heard that the *Scottish Prince* was taking on cargo and passengers in Cyprus. It was painful parting with the Altounyans: Dora, Taqui and Titty all cried and Arthur was very sad, but there was nothing else to be done. Before leaving there had been a last exchange of favours. Arthur recommended a prep. school for Roger, and Ernest read parts of *Peter Duck*, which he said he liked better than anything in the other two books. It was encouraging. On the whole the verdict on the Aleppo adventure remained favourable: 'It has been a most interesting visit, and I have got 310 pages of rough copy out of it. I've never done quite so much in the time before.' If he could keep up that rate at home there would be no trouble about having the manuscript ready for the printers in July.

Their journey home was as pleasant as the journey out, and included another enchanting experience of Cyprus; but when the *Scottish Prince* reached Rotterdam, Arthur heard shattering news. Ted Scott had died while sailing with his son Dick on Windermere.

It was the worst blow of Arthur's life. Genia said, 'I have never seen anybody so crushed at the moment of receiving bad news or taking so long to get used to live with it. It was not only the loss of the closest friend in the prime of his life but the feeling that in a way he was responsible for Ted's death.' The feeling was illogical. Ted Scott's heart had threatened trouble for at least two years. The unsinkable boat had not sunk: she had merely capsized, but instead of clinging to the hull, as Dick Scott had done, Ted had swum for the shore. The effort, and the cold April waters, were too much: he had a heart attack and died. But Arthur was obsessed by the knowledge that it was he who had urged Ted to take up sailing, he who had found the boat for him, he who had called down bad luck, in one of his letters from Syria, by writing 'Don't go and get drowned, till I am there to fish you out!!' Perhaps guilt was an emotion he could handle. His sense of regret for promise unfulfilled, of loneliness without his friend, a friend to whom he was as close as he was to anyone except Genia, might otherwise have overwhelmed him. He had been fortunate in Ted. It was not just that no other editor would have been so patient with his vagaries; or that they had known each other since boyhood; or that they had both had to struggle in the shadows of overwhelming fathers, one dead, the other, C. P. Scott, until that very year, all too much alive. By one of those lucky chances which cannot be predicted or explained, they had found increasingly that they had a deep affinity, and that such differences as separated them were trivial or even stimulating. Their careers had been opening out together; Arthur was at last writing stories successfully, Ted was at last in sole command at the *Guardian*. The future had looked triumphant, and now Ted's part in it had been cut short. No wonder the survivor suffered so keenly. He could not even bring himself to go sailing on Windermere for three months.

Scott's death led to a break with Malcolm Muggeridge. Muggeridge had got on extremely well with Ted, and occasionally visited Arthur at Ludderburn, but he had never really settled down on the paper or in Manchester. The job of writing the obituary fell to him; he resigned immediately afterwards, knowing that he could never work well with Scott's successor. He went off to Moscow, for ever as he thought, to live in the new socialist paradise, but was disillusioned even more rapidly and totally than he had been with the *Manchester Guardian*. In due course he would make his views on Stalinism known, but in the mean time he escaped the depressing world of Moscow by discharging himself of his feelings about Manchester, the Scotts and their paper. He did so in a most reckless novel, called *Picture Palace*, and it is amazing that he ever found a publisher, for the book contained scarifying portraits of the living as well as dead Scotts, of the new editor of the *Guardian*, and (especially) of Kingsley Martin, who appeared as 'Wraithly Morton'. In the end the Scott family sued and the book was suppressed. Before then the first publisher to whom it was sent had got Arthur to read it. Arthur was dreadfully upset. It was highly libellous, he reported; he thought it was a betrayal of confidence; it might do the paper, as a business concern, much harm in Manchester; it was pornographic, it was caddish. But the real offence lay elsewhere. In a letter of explanation Malcolm Muggeridge wrote to Arthur:

(*23 January 1933*) In some curious way the tragedy of E.T.S. – of his life and his death – symbolised this. I was fonder of him, I think, than of any man I have ever come across; and it seemed to me that he was a victim, directly of his father's arrogant self-righteousness, and indirectly of the hypocrisy of the *M.G.* – that he was, as it were, suffocated by the *M.G.* I know I was scarcely surprised when I heard he was drowned. I know that, blasphemously writing his obituary, I saw his death as a release from a long and unnecessary tyranny which had made it inevitable that he should always and in all circumstances do violence to his own natural honesty and sensitiveness.

There was altogether too much truth in this. Arthur could not be expected to agree that the *Manchester Guardian* was hypocritical, but otherwise, was not this his own diagnosis of Ted's case? Of course he, Arthur, would never have violated the canons of propriety by uttering such sentiments publicly, in any form; but might not such restraint resemble hypocrisy rather closely? Then there was the conflict of generations. Arthur tried to play down the fact, but there could be no doubt that he had chosen Malcolm Muggeridge as his successor and praised his work to Ted Scott before and after he joined the paper. Worst of all, Muggeridge was not the first young man to seek in Russia a refuge from intolerable personal problems. In short, Arthur's youthful self seemed suddenly to have risen in judgment against him. What with that and his sorrow for Ted and his guilt about his death, it is no wonder that he was deeply distressed. He had nothing to do with Muggeridge for fourteen years or so; but then, it is pleasant to record, they met as friends, Arthur liked him as much as ever, and was content to do no more than marvel at the 'blind spots' that had led to the unfortunate novel.

Life went on very quietly for some months after the return from the East. Arthur visited Lowestoft in search of local colour and detail for *Peter Duck*; otherwise he stayed at Ludderburn (which, on top of all other troubles, had been burgled during the Syrian visit), finishing the book. It appeared on 12 October, a few days after the death of W. G. Collingwood. This second loss was a sad one, but unlike Ted Scott, Arthur reflected, the Skald had completed his life's work. He had also lived long enough to read and approve *Swallows and Amazons*, thus seeing the first fruits of the promise which he had encouraged, so long ago, in the young Arthur Ransome. It was impossible to mourn him for long; much better to savour his obituary in the local antiquarian magazine. Then *Peter Duck* came out, and life started to move rapidly again.

The earlier books had acquired that best of all reputations, the semi-underground, word-of-mouth kind, which almost guarantee that eventually an author's work will enjoy runaway success. But if that success is to come sooner rather than later, favourable publicity is also necessary, and now Ransome received lots of it. Molly Hamilton alerted a friend, Ida O'Malley, who gave *Peter Duck* an enthusiastic welcome in *The Times*. The Junior Literary Guild in America chose *Peter Duck* as its book of the year, in succession to *Swallows and Amazons* and *Swallowdale*. (Arthur was much gratified to learn that no one had scored this hat-trick before.) Naomi Mitchison praised the book in the *Week-End Review*, Howard Spring in the *Evening Standard*. Hugh Walpole wrote what Arthur called 'an astonishing handsome thing' in the *Observer*. Arthur valued the review as much for the fact that it restored good relations with his former friend as for any other reason. He wrote to Walpole, 'Is this an olive branch?' Walpole replied, 'A twig', and the ancient quarrel was over for good. As he said to his mother, 'This will be enough to make absolutely sure of *Peter Duck*'s success. Nobody could possibly write a better review of any book, and Walpole's name carries so far today such a review signed by him, and such things said, will put *Peter Duck* safe in harbour without any sort of doubt.' But perhaps Arthur had already got beyond the point where he relied on reviews. On 12 November *Time and Tide*, which had printed an unfavourable review, had to give space to indignant letters from children: 'even mummy enjoyed reading it to us ... Black Jake is fully equal to Long John Silver in all ways, he brings such thrilling adventures that we do nothing but read all evening.' Other children even preferred *Peter Duck* to *Treasure Island*, though on shaky grounds: 'The adventures in *Peter Duck* might happen to a boy or girl nowadays.' Letters from enthralled children began to pour into Cape's office. It is not very surprising that *Peter Duck* went into a second impression less than two months after its appearance. Arthur scribbled off a note of joy to his mother as soon as he got the news: 'We shall pull through after all. I stand on my cranium' (and a sketch of himself doing so).

Peter Duck deserved its success, but as the readers' constant references to *Treasure Island* show (Arthur had had that book with him in Aleppo, and its influence, with that of John Masefield, is all-pervasive) it was not really so original as its predecessors. But even if it worked within a well-established tradition, the familiar Ransome virtues were amply in evidence. Even the waterspout, the most sensational episode in the story, was based on the one which Arthur, Genia and the Ancient Mariner had seen in the Gulf of Riga in 1923. This incident may even have been the germ of *Peter Duck*, for that grizzled mariner is of course the Ancient Mariner himself (sea-changed, rather like the Altounyans, into fiction, and made a Lowestoft man in the process) and the book is in a way the sequel to *Racundra's First Cruise*. As Arthur well knew, the contrast between the rash, enthusiastic, romantic Captain Flint, hankering for treasure, and the wise, unmercenary old sailor is the energising principle of the book: Mr Duck is never more impressive than in the glances of loathing he directs at the treasure-chest after it has been recovered, or in the rebuke he delivers to Captain Flint:

"And now," said Captain Flint at breakfast, "the first thing to do is to get across the island, find Mr. Duck's tree, and bring the stuff aboard."

"Begging your pardon, sir," said Peter Duck, "the first thing's the ship."

Peter Duck's own romanticism shows unforgettably when they see the Yankee clipper homeward bound. ' "Rot screw steamers," he burst out fiercely, "driving vessels like her off the seas where they belong!" ' The 1930s were the last decade of regular clipper trade, and both Arthur and Peter Duck knew it. But Ransome was just as concerned to show the greatness of the old *Thermopylae* hand as the beauty of sail, and nobly achieved both.

Arthur's life changed for good that winter. In the first place, Forest Smith told him to give up journalism entirely. The ulcers were cured, the doctor said, but they had been caused by excess stomach acid, which had been precipitated by anxiety of the sort that the hurried work of a newspaper was bound to bring on in a temperament like Arthur's.

(*To his mother, October-November*) Books are all right, but I must manage not to have a rush with them ... All I have to do is to recognise my limitations, and go on writing books without letting myself get worried by time limits, and to refuse all other sorts of writing whatsoever.

Vain hope: if Arthur had been the sort not to be bothered by deadlines, he would never have contracted ulcers and could have been a journalist for ever. As it was, he gave up journalism and instead tortured himself about his fancied inability to write good books or to deliver them in time.

It was no sorrow to give up the *Guardian*, Ted Scott being dead; but he did not break off relations. John Rowe Townsend remembers seeing him, years later, after the Second World War, keeping a table of young reporters in a roar at Manchester, pink and white and Falstaffian. But it was delightful to know that financially he could at last afford to do without the paper: 'Cape says that he is now confident that I have only to keep it up for another few years to be getting a respectable income from the books alone.' This prophecy came true to the letter; and Arthur, or rather Arthur and Genia, got all the benefit of the new prosperity, for in April 1935 Ivy renounced all claim on Arthur's income except for £100 *per annum*. This decidedly generous action, and a shared anxiety about Tabitha (who, in her twenties, was going her own way without consulting either of her parents), brought peace at last between Arthur and his first wife. Life had indeed entered upon a new phase.

Arthur got in some fishing in November, and visited Roger Altounyan at his boarding school:

> We went down to Abbotsholme, looking for grayling, but met none but trout. After fishing, I went up to the school for tea and saw Roger and nine other small boys of the junior school, plus three particoloured mice. Roger looking very well fed and well.

Then back to Ludderburn, quite eager to start work on a new book. With his memory full of the Great Frost of his boyhood, and ice yachts on the Stint See, and the freezing of Windermere in 1929, Arthur wanted to write a lake winter story; but (he assured Miss Helen Ferris of the Literary Guild when it was finished) it was to be the last of the Swallows and Amazons.

> I wanted to use the houseboat, frozen-in, with Captain Flint abroad, and, oh, a lot of other things. It would have been impossible to rig up a new lake, and as impossible to use the old lake without the Amazons, etc. But I hereby solemnly promise, bearing in mind what you said some time ago, that they shall NEXX NEVER (observe how even the typewriter jibs at the word. But I mean it all the same) APPEAR AGAIN.
> (*To his mother, 2 March*) The main point of the new book is two other children turn up and get acquainted with the Swallows and Amazons in a rather amusing way, and then get involved in one of Captain Nancy's colossal plans for adventure. The details I will not tell you. All the others are in it too, but the main character interest of the book is in the new couple, and in Peggy, who in the previous books has never really had a fair chance, being so much dominated by Nancy. One at least of the two new characters you won't be able to help liking. I find her a most entertaining companion.

A cheerful beginning. And the thing was helped on its way by the presence of the Altounyan girls at a nearby school. On 28 January Arthur skated with them at Tarn Hows. 'Sunshine', he recorded in his diary. 'Snow on hills but only on the tops. Titty kicking with one leg. Taqui and Susie getting on pretty fast.' This was the germ of several pages in *Winter Holiday*.

Unfortunately Arthur had now fallen into an invariable pattern of composition: the longer he worked at a book, the less he believed in it. It was all very well for Forest Smith to tell him not to worry, but such an expert could always find reasons and opportunities. On this occasion things were made worse by an accident. Out walking on 22 February he broke his ankle and stunned himself a few hundred yards down the hill from his front door. He had to crawl home and go to bed, where he lay for a month or so, churning out his book and groaning because it was so bad.

(*To his mother, 5 March*) I grimly keep up my five pages a day, but they are dull pages without the peripatetic stimulus. I need a floor to prance on and legs to prance with before I can get things going.

He need not have worried. He had served his apprenticeship, and *Winter Holiday* is the first of his books without a false note from beginning to end. The evocation of the snowbound fells and the icebound lake and all the delights of such a season is captivating, and he himself in later years confessed to 'a sort of tenderness' for the book. With *Swallows and Amazons* and *We Didn't Mean to Go to Sea* it is also one of the key sections of the hidden, and perhaps unconscious, autobiography that Ransome put into his children's stories. Dick and Dorothea are delightful additions to his cast of characters, as he well knew ('if people don't like my little astronomer and scientifically minded Dick, I'll eat ten new hats at a sitting') and Dick has proved a most popular model for young readers: one boy I knew acquired the habit, which proved lifelong, of always carrying a pocket notebook, from Dick; another seemed at times to be trying to turn himself *into* his hero. The brother and sister appear to be projections of two sides of Ransome's own character. Dick is the young Rugbeian Arthur, bespectacled, with a strong scientific bent, deaf and blind to everything except the matter in hand. His triumph in the story is also a triumph of the author's wish-fulfilment. Dorothea, the future writer, has been denigrated for being Titty's inferior in intuition. Actually, Dorothea has plenty of insight into people and situations; but what sets her apart from all the others, including Titty, is her concern with language. She alone constantly tries to find the right phrase or word; and although the style she evolves for herself could hardly be worse (' "In you go," said the gaoler, and, as the unsuspecting maiden crept into the darkness, the gate clanged behind her, and she heard the rusty key grate in the lock') it is something to have any style at all at the age of eleven. There can be no doubt that Dorothea's vocation was a true one; and the skill with which Ransome displays it tells us much about his own. To clinch the identification, there is the fact that the Callums are academic brats: their father is a Professor of Archaeology.

In late May, when his ankle was fully mended, Arthur took a week off to go cruising on the Broads. He enjoyed himself very much, and looked forward to writing a Broads book one day. But *Winter Holiday* was still unfinished, and a new difficulty had been added: Cape wanted him to draw the illustrations as he had for *Peter Duck*. This suggestion caused frightful trouble. Arthur was not without all ability as an artist. He knew how to compose a picture, he was a fanatic for visual accuracy, and he had always enjoyed doodling little drawings. He could depict boats with feeling and accuracy. But his ability, such as it was, only made him the more aware of his many deficiencies. In despair he called in outside aid.

(*To his mother, 24 September*) I swiped one of your sheep sketches and did one from it for one of the tailpieces, and for another I collared a rock or two, and a curving road from one of your sketches which I liked very much. It does not look so nice in my version as it did in yours, which is, alas, not surprising. Then I got Barbara to do a kettle and a few other details, which I similarly swiped. But these few things stolen from artists do not make up for the great mass of bad drawing contributed by myself. Genia says I must never try to illustrate a book again, unless exclusively with boats and sea.

Genia had been horrible about *Winter Holiday* from start to finish.

The work being complete at last, Arthur went off for another holiday on the Broads with a friend and fishing pupil, Charles Renold. They arrived in Potter Heigham on 27 September; next day, without warning, Arthur was struck down with acute appendicitis, and but for Renold's good sense and the skill of the surgeon, Blaxland of Norwich, who operated on the 29th, he would have died. As it was he had a particularly nasty time, for the Norwich hospital did not know about his duodenum and the need for Maclean's powders.

In November *Winter Holiday* was published, and sold 1,500 copies on its first day—as many as *Swallowdale* had sold in its first year. In celebration, and to convalesce, Arthur and Genia sailed on a little coastal steamer from London to St Mawes, where they stayed for six weeks or so. Arthur's health returned rapidly, and he began to plan the next tale.

(*To his mother, 21 November, The Watch House, St Mawes*) Our bedroom window looks out on the little harbour, and from the window of the room in which I am writing, I look up the creek at boats at anchor and green pine-covered hills, and rocks and seaweed, and (through glasses) gardens with palm trees. Why on earth we never explored down here before I really cannot think.

(*1 December*) I wish I had a good plot for my next book. It is to be placed on the Broads, with all those rivers, and hiding places in the dykes and the little stretches of open water. Really a lovely setting, with herons and bitterns, and fish, very wild except just in the holiday months. But, as usual, though I have five youthful characters and one old lady, I haven't a glimmering of a plot. (Keep this secret: about the Broads, I mean.)

He wrote to Charles Renold's wife Margaret, asking for suggestions for a plot: he was obeying a sound instinct, and one day she would suggest the idea for *The Big Six*. On this occasion, however, her offerings were politely declined:

(*To Margaret Renold, 8 December*) The essential point of a plot is a change of relationship between the characters. Some kind of stresses and strains have to be set up between hero or heroes and other children or grown ups. That is my real problem. E.g. in S and A; S. v. A. S v Cap. F. S and A v. Cap. F. All the lot v. burglars. Billies v. burglars and pro Cap. F.

S and A and Cap F all in the same boat. You see what I mean.
The story such as it is puts into the concrete one after another
of a series of different relationships.

In the end, in spite of all the usual difficulties and more than the
usual doubts (Wren Howard had to drag the book out of his
clutches so that the reading public could have what was by now
its customary new Ransome at Christmas), Arthur somehow produced *Coot Club*. Such records of the struggle as have been
preserved show with uncommon clarity how Arthur wrought
himself up to creative pitch.

He truly believed that he had done with the Walkers, Blacketts
and Callums, but like many writers he looked for inspiration,
positive or negative, to themes and situations in the earlier work.
Thus, Nancy and Peggy's prim and domineering Great-Aunt had
been very unlike his own Great-Aunt Susan. Were not old people
sometimes lively and children priggish? And then there had been
the idea he had toyed with for *Winter Holiday*, a contrast between
two sets of children, a town pair and a country pair, 'complete
savages and contrast to the townies, but with less ingenuity in
devising adventures, but greater practical power of carrying them
out'. Suppose the two ideas were merged? The book could be
called *Webfooted Grandmother*. 'Grandmother's relations to her two
are precise opposite to those of the G.A. to the Amazons. That is,
she regards them as too desperately proper and is doing her best
to tone them up to the less civilised life of Tom, Port and Starboard and the Pirates.' The theme of the book, then, would be the
conversion of the Propers to web-footedness. At the end of the
book they could start to pull on gloves 'and then refrain on seeing
the faces of Port and Starboard, the fear is expressed privately
among the Coots that the Propers may "relapse" '. So far so good:
but what was to happen between the beginning and the end?

It could be something of a cruise book. The children would
have to travel all over the Broads, experiencing as much of the life
of the region as possible. So, quite early, Ransome had the idea of
Port and Starboard missing their ship and having to beg their
passage on a wherry and a Thames barge. Tom Dudgeon was
invented, so far as can be discovered, for the express purpose of
casting off a motor-cruiser full of trippers. But it was a long time
before Ransome saw the full significance of the Hullabaloos. It
took him some time even to say, tentatively, 'I think perhaps the

same motor cruiser with crowd of Hullabaloos should wander in and out from chapter to chapter, so that there is always a danger of Tom being recognised by them. This would give a sort of feeling of outlawry to Tom and in lesser degree to the three pirates.' Thinking about Tom and the Hullabaloos at a very early stage, before his hero even had a name (in the end 'Tom' was suggested by Genia), he jotted down:

> Boy in canoe approaches ?houseboat ?yacht? with someone on board (assuming that the someone is known to him, as the owner is), collars a heavy anchor weight, puts it in his canoe, sinks the canoe close by the moored yacht, & himself hides among the reeds on shore. Pursuing motor boat turns up, & inhabitant of yacht, willy nilly, makes accomplice. Explanations follow.

A good incident (and one that would appear, with little change, in the published book) but he still hadn't got a plot to fit it.

He tried out names. What were the Propers to be called? Mary and Jane? (This unimaginative suggestion looks even worse in light of the fact that the same two names were originally those allotted to the Amazons.) Prudence and Grade? ('Prue' and 'Grue'). 'Genia suggests Dick and Dorothea.' It was of course a brilliantly right suggestion, but it struck no immediate sparks. Instead Arthur set down triumphantly the full names of his pirates, never given in print: 'Bill Jenkins. Peter Woods. Joe Southgate.' For a moment he wondered if Peter Duck could be brought in (after all, the old sailor worked a wherry on the Norfolk rivers, and had three daughters, at Beccles, Acle and Potter Heigham respectively). This idea was quickly dropped: Peter Duck had been identified too precisely as a figure of fantasy, and especially of Titty's fantasy, to be let loose in a book about what Arthur once called 'straightforward, possible events, in a world outside the door'. But Arthur borrowed his, or rather the Ancient Mariner's, views on bacon, and bestowed them on Jim Woodall's mate Simon. Tom's parents were awarded a new baby, to keep them out of the way. Thinking of the villain, the treacherous Norfolk Coot, he wrote that George Owdon must never be heard to speak throughout the book '(like the G.A. in *Swallowdale*) but seen'.

He accepted the idea that the Propers should be a boy and a girl ('Prudence and James') but resisted the Callum suggestion. For

Dick and Dorothea were not figures who could be allotted minor parts in a moral scheme of the sort he had in mind. Besides, he was trying to make a new departure, to avoid exclusive identification with the Swallows and Amazons. 'Beginning. The Propers in the train from Norwich to Wroxham with in corner of carriage Tom with pot of paint?' In spite of himself, however, the seed began to germinate. He knew and loved the *Winter Holiday* children so well. He began to imagine how they would respond to the Norfolk experience, and how affect it: 'Dorothea enhances the outlawry of Tom for all of them.' (In the end, more subtly, her fantasy just makes Tom uncomfortable.) He jotted down scraps of things they would say: Dorothea, thinking about Tom, 'Nancy would have done just the same.' It dawned on him that the Callums would provide two admirable pairs of eyes for observing the Broads: new to the country, explorers (like the Walkers in *Swallows and Amazons*); and then, a much better theme than the de-civilising of the Propers, something arising directly out of *Winter Holiday*, something so close to his heart as to set his imagination roaring forward,

Dick's stars   Dorothea
\   /
Learning sailing

Let it be Dick and Dorothea, on their way to visit Mrs Barrable (once the webfooted grandmother, now their mother's former teacher), who meet Tom in the train. Let them be desperate to learn to sail because of their exposure to the Swallows and Amazons. Let it be Mrs Barrable's yacht which Tom invades while fleeing from the Hullabaloos. Let the Coots undertake to teach the Callums in return for helping the outlaw. Everything fell into place.

The result was a worthy successor to *Winter Holiday*. If at times it touches greatness, it is for a reason barely to be glimpsed in Ransome's working notes. In the writing, the war between the bird-protector Tom and the motor-cruising Hullabaloos, with their gramophone, radio, yachting-caps and beach-pyjamas, became symbolic of the forces contesting the future of the Broads. The more Ransome detailed the society of the Bure, the Thurne and the Waveney the more clearly he showed that more was at stake than the future of a child-outlaw. The book gained greatly in force since Ransome scrupulously accepted the constraints of chronology and geography. The result was a wonderful picture of the Norfolk waters at a crucial moment of transition. The activities of the RSPB had brought back the bitterns, but the day of the wherry was almost over. The lorry, the radio (later, television), the motor-car, agrarian greed, government policy, sewage and artificial fertilisers were going to do more to undermine the social and natural life of the Broads than Ransome began to guess. In life, the Hullabaloos were going to win. That does not make their defeat in fiction less pleasing; it makes Ransome's scrupulous portrayal of the Broads in 1933 all the more valuable and interesting; and it reminds us that the issues he chose to write about were not trivial: especially not to him. As he had loved the old Russia and the traditional Lake District, so he loved the old Norfolk. *Coot Club* and certain passages of *The Big Six* are his vindication of that love.

Arthur and Genia both felt agonised misgivings over the finished *Coot Club*: about the only quality the author felt ready to vouch for was its accuracy, for he had toured the Broads for three weeks in April to verify details, whether in the text or in the pictures. Yet *Coot Club* did even better than its predecessors: by Christmas it had sold more than 5,000 copies and was still going strong. *Swallows and Amazons* was in its eighth impression (there were three in 1934 alone); it, and all *Coot Club*'s other predecessors, would be reprinted in the course of 1935. Prosperity was assured. Arthur and Genia, made restless by money, decided to leave Ludderburn.

It would be presumptuous to call this a mistake. They were old enough to know their own minds and interest. Still, the cost of this decision would ultimately be high. They would never again own a house which suited them so well in so many respects, and only once, briefly, would they be tenants in such a one. It would not have required more money than Arthur could now spare to do what later owners of Low Ludderburn have done: to introduce running water and electricity; and to gain a little extra space by discreet building additions. It might at least have been prudent to let the cottage (rather than sell it) until they could be sure they would never want it again. The trouble was, they were already sure. Both have left accounts of the decision to move.

[Genia] We began to consider our ages ... and the suitability of

our romantic but primitive cottage for housing an invalid during the worst of the winter if it happened to be a severe one;
the earth closet at the bottom of the garden and every drop of
water to be brought by hand from the well up the hill ... We
could afford to build-on or lift the beams in downstairs rooms
but there was one drawback to the place – there was no proper
water supply at that time. Reluctantly we decided that much as
we loved the place we must move somewhere else, the decision
was more difficult for Arthur than for me.

[Arthur] We had made up our minds now to have a few more
years of sailing before it was too late. Genia, always a great
designer of houses, was now busy with accommodation plans
for boats, though it was not until 1938 that we actually built
another boat for ourselves. Further, the damp climate of my
lake country did not suit her and repeated experiment had
shown that my own troubles were instantly relieved by getting
to sea. We had made up our minds to sell Ludderburn and get
to the East Coast.

The fact was, neither of them had ever been wholly reconciled to
the loss of *Racundra* and the life they had led in her.

Parting from Ludderburn was a sad business. It was a savage
little place, but the books would now have let us improve it and
I have never had nor ever hope to have such another workroom
as the old barn. Visit after visit to the East Coast brought us
back in despair to look out once more down that lovely valley
and at the distant hills. There was nothing on the East Coast
like that.

But there were big boats. Not to put too fine a point on it, Arthur
was bored with *Swallow*, which was only a dinghy, after all, and
with the limited cruising which was all that was possible on
Windermere (though in August he had written an exulting
description to Wren Howard of a race in rough weather in that
little boat, on that water). So in 1935 Ludderburn was sold, and
Swallow too: to the great indignation of the young Altounyans,
who would not have let him have her if they had known he would
ever part with her.

XI

At Pin Mill

In the afternoon we may have to go across to the *Nancy Blackett*,
who is being got ready for sea. We might have tea aboard ...
Bring sandshoes in your pocket.

ARTHUR RANSOME to Katharine Hull and Pamela Whitlock,
29 April 1937

The attraction of the East Coast was obvious. They had been sailing on the Broads, in bigger vessels than poor *Swallow*, for years.
Arthur remembered that in the sixteenth century one of his
ancestors had been a miller at Norwich. 'He may have helped to
make me feel no stranger.' Genia studied the map closely, and
eventually announced that the Shotley peninsula – she put her
finger on the map – was the place. It lies between two rivers, the
Orwell and the Stour, and is an excellent base for the sea-voyaging
which Arthur at last felt strong enough to resume. Pin Mill, on the
Orwell below Ipswich, is an excellent anchorage, and Arthur soon
lost his heart to it. He was always susceptible to places.

To begin with they could not find any satisfactory accommodation on the peninsula, and had to make do with a house on the
north side of the Orwell: Broke Farm, at Levington, convenient
for Pin Mill, but not for much else. More important, they procured a boat. On a recommendation from a yacht-designer friend
Arthur went down to Poole in Dorset and bought a fairly new,
little-used seven-ton cutter with a horrible name that he promptly
changed to *Nancy Blackett* 'feeling that but for Nancy I should
never have been able to buy her'. With a strong young man for
crew (Genia was packing up at Ludderburn) Arthur sailed her

through wild weather to Pin Mill. He was pleased with her performance. 'We had suffered no damage beyond loss of paint and varnish and the smashing up of the dinghy.' He soon got a new dinghy, *Coch-y-bonddhu*, for boarding *Nancy* when the tide served. And presently the household goods arrived from the North in a lorry. The driver, from Kendal, was offered a bed for the night. 'Nay, Mr Ransome,' he said with a shudder, 'I want to get back to England.'

By the end of 1934 *Coot Club*'s successor had begun to move. 'I don't suppose I shall begin the writing for some time yet. What's happening now is sheer fun, with the dim cloudy thing beginning to get outlines, and odd little details coming to life.' The process was to be even more protracted than he expected. First there were the interruptions of house-hunting and moving and boat-buying. Then in January Arthur had a motor accident in which he was flung out of the car and, hitting the ground with his head, suffered concussion. Then there was the decision to produce a set of drawings for *Swallowdale*, which had originally been illustrated by Clifford Webb. Arthur approached this task with relish, his doubts about his draughtsmanship forgotten. Eventually he was to replace the Webb illustrations to *Swallows and Amazons* as well. The result was a completely uniform series, and it must now be impossible for most readers to imagine the Ransome books without the Ransome pictures. Still, there was loss as well as gain. Worst of all was the disappearance of Stephen Spurrier's splendid maps for *Swallows and Amazons*, maps which had enthralled at least one child on opening the book for the first time. Their replacements are agreeable but unremarkable, and not even the author's work. The Webb drawings, which were praised by the reviewers, also deserved a better fate. They had all the strength of professionalism, and something more: Webb had a true eye for the Coniston and Windermere landscape, and by expressing it added a valuable adornment to the texts. But Ransome was not looking for adornments. He had quite a different theory of illustration, and had earlier rejected Spurrier's commissioned drawings for *Swallows* because they did not match it. He seems to have held that pictures in a story should be there merely to help readers' visualisation: they should meticulously depict details of the narrative, and nothing else. Decorative tailpieces were the only graces he was prepared to admit. The effect of this theory can best be made clear by comparing his drawing, 'The Enemy's Boathouse'

4 Clifford Webb's 'The Amazon River at Dusk'

5 Arthur Ransome's 'The Enemy's Boathouse'

(*Swallows and Amazons*, chapter 19) with Webb's 'The Amazon River at Dusk'. As the very titles show, the artists were aiming at different things, though drawing the same scene. Ransome stole Webb's composition, but made significant alterations. Whereas Webb had been chiefly concerned to catch the look of the gloaming on lawn, wood and water, and suggested, wonderfully well, the silence of day's end on a river when the wind has dropped, Ransome wanted to show the skull-and-crossbones on the boat-house, the lights in Beckfoot beyond it, and Roger's exact position before the mast in *Swallow*. Whether this additional information is worth the loss of Webb's atmospherics and strong line is something for readers to settle for themselves.

Ransome complained that neither Spurrier nor Webb drew his boats accurately unless he stood over them ('IT VERY RARELY HAPPENS THAT THE STEERSMAN SITS AS YOU HAVE DRAWN SUSAN') but the essential truth seems to be that Arthur, who had always liked drawing, however incompetently, came to enjoy producing his own illustrations, finding that they made the books feel more entirely his own than they had before, and more completely realised. So he put an end to intruders, and invented reasons for doing so afterwards. When he needed expertise, he turned to his mother or the Collingwoods. He did not mind accepting help from them: they were so close to him, and could be relied on to do exactly as they were told.

Not until March was he able to tell Wren Howard that it was safe to begin writing the new book: 'about ten pages done so far.' It was to be called *Pigeon Post*, or *The Grubbers*, or *Grubbers All*. (Later on he wanted to call it *High Topps*, but the publishers insisted on the first, best title.) It made a slow start. By 14 March it was, he said, moving dimly in a cloud of dust, 'not due to any great speed'. It was largely concerned with mining, and Arthur found that he had a lot to learn. Fortunately there was a friendly expert at hand, Oscar Gnosspelius, Barbara's husband.

He had worked as a mining surveyor in South Africa, and he gallantly threw himself into the business of my prospecting children, lecturing me on gosson, veins, reefs, pyrites and what not, demonstrating, with the tools he had himself used, the methods of panning and washing, and taking me up Weatherlam to make sure of the details of Slater Bob's activities and the ancient tunnels on the hill. This last expedition cost me dear in resultant internal pains but, thanks to Oscar Gnosspelius, I believe there are no mining errors in the book.

Pigeon Post was eventually dedicated to Gnosspelius. But meanwhile Arthur found it impossible to finish, so as soon as Ludderburn was sold and the rough draft completed, he put it aside. There was to be no Ransome for Christmas in 1935.

The move to Suffolk was immediately followed by what can only be described as an orgy of yachting. After a little autumnal cruising *Nancy Blackett* was laid up for the winter.

All her gear was brought round to Broke Farm, and, in the intervals of work, I had a happy time in the attic scraping and varnishing blocks, painting lanterns, greasing wire rigging, making up new halyards and getting through all those other small jobs that make the care of a boat so satisfying an occupation ... There were always web-footed children to help with the rigging, or to drink ginger pop in *Nancy*'s cabin, while I lit a stove to dry her out. Nor was the East Coast winter anything like as bad as we had been told it would be. *Nancy* was laid up, but I was able to sail *Cocky* all through the coldest weather. Pin Mill is the best anchorage on the whole of the East Coast, and when Spring came there were always the little ships of our friends coming in for a day or two before going on elsewhere ... I would work all through the week, and at the weekend we would be off in *Nancy* to one or other of the many anchorages that invite small boats on that coast.

It was delightful to be going to sea again, and his happiness gave him the first flash of pure inspiration he had had since beginning *Swallows and Amazons*.

(*To G. Wren Howard, 15 January 1936*) Spirits here are rising again at last. During the last four days I have seen, grabbed, clutched and pinioned a really gorgeous idea for another book. Swallows only. No Nancy or Peggy or Captain Flint. But a GORGEOUS idea with a first class climax inevitable and handed out on a plate. Lovely new angle of technical approach and everything else I could wish. So I breathe again. I was really afraid I'd done for myself or rather for these stories by uprooting, but I haven't ... And, here's something to sadden niggards

With love from Arthur Evgenia and best wishes for Christmas. & New Year. and fishing and sailing and everything else worth doing.

Coch-y-bondhu

All Good Wishes

6 Undated Christmas card to Charles and Margaret Renold

in gold leaf (I name no names), there are EIGHT words in its entirely admirable memorable and inevitable title .... EIGHT! Cheer up. Monosyllables only. But eight of the very best.

Actually, there are only seven words in the title of *We Didn't Mean to Go to Sea*: perhaps it was originally *Did Not*. Arthur was not wrong about the excellence of his notion. He made his usual thorough synopsis of the book, finished off the pictures for *Swallowdale*, and then resumed work on *Pigeon Post*.

Genia was no more encouraging than usual, and he himself was frequently prostrated with headaches or duodenal pains or both. On one of these occasions he lay in bed reading Galsworthy's letters, and reflected that the author was in many ways a fortunate man. 'E.g. complete faith in himself, his own, his wife's, and his friends'. Never a suggestion that he might fail, or that what he was doing was not worth doing.' Next day he felt 'snivelish and slack'. He went down to Levington Creek and watched birds at low tide, but felt horribly homesick for Ludderburn. 'I am written out and done with; no other explanation for my complete inability to concentrate.'

It says something about the writer's art that this protracted and painful genesis left no mark on the text of *Pigeon Post* (the fact is perhaps also a warning not to take the lamentations in the diary over-seriously). Arthur might abuse the story to his mother ('It is as long as *Peter Duck* and much duller') but it is one of his richest achievements. It is full of lively individual characterisation and fascinating technical detail. It contains a vivid depiction of the impact of drought on the Lake District, to set beside the earlier portrayal of a hard winter. With many slow, small, skilful turns of the screw, it arrives at the terrible climax of fire on the fells. Ransome's hard work was well rewarded.

Even before *Pigeon Post* was out of the way Arthur busied himself about its successor. On 1 June he took *Nancy Blackett* across to Flushing to make sure that his account of the Swallows' latest adventures would be accurate. This voyage proved more of an adventure than he had bargained for. His crew was a man quite without adequate experience, who seems to have spent most of the night passage across the North Sea cowering in his bunk. Arthur was at the helm for nearly twenty of the twenty-five hours it took to reach Flushing, and even so had to give up some of his watch below to feeding his crew. Once in Holland he put the broken reed aboard a mail steamer for Harwich (paying his passage, and happy to do so as it meant getting rid of him) and hired a reliable young Dutchman in his place. They cruised to Zeebrugge and Ostend, then back to England, where Arthur had to pay for another steamer ticket to get his Dutchman home (later on he sent him a copy of *Racundra's First Cruise* as a reward).

On 1 August he left the manuscript of *Pigeon Post* for Genia to read ('I could not have borne being in the house during that grim process') and went cruising for three days with his friend P. G. Rouse. They went down the coast to the Colne, and spent the first night in the Pyefleet behind Mersea Island. The next day, with three reefs in the mainsail and a little storm jib hoisted, they had a most enjoyable, lively time, 'the best run I've had since coming home to Riga in the gales back in 1922'.

With the storm sails she was quite happy, and fairly flew, big waves picking her up, and she riding the top of them in a flurry of white foam until they passed her and she slipped down to be picked up by the next. It really was gorgeous. We did not see any other yachts on the whole passage, just one steamship and two barges, which looked very fine indeed. The three of us, the

two big Thames barges and my little *Nancy*, all came storming
round the Naze together, and we got good shelter down at
Shotley at the mouth of the river, where we lay all night, coming back to Pin Mill yesterday.

He was more and more pleased with his *Nancy* as a sea-boat: she
fully deserved to figure in the next book, under the pseudonym of
Goblin.

Meanwhile Genia had given, by telephone, what, for her,
amounted to warm praise of *Pigeon Post*: 'not very much worse
than the worst of the others.' Three chapters, she said, would need
complete rewriting, but otherwise a few minor alterations would
be enough to justify Arthur in getting the damned thing out of the
house. That was enough to warrant a celebration with hot rum,
in which Rouse shared.

Arthur and Genia were by now very well established in Suffolk.
An unacknowledged gap in their lives had been filled by the
acquisition of two cats during their last year at Low Ludderburn:
Genia's Polly and Arthur's Podge. The Ransomes had no children,
whether from choice, or disability, or all the complications—
politics, ill-health, uncertain income, foreign residence, marital
status or lack of it – which bedevilled their lives for so long. In
1934 Genia was forty, Arthur fifty: if they had ever thought of
raising a family they had left it too late. They expressed an interest
in adopting a little girl of whom both, but perhaps especially
Genia, were fond; but she had sufficiently loving and adequate
parents, so the idea was never realistic. Polly and Podge, cats of
enormous character, intelligent and affectionate, supplied something of what was missing. In this they were not alone. The years
of comparative isolation were at an end: Arthur could easily get
up to London, and Londoners could easily visit him – Londoners
such as the young Rupert Hart-Davis, who had joined Cape in
1933 and been put in charge of the 'difficult' authors, among whom
Arthur, in large part thanks to Genia, was inevitably reckoned.
Then there were the members of the Pin Mill community, ashore
and afloat, among whom, from the moment that Arthur arrived
in *Nancy* in September 1935, they found friends: above all, the
King family of boatbuilders.

Knowing that Genia had set her heart on finding a home on the
[Shotley] peninsula, they once asked, 'When are you coming

home?' This startled Genia, who said, 'But I'm a foreigner.' 'No matter for that,' said Mr King smiling, 'We've always counted you as natives.' There was an ancient tribal feud between the two banks of the river and they said we should never have gone to Levington. 'Didn't you know they was cannibals at Levington?' said Norman King. 'We send three missionaries to them once, but they never come back.'

The Ransomes had some reason to share the Kings' dislike of Levington. True, there was a garden which Genia, according to her husband, dealt with ruthlessly. He hoped it would be very nice in the end, meanwhile it kept her thoroughly occupied. But next door to the farmhouse was a cottage occupied by, among others, a child

> whose pleasure it was to lean out of a window and shout at nobody in particular for hours on end. I happen to like children in general and have always had many among my friends, but if that child had fallen out of her window and broken her neck I think I should have regarded it as a dispensation of Providence and a kindly dispensation too.

Arthur escaped from this odious brat by taking his work to the *Nancy Blackett* and sailing her single-handed down to Hamford Water behind Walton-on-the-Naze. Unfortunately, once he was afloat temptation was too much for him, and instead of writing after mooring *Nancy* he would potter about in the dinghy, using the cutter to sleep in. 'Such is the fraudulent nature of a writer's work that even this truancy (though not so intended) turned out to have been useful.'

The work of 1936-7 was the writing of *We Didn't Mean to Go to Sea*, which seems to have gone through the usual evolution.

> (*To Miss Ferris, 18 March 1937*) I think you'll probably not like the book. It's a dreadfully seasick book, and the formula is not that of the others and may not work out right at all. At the moment it seems to me a failure, but of course it may come out better than I fear. The trouble is that one single incident fills the book, that reality presses so hard on the children that there is no room or need for romantic transfiguration of fact, and so on.

It fairly bristles with difficulties, but I've had it simmering a long time and I've got to do it as best I can.

The gloom of creation was lightened by the news that the Junior Literary Guild had taken on *Pigeon Post*, 'making the sixth running, and, says the Yank publisher, "agrees with us that it is one of your very best tales"!!! Well,' Arthur wrote to his mother, 'after that, I can only marvel and rejoice. I had made up my mind absolutely that they would not take it and that the publishers would be very disappointed – *as they ought to be*. But they aren't. So Hi Cock o lorum!'

Then in early 1937 came the news that *Pigeon Post* had won the Carnegie Medal for the best children's book of the year – the first ever awarded. On 9 February Jonathan Cape Ltd sent Arthur a round robin of congratulation, signed by every member of the firm from Mr Cape himself to the tea lady. Arthur was delighted, and hardly knew, he said, whether he valued most the unexpected expression of good will from his publishers or the equally un-expected expression of good will from the Library Association. He acknowledged the round robin suitably in a thank-you letter addressed to every single signatory ('If some of the names and initials are wrong, it's only because the signatures were too full of character'). On 1 June, in Scarborough, he received the Medal at the hands of his former schoolfellow, the Archbishop of York; and it is to be hoped at last thought of *Pigeon Post* as it deserved.

There was plenty of other evidence of his mounting success. His income from writing had passed the £1,000-a-year mark for the first time in 1934; in 1937 it jumped again to £1,583 12s. 10d.; in 1938 it would be £2,066 13s. 6d. He was getting innumerable fan letters, which would continue to flow until his death, and after. Much the biggest category of these letters testified to the uncanny power of the Ransome books. Adventures, settings and especially characters seemed so real and so attractive that numberless young readers found it almost certain that the Swallows and their friends must be 'real' and wrote to find out. Sometimes they succumbed entirely to the spell ('I believe that the stories about the Swallows and Amazons are true') and wrote for further information or for introductions to the ideal playmates. There seemed to be no boundaries which the books could not cross. Two letters survive from Czechoslovakia in the 1960s, asking the same old questions and reporting the same old reactions. 'We have liked Nancy and

Peggy Blackett especially, because we are 2 too, that we have been quarrel sometimes as Amazons.' Sometimes they wrote simply to thank Arthur: 'The books seem to send the class into a dream when we have them read to us. Your publisher Jonathan Cape has got a lot of sense. You are the best Author in the world.' Some children played at being Swallows and Amazons, and wrote to tell the author so, or to try and involve him in the game: they might put 'Pirate Post', a flag, or a discreet skull-and-crossbones on the envelopes. A chosen few wanted to go beyond Ransome's fantasies into their own. The McEoch family of Boston, Massachusetts, so impressed Arthur with their account of play-acting at savages that he dedicated *Winter Holiday* to them (and stole some of their notions for *Secret Water*).

Arthur answered almost all the letters until his old age; and the process of doing so seems to have fixed in his memory the names and personalities of at least some of the fans. He therefore recognised the name 'Whitlock' when, in March 1937, the bulky manuscript of a complete children's story arrived at Levington, sent with a covering letter from Pamela Whitlock and Katharine Hull, two schoolgirls who had composed a tale about ponies and Exmoor in such intervals as they could snatch from their official business of preparing for Higher Certificate. Pamela Whitlock had written to Arthur a couple of times before, and some quality about her letters had stuck in his mind. So it was unworthy of him to suspect that he was now the victim of a dark adult hoax. He wrote for reassurance on the point; got, in reply, a splendid *apologia* (unfortunately it is now lost); but, before it arrived, began to read *The Far-Distant Oxus*. As he did so he realised that he had just received the greatest compliment of his career.

For the *Oxus* and its successors (there were to be three before the Hull-Whitlock partnership broke up) were books alive with original talent; yet the talent might have taken years to express itself, if it had ever done so, without its discovery of the literary form invented by Arthur Ransome. Far too many professional authors were trying to reduce that form to a formula guaranteeing success in the children's market every Christmas. Hull (aged fifteen) and Whitlock (aged sixteen) seized on it as the perfect vehicle for their own literary needs and powers. They too wrote books about middle-class children on their summer holidays; they too blended imaginative fantasy with the commonplace life of the English countryside. They could never have done so without the example of the Arthur Ransome books (to which explicit tribute is paid in their pages); yet they did all this while remaining themselves, and so, originals. There were things they could not do very well: their dialogue is often unconvincing to an adult, their characterisation is thin. They often unconsciously betrayed their age, whether by giving Peter and Jennifer an impossibly complaisant father ('he doesn't mind what we do') or, as the publisher's reader noticed, building a log house complete with glazed windows between lunch and tea-time. Arthur said firmly of this last point that it would not disturb a child reader in the slightest; all the same, dialogue, characterisation, social reality and technical detail were some of the things he did best himself. Hull and Whitlock, though, were nearly his equals in poetic response to landscape, in the invention of thrilling adventure, and in the construction of narrative. And there is an authenticity about their tale which makes it in some ways the most searching critique that the Swallow books have ever received. The Oxus children, for example, do not leave the world of school almost entirely behind them as the Swallows do. They carry it with them, as real teenagers do; it is a frequent topic in their talk, and by no means wholly a negative one. They talk about the future, too, in a way that convinces the reader that they have one: Anthony means to be a Rugby international, Frances to keep a sweet-shop. This is more convincing than the male Walkers' dutiful expectations of careers in the Navy, or even the Callums' vocations as scientist and novelist. Most of all, there is a discreet, possibly unconscious, tug of eroticism which has no place in the world of the Swallows, but which is an inescapable and incessant part of adolescence. It was something that Arthur never felt able to tackle in any of his published writing.

It is truly remarkable that in six years Arthur Ransome should have attained so unique a standing in children's literature that such a successful piece of sincere flattery was possible. Arthur cannot really be blamed for his suspicions. The thing was quite unpredictable, wholly unlikely. His own Dorothea had not yet finished her masterpiece, *The Outlaw of the Broads*, though she had had two volumes to do it in. And Dorothea was much more dedicated to her craft than most child authors.

What followed showed Arthur at his best. The girls had been gifted enough to write a full-length children's book that could be sure of a creditable reception; in all else they were babes. Arthur

undertook to be their Virgil in the book-trade. The manuscript
had not been in his hands for very long before he was deep in
consultation about practicalities.

(*To Katharine Hull and Pamela Whitlock, 14 March*)
Dear Fellow-authors, The maps are very good indeed. Let me
see a sketch for an illustration. Don't waste more than ten minutes
on it. Think of those Higher Certificates. You won't get them
unless you make a new vow to cut off your hair if you don't[1]
... your respectful colleague, Arthur Ransome.

On 17 March he took the manuscript to London, and walked into
Jonathan Cape's office announcing, 'I have here the best children's
book of 1937.' 'When did you write it?' said Cape politely. He
was disabused; soon he had read, and agreed to publish, the manuscript. The next step was for Arthur to break the news to the girls'
parents, and to make various suggestions as to terms and arrangements. Mr Whitlock replied as a proud father would, but said he
was a little alarmed at the idea, put forward by Arthur, that he
should be his daughter's agent. He knew nothing of professional
authorship. Arthur replied reassuringly:

(*12 April*) I'll look after the book all right. The only difference
will be that the contract with the publisher will be signed by
you, for Pamela, instead of by me. I think that is better from a
legal point of view. For example, I might slip overboard off my
boat or something like that, which would cause quite unnecessary complications.

He fended off the Cape reader, who recommended some retouch-
ing by an adult hand, to make the details more credible. Such
tinkering would destroy the whole interest of the experiment, as
well as ignoring the authors' slogan, 'By Children, For Children
and About Children'. 'For that very reason, I think they should be
given as near as possible NO opportunity for serious revision.
Otherwise nothing will prevent the fathers from butting in.' He
sent the manuscript to his own inexpensive Ipswich typists to be
prepared for the press.

1 Originally they had vowed to cut off their hair unless the *Oxus* was finished by
a certain date.

He made himself equally busy advising Pamela about the illustrations she was preparing. He got Cape to agree to pay her an illustrator's fee, as he paid Arthur for those to the Swallow books, on condition, of course, that the drawings were usable.

> (*29 April*) PICTURES! I do hope you have done a really good lot, because I want to be able to show them to Cape ... they must be full of larkiness. Keep the idea firm in your mind that you are telling the story in the pictures to Katharine, both you and she being deaf and dumb. Thickish nib. J or Relief. Indian ink. White paper. No scratchiness.

Whether Pamela needed this advice or not, the outcome was a set of most vivacious pictures, in which the ponies are drawn with the same flair with which Arthur drew boats. There is certainly no scratchiness (which is more than can be said for the author's illustrations to *Swallows and Amazons*) but possibly there is too much Indian ink.

Then there was the book jacket to consider.

> (*29 July*) Do something that looks really *gaudy* WHEN SEEN FROM THE OTHER END OF A LONG ROOM. This is important, because only that way does a book show up among all the others in a shop.

Page proofs.

> (*12 August*) You must sit down to it right away and not stop till you have finished, and then send it back to me just as fast as ever you can. Tomorrow if possible. If not, the next day.

The jacket design arrived, and was warmly approved.

> (*22 August*) It's very very good ... I've told them I don't think my name is necessary on the jacket, but that I don't mind if they want it for the booksellers. I wish you could have done the pictures for WDMTGTS, but it's all boats.
> You must come and sail in *Nancy* and see something of her. DID YOU GET YOUR HIGHER CERTIFICATE?

A design was needed for the spine of the jacket.

(*25 August*) I'm quite sure you'll be able to think of something jolly. Ponies. Or Peranwisa or what not. Or just a bit of country in the same jolly style as the side of the jacket, with a couple of explorers silhouetted on a hill looking at it. But you'll know best.

(*2 September*) I was delighted to hear that you both got your Higher Certificates in spite of turning authors.

It was all even more absorbing and amusing than teaching young people to fish.

The Far-Distant Oxus appeared that autumn, with an excellent introduction by Arthur Ransome, an essay which throws some light on his own art as well as on that of Katharine Hull and Pamela Whitlock. The book was a great success, just as he had foreseen. But perhaps it was not, after all, the best children's book of 1937: for that was not only the year of *The Hobbit* but also, at last and in spite of all delays, interruptions and discouragements, the year of *We Didn't Mean to Go to Sea*, which many rate Arthur Ransome's masterpiece.

Four months' fairly steady labour between the beginning of November and the end of February had produced, according to the diary, '241 pages of very rough bilge'. Then, as well as the *Oxus* business, and getting *Nancy Blackett* ready for sea, and cruising in her, and occasional duodenal tortures, there was the journey north to receive the Carnegie Medal – an affair which Arthur thought was badly under-publicised – 'It would have been better to send the blessed thing by post.' Work went on nevertheless, and on 14 June the rough draft of *We Didn't Mean* was finished. Once more Arthur went sailing while Genia read his manuscript. He got back from Walton and Brightlingsea on 17 June, to be told that the book was flat, not interesting, not amusing: 'No dialogue. Skeleton only.' 'I was too tired really to hear the bad news and should have waited till morning. Asked if any good chapter? Answer, "No." '

It is difficult to know what Genia got out of these performances. No doubt the first drafts had their defects (we can only guess, for Arthur always destroyed them after the books were published) but it is quite unbelievable that they were as wholly without merit as she asserted. On this occasion Arthur pulled himself together four days later, and began typing a revised version. On 2 July Molly Hamilton, a truly helpful critic (she was a writer herself), came to stay, read the manuscript, and discussed its weak points. She thought that there ought to be more emphasis on Jim Brading in the scene where Mrs Walker confronts her returned delinquents. Titty should be given more to do in the book as a whole. Most valuably she suggested that the account of Jim's accident should be deferred till the last moment, leaving the reader as much in the dark as the Swallows themselves. Arthur worked steadily, and the second version was ready by 5 September. He sailed off to Kirby Creek. Next day Genia conceded that the book did not need much further revision and on 15 September it was posted to the printer – a happy moment, marred only by Arthur's discovery that he had left the first two chapters out of the parcel ('IDIOT!!'). Presently the proofs came back, and though he found the book dull in this form his friend Miss Muriel Wiles, a champion yachtswoman (now Mrs B. H. C. Russell), remembers cheerful sessions correcting them aboard the *Nancy* at her Pin Mill moorings. Arthur would call to Miss Wiles's boat, she would row over to his, and there they would sit to their work in the cockpit, at peace with the world.

In the middle of October Arthur was cruising on the Broads. Apart from occasional duodenal bouts and a tendency to bang his head when aboard ship he had had no illnesses or accidents for nearly three years, his best run of health since leaving the Baltic; but now, while lifting a weight or pulling a rope, he suffered an internal injury which Dr Blaxland diagnosed as an umbilical hernia. On 23 November he was back in the Norwich hospital.

(*Diary, 24 November*) Operation. Ow!
(*20 December*) Embolism and general hell.
(*21 December*) Coughing up the black bluid.

At least this time his duodenum gave no trouble: he made sure to keep up his intake of milk and Maclean's powders throughout his stay in hospital. He felt extremely grateful to Blaxland. The surgeon said he survived the embolism because he was an extremely large-hearted fellow. 'I know only one thing about that. I had a very large-hearted surgeon. Blaxland had come across the road on the run, I believe in his dressing-gown, and somehow or other had managed to keep me going. He must be blamed for the fact that *We Didn't Mean to Go to Sea* was not my last book.'

Another consolation in infirmity was that *We Didn't Mean* was received extremely well. *The Times Literary Supplement* said that Ransome's books had become an institution. The *Sunday Times* thought the latest was the best of the lot (and gave a good notice to *The Far-Distant Oxus* as well). The *Observer* said it was Ransome at the top of his form, 'and so needs no further recommendation from me.' Howard Spring, in the *Evening Standard*, perhaps captured the appeal of the work best, calling it

> the record of that uncovenanted voyage ... of the rain and the wind, the darkness and the wild water, the escape from buoys and from ships crossing in the night, the courage and resource of the children, especially of John and Susan, who, faced with the necessity of doing something they had never done before, made a job of it by using their brains.

The only sour note, at any rate the only one which bothered Arthur, was struck by David Garnett in the *New Statesman*. Garnett had reviewed the earlier books favourably, and had many kind things to say about *We Didn't Mean*; but in a long 'Books in General' article in which he waged war on insipid children's literature and grown-up manipulation of children's responses, he found it necessary to say that Ransome's books supported 'the washy pretence' that children and parents were never at odds. Arthur scribbled indignantly on his copy of the review that David 'must have had a queer time with Edward and Constance Garnett!' He was right to be cross, since the deepest theme of his new book was precisely the tensions that arise between even the nicest children and the most loving parents.

In *We Didn't Mean to Go to Sea* he at last directly confronted the ghost of Cyril Ransome. As his letter announcing its conception makes plain, the climax of the turbulent voyage was from the first to be the meeting with the children's father. And so it was carried out. John is very much the hero of the book, and gets his reward for his courage, initiative, steady nerves and good luck when his father, after listening to the tale of his adventures, squeezes his shoulder: '"You'll be a seaman yet, my son." And John, for one dreadful moment, felt that something was going wrong with his eyes. A sort of wetness, and hotness . . . Partly salt . . .' For one dreadful moment it seems that something is going wrong with the book; but the author quickly recovers his usual poise. He can be forgiven his lapse. For his daydream of at last earning and winning the approval that had been so rigidly withheld had at length given him the theme for a book of which Conrad would have been proud.

Ransome brought all his seasoned skill to the job of making his tale of childish heroism plausible: all his knowledge of the land and sea. But the chief instrument of his success is the character of Susan. In earlier books she had always been something of a propitiatory sacrifice: without at least one preternaturally good and domesticated child no one would have believed that the Walkers would have been allowed to become the Swallows, sailing off on adult-free adventures. But in *We Didn't Mean*, Susan, without for a moment ceasing to be herself, is fully human at last, and it is through her seasickness, her anxiety, her fear and tears that the dangers of the night sea are brought home to the reader. The book belongs to her as much as to her brother, for she overcomes nearly disabling terrors and proves, at last, as reliable a Mate as ever. This was perhaps Ransome's greatest triumph of psychological portraiture; a triumph that as usual he makes seem quite effortless.

Arthur was discharged from hospital on 4 January 1938. As always, his recovery was astonishingly rapid, and he got back energy and spirits together. He had various ideas for a possible successor to *We Didn't Mean*. There was a tale about a Mastodon living on Hamford Water; there was Margaret Renold's attractive suggestion that he write a detective story. What he wanted most was to commission a boat. 'Fools build and wise men buy.' As before, he ignored his own maxim. Genia had never really taken to the *Nancy Blackett*: the galley was too small for the feats of cooking in which she excelled. Now she told Arthur that if he gave in to his hankerings the Cook of *Racundra* would go to sea again in her old capacity. At hand was that admirable firm of boatbuilders, King of Pin Mill. It was all irresistible. Genia and Arthur had a wonderful time for the next nine months as the new vessel took shape at the yard. They only occasionally let themselves wonder whether, in view of the European situation, they were not mad to sink their money in a boat they might never be able to sail.

Life on the Orwell was particularly agreeable that year, even for Annie Powell, who had to learn to cook omelettes. For Arthur had given her a walk-on part in *We Didn't Mean to Go to Sea*, in which he said she served omelettes at her Pin Mill cottage, where she kept a tea-room. Youthful visitors turned up, eager to cross-examine her about the book, and to eat her omelettes. She got no peace until she produced them.

Generally, there was no shortage of small boys and girls for Arthur to play with, which was just as well, for the Altounyans were now grown up, and although Titty, Taqui and Roger all visited Levington and the *Nancy Blackett*, the old relationship, so important to Arthur creatively, could not be sustained. Like Peter Pan, he found a new generation for his games. There were the children of Colonel Busk, who owned *Lapwing*, an eight-ton cutter. There were 'the buccaneering, gun-firing young Youngs whose home port was Maldon' and their friend Nigel Arnold-Forster. John, James, Thomas and Roger came from the brewing family of Wandsworth, but it was Arthur who introduced them to the joys of beer and darts. On one occasion Thomas (aged about eight) went home drunk, and today wonders that his mother ever allowed him to return. But she was not called 'the Iron Woman' (by Arthur) for nothing.

Arthur had a rigid rule that at tea-parties cake must be eaten before bread-and-butter. 'Children?! I can't stand them,' he would mutter,[2] but he made the Youngs useful in what he called fo'c'sle parties: the boys sat in a circle on the floor, painting, varnishing and mending while he told them Anansi stories.

And there were George and Josephine Russell, the youngest members of a family which in 1937 took Broke Hall at Levington for a year. Ransome met them one day when, returning to land in *Coch-y-bonddhu*, he found them waiting on the shore, ready to catch a rope and help him ashore with his gear. Josephine Russell remembers the incident perfectly. When the little boat appeared she seemed to have a brown plum pudding bobbing about inside her: it was the helmsman's stocking cap. After he had landed, he introduced himself: 'My name's Ransome', and went off. Josephine suggested that it might be the great Arthur Ransome, and was properly snubbed for such a stupid suggestion by her elder brother. But she was right all the same, and the friendship ripened rapidly.

He taught them to sail, and took them on as crew. Looking

2 Arthur was all too fond of making this rather misleading statement. For instance in 1934, he took the eleven-year-old Wayland Young (no relation to the Youngs of Wandsworth) sailing on Windermere in *Swallow*. When they landed he remarked gruffly, 'I'm supposed to love children because I'm a children's author, but really I hate them' — which embarrassed the boy greatly.

back, Miss Russell, who as crew has had to endure torrents of abuse and bad language from the sort of man who becomes a monster when he gets his hands on a tiller, is grateful for and impressed by the fact that Arthur never lost his temper or raised his voice. He would explain in advance the order he was about to give, so that it was easy to obey promptly and successfully. If you failed to dodge the boom after the boat went about, he always said 'Bad luck' instead of 'You idiot'. In the winter, when there was tackle to clean and varnish and prepare for spring, he read them books or told them stories as they worked for him. He was, in short, an admirable skipper.

George Russell was a boy absolutely after his own heart. For one thing he was totally blind without his spectacles, like Dick Callum and Dick's creator: and, as with Arthur, it had taken years for his myopia to be diagnosed. For another, he became passionately devoted to sailing. He and Josephine saved up ten pounds, which George took up to Yarmouth, where he found a derelict old boat on the beach (it was like the discovery of the *Slug*). *Coch-y-bonddhu*, which Arthur had lent them, was restored to her owner, and George and Josephine worked devotedly at making their ship seaworthy again. In 1938 George went on one of Arthur's cruises on the Broads, and kept a conscientious log, which shows how entirely he had absorbed his master's outlook: 'We tacked and tacked and quanted and quanted till we came in sight of Wroxham and in the excitement of crying "Land Land" and smacking our parched lips we were nearly rammed by a convoy of Hullabaloos towed by a motor launch.'

Cruises on the Broads had now developed into major expeditions. In both 1938 and 1939 the Ransomes led a fleet about the northern waters for a week in spring. Arthur was admiral; in his train came four Fairways and a Whippet (sailed by Taqui and Titty, who proved to be the most efficient of the younger sailors). The rule was that every boat could do more or less as she liked during the day, but all had to arrive at the same rendezvous for the night. In practice the boats stayed pretty much together, and Arthur was usually at hand to help in misadventures, of which running aground seems to have been the most common. To aid identification every ship had to fly a Jolly Roger (according to Arthur, his own, made by Genia, was much the best): many crew members fell overboard, stepping backwards on narrow counters to get better views of their magnificent flags. On one occasion an inquisitive grown-up, seeing so many skulls-and-crossbones, asked Arthur if it was a secret society. 'Yes.' Eagerly: 'Oh do tell me all about it!' 'Since it's a secret society, I can't.' Sometimes Genia would invite guests to supper, and feast them (if George Russell's experience was typical) with plum pudding, cold tongue, tomatoes and hot potatoes. To add to the zest of life, at any rate in 1939, the sailors turned pirates and doused each other with buckets of

THE 3 LB GRAYLING YOU ARE GOING TO CATCH

7 Christmas card, 1938, to Charles and Margaret Renold

water when they met on the river: once George and Josephine captured a mop from the Youngs and hoisted it to their masthead as a trophy.

This, one cannot help feeling, is how the author of *Swallows and Amazons* ought to have behaved. In *Nancy Blackett*, with *Lapwing* as a sister ship, he also led expeditions to Hamford Water and Kirby Creek. The elders remained afloat in their cutters, while the small boats took the children off to camp on Horsey Island. 'Tents sprang up. There were fires at night and, during the days, great exploration of all the intricate waters that lie, hidden from the sea, behind the Naze.' It was idyllic.

There were undercurrents. Arthur was a fusspot, so, in her way, was Genia, and when Taqui untidily left a banana-skin on deck, her crime was forgiven, but never, never forgotten. The Russells noticed that the Ransomes were not so polite to each other as they were to their crews, and that Arthur went in terror of the Cook's whistle. Josephine did not feel so close to him as her brother, partly because at first her mother constantly worried about her health, tried to keep her at home when expeditions were afoot, and was not mollified by remarks from Arthur like 'Don't worry, she can sleep on the sand.' Neither was she so wholehearted about sailing as George: she disliked such experiences as bobbing up and down for six hours outside the Beach End Buoy at Harwich, desperately seasick, while waiting for the right combination of wind and tide. She was entering adolescence, with the usual turbulences, and noticed that Arthur did not seem interested in her except as a sailor, and in so far as she was willing to play his games. Kind though he was, he never asked her about her life away from the water, and so never discovered, for example, that she had ambitions to be a pianist. She felt a fundamental reserve in his attitude towards his child crews, which she was tempted to interpret as lack of interest. Did he understand, for example, what a difficult time she had of it as the youngest in her family (a family, furthermore, which, except for George, was bored by sailing)? Today she thinks he did understand, and was only sensible in minding his own business.

She and George had slight reservations about Genia. They thought she looked like a large fat slug, and her heavy Russian accent was a gift to young mimics (but decades later, when Josephine visited the Soviet Union, she was unexpectedly moved when her middle-aged Intourist guide proved to have the same accent). She was a wonderful cook, and was a necessary part of their pleasures when afloat. Essentially it was a happy friendship for everybody. Josephine recalls with particular pleasure a day when they cruised in the Orwell, came back to Pin Mill, supped at the Butt and Oyster, and then went to the circus. The clowns were so funny; and part of her delight was in Arthur, who beamed all the time, and enjoyed the circus as much as any of them. On his side, he had no doubts about the Russells: he regarded them as invaluable allies, and as George began to shoot up he had six inches' clearance added to the quarters planned for the crew in his new boat.

The vessel was to be called *Selina King*—*Selina*, because that was the name Genia preferred; *King*, after the boatbuilders, and to distinguish her from other *Selinas* in the registry. Old Mr King promised that his next grand-daughter would be christened Selina, and his wife had the naming of the ship. Mr King taught her carefully what to say at the launching, but at the critical moment she remembered none of his lessons, only the solemnity of the occasion: ' "I baptise thee SELINA KING," and any disapproval Mr King felt was drowned in a general shout of laughter as the bottle crashed on the stern.'

27 September 1938 was not otherwise a day for much laughter. That night Arthur wrote in his diary the stark word, 'War'.

Two days later Neville Chamberlain flew to Munich, and Arthur gave a dinner for all King's workmen at the Butt and Oyster. On 30 September came the news of Chamberlain's return, and Arthur wrote, 'Peace'.

Since Ted Scott's death he had been able to shut out politics from his life almost entirely. 'Just as I think that country best governed in which most people are able to forget that they are governed at all, so I think those times are best in which most people need not bother their heads about "the news".' The 1930s were hardly one of those times, but to judge from his surviving papers Arthur managed to exclude 'the news' from his life to an amazing extent. The autumn of 1938 burst the bubble.

XII

Ebb-Tide

His mother wanted his views on the crisis just past. He replied, on
2 October, that it was useless to comment on the political situation, 'except that in spite of all that was said against him, I think
Chamberlain has done extremely well.' Nevertheless he went on
to give his views with the tone of insight and authority, but without, any more, their substance. He was only the ghost of a Special
Correspondent, and does not seem really to have grasped how the
world had changed. To put it bluntly, he had quite failed to
recognise the nature and extent of Hitlerian evil, and thought that
'a general appeasement' was now possible if the errors of the
Versailles Treaty could be rectified. He was more at home writing
about his boat.

> *Selina* is launched. It looked as if she would be just in time for
> the war. Mrs King bust the champagne and under protest agreed
> just to sip a little. 'Like Holy Communion,' she said ... *Selina*
> seems most awfully big. Comfortable to live in, but a bit of a
> handful to sail. However, if war does come there won't be any
> sailing.

It turned out that there was to be an Indian summer before
Chamberlain's settlement collapsed. Nevertheless, the years which
had nurtured the Swallow stories were nearly over, as was symbolised by the sale of the *Nancy Blackett*. Arthur saw her go with
deep regret, but took some comfort in seeing how well her new
owner looked after her and sailed her (he even named his house
'Blackett Cottage'). Arthur presented *Coch-y-bonddhu* to the
Russells, and on 15 October launched and sailed a new dinghy, yet
another *Swallow*. 'Great fun,' says the diary. During October he
also went cruising in *Selina* — Genia gladly kept her promise to

serve as cook – and the yacht was not laid up for the winter until 17 December. Arthur gave up his idea of writing a book about her building (instead he lent his notes and photographs to Uffa Fox, who included a flattering account of the boat in his *Thoughts on Yachts and Yachting*) and went seriously to work on his story about the Mastodon on Hamford Water.

War held off long enough for Arthur and Genia at last to find a house which suited them better than Broke Farm. It was Harkstead Hall in the Shotley peninsula, a few minutes' drive from Pin Mill. In spite of its grand name it is no more than a pleasant, square, red-brick farmhouse overshadowed by some magnificent cedars of Lebanon. They moved in on 3 April. 'I had a very good room to work in, Genia had a garden in which she did wonders with roses, and Polly and Podge much preferred it to the noisy Levington.' The trouble was that they could only rent the house, on a very insecure tenure: at any moment the owner was likely to decide to live in it himself, and he spurned all their offers to buy. However, *Selina King* was afloat again, the new book was progressing in the usual fashion (in late December Arthur had been telling Wren Howard that it was not much good; the rest can be imagined) and although, with the occupation of Prague in March, it became clear that the hopes of Chamberlain and his admirers had been in vain, the little yachting community of Pin Mill merely resolved to wring the last drop of sweetness from what might be their last happy summer. Every week Genia took baskets of roses from the Harkstead garden to the anchorage, where she and Arthur rowed through the fleet distributing bunches among their friends. The second expedition to the Broads with the pirate flotilla took place, and was as great a success as the first. Plans were laid to sail *Selina* to Holland in the late summer, with George and Josephine Russell for crew; but the Ribbentrop-Molotov pact put an end to the scheme.

Arthur clung to the illusion that some reasonable bargain could be struck with Hitler that would preserve the peace. When the Nazis started their diplomatic campaign for the repossession of Danzig and the Polish Corridor, he suggested to Francis Hirst that they were right, as Yorkshire would be in resisting any similar arrangement cutting her off from the sea. Hirst showed this letter to Philips Price, now a Labour MP, who firmly squashed its argument. The Yorkshire analogy, he said, applied to Poland rather than to Germany. Neither did he think much of Arthur's notion that Stalin wanted to see Germany at war with England while he kept clear himself. The Russians, he said, knew that German expansionism in the east at their expense was part of Nazi foreign policy. No doubt: but the Ribbentrop-Molotov pact showed that Arthur had a shrewder insight into Stalin's calculations than Price. He may well have been influenced by the fact that so many of the Russian Communists he had known and admired had by now fallen victim to the Stalinist purge: Radek, Rykov, Bukharin. Probably the same factor explains why he took so long to recognise the true nature of the danger from Hitler.

All such points were made academic by the outbreak of the war. Arthur had hoped that his long experience of boats and navigation might offset his physical disabilities, such as 'being dependent on a handy cow ... being unable to lift even a chair without paying for it, and ... being fairly often put out of action altogether', but this hope, though abetted by the efforts of his friend Captain, later Rear-Admiral, Corson (who had named his cutter *Wild Cat* and his dinghy *Titmouse*), unsurprisingly came to nothing. Instead, on the first day of war, Arthur was told by the local chemist that there had been an unusual run on California Syrup of Figs; and the next day Genia had to cope with the arrival of four evacuees from London – a woman and three small children. Arthur was indignant about the imbecility of sending children to an area stiff with important naval bases; it was the equivalent of evacuating them to the front line; but the problem solved itself, for after twenty-four hours in the country the woman took her brood back to London – 'fed up with country life,' says Genia, 'and leaving an incredible mess.' A more intractable difficulty, the question of what to do with *Selina King*, was solved even more happily. Captain Corson got Arthur permission to sail her to Lowestoft to be laid up 'for the duration'.

(*To Katharine Hull and Pamela Whitlock, 31 December*) She carried a special permit for a war-time voyage by a British merchant vessel, cargo ballast, a beautiful green paper with about a ton of sealing wax on it. I did not sight a submarine, but sailed close by the tops of the masts of one of our sunken ships – very beastly to look at.

The voyage was quite adventurous. *Selina* was forbidden to sail by night, and contrary winds eventually made it clear that she would not be able to reach Lowestoft from Pin Mill in one day. There was nothing for it but to try to berth in Southwold, the notoriously tricky entry to which Arthur had carefully avoided in all his years of East Coast navigation. Now, sailing single-handed, he most creditably brought his boat in, to the stupefaction of the harbour-master. But even this feat was an ill-omen: it was to Southwold that Adlard Coles had brought *Racundra* on her first voyage after Arthur sold her. Arthur did not reflect on the coincidence. There was a strong gale on 28 September; on the 29th he went up the coast and soon had *Selina* tucked under cover in a shed by Oulton Broad, where she sat out the war in safety. But he was never going to sail her again.

Back at Harkstead, he was soon working hard on *The Big Six*. In the mean time, in November, *Secret Water* was published, and before the month was out had gone into four impressions. No doubt this immediate success occurred because *Secret Water* was the first Ransome book to appear for two years. Arthur would benefit from these encouraging sales more than ever before because in January Wren Howard had offered him the extravagant royalty of 20 per cent – the same as Ernest Hemingway's. It was a generous gesture that would, in the end, cause trouble to everybody and not do Arthur much good. Meanwhile he had been happy to agree to the terms. During the autumn he made sure that his American royalties paid full tax to the Chancellor of the Exchequer, for he had decided patriotically that his war work would be to earn hard currency for his country. He was unresponsive to another Howard suggestion, that he should write his autobiography.

Secret Water, set in empty Essex marshlands, is the quietest of all the Swallow books. It is dedicated to the Busk family, and their yacht *Lapwing* figures prominently in the story, which is largely a distillation of Arthur's happy voyages with them to Hamford Water. Perhaps the opening pages are too quiet: they are some of the most stiffly awkward that Ransome ever wrote. He did not find his form till he had got the Swallows safely marooned on Horsey Island. The technical challenge, even the business of handling a cast of eleven children (the largest number he ever tackled), was not particularly formidable. Considering how children's books are infested by twins (usually identical) it was witty of him to include two brothers, Dum and Dee: 'they're not twins, but everybody thinks they are.' The glory of the book, apart from the

Swallows' fall from grace (even Susan ends up a savage, wallowing in the mud), is the character of Bridget. The book belongs to her even more entirely than *Winter Holiday* does to Dorothea. She has her own well-defined point of view, which throws a quite new light on, for example, the characters of Titty and Roger.

> "Don't forget to wash behind your ears," said Roger.
> "Used they to say that to you?" said Bridget earnestly, and wondered why Roger grinned a little sheepishly and Susan laughed.

She has the time of her life, fairly revelling in her capture by the Eel tribe (thanks to Titty's negligence) and in being condemned to be a human sacrifice. Her brothers and sisters, who do not realise how fast she is growing up (the year before last, in *Swallows and Amazons*, she was two, now she is seven or so), hurry to rescue her, but are unwelcomed by the captive: ' "Oh go AWAY," shrieked Bridget. "Go AWAY. They're just in the middle of it. I don't WANT to be rescued." ' By the end of the book she has decisively established her own position in the family. She seems to have a stronger character than any of the others, except perhaps Susan. Yet she remains very much the young child: her relationship with the kitten Sinbad is particularly well-observed.

> "Sure you wouldn't rather sleep comfortably in a bed at Miss Powell's?" said Mother.
> Bridget sat up suddenly. "Oh, Mummy!" she said.
> "Oh well," said Mother. "I suppose you have to grow up some time."
> "Sinbad's the youngest now," said Bridget.

It is a pity that Ransome never put Bridget in a book again.

The success of *Secret Water* must have pleased Arthur. Otherwise there was less and less to be cheerful about. He could not forget the Bolshevik prophecies that the next general European war would be followed by Communist revolution in every belligerent country. 'If we win ... we shall be faced by a Communist block extending from the North Sea to the Pacific. Cheerful outlook.' He was no longer any sort of Red or Pink. His health deteriorated: 'Worry stirs up duodenal trouble and duodenal trouble brings on worry.' When he went to London for the monthly dinners of the Royal Cruising Club and stayed overnight at a hotel, he soon found himself the only civilian. He loathed being on the side-lines, but 'I had, in the most literal sense, "no stomach for the fight".' The thought that his writing could earn dollars was thin comfort, but it spurred him on to unusual speed in composition. The first draft of *The Big Six* was ready in April 1940. There could be no question of sailing while Genia read it, so Arthur went off to fish the Meon with Francis Hirst. When he came back he got a uniquely favourable verdict: 'the framework is better than usual.' Much cheered, he settled down to prepare the final version; then the phoney war came to an end, and the difficulties of life multiplied overnight.

The Germans pushed into France, and the Admiralty issued a sudden, unexplained appeal for small boats. Arthur offered *Selina*, but she was rejected: he realised afterwards that her tiny engine, useful only in a calm, would have been no good at Dunkirk. France fell and air-raids began.

(*To his mother, 26 May*) The row from the battle here is terrific. Our windows rattle till they roar, and we can feel the tremors when standing on the drive. Due to some trick of the earth's strata, I fancy. At a house near by a farmer has a watercloset directly connected by a drain to the river, and the locals appear to take turns in going there to experience the odd effect of the violent vibration transmitted to their behinds. Poor Genia is getting very little sleep at nights with the row from the aeroplanes and their resisters. The cats, however, are already inured, and merely curse silently out of the corners of their mouths ... I go on driving at my infernal book.

Arthur began to feel horribly isolated. A bellicose local parson gleefully recounted tales of Dutch partisans cutting the throats of German parachutists 'while they were still stunned by their descent' and talked of starving all Europe to save civilisation. 'Christian civilisation, I supposed.' Colonel Busk left Shotley, and Arthur had no one with whom he could talk frankly about the war: his views were so extremely gloomy that, had they been known, he might have been denounced as a traitor.

(*To his mother, 1 June*) Dick Stokes, the Ipswich M.P., was here to supper last night, full of beans and jokes as usual, and as furious as I am with the fools who (a) arranged a war without making sure that Hitler would have to fight on two fronts, and (b) did so when they knew we were in no condition to fight and (c) failed to give our splendid chaps the weapons to match those of their enemies. And to think that Halifax is still in the Government!!

(*16 June*) How soon shall we call in old Lloyd George who alone had the courage to speak out at the time and tell them what lunatics they were. He is, I am told, in constant touch with Churchill. I regard it as a blessing that there is one man of common sense still extant.

The matter of Genia's interrupted nights was serious. 'She was one of those unfortunate people who when someone drops a boot on the bedroom floor above them spend the rest of the night awake, listening for the other boot to drop.' With the Battle of Britain now taking place overhead, Harkstead Hall was no place for her. She was not much disturbed at the slight chance of being hit by a bomb, but she did miss her sleep. Then there was the possibility that the army or the navy would decide they needed the house, so that Arthur and Genia would have to move out at a moment's notice: and where could they go? They began to think seriously of moving away altogether. But that was easier said than done, and in the meantime the war continued to fill their lives with incident.

(*To his mother, 24 June*) The funniest episode was Friday night. Stokes the Ipswich M.P. had mentioned to me that if you have no cellar the best thing to do in an air raid is to make up a bed under the table. Well, on Friday night he rang up to say he was coming round in the evening, and Genia mischievously put a mattress under my worktable with a roll of blankets and a large placard 'RESERVED for R. R. Stokes, M.P.' He came in and roared with laughter. He hadn't been in the house twenty minutes before the warning went, and, as you may not move a car during the raid, there he had to stay, and under my table he had to sleep, and did, until about half past three next morning when the all clear went.

(*30 June*) I wonder very much what is happening in Aleppo, with the French army 'at peace', and Italy and Turkey watching. I think Turkey has a good chance of getting Syria back.

Well, Ernest Altounyan and his father did pretty well under the old regime before the last war, and I suppose they can do it again.

This was unworthy: the Altounyans had to flee at a moment's notice. Ernest lost his hospital and almost everything else. He never really recovered from the blow. The fact that Arthur could so mis-estimate the likelihoods is one more indication of how out of touch he had become.

He was better off dealing with brats and books. For instance, ever since the publication of *The Far-Distant Oxus* he had been showered with children's manuscripts – so many that in the end he had to refuse to read any more. How he dealt with them before reaching that extremity is well illustrated by a letter which survives from this summer. It is surely admirable, in both matter and manner.

(*28 June*)

Dear Helga and Brenda,

You are a pair of unmitigated pests.

But, in spite of being exceedingly busy, I have found time to look carefully through your manuscript. You ask me to answer two questions.

Is it good? Answer: Not very.

Is it fit to publish? Answer: No.

The reason for both these answers is that so much of it is simply cribbed or copied or reflected from other books: the method, the main idea, the dialogue, the details, almost every incident, so that if it were to be published you would be inviting very unkind criticism. N.B. I think you probably do not realise H O W imitative it is, and my best advice to you is to lock it up for a year or two and then have a look at it with fresh eyes, when you will see what I mean.

It must have been fun to do, so that it was not waste of time, and even if it had been very good it would not have had much chance of being published till after the war. It was nice of you to dedicate it to Bridget.

I think the pictures are on an altogether different level, and very good indeed. I think you ought to go ahead with your drawings for all you are worth.

Arthur also continued to observe his neighbours' reaction to the war with amusement and affection.

(*To his mother, 9 July*) People here are, as I told them they would, getting entirely accustomed to air raids, and trouble about them little more than they do about thunderstorms, which in these parts are always called 'tempests'. Our beloved Charlie Burgess, the farm bailiff, invited me to see his dug-out. He has dug a deep pit and sunk a chicken hut in it, putting logs over the top and a lot of earth. It has a bench in it and a chair, and he and his wife and his brother-in-law (Genia's gardener) and his wife all crowd in and play cards by the light of a candle. He is laying down a little cellar in one corner for the beer he brews himself. I suggested planting nasturtiums overhead, but Charlie very gravely said he thought them Germs might see 'em, so he is sowing speargrass instead. Very soon, I think, there will be resentment on those nights if any when 'them Germs' don't show up. During yesterday's go the managing director of one local firm was in the middle of a business conference which was cheerfully continued under the table. And everybody gets a sporting pleasure out of the searchlights, which really are a wonderful sight and extraordinarily quick in picking out the planes.

It begins to look as if we may be driven out of here and have to go to London if they do indeed prohibit the use of cars. We use ours only to go shopping once a week, but if we aren't allowed to do that things will be so awkward living as we do miles from any shops, that we may have to close down temporarily. Though we don't want to if we can possibly help it. I am sure things are much more cheerful here than they could be elsewhere.

Nevertheless, they began seriously to discuss a retreat to the lakes. Genia laid down conditions. There was to be no return to Ludderburn: if she went it would have to be to a house with electricity and running water. Inquiries were put in hand, but it was some time before they yielded a result, and in the mean time the war continued to batter them at Harkstead Hall, though they were thankful not to be enduring the agony of London, and Arthur still found private sources of consolation and renewal.

(*To his mother, 15 September*) Caterpillars are a great consolation.

I have got a couple of Pale Tussocks, which I never knew as a boy, beautiful pale green creatures with white hair and tufts and bits of velvet black with a plume of red hair for a tail. The first one I got went off its food, but as soon as I got a second it set to again and they are both in great form. Lime leaves, luckily, are not rationed. I have also a couple of woolly bears, brown ones ... I think drawing is a very good way of dealing with the situation: at least it concentrates your mind on things that are not affected by any idiocy of human beings. Anyhow making careful drawings of caterpillars has that effect on me.

(*20 September*) The cats are well. We now call Podge the Air Raid Warden. She comes dashing in the moment the sirens go. Polly has to be called, and Podge, in shelter, watches anxiously for her arrival. Podge, from the start, has taken aeroplanes seriously, and while anything is overhead, lies with her eyes anxiously looking up at the ceiling.

At last news arrived of a suitable house in the Lake District. At the same time Jonathan Cape told Arthur that all the blocks of the illustrations for *The Big Six* had been lost in an air raid. He wrote back to borrow £1,500 from his publishers towards the purchase of The Heald on Coniston.

(*To Wren Howard, 26 September*) Let me say how impressive we found the imperturbable resolution and calm of your letter with the news of the blocks gone west the blockmakers' plant ditto Bedford Square windows ditto and otherwise nothing to report. Hitler simply doesn't know what he's up against.

... The house is a stonebuilt one (about 18 or 20 years old) ... The actual ground happens to be a bit that I have been a bit in love with since the age of nine. It has a view across the lake to the mountains better even than the view from Brantwood. It is property that can never go down in value and must eventually go up ... The place has its own electric light, central heating, and, Gosh, that bit of land, going right up from the lake (1 mile from the original Wild Cat Island) to the sky-line of the fells; grouse, pheasant, blackcock. One thing certain is that it will mean a fresh lot of lake country Swallows and Amazons.

The next day he announced the impending purchase to his mother. Even in the middle of the Blitz she could not throw off a lifetime's habit of anxiety about Arthur, and wrote to him cautioning against the Heald project.

(*To his mother, 3 October*) Your warning came too late! Your son is once more a lake country landowner.

I have bought seventeen acres, with *half a mile of lake frontage* at the bottom of what used to be the Heald Wood ... The whole of the land on both sides of it and above it belongs to the Forestry Commission, so that it can never be spoilt. And the shoulder of the hill on the other side of the lake just hides Coniston village, so that you can see the Old Man and all that as if there were no village at all. It has its own boat harbour, and a small wooden pier. The buildings are of grey Coniston stone and they are roofed with green slate from the Old Man. You will probably remember where there is a sharp bend in the road above the lake a bit above Peel Island and a particularly lovely little wood between the road and the lake. That little wood is inside the southern boundary, and I have the whole strip between lake and road for about half a mile, the bulk of the land of course being above the road where the old Heald Wood used to be.

He had used 'the Heald Wood' in *Swallowdale* as the name of the place where Titty and Roger met the charcoal burners. The actual move is described in the draft *Autobiography*.

In October we put back the bits missing from our demobilised car, packed books and furniture into pantechnicons, and set out by road with Polly and Podge, arranging to meet the vans at the other end. We spent a somewhat noisy night in the Midlands, but next day, as we passed through Leeds, and saw once again the Wharfe, climbed the hill beyond Settle, crossed the Devil's Bridge over the Lune, and saw once more the Lake hills, I had as always, coming north, the feeling of coming home.

Arthur had the capacity to enjoy life almost anywhere he set-tled. He certainly meant to be happy at the Heald. Genia was pre-pared to lump the Lake District rainfall because it was less injurious to her health than the din of aerial battle on the East Coast. The sojourn at the Heald got off to a bad start when the vans with the furniture failed to arrive for twenty-four hours after they were due (and might not have arrived then had Arthur not asked the police for help) but they soon put that difficulty behind them. More permanently troubling was the question of how to fit all their furniture, or even their own large selves, into rooms so much smaller than they had grown used to at Harkstead. And it might be hard to ensure their supplies: 'We are actually much further from anywhere even than at Ludderburn,' Arthur wrote to his mother. 'However Genia thinks she will manage all right, though it will be very difficult on account of having next to no petrol. We have already tried our bath, and can just get into it.' One advantage of the little rooms was that they should make it impossible for Genia to overwork, as she was chronically inclined to do. No small drawbacks could dent Arthur's good humour; nor did the discovery that five original drawings for *The Big Six* had been destroyed in the raid on the blockmakers' and would have to be replaced.

(*To his mother, 21 October*) Your welcome letter arrived this morning when I was pounding through the bracken on top of the Heald. I found it here when I came rolling back, a dripping mass of fat. I think I must be losing about a pound a day. Besides our own seventeen acres I have bought the shooting in Machell's Coppice, a very lovely bit of woodland between us and Brantwood. Got it very cheap because it is not worth anything: too much poached, I think. But it is a lovely wood for birds etc., and I daresay I shall get a rabbit now and again ...

Genia is hard at it from morning to night, fitting black outs and trying to squeeze our stuff in. But as soon as that is done and the place is in working order she does not think the actual house will be hard work, though with seventeen acres to play with she'll find plenty to do outside. Still, we shall plant trees rather than try to garden. One of our boats has arrived, pretty leaky, and I caught four perch and a minnow just to show that it could be done, in our own bay. There is good trout ground all along our half mile ...

I must say I rather miss the bangs and bumps and the rest of it as well as the spectacular side, which was very fine.

This serene mood was soon violently disturbed. Tabitha, now a married woman, with a low income, a small son to look after and a husband in the services, needed money to see her through a second childbirth. She wrote to her father saying that she had decided to sell the books, 'now legally mine' (Ivy had died in 1939), and suggesting that he be the purchaser. As she received no answer (there is no reason to believe that Arthur wrote one) she went ahead with the sale in the usual manner, and was badly cheated. A local dealer, pleading the difficulties of the book-trade in wartime, took all the hundreds of volumes off her hands (and also, though she did not know it, some of Arthur's notebooks) for £25, and let her think he was doing her a favour. He then advertised the books for sale, and a kind friend sent Arthur a copy of the catalogue.

This episode made Arthur acutely angry and miserable.

After my first wife's death I had hoped to recover my daughter and had purposely said nothing to her about my books so that she might on her own initiative put right the cruel act of depriving a writer of the library he had collected in thirty years ... the catalogue that came to me at the Heald described some of them in painful detail, even mentioning the inscriptions in them from my friends. I bought from the bookseller some of my own manuscript notebooks which, of course, she had not had ever a legal right to sell. Apart from the sale of the notebooks, and some letters from my friends, she was, of course, within her legal rights.

He was long past reasoning on this topic. It is noteworthy that he talks (as elsewhere) of having collected the books for thirty years. Since the last possible date at which he can have added significantly to the collection was the winter of 1914–15, when he turned thirty-one, it is clear that the books must really have been amassed over a much shorter period; indeed, the bulk of the library can only have been assembled after his move to London in 1901. He may unconsciously have exaggerated the period concerned, in order to justify his sense of grievance. Neither did he mention anywhere that Tabitha had given him first refusal.

His account of the business is, I think, vitiated by his complete inability to enter into Tabitha's point of view. She might perhaps have been well-advised to write to her father again after getting no answer to her first letter. Otherwise it is impossible to fault her conduct. Arthur's idea that she should spontaneously offer to return the books to him as a peace-making gesture was pure fantasy. Even if it had not been, his total passivity, resembling that which he had displayed earlier, when he thought that Ivy was going to send him the books by train, is the conduct of a man nursing a grievance, not that of one really concerned either to get his library back or to restore peace in his family. Arthur would not ask for the books, let alone buy them: that would be to acknowledge Tabitha's right to them, and therefore would be an admission that to some extent he had treated her and her mother badly. It never occurred to Tabitha to make a present of the books to her father: even if she could have afforded to do so, it would have been an admission that she and her mother had been more sinning than sinned against. Impasse.

Not knowing about the £25, Arthur may also have thought that he actually had no money to spare for the re-purchase of his library: every penny had gone into buying the Heald and the seventeen acres of which he loved to boast.

Among the consequences of this unhappy incident must be reckoned Arthur's decision, announced in a letter to Wren Howard on 6 December, to make Jonathan Cape Ltd his residuary legatee in respect of his copyrights. For he decided that Tabitha was heir and party to her mother's alleged conspiracy to stop him writing, and so ought not to benefit from the literary works that, nevertheless, he had produced. For the rest of his life his attitude to his daughter was one of civil coolness, and nothing she could do altered that. She had disappointed her father once too often. It was an unhappy ending to the long sad tale of Arthur's first marriage. Fortunately the happiness of adult children does not, as a rule, depend on their parents, and did not in this case.

The publication of *The Big Six* must have somewhat lightened all this gloom. The reviewers were as enthusiastic as ever, and it was destined to receive five impressions in four years: not as good as *Secret Water* (five impressions in two years) but still satisfactory. The book was the long-planned detective story, a sequel to *Coot Club*. It is difficult, still, to better *The Times Literary Supplement*'s account of it:

> an affair of casting boats adrift on the Broads. But the adventure, though engrossing, is only part of a book in which the cry and flight of birds, the smell of water and tarry ropes, and the jargon of men and boys brought up to use their hands and senses are all delightfully plain to us.

The book is a true sequel, in that it completes Ransome's picture of Norfolk life, especially in the chapters on night-fishing for eel and on catching a monster pike – the first parts of the book to be written (it also contains cautionary tales on how not to smoke eels and set light to Christmas puddings). The main theme of the book resembles that of *We Didn't Mean to Go to Sea*, for it too concerns the placing on young shoulders of a burden of anxiety and difficulty almost too heavy for them to bear; but the burden is imposed by an enemy, not a father; is shared between three – Joe, Bill and Pete – the whole Coot Club rallies to lift it, and by superior intelligence, devotion and energy, does so. The book is thus a celebration of solidarity, not of individual courage and resourcefulness. The screw of suspense is tightened relentlessly until the very last chapter (if we don't count the postscript on 'What Happened to the Fish'), indeed almost to the last page. The plot of *The Big Six* is perhaps Ransome's most ingenious contrivance, and the book ought certainly to figure in any list of classics of detective fiction. It also refutes completely the canard that Ransome's stories are only for and about middle-class children. Joe, Bill and Pete, boatbuilders' sons, who speak and think in Norfolk dialect (Ransome's ear for regional speech was excellent), are the heroes of the book even though, unsurprisingly, it is Dorothea who organises the detection and Dick who brings about the villains' destruction with his camera. They are treated with complete straightforwardness, subtly individualised, with no restraint of the author's characteristic humour. Ransome grew increasingly fond of the Death-and-Glories, and his last attempt at fiction for children would again put them at centre stage.

Meanwhile a successor to *The Big Six* quickly got under way. For the third time Ransome was inspired to write a book of startling originality. In what circumstances he conceived *Missee Lee* (or rather, *Poor Miss Lee*, his original title) we do not know. He had not needed to think up a new tale since early 1938, when both *Secret Water* and *The Big Six* were started. Perhaps, reflecting on *Peter Duck*, he fell to wondering what would happen to the Swallows and Amazons if they ever came across pirates of a less familiar type than Black Jake – say, the ones who had infested the South China Sea, of whom he learned something during his visit to the Far East in 1927. However it was, he was hard at work by February 1941. As usual, he said he was not satisfied either with the idea or with its execution. He apparently asked Charles and

Margaret Renold, the inspirers and dedicatees of *The Big Six*, to make a fresh suggestion. But when they did so his comment shows that he was thoroughly and (in spite of himself) happily wedded to the new pirate book:

(*To Charles Renold, 19 February*) The evacuee story won't do. Questions of ages for one thing. My publishers would have a fit for another. They say, 'Steer clear of the war at all costs.' No, it has got to be *Poor Miss Lee*.

The same day he wrote to Margaret Renold asking for help with Miss Lee's Cambridge background. And could he be sent a Latin grammar containing the gender rhymes? Mrs Renold and a friend, nicknamed 'rude Lady Barlow' by Arthur, found out what they could and sent answers to his questions, and were immediately besieged with more:

(*To Margaret Renold, 24 February*) Hi! Hey! You know Hans' oars. Well coxes preserve their rudders. Does Newnham have a college boat and could my Miss Lee cox it, and bring a rudder proudly back to China to hang on her wall, just as the Troutbeck vicar, who coxed his college boat, has his rudder hung up on the wall of his study to help inspire his sermons? This would be fine for a whole lot of reasons.

Poor Miss Lee is trudging along ... there really are points about it if only I can put the bones together so as at least to look as if the tale had an articulated skeleton.

Thinking of illustrations as well as text as he went along, which had become his usual practice, he decided he would need specimens of Miss Lee's English signatures, and asked Margaret to supply them: 'I can't do them myself because mine would approximate too closely to those of Nancy Blackett.' She did as requested, and received warm thanks.

(*6 March*) You really are a go-getter with a golden heart. Thank you very much indeed. Delighted with the signatures. And thankful that, *pace* Rude L.B., instinct was right in whispering about crests, etc., and their enjoyment by the youthful patriots. It's just these bits of colour that are nothing and yet everything.

Sure enough, among the furnishings of that room, walking into which was like walking into Europe out of Asia, was a varnished oak plaque over the mantelpiece, 'with a shield painted on it with a lion flourishing a forepaw in each of the quarters.' And Miss Lee, it turns out, had coxed Newnham's second boat.

(*15 March*) Gosh! What a book! One of its troubles is that Miss Lee is merely a name of dread in the background for at least the first 150 pages. Oh well. You don't happen to know of a picture of a Chinese riding-donkey, showing the queer, wide wooden saddle?

(*26 March*) My worst mess now seems to be the pictures. No material. I am appealing in all directions for photographs of subtropical scenery – mangoes, bamboos, bananas – houses – clothes. Trouble is there is one of those infernal zoological divides just about there. I wanted a cloud of parrots, and it appears that whereas the Malays swarm with parrots there ain't none in South China. What are the damned birds there? Wanted some chopsticks. Wanted God knows what. Every kind of detail. My natural history books are useless: all confined to the British isles.

(*To Wren Howard, 17 May*) The verdict of the first draft of *Miss Lee* is awful. 'Good first two chapters – then bad – end poor.' I am starting revision at once. Some of the critic's points are good ones, particularly about Miss Lee's own language which, thanks to my abominable method of building books, is inconsistent.

This 'abominable method' was Arthur's habit of drawing up a detailed scenario of a new book, and then writing the chapters in whatever order he felt like. 'The critic says the actual skeleton of the book is much better than most of the others. I take comfort from that.' Miss Lee's success in getting under Genia's guard must rank as her most striking victory: this is by far the most favourable of the verdicts on Arthur's first drafts that has been preserved. Yet it is plain from the way he writes, with its cheerful swing and casual acknowledgments ('some of the critic's points are good') that even a more severe judgment would not have destroyed Arthur's faith in the book. He knew he was at the top of his form.

(*To Margaret Renold, 13 August*) *Missee Lee* is now being printed, or rather set up while I am desperately trying to get pictures done before the proofs arrive. And – I – can – NOT draw ...

The Chinese pictures are terrific. I want trees and Chinks – and donkeys – and chopsticks – and opium pipes – sampans – water kongs – costumes – what not. I got a catalogue of the Chinese Exhibition but the wretched cataloguer happened to be exclusively interested in crockery.

Poor *Missee Lee*. I wish I had the old title, but they all hate it.

This happy voyage ended in the autumn when the book was published and received with acclamation. The *Observer*, for instance, thought it the best Ransome book yet. Over the years *Missee Lee* has sold the fewest copies of all the Swallow books, but it went into seven editions in its first seven years, and has never lacked warm friends; nor is it ever likely to do so, though the China which it depicts has vanished more entirely than the Broads of *Coot Club* or the Russia of *Old Peter*.

The secret of the book's appeal is Miss Lee herself, even more than the vivid colours of the Chinese scene. Miss Lee, every inch a pirate, yet hankering for Cambridge, examinations and the degree of Bachelor of Arts, is at once a funny, sinister, touching and, by the end, curiously impressive figure. Her attempt to have the best of two worlds lands her in many comic contradictions ('She gripped her Horace as if the book were a pistol holster and she were about to pull a pistol from it') but finally, though she makes her choice, of Chinese piracy rather than Western learning, it is for reasons that the West, in the persons of the children and Captain Flint, wholly respects, and at a still deeper level she achieves, it seems, for a moment at least, the vision of a noble synthesis.

> The old amah was laughing and crying at the same time. The counsellor had come slowly down from the poop. Running his fingers through his beard, he was saying something that sounded like a charm.
>
> "What's he saying?" asked Roger.
>
> Miss Lee hesitated a moment. "Vir pietate glavis," she said. "He quotes Confucius. He speaks of duty to a father. He is light. My place is here."

Ultimately Miss Lee's passion for both Horace and Confucius is as enlightening, and as civilised, as Peter Duck's passion for tall ships and his contempt for the treasure brought back, at such risk, from Crab Island. He and she stand together as Arthur Ransome's most thoroughly original, satisfying and pleasurable human creations. Beside them the children and Captain Flint seem a little pallid, a little lacking in the vigour of life.

Like Peter Duck, Miss Lee had an original. Genia recorded, years later, that she was based on a Chinese girl whom Arthur once met who did indeed yearn for Cambridge. Possibly there was such a girl. But Arthur himself stated that Miss Lee was based on no less a person than Madame Sun Yat Sen, most attractive of all the figures of the Chinese Revolution, whom he met in China in 1927 and again in Moscow in 1928. She was never a Cambridge student, but her reverence for her husband's memory was not unlike Miss Lee's filial piety. Ransome also tells us that he got a great deal of pleasure from using the Chinese war-lords he had met as models for the pirate chiefs of Miss Lee's islands. Miss Lee's attitude of cheerful disdain towards these men closely resembles that of Madame Sun to the leaders of the Kuomintang.

1941, then, was a year of literary triumph for Arthur. In other respects he had much less to be cheerful about.

He endured two more ruptures, and the doctor advised against an operation in case he had another embolism. Much worse, the doctor forbade any sailing or fell-walking, and, in answer to the patient's protests, told him it was about time he remembered how long it was since he was born. 'There was no need for this to happen if you had not been a fool.' Arthur might fish *quietly*. There was to be no more exultant sitting on the stream in fast water. No more scrambling over rocks. 'From that melancholy day on I have had to remember to be old.' He was not yet sixty.

At least he was alive. On 1 June Hugh Walpole died, not three weeks after Arthur had gone over to Keswick to make him a present of trout. He was two months younger than Arthur. He had been a diabetic, but otherwise his general health had been much better than Ransome's: his biographer has no doubt that he was an indirect victim of the war and the strains it laid on him. Arthur was glad that they had been reconciled ten years before, and glad about the trout, and sorry for the passing of a friend and fellow-craftsman still in full possession of his powers.

There were to be other deaths. Young George Russell joined

the Rifle Brigade, and was sent by troopship, all the way round the Cape of Good Hope, to Egypt. His letters to his sister were full of the sailing he meant to do when peace returned. He mentioned receiving a letter from 'Ransie'. Then he was killed at the battle of El Alamein. Robin Collingwood was forced by ill-health to give up his Oxford posts, break off his brilliant career as a philosopher, which was only just reaching its peak, and come back to Coniston, to die, in 1943, after a succession of strokes. Arthur watched Robin fade away, and could hardly be sorry when death put an end to his sufferings.

Genia was unhappy. She took against the Heald as soon as she was settled there. It is not entirely clear why. For such a fanatical housekeeper the small size of the house was not so much a relief, perhaps, as the loss of a welcome challenge. For such a fanatical gardener the impossibility of doing much in the grounds (rock was only an inch below the surface everywhere) was maddening. She was ill the first winter after they moved to Coniston. The mountains to east and west meant that the Heald got comparatively little sunlight. Finally, wartime shortages made running so isolated a house exceedingly difficult. When the electric engine failed, for instance, on which all their lighting depended, there was no one to mend it but Arthur: fortunately he was a good mechanic. Genia could hardly be blamed if she felt she was living all the time on the edge of emergency.

The difficulty of transport had one comic result. Arthur wrote to Charles Renold to ask for his help in buying a motorbike for Genia. When the thing arrived Arthur promptly christened it the Monster and began to ride it himself.

(*To Charles Renold, 2 March 1942*) I have actually done five miles on the Monster. He is A1 on the flat, but I think I shall have to go in for intensive slimming to give him a chance on the hills. I weigh too much ...

    Comment of local village dame on meeting me and the Monster. 'Eh, Mr Raaaansome, but you did look scared.'

At times he seems to have lived wholly for pleasure. There is no record of Genia trying to ride the machine.

Equally, there is no evidence that Arthur was unhappy at the Heald, in spite of all his trials, except when Genia lost her temper, which she could do devastatingly.

(*Diary, 19 November 1942*) I squeaked when I got a sudden twinge with my teeth taking a rash bite at breakfast. 'For the last ten or twelve years the house has been like a hospital and I simply *loathe* it.' There is nothing I can do about it. This came out of a blue sky when we were talking cheerfully about her poultry. I am too old. And G. is terrifically over-working. But there's no way of easing things until the war is over.

His letters to his mother and other friends all display an alert, cheerful interest in life; as always, the lake country suited him. Only when his cat Podge was killed by a fox was he miserable: he missed the clever, affectionate little creature intensely.

Missee Lee was hardly published before Jonathan Cape began to hound him for its successor. By Twelfth Night 1942 he was hard at work, not altogether to his satisfaction.

(*To Margaret Renold, 6 January*) I am pounding out the stuff for the new book in the worst possible manner, before I'm ready with the story. Absolutely damnable. The result will be awful. I wish I had a decent yarn in my head. But I haven't. It's high time I took a year off for experiment, but with this beastly war on I can't, but must go on pounding out, if only for export to the Yanks. What a motive!

He had announced his new theme to Margaret months before.

(*13 August 1941*) This winter will probably be my last, because my method of keeping going by pouring down milk will be brought to an end by that damned grocer Woolton and that means the end of me. I've tried the experiment of stopping the milk three or four times and each time the result has been pretty disastrous. However, anyhow that'll mean an end to having to write book after book.

None the less, I am hunting round for a new one ... Subject: I think the Great Aunt of *Swallowdale*. Captain Flint takes Mrs Blackett off for a jaunt abroad, leaving Nancy and Peggy in charge of Beckfoot. Damned good for them. The G.A., hearing this, writes a letter to them refraining from giving her opinion of their mother but making it very plain, and invites herself to Beckfoot to look after them. Now then: WHAT? Or have you an immense idea of your own?

When *The Picts and the Martyrs* was published Mrs Renold wrote to say that although it was full of good things, 'the *reason* for all the story is a poor one. Great Aunts of that kind must have died out about 40 years ago. And you make Cook and her children so convinced that Mrs Blackett is a spineless creature and they have to protect her – I ask you! I don't think grown-ups are your strong point.' The observation about Great Aunts is interesting but irrelevant. So far as readers of *Swallowdale* were concerned, Great-Aunt Maria already existed in full rigour, and poor Mrs Blackett's character was beyond saving. Arthur was simply exploiting material which he had not yet used up; and the creator of Black Jake and Missee Lee was not likely to let mere implausibility stand between him and a literary project.

Ransome knew quite well what he was about when he planned *Picts*. His child readers were clamouring for another book about the lake; he had just returned there; it was good for business to continue to spring surprises on his public. It seemed entirely proper to follow up a thrillingly exotic tale with a story about the quietest of domestic crises; and with Nancy Blackett on hand, in her first leading role since *Pigeon Post*, there could be no shortage of excitement. Indeed, although *The Picts and the Martyrs* was planned as a mere farce, by the end of the book it had developed a comic life of its own; Nancy, whose character had come to seem so predictable, had developed new and interesting traits; and the Great-Aunt herself had become, for a moment, sympathetic. Her tribute to her niece was well-earned ('Ruth showed that she possesses much of the tact that was characteristic of your grandfather'), and so was Timothy's comment ('I think your Great-Aunt is remarkably like her Great Niece'). Who would have thought that Nancy could ever display tact? The farmer's boy Jacky, another *revenant* from *Swallowdale*, is a delightful character; Dick and Dorothea are, as usual, admirable figures through whose eyes to observe and respond to the action. *The Picts and the Martyrs* is the shortest, and one of the simplest, of the stories; but it is also one of the most immediately enjoyable.

Arthur (of course) did not enjoy writing it.

(*To Charles Renold, 26 February*) My mucky book has reached page 232 in the rough squish. Well ahead of any previous year. But what squish. Still it's got to be done somehow for export,

even if things get too hectic here, and publishers give up and
leave the field to the B.B.C. and the M.O.I.

(*23 March*) I wish I had another wild Peter Duck or Missee Lee
plot. The new book with strictly domestic interest is damnable.
I hate it and so will everyone else.

And so on. As usual he welcomed diversion from the grim task of
pounding out words. A Brownie patrol detected no less than
eight mistakes (L for M, and so on) in the semaphore message
from Captain Flint in *Missee Lee*, and the matter was reported to
Wren Howard.

(*To Wren Howard, 4 February*) Curse and confound Captain
Flint. It isn't the first time that fellow's carelessness has got me
into trouble. What's to be done? I have corrected the original
and should like a new block made at Captain Flint's expense,
damn him. Or, if there's not time for that, remove the title
from under the illustration (page 190) and print in very small
type the following note: *This is not the original S.O.S., which is
somewhere in China. Captain Flint had to make a copy of it for this
book. While he was doing it Roger was playing the penny whistle
and somebody else was not doing any harm just fingering Captain
Flint's new accordion. He says that is why there are at least eight
mistakes in the signals. Really of course his beastly carelessness. N.B.*
I do hope you'll manage the block in time for the reprint. Fry,
frizzle and broil that fellow Flint. What's the good of my
taking trouble, when he goes and lets me down like this?

A fortnight earlier, in another letter to Howard, Arthur had
made a Quixotic agreement. The price of his books was to go up
to 8s. 6d., but in view of wartime difficulties he consented to be
paid his 20 per cent royalty as if the price were still 7s. 6d. In other
words, his income from his books would remain static (unless sales
improved) while his publishers' take would go up. Arthur stipu-
lated only that if the price had to be raised again, 'as I expect it
will', the question would have to be considered *de novo*. He said
nothing about what he expected to happen when the war ended,
and the publishers did not raise the question.

The Picts and the Martyrs was finished by the beginning of
August, and as usual Arthur decamped, leaving Genia to read the
rough draft. He went up to London and dined with Richard

Stokes, another of whose guests was Aneurin Bevan. Then down to Hirst at Droxford for two days' fishing. On his return to London he found a letter from Genia waiting for him, with her opinion. It was of course unfavourable – immensely so – she had never been ruder about one of his books. 'My dear darling: I am very sorry I am going to hurt you very much – but I don't believe in Fools Paradise or in beating about the bush.' The book was dead, repeating worn-out situations: 'pale imitations of something that happened many times before.' The adventures were spurious, dragged-in, unconvincing, farcical, grown-up affairs. After *Peter Duck*, *We Didn't Mean to Go to Sea* and *Missee Lee*, even faithful readers would find it dull.

> I hope Howard will use such paper as he saved up for it in reprinting the others. But if not – and if as a result our income drops down with a bump – never mind. Anything is better than to have a book to your name of which you are ashamed. So cheer up!

Genia was entitled to have a poor opinion of *The Picts*, and entitled to stick to it however many people disagreed with her (though eventually, as with all Arthur's works, she came to think it a masterpiece and to defend it against all criticism). What she was not entitled to do was to try to impose her views on Arthur, not to mention his unlucky publishers.

She might at least have remembered the awful things she had said about *Peter Duck* while it was being written, and how dismissive she had been of *We Didn't Mean to Go to Sea*, and how she had praised *Missee Lee* with faint damns. But she never allowed the expression of her views to be tempered by judgment. She was incapable of understanding that although Arthur's art was a small one, it was genuine; and when an artist has settled upon a subject, has chosen, or been chosen by, an idea, there is no alternative for the wise critic to trusting the artist's instinct and trying to understand where it is leading him. Genia's arguments amounted to an assertion that *The Picts and the Martyrs* should never have been written. Yet today it is clear that, like its predecessors, it has an inevitability about it: it grows out of *Swallowdale* and *Pigeon Post* as naturally as *The Big Six* grew out of *Coot Club*; it is a corrective to *Missee Lee* as *Peter Duck* was a corrective to *Swallowdale*. Genia would have been wise to welcome it as evidence that her husband's talent was still growing and diversifying.

Instead she stopped him in his tracks. For Arthur, the composition of each of his stories was an act of desperate faith in himself; a faith which had been cruelly tested in the course of his life, most of all at its beginning, when his parents had so little belief in him. By taking their tone with him, by stressing his imprudence and incompetence and played-outness, by viewing with alarm, by wallowing in a truly Russian gloom about money and competitors ('Your rivals would be very happy and well justified in saying that you "missed the bus" '), Genia was cutting at the tap-root of his creativity. His anxiety was a light sleeper, even after years of success; it always woke and tormented him while he worked at a story; an attack like this one could only stir it up to raging activity. Besides, of late he had had to drive himself to work in a way that suggests he may have begun at last to tire even of his life-long commitment to writing stories for children. Genia did not have the insight to see that her letter might destroy, not *The Picts and the Martyrs*, but its successor. How could Arthur set out to create another book if he had to face this sort of thing when it was finished?

Yet it was all done with such total unconsciousness that one cannot help warming to Genia. She was so obviously devoted to Arthur. 'My dear darling.' Sincerity is always winning. If only she had not been such an abominably bad critic.

Arthur annotated her letter 'I stopped it for a year but in the end let Cape have it'; but he was actually much less supine than this account suggests. Cape got *The Picts* after five months.

At first Arthur had been completely conquered by Genia's assault on his poor book.

(*To Margaret Renold, 15 August*) I have come a cropper with the new book. I had plenty of suspicions about it, but talking about it is not allowed, and there was nobody handy for reading bits of it aloud to (another way of testing the ice) and so, with my mind more than half set on the patriotic pursuit of American dollars, I plodded doggedly on with dreadful result. I finished the beast, as far as the second complete typescript, sent it to Howard of Cape's who (no doubt blinded by the prospect of selling 20,000 copies before Christmas) said he liked it, agreeing to let me have a few more days to telescope two chapters somewhere in the middle. I had just got to the end of five days in town on that and other business and had gone to Cape's office on the last day to say goodbye when I found the bombshell in the shape of Genia's verdict (she read it for the first time) ... Consternation and monkey-house at Cape's! Howard, after telling Cape it was all right, had gone off on holiday. Paper for 25,000 copies already at the printer's waiting for it. Etc. etc. etc. I think I was more cheerful than any of them. But it is pretty ghastly after putting in such an awful period of non-stop sweat ... I feel as if with much thought and trouble I had built a motor car, and painted and varnished it all pretty, only to find that it wouldn't move and never could.

And the maddening thing is that I can't pretend to myself that Genia's wrong. She is right.

In other words, she had articulated his fears about the book. But how strong his hopes had been! Strong enough to permit Howard to begin the process of publication without waiting for Genia's verdict. Arthur must have been confident that it would be like her first verdicts on *The Big Six* and *Missee Lee*: negative, but endurable. In other words, he had to a large extent discounted her opinion in advance. When it came it was so atrocious that it halted him; but it was not long before hope stirred again, though he would not acknowledge it. The trouble was that it would be no easy matter to circumvent Genia's veto, since doing so might make life with her unendurable. But at least the manuscript could be revised, pending a resolution of the affair.

By a sweet irony his mother, who had been so unencouraging when he was young, now saved his book. Early in December he went to visit her at Kew, where she had lived since 1939. He showed her *The Picts*, and her liking of it gave him the excuse he needed to have the book printed.

(*To his mother, 10 December, Coniston*) Well, on your decision, the book has actually gone to the printers, and I have to work like smoke to have the illustrations ready before the proofs begin to arrive. They have got the paper for printing. And they have also (even more difficult) got the zinc for making the blocks.
PLEASE WHATEVER YOU DO, DON'T MENTION TO ANY-ONE MY PROJECT OF DEDICATING THE BOOK TO AUNT

HELEN. I want to surprise her with it: she suggested a great deal of it ...

It was very jolly seeing you and Aunt Kit. You would have been amused if you had seen the relief your letter caused at the office. One of the partners rushed off to the room of the other with 'We've got the Ransome manuscript.' 'God bless his Mother', was the reply.

(*17 December*) I am covered with ink, fingers, nose and forehead, in the efforts to catch up the book with the pictures. The book is being set up now, and of course Cape's are howling for the pictures so that they can get the blocks made by the time the proofs arrive. Impossible. And my word I wish you were at hand to tell me what's wrong with perspectives. So far, eight inked, seven pencilled: five not even in the air, and only one tailpiece done.

(*29 December*) PLEASE do not mention my wretched book in your letters. Genia was completely miserable because in the end I decided to publish it and every mention of it reopens the wound.

So Arthur won the battle although, privately, in his usual gloomy fashion, he was still more of Genia's opinion than his mother's. *The Picts and the Martyrs* was published the following June, to the usual round of applause. Everyone seemed pleased to meet the old friends in the old setting again. As the *Glasgow Herald* put it, 'to all old Ransome devotees the return to the lake of the first novels gives an added pleasure.' One of the many things that Genia had forgotten in her onslaught was that there is a delight in return as well as in discovery. And not everybody had already met the Ransome children. T. H. White, exiled in Dublin, was urged to write a book 'like Arthur Ransome's' by the bookseller-publisher Basil Blackwell. He bridled at the idea, but when he came across a copy of *The Picts and the Martyrs* he read it, and liked it enough to commend it to David Garnett:

He does not write with one eye on the grown-up, as I do, but seems to be a pleasantly childish man himself ... As a parent I consider it your duty to read it, if you haven't. Of course it isn't within miles of the great books, like *Treasure Island*, but it is a good, simple second ranker.

The verdict seems just, the more so as it contains an admission of precisely that point in which White's books, even *The Sword in the Stone*, are inferior to Arthur Ransome's.

Yet Arthur was now in acute literary difficulties. Even before the fate of *The Picts* was settled he had resurrected a project, very dear to his heart, which he had first mentioned as long ago as 1931. After he finished work on *Peter Duck*, he told Ernestine Evans (in a letter dated 12 January 1931), 'I've a lovely book about an old schoolmaster and a fisherman and a boy and a river. This is going to be my very best book!!! But I want to keep it fermenting for a bit yet.' In the event it had to ferment for twelve years. Arthur had looked through his notes for it in 1938, when he was casting about for a successor to *We Didn't Mean to Go to Sea*, but the book he had in mind was set in the mid-nineteenth century. He wrote to Margaret Renold (on 24 January 1938) that Genia was strong against it,

> on the ground that the reason my brats like my books is that they are all something that happens today and MIGHT happen to themselves given only some quite small modification in their circumstances, such as a different mother, or a reformed father, or living a bit nearer a lake, or something like that. She thinks there'd be an awful disappointment if I go and tell a story that happened long ago, and in circumstances that can never be the same again.

Characteristically, Genia had no faith in her husband's ability to create the taste by which he might be enjoyed, even though he had done it once already, and she tried to choke an artistic impulse by commercial calculations. But by 1942 the time had come to take up the idea in earnest. Arthur was probably getting a little tired of his Swallows and Amazons, as so many authors have got tired of their most popular creations: he had already said that he ought to take a year off for experiment. The row over *The Picts* no doubt reinforced these feelings. Once the *Picts* revision was complete, he took up the project of his very best book again. By the end of November he had drafted six chapters.

'An old schoolmaster and a fisherman and a boy and a river.' The casual phrase gives little sense of what Arthur had in mind, and no clue at all as to how he came to have it there. But when he wrote those words he was hard at work on *Swallowdale*, that seed-bed of a book, in which his knowledge and love of the Lake District's past found partial expression. He may have discovered that a second book would be necessary to do it justice, as he was to find that *Coot Club* did not exhaust all he had to say about the Broads. Then there was Tom Stainton the gamekeeper, and Arthur's Ransome grandfather.

> When I first came to fish the Beela (my father's and my grandfather's favourite river) in 1930 or thereabouts, the old keeper, Tom Stainton, told me of a remark of my grandfather's sixty years before. Tom was appointed keeper of the Beela by the little club that controlled the water, and one of the committee raised the question as to what was to be done about a superannuation fund. 'Superannuation!' exclaimed my grandfather. 'No man appointed beck-watcher on the Beela will ever want to be superannuated.' 'And by gum,' said old Tom to me, 'I never have and never will.'

Saying good-bye to Tom Stainton was to be one of the more important distresses resulting from the sale of Low Ludderburn. So it seems altogether likely that it was in 1930 or January 1931 that Arthur decided to put the old man in a book, as he had put the Swainsons of Nibthwaite into *Swallowdale* and planned to put the Ancient Mariner into *Peter Duck*. But a tribute to the older generation could not be set in the present. The book would have to be a historical novel: a form which had always attracted Arthur.

The return to Coniston revitalised the old project. In spite of doctor's orders Arthur was again fishing the waters so dear to his family; he wanted to celebrate them, and the country people of the region whom he knew so intimately. He began to shove ideas down on paper, and before very long had drawn up one of his usual synopses, and a list of chapters.

He ran into difficulties — real ones, not the sort that daunted Genia. His original notion was to write Tom's autobiography. Arthur's ear for dialect and the lucidity of his prose meant that he would have no trouble in devising a readable yet authentic-sounding language for the gamekeeper; yet over the entire length of a book the element of cod in such an enterprise could not but become apparent. Besides, Tom Stainton was not the man to write an autobiography. He was rather more likely to keep a nature diary. For a moment Arthur thought he had hit on the answer. He would pose as editor of the manuscript, supposed to have been written on the unused backs of pages in an old notebook. He went so far as to draft a cod introduction, but this idea was also dropped: it too would have introduced an element of insincerity into a book whose very essence ought to be the opposite. Ransome reverted to the plan of writing a straight autobiography, and drafted several chapters, in whole or in part, of first-person narrative. One of these, describing a cloudburst on a river island where two children are playing, is thrilling reading. But at length Arthur decided to write a third person narrative, always keeping as his main object the portrayal of his hero's character and, particularly, the indication of what it was in him that made him so supremely fitted to be a gamekeeper. The plan had come clear. It was for the sort of book that Sylvia Townsend Warner, or, in the Richard Jefferies tradition, T. H. White, wrote so well. Its theme would be the necessity of subordinating human selfishness, whether incarnate in poachers or sportsmen, to the wellbeing of the natural order: its title would be *The River Comes First*.

When Arthur visited London at the beginning of December and settled the fate of *The Picts*, he also discussed 'the gamekeeper book'. He was far from sure that Cape would want a Ransome book that had nothing to do with the Swallows, or sailing, and was as much for adults as for children. So he approached the house of Collins, which was enthusiastic. Still doubting whether he should do the book, and, perhaps, a little disturbed in his conscience, he told Jonathan Cape about the project, and they, too, welcomed news of it, and offered to commission illustrations from the celebrated bird artist C. A. Tunnicliffe. There would be no difficulty about publication, if the book were ever finished.

Nevertheless he did not resume work straight away. His outlook on New Year's Day, as he summed it up in his diary, was gloomy.

One bad book at the printers. 18 full-page pictures sketched, of which 11 are inked. 2 tailpieces inked. About another month's work, with proofs. Possibles for this year: *The River Comes First* – very rough beginning in the first person.

Last year was the worst yet, and it begins to look as if I ought to shut up shop. Still, I may get another book or two done yet in spite of all.

'All' undoubtedly included Genia. If, however, her usual rule about not discussing work in progress still applied, she may not yet have known what Arthur was up to.

January, February and March went by: it seems likely, from the state of the manuscript, that he made notes towards *The River* quite frequently during these months. Yet he was still uncommitted to it. On 2 January he wrote to Margaret Renold asking for suggestions 'for a *lively* yarn ... As wild as you like. Free from S's and A's. But a real wild yarn.' And he had other things to think of. Pamela Whitlock, for instance, was consulting him during this period both about what she should do for war-work and how she should launch herself as an adult writer when the war was over.

(*To Pamela Whitlock, 24 December 1942*) Thinking of it from the point of view of your future as a writer, you might come to feel that you had missed something of general experience by not having buttons to polish and sergeants to salute. On the other hand you might not. This amounts to saying you ought to follow your own internal compass and nothing else. Which you will do in any case. Good luck to you whatever you do.

She decided to enlist.

The River Comes First was eventually tackled again on 3 April. During the next month he wrote six complete chapters of third-person narrative, with as much speed and concentration, and, one may guess, from what he put into them, as much enjoyment as ever in his life. It seems likely (though the diary throws no light on the matter) that it was during the rest of May that he wrote two more. Then he broke off.

There is no certainty as to why. On 2 June he and Genia went to London, staying at the Park Lane Hotel. On 4 June he was off down to Droxford for a week's fishing and chess in the old style with Francis Hirst. On the 16th he was back at Coniston. He had taken a rest that was perhaps necessary. At some stage he recast the first chapter; in July he wrote four more pages of the *River*; and that was that. He fished, he sailed, he watched squirrels, shot rabbits, and in his diary recorded the depredations of youths from a nearby holiday camp: they tore up his water-lilies and submerged his dinghy at her moorings. But the next exciting thing that happened to him was in London, where he solved, or thought he did, one of the mysteries of salmon-fishing, and dashed it down in his diary. '(*1 December*) American soldiery revealed the secret of the salmon, who does not eat in fresh water, but does CHEW GUM', or rather, flies, of the sort with which fishermen try to tempt him. This was to lead to the one creation of which he said, in later years, that he ever boasted: the Vulturine Guinea Fowl Elver fly. And in 1944 he began to write *Great Northern?* – another Swallow book. *The River Comes First* dropped into limbo, like so many books in the past.

It was a serious defeat. The story, fully planned, was an excellent one. Young Tom, son of a gamekeeper in about 1850, is slowly establishing himself in his native village on a Lake District river. He has an enemy who becomes a friend, Bob Lidgett the poacher's son, and a worshipping playmate in Jenny, a farmer's daughter. Together the three children foil a gang of poachers, and as a reward Tom is carried off to London to better himself, by a gentleman visiting the Hall. He would not go, only his mother is ambitious for him: has not the old parson taught him Latin? In London the gentleman proves to be useless: Tom is reduced to becoming an assistant in a fishing-tackle shop in Long Acre where, it gradually dawns on him, he is being set up by the sadistic proprietor to be accused of theft. He decides to run away, and after various adventures on the Great North Road reaches the river again.

> As he gets near is afraid to go home [says the synopsis]. How he finds the old parson fishing and tells him the whole story. How the old parson blames himself for having indirectly brought about Tom's exile, and himself first sees the squire, and then takes Tom home, and tells the old gamekeeper that he is to have an underkeeper.
> 'What's the name of the chap? There's not many lads I know at wouldn't be more trouble nor help.'
> 'I was coming to that,' says the old parson. 'You've known the lad a long time, both of you.'
> 'What's the name of him?'
> 'I think it's the same as your own.'
> 'Where is he?' asks his mother.
> 'Not far off,' said the old parson. 'If you were to call, "Tom".'

A rich tale, made the more so by the skill with which Ransome

crams it with feeling and detail. There is scarcely a page of the
unfinished manuscript that does not shine with life. For example,
he never caught the hush and glare of noon better than he did at
the beginning of chapter two, 'Canon John William's Conscience'.

Nobody would have guessed that there was a human being
anywhere near the Oaks pool. The deer who had watched Tom
crossing the field on the other side of the river had long ago
forgotten about him and were grazing quietly or rubbing their
heads against the trees, the solitary, large trees in the open park
land between the river and the wood. The hawk that had flown
away on seeing him had long ago come back and was quivering
high overhead, and now and again with still wings gliding,
before hanging again a quivering speck, a black star twinkling
in the dazzling sky. The only thing that betrayed Tom was a
schoolbag, made for him by his gamekeeper father from a deer-
skin he had cured himself. This, with a Latin grammar in it and
Tom's slate and slate pencil, lay at the foot of a big oak tree on
the river's bank. Tom had cursed himself for leaving it there
when the cows came up to it, pushed at it with their noses and
turned it over with their rough tongues. He dared not move to
shoo them off, and had been glad when at last they had lost
interest in it and moved slowly off the field.

To shoo off the cows would have been to show himself to the
very thing from which he wished to keep hidden. He did not
mind being seen by the deer, the hawk, or the cows, but he did
not want to be seen by the salmon that was lying not ten feet
below him in the clear smooth water under the bank.

Ransome was here doing something entirely new, and doing it
with supreme success: it is impossible to believe that more than a
word or two of the above would have been altered in any revision.
Why could he not complete it?

Circumstances and the one item of positive evidence point at
Genia.

(*To his mother, 17 August*) I have had an extraordinarily nice
letter from the Vice Chancellor of Durham, or Warden, or
whatever he is, on adding *Picts and Martyrs* to the shelf. He says
Vaughan late Headmaster of Rugby put him on to the books
with *Peter Duck* and that he began by getting them for young

relations but found that he wanted to keep them himself and has now got the whole lot and re-reads them at intervals. Really a very encouraging letter, and God knows I need a bit of encouragement, if, in spite of local veto, I am to produce any more.

This suggests that Genia, still enraged by the publication of *The Picts*, had been further incensed by the discovery that Arthur was now at work on a project she had always opposed. What other motive could she have had for imposing a 'local veto' on all fresh stories?

Ultimately the responsibility for what he wrote was his, and he knew it. In May he had been giving excellent advice to Pamela Whitlock.

In your letter before the last you talked of the perfect public for which you wanted to write books. Now, do get it into your head that to think of your public is the way NOT TO BE ABLE TO WRITE BOOKS. Good books are not written FOR anyone. They are OVERHEARD. If you want to make sure of becoming just one of the many manufacturers of passable books you will choose a public and write books for it. But, surely, you want to do better than that. You are a person in your own right and you are the only public you ought to consider.

How well did Arthur heed his own maxims? Genia had constituted herself a vociferous one-woman public, and as her *Picts* letter shows, used the privilege of overhearing an author at work to bully him. Arthur himself dreaded disappointing the public he had created, in Britain and America. He was always disenchanted with his creations while shaping them. In short, what he needed, as he said to his mother, was encouragement; yet in his isolation at the Heald there was no one to encourage him, least of all Genia. He had shown what he thought of her views by publishing *The Picts* against her wishes.

So Arthur got into what he would have called a stew. He allowed his emotions to overwhelm his intellect, so that the poised, mature, skilful and sensible artist was silenced by the anxious boy. And just as he had allowed Ivy Walker to bully him into marrying her, he allowed Genia to abort his new book.

His age and infirmities no doubt explain much. But he still had many years of mental vigour ahead of him. The essential fact was that his art itself needed a new departure. The Swallows were indeed stale. For instance, a most interesting passage in *The River Comes First* describes one of Tom's adventures on his road homeward. He meets Finella, the girl fortune-teller of 'Stanley's Original', and in her flirting, jousting talk with him there is an unmistakable tang of dawning sexuality unlike anything else in Ransome's writing, and quite unlike the rigidly pre-pubescent relations of the Swallows and the Amazons. Genia was stating no more than the obvious when she remarked that he was not allowing his children to grow up. By the time of *Great Northern?* Nancy and John are allegedly about sixteen. Yet they show no signs of emerging from childhood, let alone of the stormy adolescent emotions that Hull and Whitlock had made the theme of their *Oxus in Summer*. As in life, so in fiction: Peter Pan's playmates were outgrowing him, or should have been. Only his timidity (that child-public) kept the Swallows and the Amazons from developing naturally. In *The River Comes First* he felt free to explore this new territory. Genia's assertiveness and his own weakness then decreed that he was not to do so. From that moment the end of his creative career was in sight.

XIII

Journey to Rusland

We'll have a bit of Paradise yet in spite of everything.

ARTHUR RANSOME to Charles Renold, 1943

Arthur at the Heald was isolated, but not exactly lonely. He and Genia still had many friends in the lake country, and Arthur's correspondence kept him in touch with the wider world. The publication of *The Picts and the Martyrs* provoked a flurry of letters; and occasionally the wider world came to visit him. Pamela Whitlock wrote congratulating him on *The Picts*, and asking why he had given it a sub-title ('Not Welcome At All').

(*12 July 1943*) You are a kind-hearted child. The sub-title was simply a betrayal of the author's mistrust of the book, of the title and of himself. That's what sub-titles nearly always are. My next book will probably have two sub-titles, and the one after that, three, and so on till the whole page is a nervous stammering mass of them.

In a review Janet Adam-Smith raised a question which has never quite died since; indeed, among writers less fastidious and tentative than she, has become something of a commonplace about the Ransome books. Who reads them? she wondered. Two books with working-class heroes, which she was also reviewing, must appeal, she thought, to any intelligent child, however rich; 'but I wonder whether Mr Ransome's stories appeal to children who live entirely outside the world of nannies, cooks and private boat-houses? Or may the line between Ransome readers and non-readers be drawn between town and country-minded children, and have nothing to do with class and income? It would be extremely interesting to know; perhaps the children's librarians could tell us.' This appeal was answered by Mary E. C. Fletcher, librarian of a county secondary school in Shrewsbury for girls from both town and country. She wrote to say that Ransome's books were popular with girls of all types and ages. 'The books are read so vigorously that they have to be replaced or rebound more often than the books of other authors. Few of these girls "live in the world of nannies, cooks and private boat-houses." It would, therefore, appear that the young, as do their elders, read to escape from everyday life, and so prefer to read about the kind of people they are unlikely to meet.'

Jonathan Cape sent Arthur a cutting of Mrs Fletcher's letter, and he was extremely pleased. He wrote to thank her.

(29 July) I should be very sorry indeed to think that only children of one particular background can share the fun of open air doings, and the feelings that have been common to all young human beings from the beginning of time.

But I think I recognise in the complaint that called forth your letter something that I watched with great interest in Russia in the early years of the Revolution there. Young devotees quite honestly believed that after 1917 literature must concern itself exclusively with the 'proletariat', and some of them went even further and believed that it must be written only by the 'proletariat'. It was a sterile and short-lived movement and was killed by the 'proletariat' itself which preferred to read the best books it could get and was not in the least interested in books that tried to be 'proletarian'. Within a very few years that movement became a memory and a joke, and the same thing will happen here.

... It is a great pleasure to me to know that my books are liked in such a school as yours.

Chess still provided some stimulating contacts. One day Kingsley Martin, the editor of the *New Statesman*, turned up for some games.

(*To his mother, 17 August*) As a human being I don't like him any more than I did when I was working in the *Guardian* office and Ted Scott and I both loathed him. Superficial, clever, and conceited, with a hide like that of a rhinoceros. Still, it was pleasant to have a game or two with a really good player.

A really bad player was Liddell Hart, who was regularly defeated because, as an entry in the 1942 diary remarked, 'he will dash into attack in a Churchill manner with insufficient concentration of forces' – thus forgetting his own military doctrines. Lady Liddell Hart recalled that she and Genia competed, not over the chess-board, but over the rearing of poultry.

Evgenia was a very practical sort of woman and she was very interested in hens, and she trained her hens so that, when they laid an egg, they came to the back door, and she rewarded them, and my hens were very poor creatures, and she would look at them very critically and she would say 'That one's not worth its ration,' because each hen had its ration then, in those days. 'I will come and kill it in the Russian way', so my hens were slaughtered, quite a lot of them.[1]

And Arthur clung to other pleasures.

(*To his mother, 14 September*) This is to report a joyful discovery, namely that though I can no longer row a boat at all, I can catch char by sailing. The method is that of the Bay of Biscay tunnyfishers, you must have seen them, with mast-high rods, trolling under easy sail. The whole difficulty is to sail slow enough. Finally, after a lot of experiment, I have got the thing to work, and last night we had a most luxurious supper on a brace of char, each close on half a pound (big for Coniston) caught by sailing. The trouble comes when you hook your fish, sixty to eighty yards away, and have to manage sail, rudder, rod, reel and net all at the same time with only two hands and false teeth. But the thing can be done and last night's supper was the proof of it. It can only be done during the two short seasons when the char come up from the deeps, June and again in September.

1 From an interview in the transcript of 'The Improbable Life of Arthur Ransome', a radio programme made by Peter Windows and broadcast in summer 1980.

The only possible word is indomitable. Next year the diary shows Arthur defying his ailments and fishing for trout on Coniston and salmon at Cockermouth – where on one occasion his ruptures 'came out' so that he felt very bad. He proposed to Charles Renold that they collaborate on a book on fly-fishing, to be called *A Plague of Flies*, which would concentrate on the history and making of the things. Jonathan Cape were enthusiastic, 'planning something monumental, to beat in coloured pictures of flies anything that has ever been done before.' Unfortunately they were in the end defeated by problems of colour reproduction, and the plan came to nothing.

Arthur was in London on 6 June, and heard at the Cape office of the Normandy landings. The end of the war was nearing; and in consequence a move from the Heald could be realistically contemplated.

Genia may have let herself believe that hostilities would be over sooner than in fact they were. At any rate on 29 July Arthur, returning from a visit to his mother, was met by Genia at Windermere station with a letter from a Mr Hunter asking formally to buy the house. Genia had been having a meal in a local hotel, and grumbling about her property: 'I shall sell the damned place for what we paid for it the moment the war's over.' Mr Hunter at the next table came over and said, 'I should like to take you at your word.' They shook hands on the bargain, and presumably Hunter's letter was the follow-up. This impulsive transaction was perhaps a little hard on Arthur, who had bought the Heald partly as an investment (its price would certainly have gone much higher had he held on to it) and had occasionally talked of leaving the land to the National Trust. But the episode was entirely characteristic of Genia. On 31 July Arthur wrote to Hunter accepting the offer. It was an easy way to achieve what he and Genia both wanted: to get back to the East Coast and to sailing.

Three weeks later he started to write *Great Northern?*. Nothing survives to explain this return to story-telling and the Swallows. Nearly two years had passed since the revision of *The Picts and the Martyrs*, more than one since the abandonment of *The River Comes First*. Presumably Genia had lifted her veto. Arthur did not yet think he was a spent force. He began again.

According to Genia, one of his favourite fishing resorts before the war had been his friend James Dobson's place at Uig on Lewis, 'where the family, father, mother, three adult children (and later their spouses) were so completely absorbed in their salmon fly-fishing that they had not time for any non-fishing guests.' Casting about for a background to inspire him (all his books depended on a strong sense of place) it was natural enough for Arthur to pick on the Hebrides and think about sending his children there. '*Time.* June would be best. Why they are not at school, *heaven only knows*!!!!!' (He got round that difficulty by never mentioning the date.) '*Place.* Well *north* in the Hebrides. Isle of Lewis, or Shet-lands. Dot, writing a story of the Isles. Titty's romantic view contrasting with Dot's melodramatic.' He started to read Osgord Hanbury Mackenzie's *A Hundred Years in the Highlands* for background information, and momentarily allowed himself to be distracted: 'Her recipe was to boil the salmon overnight and leave it all night in the water it was boiled in. In the morning each slice was encased in its own jelly.' Another recipe worth copying was for trout: 'Split. Backbone removed. Pepper. Salt. Then dust-ing with oatmeal. Finally fry in any fat you happen to have (and rejoice).' Back to business. The Gaelic for Great Northern Diver was *Muir Bhuachaill*, 'sea herdsman': Mackenzie had shot one. It was a bad business to disturb deer in June, when hinds drop their fawns. 'That would upset the keepers and if repeated they might well try to round up the offenders.' The heather was not really purple until July or even August.

Stray remarks in his diary and in his letters to Charles Renold (which were otherwise almost entirely taken up with the minutiae of fishing) show him suffering the usual pangs of composition.

(*Diary, 13 November 1944*) I think perhaps I should get the Laird and the Gaels side of the affair concentrated into a boy who, not knowing what the *Sea Bear* crowd are doing, is himself enjoying the generalship of their discomfiture, regarding them simply as invaders.

(*4 January 1945*) Page 295 and stuck again. I am TOO OLD.

It was a relief to write to Pamela Whitlock about plans which she and Katharine Hull had for a new children's magazine.

(*23 October 1944*) Get into your head the melancholy fact that children are omnivorous. They will like almost anything. They cannot distinguish between originals and imitations because all alike are new *to them*. They have no standards. And anybody who is such a fool as to try in editing a children's magazine to 'give them what they want' is trying to swim in a vacuum. Give them what *you* want, and, if you are the right editor you will presently find that *they* are wanting it too (and thinking they have wanted it all the time). It is as stupid to try to 'give them what they want' as it is to try to 'write books *for* children'. Give them what *you* want. Write books for yourself. That way you may produce the best children's magazine there has ever been, or you may not. You can only try ...

Genia cannot stand the lake country weather any more, and we are planning yet another migration to London or somewhere within reach of it. No time for more. I am just off to fail to catch a salmon.

They had trouble in finding somewhere to live. On 7 December Edith Ransome died. They thought of moving to her house in Leeds, but Cecily, to whom it had been left, sold up in a hurry, afraid of bomb damage. Arthur was furious with his sister: she had not given him and Genia any opportunity to go to Leeds to see if the house would suit them.

(*Diary, 18 January 1945*) 61 and pretty rotten ... Barometer lowest yet recorded since we came. GALE.
(*19 January*) Slates gone. Chicken boxes shifted. Hurdles flattened. Top of chimney from stove bust and gone.
(*22 February*) Removed moustache, disclosing an ascetic and rather stingy solicitor.

The moustache soon grew again.

House-hunting inevitably dominated 1945. Arthur does not even mention the end of the war in his diary, and *Great Northern?* was almost entirely neglected, though he and Genia visited Lewis during the later part of May to get local colour for the book. On 1 June they moved out of the Heald and stayed for six weeks in a hotel at Loweswater. Arthur enjoyed himself there. His room was at the opposite end of the hotel from Genia's, but very good to work in. The end of the war was bound to lighten his heart. It brought Rupert Hart-Davis back to civilian life, and Arthur got it into his head that he might teach both Hart-Davis and his son to fish. He wrote a warm letter on the subject, ending with the salutation, 'Tight lines to you both!' A few days later the proselytiser wrote again, urging a study of Bickerdyke's *The All Round Angler*. 'We are going to have a lovely time.' Arthur was in such good form that he even did a few days' work on *Great Northern?*.

The jovial mood lasted even after they left the lakes. They drove three hundred and twenty-seven miles in one day, reaching the Marble Arch at 9.30 p.m. on 16 July. On 18 July they moved into Jonathan Cape's flat, which he had kindly lent them while they looked for permanent accommodation. A week later Arthur told Hart-Davis that he found it rather fun being in London. 'I'm not going to hate it as much as I thought I should.'

Then the difficulties began to mount. They went to the East Coast for a few days. It was very pleasant to meet old friends again at Pin Mill, and their wish to settle again in Suffolk was reinforced; but Genia proved implacable in the matter of houses. She disliked Felixstowe very much, and decided against Woodbridge. Arthur had his mind rather on boats. His doctors, knowing their patient, were afraid that if he tried to sail *Selina King* again he would suffer further injuries. So he began to think of building yet another boat, adapted to a semi-invalid's needs. Harry King assured him he could build 'a fishing boat'. Where the material for it was to come from in that epoch of shortages is not clear: one plausible story is that Arthur had bought some timber before the war, stored it, and now could use it. He was soon deep in deliberations with the designer. By the beginning of December King's yard was hard at work.

The East Coast, or perhaps Genia, proving impossible, they accepted their fate, and moved into a flat in Weymouth Street, Marylebone. They were lucky to get it in that time of acute housing shortage: seventy other house-hunters had looked at the flat, twenty-four of whom had then offered for it. The agents, sure of their money, began to consider who would make the best tenant.

ARTHUR (offering references): If you want to know who I am —
SENIOR PARTNER : We know very well who you are. My children have talked of you for years as one of the family, and we are advising the owners to let you have the flat.

Arthur in delight told his sister Joyce the story, ending, 'there really are some points in having pumped out all those books.'

The actual move was the worst, Arthur said, in all their gipsying; he went down with flu, and Genia had a dreadful time with the removal men. Arthur did not immediately turn gloomy.

(*To Margaret Renold, 14 October*) She is alive, but only just. However, though she would like to burn or give away my fishing tackle (and send me to America) she does on the whole seem pleased at having got her way, and here we are, Cockneys, with a seven year sentence at least ...

I must admit that my big workroom is really a very good one and even at my advanced age (at which imagination cools and no kind of inspiration can be hoped for) I ought to be able to turn out some sort of substitutes for decent books. And hot water day and night is a bit of a blessing. Further, the club is within walking distance, and there will be a bit of dinghy sailing on the Thames at Hampton, thanks to my brother-in-law being mixed up with the Metropolitan Water Board. Though I can't turn out in Weymouth Street with a little rifle to look for a rabbit or a deer. Still, one mustn't be greedy, and though I shall have to work like smoke to keep solvent [This was sheer fantasy. Wren Howard would soon tell him that fifty thousand copies of his books had been sold in 1945 alone.] I daresay I shall manage it. And Genia swears that once we are straight she will be able to take things much easier than in any of our earlier camps.

He resumed work with a will, in that big workroom, on *Great Northern?*, and by mid-January had completed the first draft. Unfortunately other things began to go badly wrong.

(*To Pamela Whitlock, 31 October*) I have been and still am rather groggy, what with leaving the country, and coming here, and not being able to get a telephone, and tumbling between scaffolding and boats on the Thames, and then getting my right thumb broken by an anchor, and collecting some beastly germ, and-and-and...
(*Diary, 28 January 1946*) Genia's destruction of the bathroom completed, and the bath gone. Construction of the bedroom has now begun.
(*6 February*) Slept in bathroom.
(*7 February*) Felt pretty awful.

(*8 February*) Beastly. No work. Back at October again. I ought to have refused any changes of rooms, etc., until the second draft was done. My fault for not having refused. Too late now. (*15 February*) Genia regrets the flat and says we have moved too late (but we couldn't have moved sooner. She is as tired here as at Coniston).

Then on 5 April they were disturbed by a loud wireless in a neighbouring flat; and for the rest of their residence in Weymouth Street found one noise after another to complain of (*Diary, 19 June 1947*: 'Piano opposite made all work impossible').

The tragi-comic interplay of character and circumstance is even better illustrated by the story of *Selina King* and *Peter Duck*. Like the story of the flat, it suggests that Arthur and Genia had become the worst enemies of their own happiness.

(*To Charles Renold, 9 November 1945*) I am giving up my big ship on doctor's orders and am hoping to replace her by a much smaller, easier run vessel, a sort of marine bath chair for my old age. I shall try to catch eels when at anchor in the new boat which the designer, without consulting me, has christened *Peter Duck*. She will be P.D. among friends. A comic little boat, with two masts, so as to keep each single sail small and light to handle. She'll sleep two in comparative comfort.

Years later Genia said that it had been a great mistake to part with 'the nicest boat we ever possessed ... *Selina* was designed for single-handed use and easy moving through the water; if we cut or permanently reefed her sail we should have managed her.'

In February 1946 a yachtsman named Peter Davis expressed interest in buying *Selina*. Arthur said that if she were sold immediately his price would be £1,800. Davis accepted this, subject to a survey, so Arthur at last travelled down to Oulton Broad to see the pearl of ships once more.

(*Diary, 20 February*) *Selina* has a dried keel and garboards, so much that it will be impossible to get her in sailing trim in time for Davis. So that is off. Slept at Lowestoft.
(*21 February*) Pin Mill. *Peter Duck* planked. I begin to lose faith. Giles has *not* allowed sitting headroom under the decks. King, Norman and Giles say that they can manage to put this right.

I doubt it and wish I had not started to build ... Giles could have given four inches more room under the deck by having a 2-inch rail instead of bulwarks. Damn him!!!!!

One would not gather from this that the design of *Peter Duck* had been evolved in close consultation with Arthur, who laid down numerous specifications: a chest of drawers was to be built in, there was to be a niche where a bureau could be fitted for writing, she must be comfortable for two people, and there must be sufficient headroom below decks for him to be able to sit back without having to bend or bump his head. This last was the point that caused trouble. Arthur, on this or another early visit to *Peter Duck*, sitting down at the foreward end of his bunk, fetched his head a frightful crack, as he had done on other boats so often in the past: he was, after all, a tall man. It was a more serious matter on this occasion: the boatbuilders had disregarded his instructions! After that the whole business went sour on him. He was too fond of the Kings to quarrel with them, but he never forgave Giles. Yet the longitudinal beam with which he collided slopes elegantly upwards from fore to aft; he could easily have sat at the other end of the bunk, where there was plenty of headroom, even for him.

Selina was sold, for less than she was worth, in March ('Worth while, not to have the worry of refitting her while I am struggling with this swampy book'). On 30 March Arthur went sailing with Colonel Busk from Burnham to Pin Mill by way of West Mersea and Mistley. It was his first cruise since the war, and he enjoyed it, but although he found *Peter Duck* now decked he still grumbled in his diary about the headroom. He did not get to the Orwell again until August.

(*26 August*) Pin Mill [with] Busk; also Burnham. Genia very much against having a boat at all.

Soon Genia was displaying her special talent:

(*9 September*) Pin Mill. Genia finds no single good point in the boat, but agrees it is better to try to get it finished and experiment.

In the end *Peter Duck* proved to be one of Giles's most successful enterprises. George Jones, a local yacht-broker, commissioned and sold more than three dozen copies; the 'Peter Duck' class of yacht became famous, and the original even more so. Even Arthur gradually came to admit her merits.

> (*3 October*) Tried boat with Busk. A very good modern engine and quite comfortable roomy cabin.
> (*5 October*) Sold boat to Barton and Giles for £1,200 which should see me clear of the disastrous venture. But the boat is a very good boat and went beautifully on trials today. No more boats. Farewell to Pin Mill.

He repented at leisure.

> (*7 November*) Wrote to Barton making an offer for the ex-*Peter Duck*. Genia agrees.
> (*9 November*) Letter from Barton. Yes. Prepared to re-sell me ex-*Peter Duck*.
> (*10 November*) Finished fourth version of Chapter I. Genia approves!? *Peter Duck* to be called *Plain Jane*. Genia: 'Engliss people can't pronounce Genia. I prefer to be called plain Jane!'

He had to pay for his dithering: the boat which he sold for £1,200 cost him £1,500 to repossess. But eventually the transaction was completed.

> (*3 March*) They get the £300 for nothing, but it is better so than having a lot more trouble. Busk very pleased.

Arthur was always telling himself it was 'better so' after making large financial mistakes. But by the beginning of April he was back at Pin Mill, eager to start sailing. Even now there was a delay: the sail-makers at West Mersea had not made the sails, though they had been promised a year before. ('!!!!!!!!!!!!!!') They lent Arthur a mainsail for use over Easter. By the end of April the proper sails had arrived, and in May, when the Ipswich fleet was out in force, Arthur noted that it was 'quite like pre-war'. But he still managed to be dissatisfied with *Peter Duck*. He said that the boom had been cut too short, and that the boat would not head into a strong wind. George Jones, who came to own her in later years, told me that this was a foul slander.

The diary for 1946, while full of this ridiculous story, also records the painful emergence of *Great Northern?*:

(*22 February*) Howard very gently betrayed that the first hundred pages are pretty dull (as I knew) wanting dialogue. The Gaels too suddenly are accepted and done with. Mystery too suddenly ends in nothing. There obviously ought to be a clearer carry-over. Beginning does not show quite where they are. Of course it mustn't. Thing is to make it still vaguer ... Very useful confirmation of my suspicions of the stuff. He is all for going ahead.

(*25 February*) I think I must get the Gaels going much earlier.

(*12 April*) Nancy and John as red herrings. To be altered. No good in present form. Much better if they are duly followed by one of the *Dactyl* sailors. As it is, it simply refuses a good chance of fun.

(*2 November*) Trying a new first chapter. No good.

(*14 December*) Finished Book. Very bad beginning and end. 400 pp.

It was published in the summer of 1947 and went into four impressions that year. This must have owed at least as much to the author's reputation as to the merits of his latest work: there had been no new Arthur Ransome since 1943, an eternity to children. The reviewers welcomed it enthusiastically, and it deserved its success. It had cost Ransome more pains than any of its predecessors, but his labours were not in vain. Eric Linklater, reviewing it in the *Observer*, called it 'workmanlike' – a happy adjective. The subject, a fiendish egg-collector's designs on a pair of Great Northern Divers nesting in the Hebrides, verges on the melodramatic; the plot, which pits the Swallows, Amazons and Callums, cruising in the isles, against the egg-collector, seems to be an uneasy conflation of the mode of *Peter Duck* with that of *Coot Club*; and indeed the birds' eggs theme is too like that of *Coot Club* for comfort. Ransome has little or nothing new to say about the children's characters. But he knows his business, and by infinite attention to detail makes his commonplace tale solidly interesting and convincing. If the Hebridean scene does not wholly come to life (Ransome knew it so much less well than he knew the Lake District and East Anglia) the pictures are as good as any in the whole series. The last of all, 'Farewell to the *Sea*

Bear', showing a boy in a kilt standing on a headland and gazing out to sea, where a white sail slips into the distance, is curiously touching, showing nothing that is described in the text, but much that may be inferred, and symbolising, no doubt unconsciously, an author's farewell to his readers.

For Arthur had finally shot his bolt. He never completed another story. The last burst of his imaginative faculty came in 1948, when he started a book about the Death and Glories. Four opening chapters got Joe, Bill and Pete surreptitiously aboard a new motor-cruiser, built at Horning, which was carried by lorry to the lake in the North where the boys' friends the Callums were holidaying. A few later passages were drafted, but Ransome faced two insuperable difficulties. First, the basic idea was much too much like that of Hull and Whitlock's *Escape to Persia*, in which the Hunterley children, aided by their friend Maurice, steal out of their aunt's London house, through the coal-hole, by night, and then make their way to Exmoor by bus, hitch-hiking, train and bicycle. Second (this was a difficulty which had bothered Hull and Whitlock too) once you have got your heroes to their destination, what do you do with them? Arthur toyed with various ideas, but did not develop any of them. There may have been an answer to this problem, but he soon gave up looking for it. He did not even find a title for the book. Yet it would be a pity if it were lost to sight for ever, for the opening chapters contain some splendidly vigorous writing, the narrative verve is infectious, and the characterisation, which had become so predictable in *Great Northern?*, had recovered all its old flair. No one fully knows Joe, Bill and Pete who has not watched them setting out for their adventure in the North.

Arthur stopped work on the book on 31 January 1949. It was not quite the end of his career as a story-teller. He came across a volume of West African folk tales in a French edition, and set out to translate them into English under the title of *The Country of Wild Beasts*. His letters to Jonathan Cape about the project are full of enthusiasm, and he must have carried it well towards completion; but apparently difficulties with the French author, or her agent, made publication impossible. So Arthur was unable to bow out with an achievement to recall that of *Old Peter's Russian Tales*, his beginning. The manuscript has disappeared.

Ransome's readers had no intention of saying farewell to him. Wren Howard calculated that by 1948 Arthur's books would have sold a million copies. Arthur told his diary that this was impossible, since by December 1945 they had sold only 560,000 copies; but it came true all the same. Less agreeably, it began to appear that wartime inflation and the wartime decline in the author's position were to be permanent. In November 1946 Howard told Arthur that the price of each volume would have to go up to nine shillings. 'He wants me to take royalty on 7/6 as before,' wrote Arthur in his diary, and calculated, 'Royalty reduced from 20% to 17%.' Why he agreed to this continued sacrifice does not appear. What he thought about it in later years is shown by the heavy, angry red-ink strokes surrounding this entry in the manuscript.

Life at Weymouth Street had its advantages. Arthur was able to get to Lord's to watch England play India in the summer of 1946, and to Twickenham with Rupert Hart-Davis, where he heard that Hart-Davis was to write the biography of his old friend Hugh Walpole. The terrible winter of 1947 goes unmentioned in the diary and letters, which could hardly have been so had they continued at the Heald. Then there was the Garrick Club, a mile or so away, which became one of Arthur's favourite haunts. The great advantage of being a man of many enthusiasms is that you can usually find somewhere to indulge at least one of them to your heart's content. In the case of Arthur and the Garrick, the billiard-room was a lure, for there was always someone to give him a game; or he might play chess. He also liked the members' literary conversation. He did his best to get Genia to share his pleasure, but she remained unclubbable: 'I was one of the lucky few who meet and marry the right person. We shared so many interests, saw the same jokes, liked and disliked the same things—but Garrick was the only thing we did not see eye to eye ... but I never never tried to prevent him going there.'

This was very convenient for Arthur, but not enough to reconcile them to the flat. They decided to move once more. Being the Ransomes, they moved back to the Lake District, presumably because the climate suited Genia so little; sold *Peter Duck* a second time, because they both enjoyed sailing, and sea air was so good for Arthur; and took on not just Lowick Hall, near Nibthwaite, a large house, but the farm that went with it, although Arthur was a semi-invalid and Genia had never been able to bear servants of any kind in her home. Now she would have labourers and tenants to conciliate. They took possession on 9 June 1948, and by

11 August Arthur was writing in his diary, 'Very disheartened by Lowick.'

Settling in was of course full of horrors. The workmen called in to make improvements removed, with enormous difficulty, a worn-out cistern, and then had to put it back because a new one was unobtainable. This sort of thing drove Genia frantic, which depressed Arthur. But as usual he adapted much better than she did. For one thing he was back among the lakes. That country always brought out the best in him. Two years before, during a brief visit, he had recorded in his diary,

(*24 October 1946*) Up early and up the hill above the wood, gorgeous view over lakes and river and the big hills. Talk with a farmer who was very proud of a sheep-dog he had with him and had sold to Canada for £50. Hill dogs are no good for sheep trials. But sheep trial dogs are no good for long distance work on the fells.

While there were still such discoveries to make, he could not be unhappy in the North.

(*To Charles Renold, 27 March 1949*) Yesterday I assisted at the birth of twins — lambs. It is astonishing how good a midwife a huge clumsy farmer can suddenly become. Mother and babies doing well, though he reports the mother a laal bit stiff — and no wonder.

He had other consolations denied to Genia. Rupert Hart-Davis, for example, discovering that Jonathan Cape Ltd valued his services below what he thought they were worth, had set up his own publishing firm, which rapidly became one of the most distinguished imprints in London. Arthur was immensely interested in this undertaking, and invested £500 in the firm's ordinary shares. It would have been more if inflation, and commitments at Lowick, had allowed. 'If only people had the sense to film my books.' He helped the firm quite as much (or more) by becoming 'godfather and nanny' to its celebrated Mariners Library series, which was a wonderful expression of Arthur's mind and spirit. In the end it contained almost fifty volumes, and was in fact a collection of all the classics of cruising literature (including *Racundra's First Cruise*). Some of the titles had before been almost inaccessible to

English readers, though not to the erudite Arthur, who was as bookish a yachtsman as he was an angler. The works for which he provided the introductions himself were, with the single exception of Erling Tambs's *Cruise of the Teddy*, the originating classics of the cruising tradition: Slocum's *Sailing Alone Around the World*, R. T. McMullen's *Down Channel*, John Macgregor's *Voyage Alone in the Yawl Rob Roy*, E. E. Middleton's *Cruise of the Kate* and two of E. F. Knight's works, *The Falcon on the Baltic* and *The Cruise of the Alerte*. Taken together these six essays (the Knight introductions are virtually identical) make up a miniature history of cruising books, as the prefaces of forty years before had made up *The History of Story-Telling*. They are vastly superior work, written in the ease of old acquaintance with the books themselves and with their subject, small-boat, seagoing navigation. With unassuming authority Ransome indicates what a good cruise-book ought to be: how, for example, it ought to contain plenty of useful information for yachtsmen likely to follow in the author's track. But the strongest impression these prefaces are likely to leave is their writer's relish in human individuality. All his yachtsmen seem to be eccentric, even a little mad: Middleton was convinced that the earth was not round but flat, or disc-shaped; McMullen believed that Paradise was in the sun, which is why men rejoice in the dawn. It is a wonderful portrait gallery, and one of Ransome's worthiest achievements.

Arthur would accept no payment for these labours of love, but to his great pleasure Hart-Davis sent him a set of the *Oxford English Dictionary* as a reward.

(*To Rupert Hart-Davis, 4 June*) IT has the most extraordinary effect on me. Looking at IT full face, or even feeling ITS blue buckram presence warming my back, I have the oddest illusion that after all I must be some sort of writer.
(*15 June*) The Stupendous Dictionary is nobly housed in a built-in glass-fronted cupboard of 1748 with the bleeding heart of the Blencowes (who then owned this idiotic place) carved above it. Come and have a look at it the next time you have to go north on Walpole business.

In his will he left the dictionary to its donor, who had agreed to act as his literary executor.

For a time he had the book about the Coots in the North to

keep him busy (its theme may have been inspired by the business of moving to Lowick); and the African folk tales occupied him during an attack of shingles.

(*To Charles Renold, 27 March*) In spite of strong local opposition, I have just got to the end of a rough draft of a translation of an astonishing French book of animal stories, folklore, etc., from French West Africa. Some of it is so very good as to make the bad parts seem even worse than they are, and the ineradicable sophistication of a Frenchman can ruin almost any folk story. So I am ruthlessly turning it out of polysyllabic French into the very simplest English I can muster – more or less that of *Old Peter's Russian Tales*. I started it the day I fell ill, and have been at it, in spite of protests, ever since. But some of the black stories are grand, like that of the beginning of the world, before the sun had got regular habits, when he used to make wild leaps into the sky at evening to save himself from falling into the sea.

A much more ambitious literary project gradually took shape. To encourage Pamela Whitlock, who was struggling to write another novel, he sent her a long letter telling how long it was before he himself had found his voice as a writer. He was thinking autobiographically. Earlier that year he had set out some pros and cons.

It seems to me extremely doubtful whether to write an autobiography or not.
In favour. I should like to thank W. G. Collingwood and Mrs Collingwood for their extreme and quite unearned kindness to me. I should like to say something of my other friends, Lascelles Abercrombie, Ted Scott. So much of silliness and untruth has been said and written about my work as correspondent in Russia that, perhaps, I ought to get down the quiet, dull truth to meet any more stupid lies that may be told, really to save Genia from feeling any need to contradict them. And I suppose there may be people who will be interested to read of what I saw at the time of the men who will be remembered as the great figures of the French Revolution are remembered.
Against. My memories have faded like old photographs. I may well be forgotten altogether, in which case I should certainly

not like to reach from my grave to pluck at people's skirts as they pass.

Rupert Hart-Davis encouraged him to set to work, and at last he did so, though he thought that Hart-Davis might turn out to be his only reader. 'The more I go on with it the more certain I become that I shall never want to print it.' However he went steadily ahead, and by February 1950 had written nearly fifty thousand words.

But work and tranquillity were at the mercy of Genia, and she was in a far from tranquil state of mind.

(*To Margaret Renold, 9 March 1949*) Trouble goes on. Genia worn out with a leper in the house [Arthur's shingles] and no help, and the gardener is gone too, has got a very bad influenzaish cold and cough. She also now owns a farm and about 130 acres or so, but, with such a cold, even the farm don't mean much comfort. Anyway I expect she'll have told you about that.

We had to acquire the farm, willy nilly because it so dovetailed with our own that any other buyer could have made the place intolerable. I am told we have done well, but of course are now bankrupt completely. However, if it comes to selling, we should have the whole lot to sell in one, which will be easier. And, privately, I think in the end we shall have to give in and sell. Not so long as Genia wants to stay, but when she realises that it is more than we can deal with. We not being in our thirties. Anyhow, the subject of selling has actually been mentioned. But I dare say we shall manage another few years. And then, perhaps, we may be able to collect a pair of Hottentots or Chinese to look after us.

Arthur, in spite of his ruptures, tried to help, but something went wrong with his truss. He called in a doctor, who said at once, 'You have been pulling a roller', and told him that all pulling and lifting must stop. On 27 June Genia said she would have to give up Lowick. It was impossible to run with no staff. Being herself, she recovered from this defeatist mood, but the writing was on the wall. It took over a year, but in October 1950 they moved once more – back to London. The Lake District estate was sold at the usual heavy loss. No doubt it was better so.

Arthur seems to have enjoyed his last year as lord of Lowick. Hart-Davis received letter after letter from Lowick on a wide diversity of subjects: the *Autobiography*, toy theatres, the Mariners Library, Max Beerbohm's *Poet's Corner* (Arthur wanted Hart-Davis to bring out a new, full-sized edition), Baring-Gould's *Mehalah* ('People are still calling their boats *Mehalah* along the Essex shore. And they are still pestering their booksellers to find them secondhand copies') and the importance of putting the date of first editions in reprints. There were also nature notes.

(*To Rupert Hart-Davis, 16 July*) Yesterday I saw a stoat kill a baby rabbit and killed the stoat at fifty yards with a lucky shot with a ·22. VERY pleased, because that beastly stoat is, I think, responsible for many other rabbits and for an entire brood of young pheasants.

(*21 July*) My dear though daily damned Hart-Davis: Here is the infernal Knight over which I have stewed and sweated myself into clotted and glutinous imbecility. Old age, I suppose. The thing wouldn't come right, but I think if I go on tugging it about it will get worse not better.

No one would guess, reading the easy, humorous, scholarly introduction to *The Falcon on the Baltic*, that it had cost its writer such pains.

Arthur and Genia's next home was a flat at 40 Hurlingham Court, looking straight on to the Thames alongside Putney Bridge. There, if they had been wise, they would have stayed for the rest of their lives. A new friend, Georgina Battiscombe, was pointedly asked by Genia if she had noticed the map of England in the lavatory, with a diagonal line marked on it from north-east to south-west: 'Never again will I live on the other side of that line'. But it was perfectly plain to Mrs Battiscombe that Arthur was yearning for the Lake District. In the mean time he enjoyed an Indian summer in London.

This flat, like the last, was pronounced noisy by its occupants. It had little to recommend it in their friends' eyes. Tania Rose, meeting Arthur again after many years, was struck in about equal measure by the change in him from the haggard figure of her childhood and by the hideous utility furniture with which the flat was stuffed – it looked as if it had been made on the cheap by

disabled workmen. Hart-Davis found the journey from Soho
Square to Putney Bridge tryingly long after a hard day's work (an
hour each way) but made it frequently nevertheless, to have his
plate heaped high by Genia. 'This is salmon in the Polish style,'
she would say, covering everything with a thick yellow sauce,
and then standing over him to make sure he ate it all (it must be
remembered that she had been fattening up Arthur for twenty
years). Hart-Davis, aware that he was putting on weight, didn't
especially welcome such vast, rich helpings; besides, they sometimes contained brains, which he disliked. It was more pleasant
meeting Arthur at the Garrick, where he now went every Thursday, to lunch, dine and have a game of chess or billiards.

Now that they were within reach of the sea again, they had to
have a boat, even though Arthur had to have a prostate operation
early in 1952. For the last time he built a ship. The yard (Hillyard's
of Littlehampton) which had made the *Nancy Blackett* now built
the *Lottie Blossom*, a five-ton sloop, largely to Genia's specifications
('We don't want friends,' she said, so *Lottie* has only two berths).
The name of the boat was found in *The Luck of the Bodkins* by one
of their most cherished authors. During the war Arthur had been
disgusted by what he called the 'hysterical victimisation' of 'the
unfortunate even if unwise but certainly not pro-German Wode-
house (his initials stand for anything but that)' and he now seized
the excuse for writing the master a fan letter.

> There are, of course, some ignorant persons who, knowing all
> of your books, do not know the best of all and ask 'Who was
> Lottie Blossom?' We refer them to the book, a copy of which
> is always aboard (another remaining at home in the long shelf
> of orange Wodehouses, orange but for a few regretted excep-
> tions) and tell them merely that she is a red-headed American
> film star who, to please her publicity agent, travels round with
> a small alligator in a wicker basket and, when the Customs come
> aboard to go through her luggage, asks them to begin with the
> wicker basket, after which they go no further. This usually
> raises a laugh, but on one occasion it did not. I was registering
> the name of the boat at the Customs Office, and the Customs
> Officer who was taking down the particulars for the Registrar
> asked the usual question. I, unthinking, replied with the usual
> story. It did not seem to amuse him at all. 'A very unpleasant
> young woman!' he remarked when I had done.

Arthur was so happy to have a sea-going boat again that he started an elaborate log of the *Lottie Blossom*'s voyages, an undertaking which suggests that he thought of compiling another cruise book. Abandoning the East Coast, he kept *Lottie* in Chichester Harbour, where friends frequently visited him. He and Genia sailed her to Cherbourg, through frightful weather, in 1953 and 1954, and greatly enjoyed themselves, particularly on the latter occasion, when they sat snug in Cherbourg feasting on lobsters while the gales raged; but even indominability must sometimes admit defeat. Arthur was now seventy, Genia sixty; and he was an anthology of ailments. So *Lottie* was laid up for the last time, and sold in 1954. Arthur does not seem to have been embittered by his resignation from the sea. He had had years of pleasure, and by defying his doctor's orders had had far more than at one time had seemed likely. He accepted that he was now an Ancient Mariner himself, and turned with all the more zest to fishing.

In 1951 the University of Leeds sounded him out: would he accept an honorary doctorate? He wrote back in a gratified flutter, but said firmly that he would accept the degree only in respect of his literary achievements, not in respect of his journalism. The reply must have been reassuring, for the following summer he was made Doctor of Letters at the same time as the painter and writer Wyndham Lewis. This amply made up for a muddle a few years previously at the University of Durham. Arthur's admirer, Sir James Duff, Warden of the Durham Colleges, had proposed Arthur for an honorary degree in 1948, and the proposal had been approved. Only when Arthur appeared at the ceremony did he discover that he was going to receive only an honorary MA, not being judged worthy of anything higher by the then Professor of English, one Abbott. To make matters worse, he discovered that Edith Sitwell was to get an honorary doctorate at the same ceremony, and he must have found it hard to see that she had any higher claims than his. He behaved with the utmost politeness (though he would not stay to dine with poor Sir James) and accepted the Vice-Chancellor's 'odd sort of apology', but told Cape never to mention the honorary MA in *Who's Who* or anywhere else. The Leeds degree was a different matter. He had barely recovered from his prostate operation, but all went well, and he revelled in this resumption of his academic career. As he said in his diary, quoting Samuel Johnson, 'Every man has a lurking wish to be thought considerable in his native place.' Perhaps it was the memory of the same Johnson that made him decide he liked his new academic dignity. At any rate, it was 'Dr Ransome' for the rest of his life. Genia was equally firm on the point.

Arthur was now a Grand Old Man of English letters – certainly of children's literature. He was awarded a CBE in 1953. From time to time articles celebrating his achievement were published. Sales of his books continued high. Unfortunately his relations with his publisher were clouded. For it had occurred to him in the spring of 1951 that the war had been over for six years, and yet he was still receiving a reduced royalty. Angry with Cape, and angry with himself, he began a long struggle to put matters on a better footing. He took up the matter with his accountant, William Balleny, who also did the accounts of Jonathan Cape Ltd.

Arthur freely admitted that the mess was his own fault.

> It was quite ridiculous to agree to a reduction in royalty during the war on books that were selling so well. If the sales had been small there might have been a reason for agreeing. But for an author to take a LOWER royalty because his books were selling too well was pure lunacy.

He proposed to wipe the slate clean up to 31 December 1945; but after that date he had not been properly compensated, and he wanted Jonathan Cape to make some back payments. He does not seem to have remembered that in November 1946 he had explicitly agreed to continue to accept a reduced royalty of 20 per cent on 7s. 6d., not the actual price of 8s. 6d. But Wren Howard and Jonathan Cape did not forget, and resisted Arthur's claim tenaciously. The dispute was still raging in 1955. Arthur calculated that he had sacrificed £12,000 by agreeing to the various alterations to his agreed royalty, and refused to continue them; Howard was adamant that he could no longer afford to pay a 20 per cent royalty, let alone back payments. The market for books was strongly resistant to price increases, and inflation meant that the publisher's real profit was becoming more and more precarious. Eventually a compromise was arranged, but Arthur remained convinced that he had been swindled. He revenged himself by cutting Jonathan Cape Ltd out of his will, but as he outlived Jonathan Cape, and Wren Howard was retired before Arthur's death, the blow went rather wide. Others benefited: his residual legatees were now to be the Royal Literary Fund, and also his literary executors, Rupert Hart-Davis, John Bell and his wife, the former Pamela Whitlock.

Arthur had done well: these devoted friends were more and more useful and important to him as he grew older and feebler. But in the mid-1950s he was still fairly vigorous, still working at the *Autobiography*, and still fishing.

Like so many other books, the *Autobiography* was never to be finished. We are told why by Rupert Hart-Davis, who in 1955 started his correspondence with George Lyttelton, which contains many glimpses of Arthur.

(*Hart-Davis to Lyttelton, 27 November 1955*) On Tuesday evening I journeyed to Putney (people never think their own home is far away) to dine with the Arthur Ransomes. He is a most delightful and interesting man. My present concern is that he should finish his autobiography, for he has made me promise (as his literary executor) to finish it for him if he dies too soon (he's only 71) and he has left all the most difficult bits to the last.

The most difficult bits almost all concerned the Russian Revolution.

For years and years Arthur had been professing his loathing of politics, and had kept it out of his life and work. But there had once been another Arthur, and under the stimulus of writing about the past he came to life again. Perhaps, in conversation, he had never been dead.

(*Hart-Davis to Lyttelton, 26 January 1958*) Did you read Alan Moorehead's stuff in today's *Sunday Times*? Jolly good, I thought, though I'm sure that Arthur Ransome, with whom I dine tomorrow, will pick holes in it. He was in Russia from 1913 to 1918, and nobody else is right, bless him.

This trait had its effect on the *Autobiography*. Ransome remembered far too much of what he had meant to put in his abortive history of the Revolution, and so pages that might have described his courtship of Genia, or his relations with the *Daily News*, or with the Foreign Office and the British Embassy, were sacrificed to elaborate arguments about Russian politics.

The book as we have it must have been substantially complete by the end of 1957. The style is as clear and firm as ever, the tone unmistakable, the handling of incident and individuals masterly.

Yet although the book is a delight to read, it can hardly be rated a complete success. Ransome is decently reticent about his relations with living persons (when he cannot be kind he says nothing) and his account of Ivy is truthful and fair, though necessarily painful to read. But he says surprisingly little about his mother; his account of his father seems to be an exercise in unconscious revenge; and where the Altounyans are concerned he is guilty of some suppression of the truth. The book will survive chiefly because of its vivid evocation of early childhood, its equally telling depiction of literary London early in the century and its account of episodes and personalities (especially Karl Radek) of the Russian years.

It is only fair to add that when the book was at last published, in 1976, it was warmly greeted by reviewers and sold very well. William Golding commended the book's wit and energy; A. J. P. Taylor (an old friend) said it was the most enchanting book of the year; and everyone responded warmly to its revelation of Arthur's personality.

The last book which Arthur published himself was *Mainly About Fishing*. It came out in 1959, attracting less attention than it deserved. His first idea had been to expand *Rod and Line*, but he sensibly decided to make a new book instead, and told Hart-Davis that he intended it as a tribute to his father's memory, since Cyril Ransome had himself wanted to write an angling book. It salvages the material that had been meant to go into *A Plague of Flies*. Where *Rod and Line* was chiefly concerned with coarse-fishing and trout, the new book was preoccupied with salmon, and contained full details of the Blue Vulturine Elver. For the last time Ransome displayed his magical facility for making technicalities fascinating to ignoramuses and outsiders, while at the same time making valuable observations for experts. The book was not published by Cape but by A. and C. Black, whom he had induced to reissue H. E. Morritt's *Fishing Ways and Wiles* (Cape had refused) and to publish, with an introduction by himself, the same author's *The Constant Fisherman*. But in binding and format *Mainly About Fishing* greatly resembled a Swallow book.

Fishing being impossible at Hurlingham Court, each spring saw the Ransomes setting off for the lakes again. They settled this time on the northern edge of Haverthwaite, a parish south-west of Windermere, south-east of Coniston. For the first year they rented Ealinghearth Cottage, thereafter Hill Top. From both houses they had splendid views up the valley of Rusland: etymologically Rolf's

Land or Ranulf's Land, just as 'Ransome' is 'Ranulf's Son'. Exploring up Rusland Pool they discovered Rusland churchyard, green and isolated, one of the quietest places in the world. Arthur decided that he would like to be buried there. In the mean time he fished, and revelled in his continuing vigour.

(*To Rupert Hart-Davis, 24 May 1956*) We are beginning to feel we have been in this house for a long time. Last year's cat met Genia at the farm down below, greeted her with enthusiasm, walked all the way up the hill uninvited and has taken up residence. I have been lucky with trout, but the sea trout have not yet arrived, though I saw one leap at the top of the tidal water. Genia is over-working as usual in the nettle-choked wilderness that she means to turn into a garden. The gutters round the roofs have been mended, slates placed over a yawning hole in the roof of the barn, the rodent operative has got rid of a fearful plague of other rodents as operative as himself, the barn door has been so altered as to make it easy to get my chariot in, Great Spotted Woodpeckers are busy in the oak below my windows, we see buzzards daily, the worst rush of Whitsuntide trippers has ebbed, and we want to know when Rupert Hart-Davis is coming north.

Among the advantages of having a publisher for a friend are the presents he sends you. This year Hart-Davis sent Nancy Cunard's memoir of George Moore and Humphry House's book on Aristotle. Arthur liked both, saying of the Cunard, 'a real beauty of a portrait, and done so delicately. I do like people who write with their fingertips and not with their fists.' Of Humphry House, 'I do wish I'd met him in the days when Lascelles Abercrombie and I used to walk and talk. Ass!! In those days he would have been six years old. He is interested in just the things that used in those old days to make nothing of twenty miles for us.' This delighted his benefactor:

(*Hart-Davis to AR, 18 September 1956*) It's uncanny the way in which you always pick out for special praise those books in which I myself am particularly interested and which I have almost always decided to publish on their merits, without much hope of profit. You've no idea how encouraging your approval can be.

(*AR to Wren Howard, 18 May 1957*) I think I must boast that for the first time since 1945 I have been walking a bit, with great joy. I climbed up to a very high, wild and lonely tarn without disaster and did it again the next day. Up on the top I saw a raven and the usual buzzards. It looks as if that last operation has done a miracle.

As the allusion to an operation shows (this one was for a strangu-lated hernia) nothing could keep Arthur out of hospital for long; but otherwise his health seemed fairly good. He was growing weak on his legs, though not weak enough to keep away from rivers: the same letters which tell of him stumbling after fish tell of him catching them. Neither did his weakness stop renewed house-hunting. Genia visited the Bells' beautiful house in the Chilterns and, she said, 'nearly died with envy. It is just exactly what I want.' They began to look for something in the same area. But then on 1 December 1958 Arthur slipped and fell as he left the Cape offices after lunch. It proved to be the beginning of a long and painful decline.

The fall did not seem to be much: Arthur suffered a grazed knee, that was all. But presently he began to suffer fearful pains in his back. He started going for physiotherapy to the Charterhouse Clinic where, early in the New Year, he was given an injection which completely paralysed him for two days; then the pain in his back returned, as violent as ever, or worse.

(*Diary, 9 January 1959*) Lay low, hoping for improvement. Pretty well paralysed from middle down. Rupert and John Bell came to lunch, and to talk about my will, very satisfactory. They do know what I want.

Hart-Davis reported the occasion to George Lyttelton, comment-ing, 'I hope to goodness he lives for ages: he is seventy-five next week.' Before long it began to seem doubtful if he would see seventy-six.

(*Diary, 17 January*) Worse, I think. Could hardly move any-where. From hip to toe of left leg. Duodenal horrors in the night. From 1.45 to 4.30 awake.

Three months later Arthur was still bed-ridden. Rupert Hart-

Davis, who was a faithful visitor to the sickbed, described him as bored stiff, sleepless, often in pain. He was carted off, first to a nursing-home and then to hospital, but it did no good, since the doctors could not agree on a diagnosis: sciatica? lumbago? rheumatism? slipped disc? rheumatoid arthritis? He was massaged and drugged and pulled about, to no avail. And it took Genia at least ten days to get the kitchens to understand that he must not be served with food cooked in aluminium. By July he was so weak and helpless that he could not sit up in bed or even turn from one side to the other. He begged to be allowed to go home to die in his own bed, and was allowed to do so. It was a stretcher and ambulance affair, and Genia grimly promised herself that she would sue the Charterhouse Clinic for negligence if he did die. Hart-Davis saw him soon after his return, and was distressed.

(*Hart-Davis to Lyttelton, 26 July*) He is seventy-five, and I begin to fear he will never walk again. So does he, and the other evening, when his wife was out of the room, he said in a woeful voice: 'I'd always hoped to end respectably.' His wife, a large and vigorous Russian woman of sixty-five, refuses to have any kind of 'help', and the task of nursing, cooking, cleaning, shopping is clearly wearing her out.

But then, left to himself, Arthur once more displayed his astonishing powers of recovery.

A girl physiotherapist came two or three times a week to minister to him [Genia wrote later] and it was the greatest pleasure to me to see the surprise, almost disbelief in the eyes of two doctors who had most to do with him at St Mary's when they came to visit him a month later and saw him actually walking without any crutches or being supported by a nurse on either side.

By October the patient was convalescing at Pagham in Sussex. He wrote happily to Wren Howard of meeting four cats there, one of whom, a Siamese, was in charge of their cottage, and took Arthur for walks in the garden.

But his recovery was never complete; he tired easily. In April 1960 Genia carried him off to Haverthwaite, where he pottered about, tried to get on with the *Autobiography*, thought and talked, as well as wrote, about his past, and felt his strength ebb.

(*To Rupert Hart-Davis, 23 April*) The Boss seems as usual to be exhausting herself but as this is her own peculiar method of enjoying herself, I make no protest. By keeping quiet I keep my head on my own shoulders: and I prefer it there.

This letter indicates what was to be one of the saddest turns of his senescence. He began to be afraid of Genia. They had lived together for over forty years, and he had long known her to be hot-tempered, occasionally morose, sometimes savage. From time to time her rages had cast him into the deepest glooms. But his love and respect for her, his reliance on her strength, and their innumer-able shared tastes, had made it on the whole a happy and successful marriage. Genia was still what she had always been, and just as devoted to Arthur. But he no longer had the resilience to deal with her moods. It is to be hoped that she never noticed, as she struggled with the problems of looking after him (soon she would have to take over his business affairs on top of the housekeeping), how nervous she made him.

She decided that they should buy Hill Top cottage: once more his love of the lake country over-rode prudence. The contract was signed and the deposit paid over on Friday 13 May: 'What a day to choose!' wrote Genia in her diary. Certainly they were not lucky in what followed: builders made the house more or less uninhabitable for the next two years. Hurlingham Court was not entirely given up until 1963.

Arthur struggled with the *Autobiography* and watched the natural life around him with more than his old interest. On 1 May, for instance, he reported to Hart-Davis that the story now ran continuously from his birth to the eve of the Revolution, and that in the last three minutes he had seen a buzzard, two redstarts, some jays, and a Great Spotted Woodpecker, and heard a cuckoo, '1st this year'. He began to suffer from attacks of amnesia. But as the summer wore on he revived somewhat. He began to fish again; and at the end of the season was able to make the following entry in his diary:

(*20 September*) Cockermouth. Cricket field. After unwillingly spinning fished this fly of Tom's (adviser yesterday) at 7 p.m.

Hooked a 7 lb. cock fish, firm and bright, like a spring fish. Played hard (standing on its head and boring) a beautiful fish: and it ate magnificently.

This I expect will be my last fish.

He thought much about his art in these last years. *The Soldier and Death* was to be reissued in 1962; this necessitated some correspondence with the publisher in 1961. In an undated letter to a Mr Marriott (which possibly was never sent) he held forth on some favourite themes:

I believe that no matter who reads it, a good book is always one written by the author for himself. This is true even of the good books whose authors mistakenly supposed that they were writing for children. *Alice* is a good book not because the story was first invented 'for' a young Miss Liddell, but because Lewis Carroll got a great deal of private fun out of writing it for himself. And you do not suppose that Stevenson wrote *Treasure Island* for anybody but himself. He enjoyed writing it. He enjoyed reading it aloud: to whom? To the boy Lloyd Osbourne? Not a bit of it. Lloyd Osbourne, aged about twelve, Mrs Stevenson, as old as Stevenson, and Stevenson's father and mother, older still, were lucky enough, not so much to hear a story told 'for' them, as to *overhear* Stevenson telling a story to himself ... A good book is not merely a thing that keeps a child (or a grown-up person) amused while reading. It is an experience he shares, something that he himself lives. It calls upon faculties that grow with use and atrophy without it. It peoples his world and lets him share in other lives, enriches by exercising his own power of imaginative living and so enriches life itself for him ... A man's whole life is the poorer if it has not been thus enriched in childhood and youth. For this no picture papers, no cinema films, that depend not on things imagined but on things actually demonstrated to the eye, are any substitute.

This was a noble *apologia*. Unfortunately it had a hidden meaning. As Arthur's powers failed his weaknesses took command. Always a perfectionist, he now became a ditherer (a letter about *The Soldier and Death*, for example, went through at least three drafts). His anxieties could no longer be curbed by his common sense and natural buoyancy. Small slights, real or imagined, small worries, tended to become obsessions, over which he mumbled tooth-lessly. It was a sad way to pass into extreme old age, and in at least one case had long-lasting and unfortunate consequences.

For Ernest Altounyan now became the object of Arthur's glooms. Arthur had unwisely listened to gossip, and convinced himself that Altounyan was making undue claims about his part in engendering *Swallows and Amazons*. Hidden, half-forgotten jealousies were fed by this, and the loyal friendship of a lifetime was discounted. Altounyan died in 1962. Arthur read the obituary in *The Times* with sullen indignation, for it said that Ernest's children were the models for the Swallows and, to Arthur's sus-picious eyes, even seemed to suggest that some of the credit for the Ransome books therefore belonged to their father. Matters were made worse when the *Guardian* asked Arthur to write an appreciation of Altounyan. Instead of accepting the invitation he sat and brooded over this rather small matter which, like the ques-tion of caravan sites in the Lake District, became something which could be guaranteed to provoke a burst of rage whenever, in later years, it came to mind.

He tried very hard to persuade himself otherwise, but he had borrowed a great deal more than their names from the Altounyan children when he set about creating his own; and the initial im-pulse behind *Swallows and Amazons* was the wish to tell the Altounyans a story. Neither was it just a question of *Swallows and Amazons. Peter Duck*, as we have seen, was actually written in the Altounyan home, and throughout the 1930s he had continued to see a lot of the young ones, especially Taqui and Titty. However much he might tell himself what, in a sense, was true, that they had only 'overheard' a story he told to himself for his own amuse-ment, in another sense it was *not* true, and it was unworthy to try to evade the facts.

Yet he did so. He even suppressed the dedication of *Swallows*. The fan letters seem to have originated the process. The apparent actuality of the books was so convincing that readers, whether old or young, found no difficulty in believing that in some literal sense the Swallows actually existed as he had drawn them, and could be met as friends if the author would help. One American woman wrote inviting them over for the summer holidays. Arthur might have been merely flattered by this tribute to his skill, except for the fact that there were the Altounyans all the time, seemingly verifying the fans' simple view of the nature of imaginative creation.

Still worse, they seemed to have a claim on children who were now intensely dear to him.

> My children were much more real to me than most of the people I knew. I had spent so much time with them. I knew so much more about them than ever I could put down on paper. It was a painful shock to be forced to remember that there are more kinds of reality than one. And it was made much worse when children wrote almost with indignation that they had met people who had told them that they were the Swallows and that they were not at all like the children in my books.

In all this he did the Altounyans a great injustice. To them, as the years went on and the success of the books mounted, their identification with the Swallows became something of an embarrassment, something of a distress. It was perhaps particularly felt by Taqui, who, when she went to school in England, found that she had to spend more time than was pleasant denying that she was Captain John – which she thought should have been obvious. The Altounyans suffered somewhat as Christopher Milne suffered. All this was lost on the jealous Arthur, who began to imagine that they were trying to cash in on his inventions. But that was a rationalisation, even if a base one. His fundamental motive was that which had led him to exclude the Webb illustrations from his books. He was a child protecting his own private game. Only his continuing affection for Dora prevented him making a complete ass of himself by sending a statement to the press. He excluded the Altounyans as much as possible from the *Autobiography*. He left them out completely from his account of the genesis of *Swallows and Amazons*, which begins 'I had for some time been growing intimate with a family of imaginary children ... ' Later on, when there was no getting out of describing the visit to Aleppo, he wrote of Ernest Altounyan: 'his children had identified themselves (regardless of sex) with my characters ... ' This is pretty cool, though not perhaps so much so as the prefatory note which was included in all the Swallow books from 1958 onwards:

> I have often been asked how I came to write *Swallows and Amazons*. The answer is that it had its beginning long, long ago

when, as children, my brother, my sisters and I spent most of our holidays on a farm at the south end of Coniston ... *Swallows and Amazons* grew out of those old memories. I could not help writing it. It almost wrote itself.

True, so far as it went, but it did not go more than half-way. It is as if Arthur wanted to deny the very existence of the Altounyans, as well as their importance to his imagination. When he drafted an account of the 1938 expedition to the Broads, he could not bring himself to mention Taqui and Titty by name.

It was a very sad ending to the most important friendship of his life; and the evil effects outlasted him, for Genia took up the cudgels after his death and treated the Altounyans as if they were so many pirates. 'I am going to talk to you like a Dutch aunt,' she said, in a way that might have seemed unintentionally comic but that at the time was merely distressing.

Before long Arthur would have no energy left even for the pursuit of his grievances. In the summer of 1960 Rupert Hart-Davis drove him about the lake country to take farewell of his favourite spots. Hart-Davis was touched by Arthur's love and knowledge of every place, but the trip was a nightmare, for the roads were crowded with tourist traffic, Arthur was too feeble to get out of the car very often, which therefore had to be manoeuvred right to every river's brink if he was to see what he wanted; and he was now threatened with incontinence, so the car had to keep on stopping, whatever the state of the traffic. Old age, said Charles de Gaulle, is a shipwreck.

Life was not made more bearable by his habitation, or rather his confinement, at Hill Top. In 1961 Genia dug furiously in the garden all summer and refused to listen to any suggestions of a return to London before mid-autumn, when Summer Time ended. Her instincts were probably in revolt against shutting herself up in a London flat with an elderly invalid declining into senescence; but it was hard on Arthur. His friends in the North were dead or dying, and he had no one to talk to (for Genia regarded most conversation as idle chatter). The only regular counter to his loneliness was the flow of books from Rupert Hart-Davis Ltd. When the great edition of the letters of Oscar Wilde appeared he was gratified to find that 'the biographical part of my little piece of impertinence' was justified by the facts. He liked Michael Howard's *Franco-Prussian War* ('What a mess I should be in if

your list did not carry on with my neglected education') and
Francis Steegmuller's French version of *The Owl and the Pussy-Cat*
('The Poussiquette is a creature of pure genius. How lucky you are
to have caught her'). But books cannot do everything. In November he had to have a further operation. Yet another followed next
spring. A few days after it was over Genia reported to Georgina
Battiscombe that the surgeon boasted of his success, but it seemed
likely that Arthur would take a long time to recover. Mrs Battiscombe agreed to write the introduction to the new edition of *The
Soldier and Death* which Arthur could no longer provide himself.

Nevertheless he recovered with his usual surprising speed,
though he did not recapture his former vigour. His world had
shrunk, but he could still take a boyish pleasure in it.

(*To Rupert Hart-Davis, 21 May 1962, Haverthwaite*) People have
been most awfully kind. Mrs Pedder, whom you met, had a
grandson staying with her (*aet.* 5) and he had a jar of tadpoles
from their pond. When he went home he forgot them and Mrs
Pedder by divination thought of me and brought them here,
where they are a great delight. She then went one better and
brought me a small, elegant and wholly delightful grass-snake,
which now lives on my window-sill. Genia reports that he is
showing intelligent interest in a small slug, crawling past his
nose.

But all prospect of a peaceful convalescence was shattered by the
arrival of a team to make a television version of *Swallows and
Amazons*. They began by proposing to blow up some of the rocks
in the Peel Island harbour, and went on from there. According to
Arthur their child-actors were ugly, their Captain Flint was
'common', their script a travesty of his book, their rural characters
were made to talk Cockney and they introduced some Cockney
villains. Genia missed no chance of telling him he was a fool ever
to have consented to the project, and he sadly agreed with her.

Matters were no better in 1963. He was now to be stuck away
in Haverthwaite for good, the London flat being given up. The
final move from Hurlingham Court demonstrated that, as in 1940,
Arthur had more possessions than he could fit into his new quarters. This gave him another grievance against his wife:

(*To Rupert Hart-Davis, 3 December*) As for the sorting of my books I am having to throw out a fearful lot for the retention of which I have no excuse: and, after all, how many books can on the instant offer a good excuse for their own retention. There seems to be very much less shelf-space in this cottage than I have ever had before. I am throwing out most of the sailing books and a great many fishing books. Of course I have no valid excuse for having a lot of worthless books on my shelves. But I rather like to look at them even if I can't any longer properly read them.

In fairness to Genia it must be stated that Arthur was exaggerating. No owner of books ever has enough shelf-space. Hill Top was crammed with volumes until Arthur's death (when Genia sold them on an impulse she soon regretted). His lamentations over the fishing and sailing books must be understood as symbolic assertions of his feeling that Hill Top was not the place for him, and as farewells to his favourite sports.

Neither was it really the place for Genia. Her position was exceedingly difficult. Even if she had been ready to accept domestic help, there was none to be had, so remote was the cottage from all well-populated areas. Of all their friends only Janet Gnosspelius, Barbara's daughter, was near enough to visit them regularly, and she, living in Liverpool, was hardly a near neighbour. So all the burdens of life fell on Genia's shoulders which, though as resolute as ever, were less strong: she was in her seventieth year. By now Arthur was immobilised on the upper floor of the cottage in a wheelchair, and as his faculties decayed he became, at times, a difficult patient.

There was a break in the clouds in January 1964, when he reached his eightieth birthday. Congratulatory letters swamped the local post-office. *The Times Literary Supplement* marked the occasion by a long anonymous article in his honour (it was not too difficult to discover that it had been written by Georgina Battiscombe). There was some suggestion of a party, but Genia told Rupert Hart-Davis that Arthur was more distressed than cheered if there were more than half a dozen people in the room. So at her suggestion Hart-Davis sent cigars and a *Whitaker's Almanac*, to which he added, of his own accord, a birthday card and a greetings telegram. The Bells sent letters and a book. Wren Howard sent cigars. Arthur wrote warm thanks to all of them, in a hand that had got sadly shaky.

(*To Pamela Whitlock, 22 January 1964*) I blush to read your letter but lap up the affection which prompts your exaggerations. Thank you very much ... I would like to see you both before very long. But I am losing mobility so fast I expect I shall be stuck here for the rest of my life. Nice enough place to be stuck in but difficult for friends to get to when we want to see them.

Even this cautious forecast turned out wrong. Genia suffered a bad attack of sciatica, and Arthur went to a nursing home in Grange-over-Sands for two or three weeks in March to give her a rest. And so the pattern of his last years gradually established itself.

A few more letters were written before his mind clouded over entirely. He rejoiced at the news that Rupert Hart-Davis was at last able to give up publishing and retire to be a man of letters at a former parsonage in the North Riding.

(*To Rupert Hart-Davis, 3 May*) Three million cheers for your capture of the rectory. I hope and believe that you will find such stimulation in the Yorkshire air that you will lightheartedly produce a long line of masterpieces as outstanding as your never to be too often reread *Walpole*. We enormously look forward to seeing you both, if you can bring yourselves to forgive my dodderiness. Saw a pair of green woodpeckers yesterday.

But the rest of his story would be told by Genia.

Visits to nursing homes became frequent. Then he fell into an electric fire. Fortunately he did not burn or shock himself, but he did suffer concussion. Soon after that Genia herself went into hospital for a neck operation, and for treatment of a varicose ulcer. She hated it: 'I loathe staying in bed *even when ill*,' she told Hart-Davis. Home again, she found Arthur worse than ever. Nurses had to be brought in, and were a strain on her short temper. She put Arthur into a hospital, but he was so miserable there that she brought him home in the New Year.

In the autumn she had to admit defeat at last. She had two heart attacks. Arthur would have to go to the Cheadle Royal Hospital, near Manchester.

(*Genia to Rupert Hart-Davis, 1 October 1965*) I wonder if you could come to see us before he goes. He was talking of wanting to see you, he tried even to write a letter to you – his efforts are quite pitiful – like a very small bird walking over the paper after its claws have been dipped in ink – and he just can't dictate.

Hart-Davis came, and saw Arthur for what he knew would be the last time, the day before the move to Cheadle.

He lingered there for twenty months more, sometimes alert enough to know where he was and to hold a real conversation with Genia, but mostly unaware of anything or anybody very much. He complained no more. Genia and Janet Gnosspelius visited him constantly. By May 1967, it was evident that he was rapidly slipping away, and Genia moved into the hospital to be with him. Eight days later, on 3 June, he died peacefully. He was buried, as he had wished, at Rusland; there was a memorial service at St Martin-in-the-Fields, at which Rupert Hart-Davis gave the address.

Genia survived for nearly eight years. Her chief preoccupation was to act as guardian of Arthur's reputation, writings and estate; she took especial care over the preparation of the *Autobiography* for publication after her own death. She found her relaxation in the sort of unproductive quarrelling to which, Bolshevik by temperament that she was, she was so much addicted. There were sunny interludes. A collaboration with Kaye Webb of Puffin Books in bringing out Arthur's stories in paperback gave her great pleasure. She also enjoyed herself immensely on two visits to her long-unseen family in Russia, and in a return visit from her sister, though she was embarrassed to find that she had forgotten almost all her Russian. She sold Hill Top and moved to a comfortable 'home' for rich old ladies in Oxfordshire, where she took pleasure in visits from her friends and, perhaps even more, in quarrelling with her fellow-inmates. At length, restless as ever, she decided to move yet once more, and bought a house at Girton, near Cambridge. But she was old, and very tired, and the preparations for the move overstrained her heart. She died on 19 March 1975, and on a day of rain and storm was buried beside Arthur at Rusland.

Bibliography

Unpublished Sources

There are at present five main collections of Ransome papers, all of which have been used in the preparation of this biography. By far the most important is the one in the Brotherton Collection, Leeds, where almost all the important documents remaining in Evgenia Ransome's possession at the time of her death were deposited. This archive at the time of writing is being arranged by Mrs Farr, but is unlikely to be catalogued in the near future. In the main it consists of five categories: letters; diaries; unpublished drafts and notebooks of all kinds, including sketches for stories and a large number of autobiographical memoranda; drawings, sketchbooks and photographs; printed newspaper articles, and the typewritten drafts for much of Arthur Ransome's journalism, including his reports on the Russian Revolution. These last are especially important because much of his copy was heavily censored.

Arthur's desk, some of his books, a good many of his mementoes and various papers were presented by Genia to the Lakeland Museum, Abbot Hall, Kendal. Of the papers the most important are the typed draft of *Swallows and Amazons*, unpublished chapters of the *Autobiography*, and the typescript of the unfinished story, 'Coots in the North'.

As Ransome's literary executor, Sir Rupert Hart-Davis had the duty of editing the *Autobiography*. To assist him, Genia wrote a long series of letters and memoranda, which remain in his hands, along with the letters he received from Arthur during his lifetime. Having been written mostly in the last two years of her life, Genia's notes are not always reliable; but they are nevertheless extremely valuable bio-graphical sources, and the letters to Sir Rupert from Arthur form one of the best series extant. Arthur's other executor, Mr John Bell, took charge of Arthur's business papers; he has also kept the letters which

Arthur wrote to him and, especially, to his wife, the late Pamela Whitlock.

In the files of Jonathan Cape Ltd is a lot more business correspondence, of which there are no duplicates elsewhere; the firm also possesses statements of Ransome's sales, and samples of the reviews of his works.

I have listed other MSS and interview sources in the Acknowledgments.

Published Sources

It would be impossible to attempt a proper bibliography of Arthur Ransome's works without swelling my book intolerably, and delaying its appearance. It is impossible even to guess how many hundreds of items of journalism, for example, would have to be tracked down and included. What follows is therefore confined to items which I have used in preparing this biography. Contributions to the *Daily News* and the *Manchester Guardian* are not listed. The place of publication, here and in the concluding section of this bibliography, is London, unless otherwise shown or in the case of the university presses.

The ABC of Physical Culture, Henry J. Drane, 1904.

The Souls of the Streets, Brown Langham, 1904.

The Stone Lady, Brown Langham, 1905.

A Child's Book of the Garden (on cover), *The Things in our Garden* (on title-page), illustrated by Frances Craine, Anthony Treherne & Co., 1906.

Pond and Stream, Anthony Treherne & Co., 1906.

Things in Season, Anthony Treherne & Co., 1906.

'Books and children, by a writer of children's books', *Temple Bar*, vols 1 and 2, New Series, 1906, pp. 536–52.

Highways and Byways in Fairyland, Alston Rivers Ltd, 1907.

Bohemia in London, illustrated by Fred Taylor, Chapman & Hall, 1907. New edition, Oxford University Press, 1984.

A History of Story-Telling: studies in the development of narrative, with 27 portraits by J. Gavin, T. C. and E. C. Jack, 1909.

The Book of Friendship: essays poems maxims & prose passages arranged by Arthur Ransome, T. C. and E. C. Jack; n.d., but 1909.

Edgar Allan Poe, a critical study, Martin Secker, 1910.

The Book of Love, T. C. and E. C. Jack, 1911.

The Hoofmarks of the Faun, Martin Secker, 1911.

Oscar Wilde, a critical study, Martin Secker, 1912.

A Night in the Luxembourg, by Rémy de Gourmont; translated by Arthur Ransome, Stephen Swift, 1912.

Portraits and Speculations, Macmillan & Co., 1913.

The Elixir of Life, Methuen, 1915.

Old Peter's Russian Tales, illustrated by Dmitri Mitrokhin, Jack, 1916.

The Truth about Russia, New Republic pamphlet, New York, 1918.

Aladdin and his Wonderful Lamp, in rhyme, illustrated by Mackenzie, Nisbet & Co.; n.d., but 1919.

Six Weeks in Russia in 1919, George Allen & Unwin, 1919.

'The Blacksmith in Heaven: a Ukrainian folk story', *The Wheatsheaf*, December 1919.

The Soldier and Death, J. G. Wilson, 1920. Included in *The War of the Birds and the Beasts*, Jonathan Cape, 1984.

The Crisis in Russia, George Allen & Unwin, 1921.

A Week, by Iury Libedinsky, translated and with an introduction by Arthur Ransome, George Allen & Unwin, 1923.

Racundra's First Cruise, George Allen & Unwin, 1923.

The Chinese Puzzle, George Allen & Unwin, 1927.

Rod and Line, Jonathan Cape, 1929.

'Two Shorts and a Long', *Pall Mall Magazine*, vol. v, no. 1, May 1929.

'The Unofficial Side', *Pall Mall Magazine*, vol. v, no. 5, September 1929.

Swallows and Amazons, with endpaper and frontispiece maps and title-page drawing by Stephen Spurrier, Jonathan Cape, 1930.

Swallows and Amazons, illustrated by Clifford Webb, Jonathan Cape, 1931.

Swallowdale, illustrated by Clifford Webb, Jonathan Cape, 1931.

Introduction, *Down Channel*, by R. T. McMullen, George Allen & Unwin, 1931.

Peter Duck, Jonathan Cape, 1932.

Introduction, *The Cruise of the Teddy*, by Erling Tambs, George Newnes, 1932.

Winter Holiday, Jonathan Cape, 1933.

Coot Club, Jonathan Cape, 1934.

Pigeon Post, Jonathan Cape, 1936.

Introduction, *The Far-Distant Oxus*, by Katharine Hull and Pamela Whitlock, Jonathan Cape, 1937.

We Didn't Mean to Go to Sea, Jonathan Cape, 1937.

Secret Water, Jonathan Cape, 1939.

The Big Six, Jonathan Cape, 1940.

Missee Lee, Jonathan Cape, 1941.

The Picts and the Martyrs, Jonathan Cape, 1943.

Great Northern?, Jonathan Cape, 1947.

Introduction, *Sailing Alone Around the World*, by Joshua Slocum, Rupert Hart-Davis, 1948.

Introduction, *The Falcon on the Baltic*, by E. F. Knight, Rupert Hart-Davis, 1951.

Introduction, *The Cruise of the Alerte*, by E. F. Knight, Rupert Hart-Davis, 1952.

Introduction, *The Cruise of the Kate*, by E. E. Middleton, Rupert Hart-Davis, 1953.

Introduction, *The Voyage Alone in the Yawl Rob Roy*, by John Macgregor, Rupert Hart-Davis, 1954.

Fishing, National Book League, Reader's Guides, series 2, no. 2, Cambridge University Press, 1955.

Introduction, *The Constant Fisherman*, by Major H. E. Morritt, A. & C. Black, 1957.

Mainly About Fishing, A. & C. Black, 1959.

Autobiography, edited and with an introduction by Rupert Hart-Davis, Jonathan Cape, 1976.

A fair amount of miscellaneous reading has gone into this biography, but the following is a list only of items which contain Ransome material or which I have found otherwise indispensable (for example, in helping me to understand the Russian Revolution) or to which I refer in the text.

ADAM SMITH, JANET. Review of *The Picts and the Martyrs* in the *Spectator*, 9 July 1943.

ALTOUNYAN, TAQUI. *In Aleppo Once*, John Murray, 1969.

AYERST, DAVID. *The Guardian: portrait of a newspaper*, Collins, 1971.

BAIN, R. NISBET. *Russian Fairy Tales from the Skaski of Polevoi*, Harrap, 1915.

CARPENTER, HUMPHREY (ed.), *Letters of J. R. R. Tolkien*, George Allen & Unwin, 1981.

COLES, K. ADLARD. *Close Hauled: Latvia to England*, Seeley, Service & Co., 1926.

COLES, K. ADLARD. *Sailing Years: an autobiography*, Coles/Granada, 1981.

COLLINGWOOD, R. G. *Autobiography*, Oxford University Press, 1939.

COLLINGWOOD, W. G. *The Lake Counties*, Dent, Open Air Library edition, 1938.

DAWSON, JOHN. 'Swallows and Amazons', *Lancashire Life*, September 1978.

DUKES, PAUL. *The Story of 'ST 23': adventure and romance in the secret intelligence service in Red Russia*, Cassell, 1930.

FARJEON, ELEANOR. *Edward Thomas: the last four years*, Oxford University Press, 1958.

FLETCHER, MARY E. C. Letter, *Spectator*, 9 July 1943.

FOX, UFFA. *Thoughts on Yachts and Yachting*, Peter Davies, 1938.

GARNETT, DAVID (ed.). *The White-Garnett Letters*, Jonathan Cape, 1968.

HARD, WILLIAM. *Raymond Robins' Own Story*, Harper, New York and London, 1920.

HART-DAVIS, RUPERT. *Hugh Walpole, a biography*, Macmillan, 1952.

HART-DAVIS, RUPERT (ed.). *The Lyttelton-Hart-Davis Letters*, vols I to V, John Murray, 1978–83.

HART-DAVIS, RUPERT (ed.). *The Letters of Oscar Wilde*, Rupert Hart-Davis, 1962.

History of The Times, vol. IV, part I, *The Times*, 1952.

KENNAN, GEORGE. *Russia Leaves the War*, Faber & Faber, 1956.

KENNAN, GEORGE. *The Decision to Intervene*, Faber & Faber, 1957.

KENNAN, GEORGE. *Russia and the West*, Hutchinson, 1961.

KETTLE, MICHAEL. *The Allies and the Russian Collapse*, André Deutsch, 1981.

KIPLING, RUDYARD. 'Baa Baa Black Sheep', in *Wee Willie Winkie and other stories*, Macmillan, uniform edition, 1899.

KIPLING, RUDYARD. *Something of Myself*, Macmillan, 1937.

KOCHAN, LIONEL. *Russia in Revolution*, Granada Publishing edition, 1970.

LASCH, CHRISTOPHER. *The American Liberals and the Russian Revolution*, Columbia University Press, New York, 1962.

LEGGETT, GEORGE. *The Cheka*, Oxford University Press, 1981.

LOCKHART, R. H. BRUCE. *Memoirs of a British Agent*, Putnam, London and New York, 1934.

LOCKHART, R. H. BRUCE. *Retreat from Glory*, Putnam, 1934.

LOCKHART, R. H. BRUCE. *Diary*, vol. I, Macmillan, 1973.

MANDEL, WILLIAM M. *Slavic Review*, 1968, p. 295.

'MANDRAKE'. *Sunday Telegraph*, 2 December 1982.

MAYER, ARNO. *Wilson vs. Lenin*, Meridian edition, New York, 1964.

MUGGERIDGE, MALCOLM. *The Green Stick*, Fontana edition, 1975.

NEILSON, KEITH. ' "Joy-Ride"? British intelligence and propaganda in Russia, 1914–1917', *Historical Journal*, December 1981.

NIXON, W. M. 'Memorable *Racundra*', *Yachting World*, April 1982.

PARES, BERNARD. *My Russian Memoirs*, Jonathan Cape, 1931.

PEARSON, HESKETH. *Oscar Wilde*, London, 1954.

PRICE, M. PHILIPS. 'Arthur Ransome and the Russian Revolution', letter in the *Guardian*, 27 June 1967.

PRICE, M. PHILIPS. *My Three Revolutions*, Allen & Unwin, 1969.

RALSTON, W. R. S. *Russian Folk-Tales*, Smith, Elder, 1873.

REED, JOHN. *Ten Days That Shook the World*, Penguin edition, 1977.

ROSMER, ALFRED. *Lenin's Moscow*, translated by Ian H. Birchall, Pluto Press edition, 1971.

SISSON, EDGAR. *One Hundred Red Days*, Yale University Press, New Haven, Connecticut, 1931.

SMITH, ADRIAN. 'EXCLUSIVE: New Statesman Editor in Pay of British Security Services', *New Statesman*, 22 December 1978.

'SOCRATICUS' (F. W. HIRST). 'Interview with Arthur Ransome', *Common Sense*, 15 January 1918.

STEFFENS, LINCOLN. *Autobiography*, Harrap, 1931.

STEVENS, E. S. ' — and what happened', being an account of some romantic meals, Mills & Boon, 1916.

THOMAS, R. GEORGE (ed.). *Letters from Edward Thomas to Gordon Bottomley*, Oxford University Press, 1968.

TROTSKY, LEON. *The History of the Russian Revolution*, Sphere edition, 1970.

TYRKOVA-WILLIAMS, ARIADNA. *Cheerful Giver: the life of Harold Williams*, Peter Davies, 1935.

ULAM, ADAM B. *Lenin and the Bolsheviks*, Fontana edition, 1969.

ULLMAN, RICHARD H. *Intervention and the War*, Princeton University Press, New Jersey, 1961.

ULLMAN, RICHARD H. *Britain and the Russian Civil War*, Princeton University Press, New Jersey, 1968.

WALKER-SMITH, D. *The Life of Lord Darling*, Cassell, 1938.

WARTH, ROBERT D. *The Allies and the Russian Revolution*, Durham, North Carolina, 1954.

WHEELER-BENNETT, JOHN. *Brest-Litovsk: the forgotten peace*, Macmillan, 1938.

Index